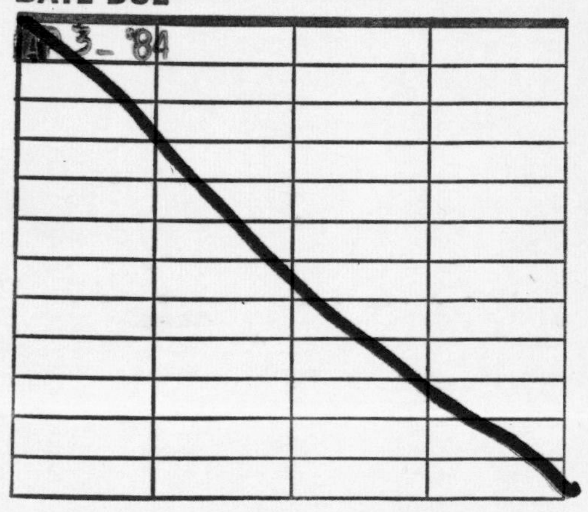
DATE DUE
AP 3 '84

BURT FRANKLIN: RESEARCH & SOURCE WORKS SERIES 873
American Classics in History and Social Science 217

THE NATIONAL CONVENTIONS AND PLATFORMS OF ALL POLITICAL PARTIES

THE NATIONAL CONVENTIONS AND PLATFORMS OF ALL . . POLITICAL PARTIES . . .

1789 to 1905

CONVENTION, POPULAR AND ELECTORAL VOTE

Also the Political Complexion of both Houses of Congress at each biennial period

BY

THOMAS HUDSON McKEE

BURT FRANKLIN
NEW YORK

Published by LENOX HILL Pub. & Dist. Co. (Burt Franklin)
235 East 44th St., New York, N.Y. 10017
Originally Published: 1906
Reprinted: 1971
Printed in the U.S.A.

S.B.N.: 8337-23316
Library of Congress Card Catalog No.: 75-132682
Burt Frankkin: Research and Source Works Series 873
American Classics in History and Social Science 217

Reprinted from the original edition in the New York Public Library.

PREFACE.

This, the latest and thoroughly revised and greatly enlarged edition of "The National Conventions and Platforms of All Political Parties," has been made as complete and reliable as possible; and to this end all available records have been searched for useful and confirmatory information; but some things connected with the earlier presidential campaigns are lost, so far as either official or newspaper record of them is concerned.

Into this little volume have been gathered such of the most important things referring to presidential campaigns as are likely to prove needful to public men in their political work. Very many of the names and incidents recited are not matters of public history, but are culled from the almost forgotten things connected with national conventions and elections.

An Appendix of useful information and an exhaustive Index add greatly to the value of the work.

Confident that it will prove helpful to students of political history and to all others desiring information on public questions, it is submitted to the consideration of the public.

T. H. McK.

TABLE OF CONTENTS.

Conventions and Platforms.

Table of Contents.

Appendix.

Index.

Election of 1789

NO CONVENTION. NO PLATFORMS. NO NOMINATIONS.

The first presidential election occurred in the states which ratified the Constitution on the first Wednesday of January, the 7th, 1789, and on the first Wednesday of February following the electors made choice for President and Vice-President.

The selection of candidates to be voted for by the electors chosen included Washington, but no agreement was reached as to what candidates were to be voted for. The names of those voted for are given in the table below.

TEN STATES ONLY VOTED. Rhode Island, North Carolina, and New York not voting at this election.

Electors were chosen by the legislatures in Connecticut, Delaware, Georgia, New Jersey, and South Carolina.

The result of the vote, as counted on April 6, 1789, was as follows:

STATES.	George Washington, of Virginia.	John Adams, of Massachusetts.	John Jay, of New York.	Robert H. Harrison, of Maryland.	John Rutledge, of South Carolina.	John Hancock, of Massachusetts.	George Clinton, of New York.	Samuel Huntington, of Connecticut.	John Milton, of Georgia.	James Armstrong, of Georgia.	Benjamin Lincoln, of Massachusetts.	Edward Telfair, of Georgia.	Vacancies.	No. entitled to vote.
Connecticut....	7	5	..	..	..	..	..	2	..	..	..	..	..	7
Delaware.......	3	..	3	..	..	..	..	..	..	..	..	..	..	3
Georgia.........	5	..	..	..	..	..	..	..	2	1	1	1	..	5
Maryland.......	6	..	..	6	..	..	..	..	..	..	..	..	2	8
Massachusetts..	10	10	..	..	..	..	..	..	..	..	..	..	..	10
New Hampshire	5	5	..	..	..	..	..	..	..	..	..	..	..	5
New Jersey.....	6	1	5	..	..	..	..	..	..	..	..	..	..	6
Pennsylvania....	10	8	..	..	..	2	..	..	..	..	..	..	..	10
South Carolina..	7	..	..	..	6	1	..	..	..	..	..	..	..	7
Virginia.........	10	5	1	..	..	1	3	..	..	..	..	..	2	12
Total..........	69	34	9	6	6	4	3	2	2	1	1	1	4	73

NOTE.—The voting at this time by the electors was according to the old clause of the Constitution (art. II, sec. 2), which required the electors to vote for two persons, the one receiving the majority to be President, and the one receiving the next greatest number to be Vice-President.

The President elect and Vice-President elect were notified of their election by special messengers of the Senate.

During this period Congress was divided politically as follows:

First Congress.

Senate—26 Federalists .... Total, 26
House—53 Federalists, 12 Democrats .... " 65

Second Congress.

Senate—17 Federalists, 13 Democrats .... Total, 30
House—55 Federalists, 14 Democrats .... " 69

Election of 1792*

NO CONVENTIONS. NO PLATFORMS. NO NOMINATIONS.

Party organization had just begun. Those acting under the general name of Anti-Federalists, although having many minor differences, were now (spring of 1792) united into one party, taking the name of *Democratic-Republican.*

The Federalist and Democratic-Republicans both supported President **Washington** for a second term.

For Vice-President, the Federalists supported **John Adams,** of Massachusetts.

The Democratic-Republicans supported **George Clinton,** of New York.

The election occurred on November 6, 1792.

FIFTEEN STATES VOTED.

Electors were chosen by the legislatures in Connecticut, Delaware, Georgia, Kentucky, New Jersey, New York, Rhode Island, South Carolina, and Vermont.

* Previous to the election in 1792, Congress passed an act (March 1, 1792) regulating the holding of elections for the selection of President and Vice-President, which act fixed the succession in the office in case of death or disability.

The vote, as counted on February 13, 1793, resulted as follows:

STATES.	George Washington, of Virginia.	John Adams, of Massachusetts.	George Clinton, of New York.	Thomas Jefferson, of Virginia.	Aaron Burr, of New York.	Vacancies.	No. entitled to vote.
Connecticut	9	9	..	..	..	..	9
Delaware	3	3	..	..	..	..	3
Georgia	4	..	4	..	..	..	4
Kentucky	4	..	..	4	..	..	4
Maryland	8	8	..	..	..	2	10
Massachusetts	16	16	..	..	..	..	16
New Hampshire	6	6	..	..	..	..	6
New Jersey	7	7	..	..	..	..	7
New York	12	..	12	..	..	..	12
North Carolina	12	..	12	..	..	..	12
Pennsylvania	15	14	1	..	..	..	15
Rhode Island	4	4	..	..	..	..	4
South Carolina	8	7	..	..	1	..	8
Vermont	3	3	..	..	..	1	4
Virginia	21	..	21	..	..	..	21
Total	132	77	50	4	1	3	135

NOTE.—The voting at this time by the electors was according to the old clause of the Constitution (art. II, sec. 2), which required the electors to vote for two persons, the one receiving the majority to be President, and the one receiving the next greatest number to be Vice-President.

George Washington was elected President and John Adams as Vice-President.

During this period Congress was divided politically as follows:

Third Congress.

Senate—18 Federalists, 12 Democrats .... Total, 30
House—51 Federalists, 54 Democrats .... " 105

Fourth Congress.

Senate—19 Federalists, 13 Democrats .... Total, 32
House—46 Federalists, 59 Democrats .... " 105

Election of 1796

NO CONVENTIONS. NO PLATFORMS. NO NOMINATIONS.

The Republicans, now organized, rallied in an effort to defeat the Federalists. It was late in the year before the Farewell Address of Washington was made public. (It was dated September 17, 1796.) Without either caucus or convention the candidates had been already designated by popular agreement.

The Democratic-Republicans supported—

For President, **Thomas Jefferson,**
of Virginia.

For Vice-President, **Aaron Burr,**
of New York.

The Federalists—

For President, **John Adams,**
of Massachusetts.

For Vice-President, **Thomas Pinckney,**
of South Carolina.

The election occurred on November 8, 1796.

SIXTEEN STATES VOTED.

Electors were chosen by the legislatures in Connecticut, Delaware, Georgia, Kentucky, New Jersey, New York, Rhode Island, South Carolina, Tennessee, and Vermont.

The following is the result of the vote, as counted on February 8, 1797:

STATES.	John Adams, of Massachusetts.	Thomas Jefferson, of Virginia.	Thomas Pinckney, of South Carolina.	Aaron Burr, of New York.	Samuel Adams, of Massachusetts.	Oliver Ellsworth, of Connecticut.	George Clinton, of New York.	John Jay, of New York.	James Iredell, of North Carolina.	George Washington, of Virginia.	John Henry, of Maryland.	Samuel Johnson, of North Carolina.	Charles C. Pinckney, of South Carolina.	No. entitled to vote.
Connecticut	9	..	4	..	..	..	..	5	..	..	..	..	..	9
Delaware	3	..	3	..	..	..	..	..	..	..	..	..	..	3
Georgia	..	4	..	..	..	..	4	..	..	..	..	..	..	4
Kentucky	..	4	..	4	..	..	..	..	..	..	..	..	..	4
Maryland	7	4	4	3	..	..	..	..	..	..	2	..	..	10
Massachusetts	16	..	13	..	..	1	..	..	..	..	..	2	..	16
New Hampshire	6	..	..	..	..	6	..	..	..	..	..	..	..	6
New Jersey	7	..	7	..	..	..	..	..	..	..	..	..	..	7
New York	12	..	12	..	..	..	..	..	..	..	..	..	..	12
North Carolina	1	11	1	6	..	..	..	..	3	1	..	..	1	12
Pennsylvania	1	14	2	13	..	..	..	..	..	..	..	..	..	15
Rhode Island	4	..	..	..	..	4	..	..	..	..	..	..	..	4
South Carolina	..	8	8	..	..	..	..	..	..	..	..	..	..	8
Tennessee	..	3	..	3	..	..	..	..	..	..	..	..	..	3
Vermont	4	..	4	..	..	..	..	..	..	..	..	..	..	4
Virginia	1	20	1	1	15	..	3	..	..	1	..	..	..	21
Total	71	68	59	30	15	11	7	5	3	2	2	2	1	138

NOTE.—The voting at this time by the electors was according to the old clause of the Constitution (art. II, sec. 2), which required the electors to vote for two persons, the one receiving the majority to be President, and the one receiving the next greatest number to be Vice-President.

John Adams was elected President and Thomas Jefferson as Vice-President.

During this period Congress was divided politically as follows:

Fifth Congress.

Senate—21 Federalists, 11 Democrats .... Total, 32
House—51 Federalists, 54 Democrats .... " 105

Sixth Congress.

Senate—19 Federalists, 13 Democrats .... Total, 32
House—57 Federalists, 48 Democrats .... " 105

Election of 1800

NO CONVENTIONS. NO PLATFORMS.

Early in the year 1800 the Federalist members of Congress held a conference in the Senate chamber for the purpose of settling the candidacy of Mr. Adams for a second term. No account of the proceedings of this conference was ever published.

The Federalists selected—

For President, **John Adams,**
of Massachusetts.

For Vice-President, **Charles C. Pinckney,**
of South Carolina.

The Democratic-Republican members of Congress held a caucus and secret meeting somewhat later, probably the last of February, 1800. The candidates selected at this caucus were—

For President, **Thomas Jefferson,**
of Virginia.

For Vice-President, **Aaron Burr,**
of New York.

The election occurred on November 4, 1800.

SIXTEEN STATES VOTED.

Electors were chosen by the legislatures in Connecticut, Delaware, New Jersey, New York, Pennsylvania, South Carolina, and Vermont.

The vote, as counted on February 11, 1801, was as follows:

STATES.	Thomas Jefferson, of Virginia.	Aaron Burr, of New York.	John Adams, of Massachusetts.	Charles C. Pinckney, of South Carolina.	John Jay, of New York.	No. entitled to vote.
Connecticut	..	..	9	9	..	9
Delaware	..	..	3	3	..	3
Georgia	4	4	..	..	..	4
Kentucky	4	4	..	..	..	4
Maryland	5	5	5	5	..	10
Massachusetts	..	..	16	16	..	16
New Hampshire	..	..	6	6	..	6
New Jersey	..	..	7	7	..	7
New York	12	12	..	..	..	12
North Carolina	8	8	4	4	..	12
Pennsylvania	8	8	7	7	..	15
Rhode Island	..	..	4	3	1	4
South Carolina	8	8	..	..	..	8
Tennessee	3	3	..	..	..	3
Vermont	..	..	4	4	..	4
Virginia	21	21	..	..	..	21
Total	73	73	65	64	1	138

NOTE.—The voting at this time by the electors was according to the old clause of the Constitution (art. II, sec. 2), which required the electors to vote for two persons, the one receiving the majority to be President, and the one receiving the next greatest number to be Vice-President.

Thomas Jefferson and Aaron Burr having both received the same vote, and therefore, under the law then in force, no choice having been made by the people, the House proceeded on the same day to elect a President and Vice-President, as follows:—On the first ballot eight states voted for Thomas Jefferson, six for Aaron Burr, and the votes of two were divided. The balloting continued until Tuesday, February 17, 1801, when, on the 36th ballot, ten states voted for Thomas Jefferson, four for Aaron Burr, and two in blank. Thomas Jefferson, having received the votes of a majority of the states, was thereby elected President, and Aaron Burr, Vice-President.

During this period Congress was divided politically as follows:

Seventh Congress.

Senate—13 Federalists, 19 Democrats ....Total, 32
House—34 Federalists, 71 Democrats .... " 105

Eighth Congress.

Senate—10 Federalists, 24 Democrats ....Total, 34
House—38 Federalists, 103 Democrats .... " 141

Election of 1804

NO CONVENTIONS. NO PLATFORMS.

The first regular caucus of members of Congress for the nomination of presidential candidates was held in Washington, D. C., February 25, 1804, by the Democratic-Republicans, who unanimously nominated—

For President, **Thomas Jefferson,**
of Virginia.

For Vice-President, **George Clinton,**
of New York.

The Federalists, by agreement, without holding a congressional caucus, supported—

For President, **Charles C. Pinckney,**
of South Carolina.

For Vice-President, **Rufus King,**
of New York

The election occurred on November 6, 1804.

SEVENTEEN STATES VOTED.

Electors were chosen by the legislatures in Connecticut, Delaware, Georgia, New York, South Carolina, Tennessee, and Vermont.

The vote, as counted on February 13, 1805, showed the following result:

STATES.	PRESIDENT.		VICE-PRESIDENT.		No. entitled to vote.
	Thomas Jefferson, of Virginia.	Charles C. Pinckney, of South Carolina.	George Clinton, of New York.	Rufus King, of New York.	
Connecticut	..	9	..	9	9
Delaware	..	3	..	3	3
Georgia	6	..	6	..	6
Kentucky	8	..	8	..	8
Maryland	9	2	9	2	11
Massachusetts	19	..	19	..	19
New Hampshire	7	..	7	..	7
New Jersey	8	..	8	..	8
New York	19	..	19	..	19
North Carolina	14	..	14	..	14
Ohio	3	..	3	..	3
Pennsylvania	20	..	20	..	20
Rhode Island	4	..	4	..	4
South Carolina	10	..	10	..	10
Tennessee	5	..	5	..	5
Vermont	6	..	6	..	6
Virginia	24	..	24	..	24
Total	162	14	162	14	176

NOTE.—By article XII of the amendments to the Constitution, which was declared in force September 25, 1804, the electors are required to ballot separately for President and Vice-President. The election of 1804 was the first held under this amendment.

Thomas Jefferson was elected President, and George Clinton as Vice-President.

During this period Congress was divided politically as follows:

Ninth Congress.

Senate— 7 Federalists,	27 Democrats,	Total,	34
House —29 Federalists,	112 Democrats,	"	141

Tenth Congress.

Senate— 7 Federalists,	27 Democrats	Total,	34
House—31 Federalists,	110 Democrats	"	141

Election of 1808

NO CONVENTIONS. NO PLATFORMS.

The Democratic-Republicans nominated—

For President, **James Madison,**
of Virginia.

For Vice-President, **George Clinton,**
of New York.

The above-named candidates were nominated at a congressional caucus of Democratic-Republicans held January 23, 1808, James Madison receiving 83 votes out of a total of 89, and George Clinton receiving 79 votes out of a total of 88.

The Federalists nominated—

For President, **Charles C. Pinckney,**
of South Carolina.

For Vice-President, **Rufus King,**
of New York.

The Federalists, without holding any caucus, by some method concentrated their votes on these candidates, who had been the Federalist candidates in 1804.

The election occurred on November 8, 1808.

SEVENTEEN STATES VOTED.

The states choosing their electors by the legislatures were Connecticut, Delaware, Georgia, Massachusetts, New York, South Carolina, and Vermont.

The result of the vote, as counted on February 8, 1809, was:

STATES.	PRESIDENT.				VICE-PRESIDENT.						No. entitled to vote.
	James Madison, of Virginia.	Charles C. Pinckney, of South Carolina.	George Clinton, of New York.	Vacancies.	George Clinton, of New York.	Rufus King, of New York.	John Langdon, of New Hampshire.	James Madison, of Virginia.	James Monroe, of Virginia.	Vacancies.	
Connecticut	..	9	..	..	..	9	..	..	..	..	9
Delaware	..	3	..	..	..	3	..	..	..	..	3
Georgia	6	..	..	..	6	..	..	..	..	..	6
Kentucky	7	..	..	1	7	..	..	..	..	1	8
Maryland	9	2	..	..	9	2	..	..	..	..	11
Massachusetts	..	19	..	..	..	19	..	..	..	..	19
New Hampshire	..	7	..	..	..	7	..	..	..	..	7
New Jersey	8	..	..	..	8	..	..	..	..	..	8
New York	13	..	6	..	13	..	..	3	3	..	19
North Carolina	11	3	..	..	11	3	..	..	..	..	14
Ohio	3	..	..	..	..	..	3	..	..	..	3
Pennsylvania	20	..	..	..	20	..	..	..	..	..	20
Rhode Island	..	4	..	..	..	4	..	..	..	..	4
South Carolina	10	..	..	..	10	..	..	..	..	..	10
Tennessee	5	..	..	..	5	..	..	..	..	..	5
Vermont	6	..	..	..	..	..	6	..	..	..	6
Virginia	24	..	..	..	24	..	..	..	..	..	24
Total	122	47	6	1	113	47	9	3	3	1	176

James Madison was elected President and George Clinton as Vice-President.

During this period Congress was divided politically as follows:

Eleventh Congress.

Senate—10 Federalists, 24 Democrats ....Total, 34
House—46 Federalists, 95 Democrats .... " 141

Twelfth Congress.

Senate— 6 Federalists, 30 Democrats ....Total, 36
House—36 Federalists, 105 Democrats .... " 141

Election of 1812

NO CONVENTIONS. NO PLATFORMS.

The Republicans nominated—

For President, **James Madison,**
of Virginia.

For Vice-President, **Elbridge Gerry,**
of Massachusetts.

At a Republican caucus held in Washington, D. C., May 12, 1812, James Madison received the unanimous vote of the caucus (82 votes). John Langdon, of New Hampshire, was nominated for Vice-President, receiving 64 out of the 82 votes. Langdon declined the nomination, and at a second caucus, held on June 8, 1812, Elbridge Gerry was nominated by 74 out of 77 votes cast.

The Federalists nominated—

For President, **De Witt Clinton,**
of New York.

For Vice-President, **Jared Ingersoll,**
of Pennsylvania.

Clinton and Ingersoll were nominated at a convention held in September, 1812, in New York City.

The election occurred on November 3, 1812.

EIGHTEEN STATES VOTED.

The states choosing their electors by the legislatures were Connecticut, Delaware, Georgia, Louisiana, New Jersey, New York, North Carolina, South Carolina, and Vermont.

The following is the result of the vote, as counted on February 10, 1813:

STATES.	PRESIDENT.			VICE-PRESIDENT.			
	James Madison, of Virginia.	De Witt Clinton, of New York.	Vacancies.	Elbridge Gerry, of Massachusetts.	Jared Ingersoll, of Pennsylvania.	Vacancies.	No. entitled to vote.
Connecticut	..	9	..	..	9	..	9
Delaware	..	4	..	..	4	..	4
Georgia	8	..	..	8	..	..	8
Kentucky	12	..	..	12	..	.	12
Louisiana	3	..	..	3	..	..	3
Maryland	6	5	..	6	5	..	11
Massachusetts	..	22	..	2	20	..	22
New Hampshire	..	8	..	1	7	..	8
New Jersey	..	8	..	..	8	..	8
New York	..	29	..	..	29	..	29
North Carolina	15	..	..	15	..	..	15
Ohio	7	..	1	7	..	1	8
Pennsylvania	25	..	..	25	..	..	25
Rhode Island	..	4	..	..	4	..	4
South Carolina	11	..	..	11	..	..	11
Tennessee	8	..	..	8	..	..	8
Vermont	8	..	..	8	..	..	8
Virginia	25	..	..	25	..	..	25
Total	128	89	1	131	86	1	218

James Madison was elected President and Elbridge Gerry as Vice-President.

During this period Congress was divided politically as follows:

Thirteenth Congress.

Senate— 9 Federalists, 27 Democrats ....Total, 36
House—67 Federalists, 115 Democrats .... " 182

Fourteenth Congress.

Senate—12 Federalists, 26 Democrats ....Total 38
House—61 Federalists, 122 Democrats .... " 183

Election of 1816

NO CONVENTIONS. NO PLATFORMS.

The Republicans nominated—

For President, **James Monroe,**
of Virginia.

For Vice-President, **Daniel D. Tompkins,**
of New York.

A Republican caucus was held on March 16, 1816; 119 members attended this session. In the balloting for candidates for President James Monroe received 65, and William H. Crawford, 54 votes; consequently Monroe was declared the nominee. Daniel D. Tompkins was nominated for Vice-President, receiving 85 votes, as against 30 votes for Simon Snyder, of Pennsylvania.

The Federalists supported—

For President, **Rufus King,**
of NEW YORK.

For Vice-President, no particular one.

The Federalists did nothing whatever to nominate opposition candidates, but they all voted for Rufus King for President.

The election occurred on November 5, 1816.

NINETEEN STATES VOTED.

The states choosing their electors by the legislatures were Connecticut, Delaware, Georgia, Indiana, Louisiana, Massachusetts, New York, South Carolina, and Vermont.

The vote, as counted on February 12, 1817, resulted:

STATES.	PRESIDENT.			VICE-PRESIDENT.						No. entitled to vote.
	James Monroe, of Virginia.	Rufus King, of New York.	Vacancies.	Daniel D. Tompkins, of New York.	John E. Howard, of Maryland.	James Ross, of Pennsylvania.	John Marshall, of Virginia.	Robert G. Harper, of Maryland.	Vacancies.	
Connecticut	..	9	..	..	..	5	4	..	..	9
Delaware	..	3	1	..	..	..	..	3	1	4
Georgia	8	..	..	8	..	..	..	..	..	8
Indiana	3	..	..	3	..	..	..	..	..	3
Kentucky	12	..	..	12	..	..	..	..	..	12
Louisiana	3	..	..	3	..	..	..	..	..	3
Maryland	8	..	3	8	..	..	..	..	3	11
Massachusetts	..	22	..	..	22	..	..	..	..	22
New Hampshire	8	..	..	8	..	..	..	..	..	8
New Jersey	8	..	..	8	..	..	..	..	..	8
New York	29	..	..	29	..	..	..	..	..	29
North Carolina	15	..	..	15	..	..	..	..	..	15
Ohio	8	..	..	8	..	..	..	..	..	8
Pennsylvania	25	..	..	25	..	..	..	..	..	25
Rhode Island	4	..	..	4	..	..	..	..	..	4
South Carolina	11	..	..	11	..	..	..	..	..	11
Tennessee	8	..	..	8	..	..	..	..	..	8
Vermont	8	..	..	8	..	..	..	..	..	8
Virginia	25	..	..	25	..	..	..	..	..	25
Total	183	34	4	183	22	5	4	3	4	221

James Monroe was elected President and Daniel D. Tompkins as Vice-President.

During this period Congress was divided politically as follows:

Fifteenth Congress.

Senate—10 Federalists,	34 Democrats	Total,	44
House—57 Federalists,	128 Democrats	"	185

Sixteenth Congress.

Senate—10 Federalists,	36 Democrats	Total,	46
House—42 Federalists,	145 Democrats	"	187

Election of 1820

NO CONVENTIONS. NO PLATFORMS.

A congressional caucus, held in the spring of 1820, was attended by only a few members, and it was resolved that no nominations should be made.

The following candidates had practically no opposition:

For President, **James Monroe,**
of Virginia.

For Vice-President, **Daniel D. Tompkins,**
of New York.

The election occurred on November 13, 1820.

TWENTY-FOUR STATES VOTED.

The states choosing their electors by the legislatures

were Alabama, Connecticut, Delaware, Georgia, Indiana, Louisiana, New York, South Carolina and Vermont.

The vote as counted on February 14, 1821, follows:

STATES.	PRESIDENT.			VICE-PRESIDENT.						
	James Monroe, of Virginia.	John Quincy Adams, of Massachusetts.	Vacancies.	Daniel D. Tompkins, of New York.	Richard Stockton, of New Jersey.	Daniel Rodney, of Delaware.	Robert G. Harper, of Maryland.	Richard Rush, of Pennsylvania.	Vacancies.	No. entitled to vote.
Alabama	3	..	..	3	..	..	..	..	..	3
Connecticut	9	..	..	9	..	..	..	..	..	9
Delaware	4	..	..	..	..	4	..	..	..	4
Georgia	8	..	..	8	..	..	..	..	..	8
Illinois	3	..	..	3	..	..	..	..	..	3
Indiana	3	..	..	3	..	..	..	..	..	3
Kentucky	12	..	..	12	..	..	..	..	..	12
Louisiana	3	..	..	3	..	..	..	..	..	3
Maine	9	..	..	9	..	..	..	..	..	9
Maryland	11	..	..	10	..	..	1	..	..	11
Massachusetts	15	..	..	7	8	..	..	..	..	15
*Mississippi	2	..	1	2	..	..	..	..	1	3
Missouri	3	..	..	3	..	..	..	..	..	3
New Hampshire	7	1	..	7	..	..	..	1	..	8
New Jersey	8	..	..	8	..	..	..	..	..	8
New York	29	..	..	29	..	..	..	..	..	29
North Carolina	15	..	..	15	..	..	..	..	..	15
Ohio	8	..	..	8	..	..	..	..	..	8
*Pennsylvania	24	..	1	24	..	..	..	..	1	25
Rhode Island	4	..	..	4	..	..	..	..	..	4
South Carolina	11	..	..	11	..	..	..	..	..	11
*Tennessee	7	..	1	7	..	..	..	..	1	8
Vermont	8	..	..	8	..	..	..	..	..	8
Virginia	25	..	..	25	..	..	..	..	..	25
Total	231	†1	3	218	8	4	1	1	3	235

James Monroe was elected President and Daniel D. Tompkins as Vice-President.

* One elector in each of the States of Mississippi, Pennsylvania and Tennessee died before the meetings of the electors.

† The one vote for Adams was cast by Wm. Plumer, who did not consider that he was merely to perfunctorily record the choice of his party, therefore he exercised what he considered his power and duty as an elector by voting for Adams. He disapproved of Monroe's administration and also desired to draw attention to his friend Adams, who was elected President at the next election.

During this period Congress was divided politically as follows:

Seventeenth Congress.

Senate— 7 Federalists, 41 Democrats ....Total, 48
House—58 Federalists, 129 Democrats .... " 187

Eighteenth Congress

Senate—40 Democrats, 8 Whigs ....Total, 48
House—72 Federalists, 141 Democrats .... " 213

Election of 1824

NO CONVENTIONS. NO PLATFORMS.

During the spring of 1823 an effort was made to revive the congressional caucus system. On February 14, 1824, 66 members of Congress met in the hall of the House of Representatives—about one-fourth of all the members, 261 being the total membership of the two Houses. At this caucus William H. Crawford, of Georgia, was nominated for President and Albert Gallatin, of Pennsylvania, for Vice-President. The caucus adopted a resolution commending Messrs. Crawford and Gallatin as the national candidates, and added the following:

"In making the foregoing recommendation, the members of this meeting have acted in their individual characters as citizens; that they have been induced to this measure from a deep and settled conviction of the importance of union among Republicans throughout the United States, and as the best means of collecting and concentrating the feelings and wishes of the people of the Union upon this important subject."

The caucus proved to be a failure in this campaign, and as there were no recognized parties, the presidential election degenerated into a personal contest, in which the leading candidates were—

For President, **Henry Clay,** of Kentucky.
John Quincy Adams, of Massachusetts.
William H. Crawford, of Georgia.
Andrew Jackson, of Tennessee.

For Vice-President, **John C. Calhoun,** of South Carolina.

The election occurred on November 2, 1824.

TWENTY-FOUR STATES VOTED.

In six states—Delaware, Georgia, Louisiana, New York, South Carolina and Vermont—the electors were chosen by the legislatures, and in the remaining eighteen they were chosen by the people. The following is the result of the popular vote for President, being the first recorded:

STATES.	Andrew Jackson, Democrat.	J. Quincy Adams, Coalition.	William H. Crawford, Democrat.	Henry Clay, Republican.	Total vote.
Alabama	9,443	2,416	1,680	67	13,606
Connecticut	....	7,587	1,978	....	9,565
Illinois	1,901	1,542	219	1,047	4,709
Indiana	7,343	3,095	....	5,315	15,753
Kentucky	6,453	....	....	16,782	23,235
Maine	2,330	6,870	....	....	9,200
Maryland	14,523	14,632	3,646	695	33,496
Massachusetts	....	30,687	6,616	....	37,303
Mississippi	3,234	1,694	119	...	5,047
Missouri	987	311	....	1,401	2,699
New Hampshire	643	4,107	....	....	4,750
New Jersey	10,985	9,110	1,196	....	21,291
North Carolina	20,415	....	15,621	....	36,036
Ohio	18,457	12,280	....	19,255	49,992
Pennsylvania	36,100	5,440	4,206	1,609	47,355
Rhode Island	....	2,145	200	....	2,345
Tennessee	20,197	216	312	....	20,725
Virginia	2,861	3,189	8,489	416	14,955
Total	155,872	105,321	44,282	46,587	352,062

ELECTORAL VOTE.

Counted on February 9, 1825.

STATES.	PRESIDENT.				VICE-PRESIDENT.							
	Andrew Jackson, of Tennessee.	John Q. Adams, of Massachusetts.	William H. Crawford, of Georgia.	Henry Clay, of Kentucky.	John C. Calhoun, of South Carolina.	Nathan Sanford, of New York.	Nathaniel Macon, of North Carolina.	Andrew Jackson, of Tennessee.	Martin Van Buren, of New York.	Henry Clay, of Kentucky.	Vacancies.	No. entitled to vote.
Alabama	5	..	..	..	5	..	..	..	..	..	..	5
Connecticut	..	8	..	..	..	..	..	8	..	..	..	8
Delaware	..	1	2	..	1	..	..	..	..	2	..	3
Georgia	..	..	9	..	..	..	..	..	9	..	..	9
Illinois	2	1	..	..	3	..	..	..	..	..	..	3
Indiana	5	..	..	..	5	..	..	..	..	..	..	5
Kentucky	..	..	..	14	7	7	..	..	..	..	..	14
Louisiana	3	2	..	..	5	..	..	..	..	..	..	5
Maine	..	9	..	..	9	..	..	..	..	..	..	9
Maryland	7	3	1	..	10	..	..	1	..	..	..	11
Massachusetts	..	15	..	..	15	..	..	..	..	..	..	15
Mississippi	3	..	..	..	3	..	..	..	..	..	..	3
Missouri	..	..	..	3	..	..	..	3	..	..	..	3
New Hampshire	..	8	..	..	7	..	.	1	..	..	..	8
New Jersey	8	..	..	..	8	..	..	..	..	..	..	8
New York	1	26	5	4	29	7	..	..	..	..	..	36
North Carolina	15	..	..	..	15	..	..	..	..	..	..	15
Ohio	..	..	..	16	..	16	..	..	..	..	..	16
Pennsylvania	28	..	..	..	28	..	..	..	..	..	..	28
Rhode Island	..	4	..	..	3	..	..	..	..	..	1	4
South Carolina	11	..	..	..	11	..	..	..	..	..	..	11
Tennessee	11	..	..	..	11	..	..	..	..	..	..	11
Vermont	..	7	..	..	7	..	..	..	..	..	..	7
Virginia	..	..	24	..	..	..	24	..	..	..	..	24
Total	99	84	41	37	182	30	24	13	9	2	1	261

John C. Calhoun was declared elected as Vice-President. No candidate for President having received a majority, the election was thrown into the House of Representatives. Accordingly, the same day, February 9, 1825, the Senate having retired, the House immediately proceeded to elect a President. A roll-call showed that every member of the House except Mr. Garnett, of Virginia, ho s sick at his lodgings in Washington, was present. Mr. Webster, of Massachusetts, and Mr. Randolph, of Virginia, were appointed tellers. The House conducted the election according to the rules already adopted, and on the first ballot John Quincy Adams was chosen. The votes of thirteen states were given to him, those of seven to Jackson, and of four to Crawford. The Speaker declared Mr. Adams elected, and notice of the result was sent to the Senate. The votes of the states are shown by the following table, which indicates the divisions within the delegations:

STATES.	J. Quincy Adams.	Andrew Jackson.	William H. Crawford.
Alabama	..	3	..
Connecticut	6	..	..
Delaware	..	..	1
Georgia	..	..	7
Illinois	1	..	..
Indiana	..	3	..
Kentucky	8	4	..
Louisiana	2	1	..
Maine	7	..	..
Maryland	5	3	1
Massachusetts	12	1	..
Mississippi	..	1	..
Missouri	1	..	..
New Hampshire	6	..	..
New Jersey	1	5	..
New York	18	2	14
North Carolina	1	2	10
Ohio	10	2	2
Pennsylvania	1	25	..
Rhode Island	2	..	..
South Carolina	..	9	..
Tennessee	..	9	..
Vermont	5	..	..
Virginia	1	1	19
Total	87	71	54

John Quincy Adams was elected President and John C. Calhoun as Vice-President.

During this period Congress was divided politically as follows:

Nineteenth Congress.

Senate—38 Democrats, 10 Whigs ....Total, 48
House—79 Federalists, 134 Democrats .... " 213

Twentieth Congress.

Senate—37 Democrats, 11 Whigs ....Total, 48
House—85 Federalists, 128 Democrats .... " 213

Election of 1828

NO CONVENTIONS. NO PLATFORMS.

In the campaign of 1828, political parties for the first time in the century asserted themselves, and took that form which was to continue through several contests. The candidates were chosen by common consent, the legislatures of the states having indorsed and expressed a choice.

The Democrats named—

For President, **Andrew Jackson,**
of Tennessee.

For Vice-President, **John C. Calhoun,**
of South Carolina.

The National Republican candidates were—

For President, **John Quincy Adams,**
of Massachusetts.

For Vice-President, **Richard Rush,**
of Pennsylvania.

The election occurred on November 4, 1828.

TWENTY-FOUR STATES VOTED.

POPULAR VOTE.

The popular vote of the twenty-three states choosing electors was as follows:

STATES.	Andrew Jackson, Democrat.	John Q. Adams, National Republican.	Total vote.
Alabama	17,138	1,938	19,076
Connecticut	4,448	13,829	18,277
Delaware	4,349	4,769	9,118
Georgia	18,709	....	18,709
Illinois	6,763	1,581	8,344
Indiana	22,237	17,052	39,289
Kentucky	39,084	31,172	70,256
Louisiana	4,605	4,097	8,702
Maine	13,927	20,773	34,700
Maryland	24,578	25,759	50,337
Massachusetts	6,019	29,836	35,855
Mississippi	6,763	1,581	8,344
Missouri	8,232	3,422	11,654
New Hampshire	20,692	24,076	44,768
New Jersey	21,950	23,758	45,708
New York	140,763	135,413	276,176
North Carolina	37,857	13,918	51,775
Ohio	67,597	63,396	130,993
Pennsylvania	101,652	50,848	152,500
Rhode Island	821	2,754	3,575
*South Carolina	....	....	....
Tennessee	44,090	2,240	46,330
Vermont	8,205	24,784	32,989
Virginia	26,752	12,101	38,853
Total	647,231	509,097	1,156,328

* The electors were chosen by the legislature.

ELECTORAL VOTE.

Counted on February 11, 1829.

STATES.	PRESIDENT.		VICE-PRESIDENT.			No. entitled to vote.
	Andrew Jackson, of Tennessee.	John Q. Adams, of Massachusetts.	John C. Calhoun, of South Carolina.	Richard Rush, of Pennsylvania.	William Smith, of South Carolina.	
Alabama	5	..	5	..	..	5
Connecticut	..	8	..	8	..	8
Delaware	..	3	..	3	..	3
Georgia	9	..	2	..	7	9
Illinois	3	..	3	..	..	3
Indiana	5	..	5	..	..	5
Kentucky	14	..	14	..	..	14
Louisiana	5	..	5	..	..	5
Maine	1	8	1	8	..	9
Maryland	5	6	5	6	..	11
Massachusetts	..	15	..	15	..	15
Mississippi	3	..	3	..	..	3
Missouri	3	..	3	..	..	3
New Hampshire	..	8	..	8	..	8
New Jersey	..	8	..	8	..	8
New York	20	16	20	16	..	36
North Carolina	15	..	15	..	..	15
Ohio	16	..	16	..	..	16
Pennsylvania	28	..	28	..	..	28
Rhode Island	..	4	..	4	..	4
South Carolina	11	..	11	..	..	11
Tennessee	11	..	11	..	..	11
Vermont	..	7	..	7	..	7
Virginia	24	..	24	..	..	24
Total	178	83	171	83	7	261

Andrew Jackson was elected President and John C. Calhoun as Vice-President.

During this period Congress was divided politically as follows:

Twenty-first Congress.

Senate— 38 Democrats, 10 Whigs........................Total, 48
House—142 Democrats, 71 Whigs........................ " 213

Twenty-second Congress.

Senate— 35 Democrats, 13 Whigs........................Total, 48
House—130 Democrats, 83 Whigs........................ " 213

Election of 1832

For the first time, all presidential candidates were nominated by national conventions.

DEMOCRATIC CONVENTION.

Baltimore, Md., May 21, 1832.

Chairman, ROBERT LUCAS,
of Ohio.

NOMINATED—

For President, **Andrew Jackson,**
of Tennessee.

For Vice-President, **Martin Van Buren,**
of New York.

Delegates were present from every state except Missouri. At this convention the Committee on Rules reported the following resolution:

Resolved, That each state be entitled, in the nomination to be made of a candidate for the vice-presidency, to a number of votes equal to the number to which they will be entitled in the electoral colleges, under the new apportionment, in voting for President and Vice-President; and that two-thirds of the whole number of the votes in the convention shall be necessary to constitute a choice.

This was the beginning of the two-thirds rule which has governed all subsequent Democratic conventions in making nominations.

No platform was adopted.

Andrew Jackson was renominated for President without opposition. Martin Van Buren was nominated for Vice-President by the following ballot:

Martin Van Buren, of New York,	208	votes.
Philip P. Barbour, of Virginia,	49	"
Richard M. Johnson, of Kentucky,	26	"

NATIONAL REPUBLICAN CONVENTION.

Baltimore, Md., December 12, 1831.

Chairman pro tem., ABNER LACOCK,
of Pennsylvania.

Chairman, JAMES BARBOUR,
of Virginia.

NOMINATED—

For President, **Henry Clay,**
of Kentucky.

For Vice-President, **John Sergeant,**
of Pennsylvania.

Seventeen states were represented by 157 delegates. Henry Clay was nominated for President by a unanimous vote, and John Sergeant, of Pennsylvania, for Vice-President, also by a unanimous vote.

No platform was adopted.

By recommendation of this convention a national gathering of young men met in Washington, D. C., May 11, 1832, and having accepted or ratified the nominations of Henry Clay and John Sergeant, they adopted the following resolutions, which was the *first platform* ever issued by a national convention—to wit:

1. *Resolved,* That, in the opinion of this convention, although the fundamental principles adopted by our fathers, as a basis upon which to raise a superstructure of American independence, can never be annihilated, yet the time has come when nothing short of the united energies of all the friends of the American republic can be relied on to sustain and perpetuate that hallowed work.

2. *Resolved,* That an adequate protection to American industry is indispensable to the prosperity of the country; and that an abandonment of the policy at this period would be attended with consequences ruinous to the best interests of the nation.

3. *Resolved,* That a uniform system of internal improvements, sustained and supported by the general government, is calculated to secure, in the highest degree, the harmony, the strength, and the permanency of the republic.

4. *Resolved,* That the Supreme Court of the United States is the only tribunal recognized by the Constitution for deciding in the last resort all questions arising under the Constitution and laws of the United States, and that upon the preservation of the authority and jurisdiction of that court inviolate depends the existence of the nation.

5. *Resolved,* That the Senate of the United States is pre-eminently a conservative branch of the federal government; that upon a fearless and independent exercise of its constitutional functions depends the existence of the nicely balanced powers of that government; and that all attempts to overawe its deliberations by the public press or by the national executive deserve the indignant reprobation of every American citizen.

6. *Resolved,* That the political course of the present executive has given us no pledge that he will defend and support these great principles of American policy and the Constitution; but, on the contrary, has convinced us that he will abandon them whenever the purposes of party require it.

7. *Resolved,* That the indiscriminate removal of public officers, for the mere difference of political opinion, is a gross abuse of power; and that the doctrine lately "boldly

preached" in the Senate of the United States, that "to the victor belong the spoils of the enemy," is detrimental to the interests, corrupting to the morals, and dangerous to the liberties of this country.

8. *Resolved*, That we hold the disposition shown by the present national administration to accept the advice of the King of Holland, touching the northeastern boundary of the United States, and thus to transfer a portion of the territory and citizens of a state of this Union to a foreign power, to manifest a total destitution of patriotic American feeling, inasmuch as we consider the life, liberty, property, and citizenship of every inhabitant of every state as entitled to the national protection.

9. *Resolved*, That the arrangement between the United States and Great Britain relative to the colonial trade, made in pursuance of the instructions of the late Secretary of State, was procured in a manner derogatory to the national character, and is injurious to this country in its practical results.

10. *Resolved*, That it is the duty of every citizen of this republic, who regards the honor, the prosperity, and the preservation of our Union, to oppose by every honorable measure the re-election of Andrew Jackson, and to promote the election of Henry Clay, of Kentucky, and John Sergeant, of Pennsylvania, as President and Vice-President of the United States.

NOTE.—*These resolutions have been often published in mistake as the resolves of the convention which nominated Jackson and Van Buren.*

ANTI-MASONIC CONVENTION.

Baltimore, Md., September 26, 1831.

Chairman, JOHN C. SPENCER,
of New York.

NOMINATED—

For President, **William Wirt,**
of Maryland.

For Vice-President, **Amos Ellmaker,**
of Pennsylvania.

The Anti-Masonic movement dates from 1826. Its tenets were opposition to Freemasonry. As a party it held its first national convention in September, 1830, in the city of Philadelphia. Ten states with 96 delegates made up the convention. This body provided for a national convention which was held in Baltimore on the 26th of September, 1831, with 112 delegates present, representing the states of Connecticut, Delaware, Indiana, Maine, Maryland, Massachusetts, New Hampshire, New Jersey, New York, Ohio, Pennsylvania, Rhode Island, and Vermont. This convention met pursuant to the following call, issued by the prior convention held at Philadelphia, Pa., in September, 1830:

Resolved, That it is recommended to the people of the United States, opposed to secret societies, to meet in convention on Monday, the 26th day of September, 1831, at the City of Baltimore, by delegates equal in number to their representatives in both Houses of Congress, to make nominations of suitable candidates for the offices of President and Vice-President, to be supported at the next election, and for the transacting of such other business as the cause of Anti-Masonry may require.

At this convention the above-named nominations were made. Judge John McLean, of Ohio, was also considered for the nomination of President.

No platform was adopted.

The election occurred on November 6, 1832.

TWENTY-FOUR STATES VOTED.

POPULAR VOTE.

STATES.	Andrew Jackson, Democrat.	Henry Clay, National Republican.	Total vote.
* Alabama	....	....	....
Connecticut	11,269	17,775	29,044
Delaware	4,110	4,276	8,386
Georgia	20,750	....	20,750
Illinois	14,147	5,429	19,576
Indiana	31,552	15,472	47,024
Kentucky	36,247	43,396	79,643
Louisiana	4,049	2,528	6,577
Maine	33,291	27,204	60,495
Maryland	19,156	19,160	38,316
Massachusetts	14,545	33,003	47,548
Mississippi	5,919	....	5,919
Missouri	5,192	....	5,192
New Hampshire	25,486	19,010	44,496
New Jersey	23,856	23,393	47,249
New York	168,497	154,896	323,393
North Carolina	24,862	4,563	29,425
Ohio	81,246	76,539	157,785
Pennsylvania	90,983	56,716	147,699
Rhode Island	2,126	2,810	4,936
† South Carolina	....	....	....
Tennessee	28,740	1,436	30,176
Vermont	7,870	11,152	19,022
Virginia	33,609	11,451	45,060
Total	687,502	530,209	‡1,217,711

* Vote not recorded.

† The electors were chosen by the legislature.

‡ This total does not include 33,108 votes cast for John Floyd and William Wirt.

ELECTORAL VOTE.

Counted on February 13, 1833.

STATES.	PRESIDENT.					VICE-PRESIDENT.						
	Andrew Jackson, of Tennessee.	Henry Clay, of Kentucky.	John Floyd, of Virginia.	William Wirt, of Maryland.	Vacancies.	Martin Van Buren, of New York.	John Sergeant, of Pennsylvania.	William Wilkins, of Pennsylvania.	Henry Lee, of Massachusetts.	Amos Ellmaker, of Pennsylvania.	Vacancies.	No. entitled to vote.
Alabama	7	..	..	..	..	7	..	..	..	..	..	7
Connecticut	..	8	..	..	..	..	8	..	..	..	..	8
Delaware	..	3	..	..	..	..	3	..	..	..	..	3
Georgia	11	..	..	..	..	11	..	..	..	..	..	11
Illinois	5	..	..	..	..	5	..	..	..	..	..	5
Indiana	9	..	..	..	..	9	..	..	..	..	..	9
Kentucky	..	15	..	..	..	..	15	..	..	..	..	15
Louisiana	5	..	..	..	..	5	..	..	..	..	..	5
Maine	10	..	..	..	..	10	..	..	..	..	..	10
Maryland	3	5	..	..	2	3	5	..	..	..	2	10
Massachusetts	..	13	..	..	..	..	14	..	..	..	..	14
Mississippi	4	..	..	..	..	4	..	..	..	..	..	4
Missouri	4	..	..	..	..	4	..	..	..	..	..	4
New Hampshire	7	..	..	..	..	7	..	..	..	..	..	7
New Jersey	8	..	..	..	..	8	..	..	..	..	..	8
New York	42	..	..	..	..	42	..	..	..	..	..	42
North Carolina	15	..	..	..	..	15	..	..	..	..	..	15
Ohio	21	..	..	..	..	21	..	..	..	..	..	21
Pennsylvania	30	..	..	..	..	..	..	30	..	..	..	30
Rhode Island	..	4	..	..	..	..	4	..	..	..	..	4
South Carolina	..	..	11	..	..	..	..	..	11	..	..	11
Tennessee	15	..	..	..	..	15	..	..	..	..	..	15
Vermont	..	..	..	7	..	..	..	..	..	7	..	7
Virginia	23	..	..	..	..	23	..	..	..	..	..	23
Total	219	49	11	7	2	189	49	30	11	7	2	288

Andrew Jackson was elected President and Martin Van Buren as Vice-President.

During this period Congress was divided politically as follows:

Twenty-third Congress.

Senate— 30 Democrats, 18 Whigs ....Total, 48
House—147 Democrats, 93 Whigs .... " 240

Twenty-fourth Congress.

Senate— 33 Democrats, 19 Whigs ....Total, 52
House—144 Democrats, 98 Whigs .... " 242

Election of 1836

DEMOCRATIC CONVENTION.

Baltimore, Md., May 20, 1835.

Chairman, ANDREW STEVENSON,
of Virginia.

NOMINATED—

For President, **Martin Van Buren,**
of New York.

For Vice-President, **Richard M. Johnson,**
of Kentucky.

Twenty-two states and two territories (Michigan and Arkansas) were represented at this convention, and more than 600 delegates were present, but the vote was restricted in each state to the number of representatives in Congress. Martin Van Buren was nominated for President by a unanimous vote. For Vice-President, the following is the ballot:

Richard M. Johnson, of Kentucky, 178 votes.
William C. Rives, of Virginia, 87 "

Johnson having the necessary two-thirds majority, was declared the nominee.

No platform was adopted, but the Democrats of New York, in January, 1836, published the following, which was regarded as a party declaration—to wit:

We hold these truths to be self-evident: that all men are created free and equal; that they are endowed by their Creator with certain inalienable rights, among which are life, liberty, and the pursuit of happiness; that the true foundation of republican government is the equal rights of every citizen in his person and property, and in their management; that the idea is quite unfounded that on entering into society we give up any natural right; that the rightful power of all legislation is to declare and enforce only our natural rights and duties, and to take none of them from us; that no man has the natural right to commit aggressions on the equal rights of another, and this is all from which the law ought to restrain him; that every man is under the natural duty of contributing to the necessities of society, and this is all the law should enforce on him; that when the laws have declared and enforced all this they have fulfilled their functions.

We declare unqualified hostility to bank notes and paper money as a circulating medium, because gold and silver is the only safe and constitutional currency; hostility to any and all monopolies by legislation, because they are violations of equal rights of the people; hostility to the dangerous and unconstitutional creation of vested rights or prerogatives by legislation, because they are usurpations of the people's sovereign rights; no legislative or other authority in the body politic can rightfully, by charter or otherwise, exempt any man or body of men, in any case whatever, from trial by jury and the jurisdiction or operation of the laws which govern the community.

We hold that each and every law or act of incorporation passed by preceding legislatures can be rightfully altered and repealed by their successors; and that they should be altered or repealed when necessary for the public good, or when required by a majority of the people.

NATIONAL REPUBLICAN OR WHIG.

NO CONVENTION.

The candidates named by the several states were—

For President, **William Henry Harrison,**
of Ohio.

Daniel Webster,
of Massachusetts.

Willie P. Mangum,
of North Carolina.

For Vice-President, **John Tyler,**
of Virginia.

Francis Granger,
of New York.

John McLean,
of Ohio.

William Henry Harrison, of Ohio, and Francis Granger, of New York, were nominated for President and Vice-President respectively, by a state convention held at Harrisburg, Pennsylvania.

A Democratic Anti-Masonic Convention held in the same place at a different date, nominated the same candidates.

A Whig state convention held in Maryland nominated William Henry Harrison for President, with John Tyler, of Virginia, for Vice-President.

General Harrison was also nominated by state conventions in New York, Ohio, and elsewhere.

Hugh L. White, of Tennessee, was nominated for President by the legislatures of Alabama and Tennessee, as the opposition or Anti-Jackson candidate.

Daniel Webster, of Massachusetts, and Willie P. Mangum, of North Carolina, were also named as candidates for President.

No platform was adopted, but the Whigs in state convention at Albany, N. Y., February 3, 1836, adopted the following resolutions:

Resolved, That in support of our cause we invite all citizens opposed to Martin Van Buren and the Baltimore nominees.

Resolved, That Martin Van Buren, by intriguing with the Executive to obtain his influence to elect him to the Presidency, has set an example dangerous to our freedom and corrupting to our free institutions.

Resolved, That the support we render to William H. Harrison is by no means given to him solely on account of his brilliant and successful services as leader of our armies during the last war, but that in him we view also the man of high intellect, the stern patriot, uncontaminated by the machinery of hackneyed politicians—a man of the school of Washington.

Resolved, That in Francis Granger we recognize one of our most distinguished fellow citizens, whose talents we admire, whose patriotism we trust, and whose principles we sanction.

The election occurred on November 8, 1836.

TWENTY-SIX STATES VOTED.

POPULAR VOTE.

STATES.	Martin Van Buren, Democrat.	William H. Harrison, National Republican.	Total vote.
Alabama	19,068	15,637	34,705
Arkansas	2,400	1,238	3,638
Connecticut	19,234	18,466	37,700
Delaware	4,155	4,738	8,893
Georgia	22,126	24,930	47,056
Illinois	18,097	14,983	33,080
Indiana	32,480	41,281	73,761
Kentucky	33,435	36,955	70,390
Louisiana	3,653	3,383	7,036
Maine	22,300	15,239	37,539
Maryland	22,167	25,852	48,019
Massachusetts	33,501	41,093	74,594
Michigan	7,360	4,000	11,360
Mississippi	9,979	9,688	19,667
Missouri	10.995	8,337	19,332
New Hampshire	18,722	6,228	24,950
New Jersey	26.347	26,892	53,239
New York	166,815	138,543	305,358
North Carolina	26,910	23,626	50,536
Ohio	96,948	105,405	202,353
Pennsylvania	91,475	87,111	178,586
Rhode Island	2,964	2,710	5,674
* South Carolina	....	....	....
Tennessee	26,120	35,962	62,082
Vermont	14,037	20,991	35,028
Virginia	30,261	23,368	53,629
Total	761,549	736,656	1,498,205

* The electors were chosen by the legislature.

ELECTORAL VOTE.

Counted on February 8, 1837.

STATES.	PRESIDENT.					VICE-PRESIDENT.				No. entitled to vote.
	Martin Van Buren, of New York.	William H. Harrison, of Ohio.	Hugh L. White, of Tennessee.	Daniel Webster, of Massachusetts.	Willie P. Mangum, of North Carolina.	Richard M. Johnson, of Kentucky.	Francis Granger, of New York.	John Tyler, of Virginia.	William Smith, of Alabama.	
Alabama	7	..	..	..	..	7	..	..	..	7
Arkansas	3	..	..	..	..	3	..	..	..	3
Connecticut	8	..	..	..	..	8	..	..	..	8
Delaware	..	3	..	..	..	..	3	..	..	3
Georgia	..	..	11	..	..	..	..	11	..	11
Illinois	5	..	..	..	..	5	..	..	..	5
Indiana	..	9	..	..	..	..	9	..	..	9
Kentucky	..	15	..	..	..	..	15	..	..	15
Louisiana	5	..	..	..	..	5	..	..	..	5
Maine	10	..	..	..	..	10	..	..	..	10
Maryland	..	10	..	..	..	..	..	10	..	10
Massachusetts	..	..	..	14	..	..	14	..	..	14
Michigan	3	..	..	..	..	3	..	..	..	3
Mississippi	4	..	..	..	..	4	..	..	..	4
Missouri	4	..	..	..	..	4	..	..	..	4
New Hampshire	7	..	..	..	..	7	..	..	..	7
New Jersey	..	8	..	..	..	..	8	..	..	8
New York	42	..	..	..	..	42	..	..	..	42
North Carolina	15	..	..	..	..	15	..	..	..	15
Ohio	..	21	..	..	..	..	21	..	..	21
Pennsylvania	30	..	..	..	..	30	..	..	..	30
Rhode Island	4	..	..	..	..	4	..	..	..	4
South Carolina	..	..	..	..	11	..	..	11	..	11
Tennessee	..	..	15	..	..	..	..	15	..	15
Vermont	..	7	..	..	..	..	7	..	..	7
Virginia	23	..	..	..	..	..	..	..	23	23
Total	170	73	26	14	11	147	77	47	23	294

No candidate for Vice-President having received a majority of the votes cast, the Senate elected Richard M. Johnson, of Kentucky, Vice-President.

Martin Van Buren was elected President and Richard M. Johnson as Vice-President.

During this period Congress was divided politically as follows:

Twenty-fifth Congress.

Senate— 31 Democrats, 18 Whigs, 3 Independents .....Total, 52
House—117 Democrats, 115 Whigs, 10 Independents ..... " 242

Twenty-sixth Congress.

Senate— 22 Democrats, 28 Whigs, 2 Independents.......Total, 52
House—103 Democrats, 132 Whigs, 6 Independents,
1 vacancy.. " 242

Election of 1840

DEMOCRATIC CONVENTION.

Baltimore, Md., May 5, 1840.

Chairman pro tem., ISAAC HILL,
of New Hampshire.

Chairman, WILLIAM CARROLL,
of Tennessee.

NOMINATED—

For President, **Martin Van Buren,**
of New York.

For Vice-President, no nomination.

Delegates from 21 states attended the Democratic Convention. Connecticut, Delaware, Illinois, South Carolina, and Virginia were not represented. Martin Van Buren was renominated without opposition.

No nomination was made for Vice-President, but the following resolution was adopted, stating the reason therefor: "*Resolved,* that the convention deem it expedient at the present time, not to choose between the individuals in nomination, but to leave the decision to their Republican fellow-citizens in the several states, trusting that before the Election shall take place this opinion will become so concentrated as to secure the choice of a Vice-President by the Electoral College." For a list of those voted for see the electoral vote of this election.

The following platform was adopted:—

DEMOCRATIC PLATFORM.

1. *Resolved,* That the federal government is one of limited powers, derived solely from the Constitution, and the grants of power shown therein ought to be strictly construed by all the departments and agents of the government, and that it is inexpedient and dangerous to exercise doubtful constitutional powers.

2. *Resolved,* That the Constitution does not confer upon the general government the power to commence and carry on a general system of internal improvements.

3. *Resolved,* That the Constitution does not confer authority upon the federal government, directly or indirectly, to assume the debts of the several states, contracted for local internal improvements or other state purposes; nor would such assumption be just or expedient.

4. *Resolved,* That justice and sound policy forbid the federal government to foster one branch of industry to the detriment of another, or to cherish the interests of one portion to the injury of another portion of our common country; that every citizen and every section of the country has a right to demand and insist upon an equality of rights and privileges, and to complete and ample protection of person and property from domestic violence or foreign aggression.

5. *Resolved,* That it is the duty of every branch of the government to enforce and practice the most rigid economy in conducting our public affairs, and that no more revenue ought to be raised than is required to defray the necessary expenses of the government.

6. *Resolved,* That Congress has no power to charter a United States Bank; that we believe such an institution one of deadly hostility to the best interests of the country, dangerous to our republican institutions and the liberties of the people, and calculated to place the business of the country within the control of a concentrated money power and above the laws and the will of the people.

7. *Resolved,* That Congress has no power under the Constitution to interfere with or control the domestic institutions of the several states, and that such states are the sole and proper judges of everything pertaining to their own affairs not prohibited by the Constitution; that all efforts by Abolitionists or others, made to induce Congress to interfere with questions of slavery, or to take incipient steps in relation thereto, are calculated to lead to the most alarming and dangerous conse-

quences, and that all such efforts have an inevitable tendency to diminish the happiness of the people and endanger the stability and permanence of the Union, and ought not to be countenanced by any friend to our political institutions.

8. *Resolved,* That the separation of the moneys of the government from banking institutions is indispensable for the safety of the funds of the government and the rights of the people.

9. *Resolved,* That the liberal principles embodied by Jefferson in the Declaration of Independence, and sanctioned in the Constitution, which make ours the land of liberty and the asylum of the oppressed of every nation, have ever been cardinal principles in the Democratic faith; and every attempt to abridge the present privilege of becoming citizens and the owners of soil among us ought to be resisted with the same spirit which swept the Alien and Sedition laws from our statute-book.

WHIG CONVENTION.

Harrisburg, Pa., December 4–7, 1839.

Chairman pro tem., ISAAC C. BATES,
of Massachusetts.

Chairman, JAMES BARBOUR,
of Virginia.

NOMINATED—

For President, **William H. Harrison,**
of Ohio.

For Vice-President, **John Tyler,**
of Virginia.

Delegates from 22 states appeared at this convention. Arkansas, Georgia, South Carolina, and Tennessee, were not represented. A special rule was adopted at this convention which might be called the "unit rule," according to which the delegations by states selected a committee of three each, such committeemen to assemble as a Committee of the Whole. The state delegations, meeting separately, were to ballot, and then to deliver their ballots to their committee, to be later compared by the whole committee. The official proceedings of this committee are not of record. Sufficient is known, however, to say that on the first ballot in the Committee of the Whole, the following vote resulted:

Henry Clay, of Kentucky,	103 votes.
William Henry Harrison, of Ohio,	94 "
Winfield Scott, of New Jersey,	57 "

After a long struggle, on the third day of the convention, the committee reported the following vote:

William Henry Harrison, of Ohio,	148 votes.
Henry Clay, of Kentucky,	90 "
Winfield Scott, of New Jersey,	16 "

William H. Harrison was declared the nominee. John Tyler, of Virginia, received the unanimous vote of the committee for Vice-President.

No platform was adopted.

ABOLITION PARTY CONVENTION.

Warsaw, N. Y., November 13, 1839,
and Albany, N. Y., April 1, 1840.

NOMINATED—

For President, **James G. Birney,**
of New York.

For Vice-President, **Francis Lemoyne,**
of Pennsylvania.

This was the beginning of the movement which culminated in the organization of the Republican party. At first James G. Birney, of New York, was nominated for President, and Thomas Earl, of Pennsylvania, for Vice-President; but Mr. Earl declining, Francis Lemoyne, of Pennsylvania, was nominated in his stead.

The Warsaw convention of Nov. 13, 1839, adopted the following resolution:

Resolved, That, in our judgment, every consideration of duty and expediency which ought to control the action of Christian freemen requires of the Abolitionists of the United States to organize a distinct and independent political party, embracing all the necessary means for nominating candidates for office and sustaining them by public suffrage.

The election occurred on November 3, 1840.

TWENTY-SIX STATES VOTED.

POPULAR VOTE.

STATES.	William H. Harrison, Whig.	Martin Van Buren, Democrat.	James G. Birney, Abolitionist.	Total vote
Alabama	28,471	33,991	....	62,462
Arkansas	5,160	6,049	....	11,209
Connecticut	31,601	25,296	174	57,071
Delaware	5,967	4,884	....	10,851
Georgia	40,261	31,933	....	72,194
Illinois	45,537	47,476	149	93,162
Indiana	65,302	51,695	....	116,997
Kentucky	58,489	32,616	....	91,105
Louisiana	11,297	7,617	....	18,914
Maine	46,612	46,201	194	93,007
Maryland	33,528	28,752	....	62,280
Massachusetts	72,874	51,948	1,621	126,443
Michigan	22,933	21,098	321	44,352
Mississippi	19,518	16,995	....	36,513
Missouri	22,972	29,760	....	52,732
New Hampshire	26,158	32,670	126	58,954
New Jersey	33,351	31,034	69	64,454
New York	225,817	212,519	2,798	441,134
North Carolina	46,376	34,218	....	80,594
Ohio	148,157	124,782	903	273,842
Pennsylvania	144,021	143,676	343	288,040
Rhode Island	5,278	3,301	42	8,621
*South Carolina	....	....	....	....
Tennessee	60,391	48,289	....	108,680
Vermont	32,445	18,009	319	50,773
Virginia	42,501	43,893	....	86,394
Total	1,275,017	1,128,702	7,059	2,410,778

* The electors were chosen by the legislature.

ELECTORAL VOTE.

Counted on February 10, 1841.

STATES.	PRESIDENT.		VICE-PRESIDENT.				No. entitled to vote.
	William H. Harrison, of Ohio.	Martin Van Buren, of New York.	John Tyler, of Virginia.	Richard M. Johnson, of Kentucky.	Littleton W. Tazewell, of Virginia,	James K. Polk, of Tennessee.	
Alabama	..	7	..	7	..	..	7
Arkansas	..	3	..	3	..	..	3
Connecticut	8	..	8	..	..	..	8
Delaware	3	..	3	..	..	..	3
Georgia	11	..	11	..	..	..	11
Illinois	..	5	..	5	..	..	5
Indiana	9	..	9	..	..	..	9
Kentucky	15	..	15	..	..	..	15
Louisiana	5	..	5	..	..	..	5
Maine	10	..	10	..	..	..	10
Maryland	10	..	10	..	..	..	10
Massachusetts	14	..	14	..	..	..	14
Michigan	3	..	3	..	..	..	3
Mississippi	4	..	4	..	..	..	4
Missouri	..	4	..	4	..	..	4
New Hampshire	..	7	..	7	..	..	7
New Jersey	8	..	8	..	..	..	8
New York	42	..	42	..	..	..	42
North Carolina	15	..	15	..	..	..	15
Ohio	21	..	21	..	..	..	21
Pennsylvania	30	..	30	..	..	..	30
Rhode Island	4	..	4	..	..	..	4
South Carolina	..	11	..	..	11	..	11
Tennessee	15	..	15	..	..	..	15
Vermont	7	..	7	..	..	..	7
Virginia	..	23	..	22	..	1	23
Total	234	60	234	48	11	1	294

William H. Harrison was elected President and John Tyler as Vice-President.

During this period Congress was divided politically as follows:

Twenty-Seventh Congress.

Senate— 22 Democrats, 28 Whigs, 2 Independents ...... Total, 52
House —103 Democrats, 132 Whigs, 6 Independents,
1 vacancy .... " 242

Twenty-eighth Congress.

Senate— 23 Democrats, 29 Whigs .... Total, 52
House —142 Democrats, 81 Whigs .... " 223

Election of 1844

DEMOCRATIC CONVENTION.

Baltimore, Md., May 27–29, 1844.

Temporary and permanent Chairman,
HENDRICK B. WRIGHT,
of Pennsylvania.

NOMINATED—

For President, **James K. Polk,**
of Tennessee.

For Vice-President, **George M. Dallas,**
of Pennsylvania.

Every state was represented at this convention except South Carolina. 325 delegates were in attendance, but they cast only 266 votes. After a day and a half of contention the two-thirds rule was adopted.

The following is the result of the balloting:

CANDIDATES.	1st.	2d.	3d.	4th.	5th.	6th.	7th.	8th.	9th
MARTIN VAN BUREN, of New York.......	146	127	121	111	103	101	99	104	..
LEWIS CASS, of Michigan........	83	94	92	105	107	116	123	114	..
RICHARD M. JOHNSON, of Kentucky.......	24	33	38	32	29	23	21	..	..
JAMES BUCHANAN, of Pennsylvania...	4	9	11	17	26	25	22	..	..
LEVI WOODBURY, of New Hampshire	2	1	2	..	..	..	..	..	..
COMMODORE STEWART, of Pennsylvania...	1	1	..	..	..	..	..	..	..
JOHN C. CALHOUN, of South Carolina..	6	1	2	..	..	..	..	..	..
JAMES K. POLK, of Tennessee	..	..	..	..	..	..	..	44	266
Whole No. of votes, 266 Necessary to choice, 178									

In voting for a candidate for Vice-President, Silas Wright, of New York, received 256 votes on the first ballot, 9 being cast for Levi Woodbury, of New Hampshire. Mr. Wright declined the nomination.

On the following day George M. Dallas, of Pennsylvania, was nominated, receiving 220 votes. John Fairfield, of Maine; Levi Woodbury, of New Hampshire; Lewis Cass, of Michigan; Richard M. Johnson, of Kentucky; Commodore Stewart, of Pennsylvania; Wm. L. Marcy, of New York, were also voted for.

The following platform was adopted:

DEMOCRATIC PLATFORM.

1. *Resolved*, That the American Democracy place their trust, not in factitious symbols, not in displays and appeals insulting to the judgment and subversive of the intellect of the people, but in a clear reliance upon the intelligence, patriotism, and the discriminating justice of the American people.

2. *Resolved*, That we regard this as a distinctive feature of our political creed, which we are proud to maintain before the world, as the great moral element in a form of government springing from and upheld by the popular will; and we contrast it with the creed and practice of federalism, under whatever name or form, which seeks to palsy the will of the constituent, and which conceives no imposture too monstrous for the popular credulity.

3. *Resolved, therefore*, That, entertaining these views, the Democratic party of this Union, through the delegates assembled in general convention of the states, coming together in a spirit of concord, of devotion to the doctrines and faith of a free representative government, and appealing to their fellow-citizens for the rectitude of their intentions, renew and reassert before the American people the declaration of principles avowed by them on a former occasion, when, in general convention, they presented their candidates for the popular suffrage.

Then resolutions 1, 2, 3, 4, 5, 6, 7, 8, and 9 of the platform of 1840 (see pages 41 and 42) were reaffirmed, to which were added the following:

13. *Resolved*, That the proceeds of the public lands ought to

be sacredly applied to the national objects specified in the Constitution, and that we are opposed to the laws lately adopted, and to any law, for the distribution of such proceeds among the states, as alike inexpedient in policy and repugnant to the Constitution.

14. *Resolved,* That we are decidedly opposed to taking from the President the qualified veto power by which he is enabled, under restrictions and responsibilities amply sufficient to guard the public interest, to suspend the passage of a bill whose merits cannot secure the approval of two thirds of the Senate and House of Representatives, until the judgment of the people can be obtained thereon, and which has thrice saved the American people from the corrupt and tyrannical domination of the Bank of the United States.

15. *Resolved,* That our title to the whole of the Territory of Oregon is clear and unquestionable; that no portion of the same ought to be ceded to England or any other power, and that the re-occupation of Oregon and the re-annexation of Texas at the earliest practicable period are great American measures, which this convention recommends to the cordial support of the Democracy of the Union.

NOTE.—An abortive convention of officeholders met at Baltimore shortly after the Democratic Convention and renominated ex-President Tyler. He accepted the nomination, but soon after withdrew.

WHIG CONVENTION.

Baltimore, Md., May 1, 1844.

Chairman pro tem., ANDREW F. HOPKINS,
of Alabama.

Chairman, AMBROSE SPENCER,
of New York.

NOMINATED—

For President, **Henry Clay,**
of Kentucky,

For Vice-President, **Theodore Frelinghuysen,**
of New Jersey.

Every state in the Union was represented at this convention by a full delegation. Henry Clay, of Kentucky, was nominated for President by acclamation.

For Vice-President, Theodore Frelinghuysen, of New Jersey, was nominated on the third ballot, as follows:

CANDIDATES.	1st.	2d.	3d.
THEODORE FRELINGHUYSEN, of New Jersey	101	118	155
JOHN DAVIS, of Massachusetts	83	74	79
MILLARD FILLMORE, of New York	53	51	40
JOHN SERGEANT, of Pennsylvania	38	32	Withdr'n.
Whole number of votes	275	275	274
Necessary to a choice	138	138	138

The convention adopted the following platform:—

WHIG PLATFORM.

1. *Resolved*, That, in presenting to the country the names of Henry Clay for President, and of Theodore Frelinghuysen for Vice-President of the United States, this convention is actuated by the conviction that all the great principles of the Whig party—principles inseparable from the public honor and prosperity—will be maintained and advanced by these candidates.

2. *Resolved*, That these principles may be summed as comprising: A well-regulated currency; a tariff for revenue to defray the necessary expenses of the government, and discriminating with special reference to the protection of the domestic labor of the country; the distribution of the proceeds from the sales of the public lands; a single term for the presidency; a reform of executive usurpations; and generally such an administration of the affairs of the country as shall impart to every branch of the public service the greatest practical efficiency, controlled by a well-regulated and wise economy.

3. *Resolved*, That the name of Henry Clay needs no eulogy. The history of the country since his first appearance in public life is his history. Its brightest pages of prosperity and suc-

cess are identified with the principles which he has upheld, as its darkest and more disastrous pages are with every material departure in our public policy from those principles.

4. *Resolved,* That in Theodore Frelinghuysen we present a man pledged alike by his Revolutionary ancestry and his own public course to every measure calculated to sustain the honor and interest of the country. Inheriting the principles as well as the name of a father who, with Washington, on the fields of Trenton and of Monmouth, perilled life in the contest for liberty, and afterwards, as a senator of the United States, acted with Washington in establishing and perpetuating that liberty, Theodore Frelinghuysen, by his course as attorney-general of the State of New Jersey for twelve years, and subsequently as a senator of the United States for several years, was always strenuous on the side of law, order, and the Constitution, while, as a private man, his head, his hand, and his heart have been given without stint to the cause of morals, education, philanthropy, and religion.

LIBERTY-ABOLITIONIST CONVENTION.

Buffalo, N. Y., August 30, 1843.

Chairman. LEICESTER KING,
of Ohio.

NOMINATED—

For President, **James G. Birney,**
of New York.

For Vice-President, **Thomas Morris,**
of Ohio.

There were present at this convention 148 delegates representing twelve states. A platform was adopted, and nominations were made as given above.

LIBERTY-ABOLITIONIST PLATFORM.

1. *Resolved,* That human brotherhood is a cardinal principle of true democracy, as well as of pure Christianity, which spurns all inconsistent limitations; and neither the political

party which repudiates it, nor the political system which is not based upon it, can be truly democratic or permanent.

2. *Resolved*, That the Liberty party, placing itself upon this broad principle, will demand the absolute and unqualified divorce of the general government from slavery, and also the restoration of equality of rights among men in every state where the party exists or may exist.

3. *Resolved*, That the Liberty party has not been organized for any temporary purpose by interested politicians, but has arisen from among the people in consequence of a conviction, hourly gaining ground, that no other party in the country represents the true principles of American liberty, or the true spirit of the Constitution of the United States.

4. *Resolved*, That the Liberty party has not been organized merely for the overthrow of slavery: its first decided effort must, indeed, be directed against slaveholding as the grossest and most revolting manifestation of despotism, but it will also carry out the principle of equal rights into all its practical consequences and applications, and support every just measure conducive to individual and social freedom.

5. *Resolved*, That the Liberty party is not a sectional party, but a national party; was not originated in a desire to accomplish a single object, but in a comprehensive regard to the great interests of the whole country; is not a new party, nor a third party, but is the party of 1776, reviving the principles of that memorable era, and striving to carry them into practical application.

6. *Resolved*, That it was understood in the times of the Declaration and the Constitution that the existence of slavery in some of the states was in derogation of the principles of American liberty, and a deep stain upon the character of the country; and the implied faith of the states and the nation was pledged that slavery should never be extended beyond its then existing limits, but should be gradually, and yet at no distant day wholly, abolished by state authority.

7. *Resolved*, That the faith of the states and the nation thus pledged was most nobly redeemed by the voluntary abolition of slavery in several of the states, and by the adoption of the ordinance of 1787 for the government of the territory northwest of the river Ohio, then the only territory in the United States, and consequently the only territory subject in this respect to the control of Congress, by which ordinance slavery

was forever excluded from the vast regions which now compose the States of Ohio, Indiana, Illinois, Michigan, and the Territory of Wisconsin, and an incapacity to bear up any other than free men was impressed on the soil itself.

8. *Resolved,* That the faith of the states and the nation, thus pledged, has been shamefully violated by the omission, on the part of many of the states, to take any measures whatever for the abolition of slavery within their respective limits; by the continuance of slavery in the District of Columbia and in the Territories of Louisiana and Florida; by the legislation of Congress; by the protection afforded by national legislation and negotiation of slaveholding in American vessels, on the high seas, employed in the coastwise slave traffic; and by the extension of slavery far beyond its original limits by acts of Congress admitting new slave states into the Union.

9. *Resolved,* That the fundamental truths of the Declaration of Independence, that all men are endowed by their Creator with certain inalienable rights, among which are life, liberty, and the pursuit of happiness, was made the fundamental law of our national government by that amendment of the Constitution which declares that no person shall be deprived of life, liberty, or property without due process of law.

10. *Resolved,* That we recognize as sound the doctrine maintained by slaveholding jurists, that slavery is against natural rights, and strictly local, and that its existence and continuance rests on no other support than state legislation, and not on any authority of Congress.

11. *Resolved,* That the general government has, under the Constitution, no power to establish or continue slavery anywhere, and therefore that all treaties and acts of Congress establishing, continuing, or favoring slavery in the District of Columbia, in the Territory of Florida, or on the high seas, are unconstitutional, and all attempts to hold men as property within the limits of exclusive national jurisdiction ought to be prohibited by law.

12. *Resolved,* That the provisions of the Constitution of the United States which confer extraordinary political powers on the owners of slaves, and thereby constituting the two hundred and fifty thousand slaveholders in the slave states a privileged aristocracy; and the provision for the reclamation of fugitive slaves from service, are anti-republican in their character, dangerous to the liberties of the people, and ought to be abrogated.

13. *Resolved,* That the practical operation of the second of these provisions is seen in the enactment of the act of Congress respecting persons escaping from their masters, which act, if the construction given to it by the Supreme Court of the United States in the case of Prigg *v.* Pennsylvania be correct, nullifies the *habeas corpus* acts of all the states, takes away the whole legal security of personal freedom, and ought, therefore, to be immediately repealed.

14. *Resolved,* That the peculiar patronage and support hitherto extended to slavery and slaveholding by the general government ought to be immediately withdrawn, and the example and influence of national authority ought to be arrayed on the side of liberty and free labor.

15. *Resolved,* That the practice of the general government, which prevails in the slave states, of employing slaves upon the public works, instead of free laborers, and paying aristocratic masters, with a view to secure or reward political services, is utterly indefensible and ought to be abandoned.

16. *Resolved,* That freedom of speech and of the press, and the right of petition, and the right of trial by jury, are sacred and inviolable; and that all rules, regulations, and laws in derogation of either are oppressive, unconstitutional, and not to be endured by a free people.

17. *Resolved,* That we regard voting, in an eminent degree, as a moral and religious duty, which, when exercised, should be by voting for those who will do all in their power for immediate emancipation.

18. *Resolved,* That this convention recommend to the friends of liberty in all those free states where any inequality of rights and privileges exists on account of color, to employ their utmost energies to remove all such remnants and effects of the slave system.

Whereas, The Constitution of these United States is a series of agreements, covenants, or contracts between the people of the United States, each with all and all with each; and

Whereas, It is a principle of universal morality that the moral laws of the Creator are paramount to all human laws; or, in the language of an Apostle, that " we ought to obey God rather than men "; and

Whereas, The principle of common law that any contract, covenant, or agreement to do an act derogatory to natural right is vitiated and annulled by its inherent immorality, has been recognized by one of the justices of the Supreme Court of the United States, who in a recent case expressly holds that "*any* contract that rests upon such a basis is *void*"; and

Whereas, The third clause of the second section of the fourth article of the Constitution of the United States, when construed as providing for the surrender of a fugitive slave, *does* "rest upon such a basis," in that it is a contract to rob a man of a natural right—namely, his natural right to his own liberties, and is, therefore, absolutely *void;* therefore,

19. *Resolved*, That we hereby give it to be distinctly understood by this nation and the world, that, as Abolitionists, considering that the strength of our cause lies in its righteousness, and our hope for it in our conformity to the laws of God and our respect for the rights of man, we owe it to the Sovereign Ruler of the Universe as a proof of our allegiance to Him, in all our civil relations and offices, whether as private citizens or public functionaries sworn to support the Constitution of the United States, to regard and treat the third clause of the fourth article of that instrument, whenever applied to the case of a fugitive slave, as utterly null and void, and consequently as forming no part of the Constitution of the United States, whenever we are called upon or sworn to support it.

20. *Resolved*, That the power given to Congress by the Constitution to provide for calling out the militia to suppress insurrection does not make it the duty of the government to maintain slavery by military force, much less does it make it the duty of the citizens to form a part of such military force. When freemen unsheathe the sword it should be to strike for liberty, not for despotism.

21. *Resolved*, That to preserve the peace of the citizens and secure the blessings of freedom, the legislature of each of the free states ought to keep in force suitable statutes rendering it penal for any of its inhabitants to transport, or aid in transporting, from such state, any person sought to be thus transported merely because subject to the slave laws of any other state; this remnant of independence being accorded to the free states by the decision of the Supreme Court in the case of Prigg *v.* the State of Pennsylvania.

The election occurred on November 5, 1844.

TWENTY-SIX STATES VOTED.

POPULAR VOTE.

STATES.	James K. Polk, Democrat.	Henry Clay, Whig.	James G. Birney, Liberty-Abolitionist.	Total vote.
Alabama	37,740	26,084	....	63,824
Arkansas	9,546	5,504	....	15,050
Connecticut	29,841	32,832	1,943	64,616
Delaware	5,996	6,278	....	12,274
Georgia	44,177	42,106	....	86,283
Illinois	57,920	45,528	3,570	107,018
Indiana	70,181	67,867	2,106	140,154
Kentucky	51,988	61,255	....	113,243
Louisiana	13,782	13,083	....	26,865
Maine	45,719	34,378	4,836	84,933
Maryland	32,676	35,984	3,308	71,968
Massachusetts	52,846	67,418	10,860	131,124
Michigan	27,759	24,337	3,632	55,728
Mississippi	25,126	19,206	....	44,332
Missouri	41,369	31,251	....	72,620
New Hampshire	27,160	17,866	4,161	49,187
New Jersey	37,495	38,318	131	75,944
New York	237,588	232,482	15,812	485,882
North Carolina	39,287	43,232	....	82,519
Ohio	149,117	155,057	8,050	312,224
Pennsylvania	167,535	161,203	3,138	331,876
Rhode Island	4,867	7,322	107	12,296
* South Carolina	....	....	....	....
Tennessee	59,917	60,030	....	119,947
Vermont	18,041	26,770	3,954	48,765
Virginia	49,570	43,677	....	93,247
Total	1,337,243	1,299,068	65,608	2,701,919

* The electors were chosen by the legislature.

ELECTORAL VOTE.

Counted on February 12, 1845.

STATES.	PRESIDENT.		VICE-PRESIDENT.		No. entitled to vote.
	James K. Polk, of Tennessee.	Henry Clay, of Kentucky.	George M. Dallas, of Pennsylvania.	Theodore Freling-huysen. of New Jersey.	
Alabama	9	..	9	..	9
Arkansas	3	..	3	..	3
Connecticut	..	6	..	6	6
Delaware	..	3	..	3	3
Georgia	10	..	10	10	10
Illinois	9	..	9	..	9
Indiana	12	..	12	..	12
Kentucky	..	12	..	12	12
Louisiana	6	..	6	..	6
Maine	9	..	9	..	9
Maryland	..	8	..	8	8
Massachusetts	..	12	..	12	12
Michigan	5	.	5	..	5
Mississippi	6	.	6	..	6
Missouri	7	..	7	..	7
New Hampshire	6	..	6	..	6
New Jersey	..	7	..	7	7
New York	36	..	36	..	36
North Carolina	..	11	..	11	11
Ohio	..	23	..	23	23
Pennsylvania	26	..	26	..	26
Rhode Island	..	4	..	4	4
South Carolina	9	..	9	..	9
Tennessee	..	13	..	13	13
Vermont	..	6	..	6	6
Virginia	17	..	17	..	17
Total	170	105	170	105	275

James K. Polk was elected President and George M. Dallas as Vice-President.

During this period Congress was divided politically as follows:

Twenty-ninth Congress.

Senate— 30 Democrats, 25 Whigs, 1 vacancy .... Total, 56
House—141 Democrats, 78 Whigs, 6 Americans .... " 225

Thirtieth Congress.

Senate— 37 Democrats, 21 Whigs .... Total, 58
House—108 Democrats, 115 Whigs, 4 Independents .... " 227

Election of 1848

DEMOCRATIC CONVENTION.

Baltimore, Md., May 22–26, 1848.

Chairman pro tem., J. S. BRYCE,
of Louisiana.

Chairman, ANDREW STEVENSON,
of Virginia.

NOMINATED—

For President, **Lewis Cass,**
of Michigan.

For Vice-President, **William O. Butler,**
of Kentucky.

All the states were represented at this convention. Three days were spent in perfecting the organization. This convention directed the appointment of the first national committee ever organized.

The following is the result of the balloting for a candidate:

CANDIDATES.	1st.	2d.	3d.	4th.
LEWIS CASS, of Michigan	125	133	156	179
JAMES BUCHANAN, of Pennsylvania	55	54	40	33
LEVI WOODBURY, of New Hampshire	53	56	53	38
GEORGE M. DALLAS, of Pennsylvania	3	3	..	..
W. J. WORTH, of Tennessee	6	6	5	1
JOHN C. CALHOUN, of South Carolina	9	..	..	..
WILLIAM O. BUTLER, of Kentucky	..	..	..	3
Whole number of votes	251	252	254	253
Necessary to a choice	168	168	169	169

For Vice-President, William O. Butler, of Kentucky, was nominated on the second ballot, receiving 169 votes. John A. Quitman, of Mississippi; John Y. Mason, of Virginia; William R. King, of Alabama; James J. McKay, of North Carolina; and Jefferson Davis, of Mississippi, were also voted for.

The convention adopted the following platform:—

DEMOCRATIC PLATFORM.

1. *Resolved*, That the American Democracy place their trust in the intelligence, the patriotism, and the discriminating justice of the American people.

2. *Resolved*, That we regard this as a distinctive feature of our political creed, which we are proud to maintain before the world as the great moral element in a form of government springing from and upheld by the popular will, and contrasted with the creed and practice of federalism, under whatever name or form, which seeks to palsy the will of the constituent and which conceives no imposture too monstrous for the popular credulity.

3. *Resolved*, Therefore, that entertaining these views, the Democratic party of this Union, through the delegates assembled in general convention of the states, coming together in a spirit of concord, of devotion to the doctrines and faith of a free representative government, and appealing to their fellow citizens for the rectitude of their intentions, renew and reassert before the American people the declaration of principles avowed by them on a former occasion, when, in general convention, they presented their candidates for the popular suffrage.

Resolutions 1, 2, 3, and 4 of the platform of 1840 (see page 41) were reaffirmed, with the following:

8. *Resolved*, That it is the duty of every branch of the government to enforce and practice the most rigid economy in conducting our public affairs, and that no more revenue ought to be raised than is required to defray the necessary expenses of the government, and for the gradual but certain extinction of the debt created by the prosecution of a just and necessary war.

Resolution 5 of the platform of 1840 (see page 41) was enlarged by the addition of the following:

And that the results of Democratic legislation in this and

all other financial measures upon which issues have been made between the two political parties of the country, have demonstrated to careful and practical men of all parties their soundness, safety, and utility in all business pursuits.

Resolutions 7, 8, and 9 of the platform of 1840 (see pages 41 and 42) were here inserted.

13. *Resolved*, That the proceeds of the public lands ought to be sacredly applied to the national object specified in the Constitution; and that we are opposed to any law for the distribution of such proceeds among the states as alike inexpedient in policy and repugnant to the Constitution.

14. *Resolved*, That we are decidedly opposed to taking from the President the qualified veto power, by which he is enabled, under restrictions and responsibilities amply sufficient to guard the public interests, to suspend the passage of a bill whose merits cannot secure the approval of two thirds of the Senate and House of Representatives, until the judgment of the people can be obtained thereon, and which has saved the American people from the corrupt and tyrannical domination of the Bank of the United States, and from a corrupting system of general internal improvements.

15. *Resolved*, That the war with Mexico, provoked on her part by years of insult and injury, was commenced by her army crossing the Rio Grande, attacking the American troops, and invading our sister State of Texas; and upon all the principles of patriotism and laws of nations, it is a just and necessary war on our part, in which every American citizen should have showed himself on the side of his country, and neither morally nor physically, by word or by deed, have given "aid and comfort to the enemy."

16. *Resolved*, That we should be rejoiced at the assurance of peace with Mexico, founded on the just principles of indemnity for the past and security for the future; but that while the ratification of the liberal treaty offered to Mexico remains in doubt, it is the duty of the country to sustain the administration and to sustain the country in every measure necessary to provide for the vigorous prosecution of the war, should that treaty be rejected.

17. *Resolved*, That the officers and soldiers who have carried the arms of their country into Mexico have crowned it with imperishable glory. Their unconquerable courage, their daring enterprise, their unfaltering perseverance and fortitude when assailed on all sides by innumerable foes and that more

formidable enemy—the diseases of the climate—exalt their devoted patriotism into the highest heroism, and give them a right to the profound gratitude of their country and the admiration of the world.

18. *Resolved,* That the Democratic National Convention of the thirty states composing the American Republic tender their fraternal congratulations to the National Convention of the Republic of France, now assembled as the free suffrage representatives of the sovereignty of thirty-five millions of republicans, to establish government on those eternal principles of equal rights for which their Lafayette and our Washington fought side by side in the struggle for our national independence; and we would especially convey to them, and to the whole people of France, our earnest wishes for the consolidation of their liberties, through the wisdom that shall guide their counsels, on the basis of a democratic constitution not derived from grants or concessions of kings or dynasties, but originating from the only true source of political power recognized in the states of this Union—the inherent and inalienable right of the people, in their sovereign capacity, to make and to amend their forms of government in such manner as the welfare of the community may require.

19. *Resolved,* That, in view of the recent developments of this grand political truth—of the sovereignty of the people and their capacity and power for self-government, which is prostrating thrones and erecting republics on the ruins of despotism in the Old World—we feel that a high and sacred duty is devolved, with increased responsibility, upon the Democratic party of this country, as the party of the people, to sustain and advance among us constitutional liberty, equality, and fraternity, by continuing to resist all monopolies and exclusive legislation for the benefit of the few at the expense of the many, and by a vigilant and constant adherence to those principles and compromises of the Constitution which are broad enough and strong enough to embrace and uphold the Union as it was, the Union as it is, and the Union as it shall be, in the full expansion of the energies and capacity of this great and progressive people.

20. *Resolved,* That a copy of these resolutions be forwarded, through the American Minister at Paris, to the National Convention of the Republic of France.

21. *Resolved,* That the fruits of the great political triumph of 1844, which elected James K. Polk and George M. Dallas, Pres-

ident and Vice-President of the United States, have fulfilled the hopes of the Democracy of the Union in defeating the declared purposes of their opponents in creating a national bank; in preventing the corrupt and unconstitutional distribution of the land proceeds from the common treasury of the Union for local purposes; in protecting the currency and labor of the country from ruinous fluctuations, and guarding the money of the country for the use of the people by the establishment of the constitutional treasury; in the noble impulse given to the cause of free trade by the repeal of the tariff of 1842, and the creation of the more equal, honest, and productive tariff of 1846; and that, in our opinion, it would be a fatal error to weaken the hands of a political organization by which these great reforms have been achieved, and risk them in the hands of their known adversaries, with whatever delusive appeals they may solicit our surrender of that vigilance which is the only safeguard of liberty.

22. *Resolved*, That the confidence of the Democracy of the Union in the principles, capacity, firmness, and integrity of James K. Polk, manifested by his nomination and election of 1844, has been signally justified by the strictness of his adherence to sound Democratic doctrines, by the purity of purpose, the energy and ability, which have characterized his administration in all our affairs at home and abroad; that we tender to him our cordial congratulations upon the brilliant success which has hitherto crowned his patriotic efforts, and assure him that at the expiration of his presidential term he will carry with him to his retirement the esteem, respect, and admiration of a grateful country.

Resolved, That this convention hereby presents to the people of the United States, Lewis Cass, of Michigan, as the candidate of the Democratic party for the office of President, and William O. Butler, of Kentucky, for Vice-President of the United States.

WHIG CONVENTION.

Philadelphia, Pa., June 7–9, 1848.

Chairman pro tem., JOHN A. COLLIER,
of New York.

Chairman, JOHN M. MOREHEAD,
of North Carolina.

NOMINATED—

For President, **Zachary Taylor,**
of Louisiana.

For Vice-President, **Millard Fillmore,**
of New York.

Every state was represented at this convention except Texas. Two days were spent in perfecting the organization. Zachary Taylor, of Louisiana, was nominated as the candidate for President on the fourth ballot. The following was the vote:

CANDIDATES.	1st.	2d.	3d.	4th.
ZACHARY TAYLOR, of Louisiana	111	118	133	171
HENRY CLAY, of Kentucky	97	86	74	32
WINFIELD SCOTT, of New Jersey	43	49	54	63
DANIEL WEBSTER, of Massachusetts	22	22	17	14
JOHN McLEAN, of Ohio	2	..	..	..
JOHN M. CLAYTON, of Delaware	4	4	1	..
Whole number of votes	279	279	279	280
Necessary to a choice	140	140	140	141

As the candidate for Vice-President, Millard Fillmore, of New York, was declared nominated on the second ballot, as follows:

CANDIDATES.	1st.	2d.
MILLARD FILLMORE, of New York	115	173
ABBOTT LAWRENCE, of Massachusetts	109	87
Scattering	51	6
Whole number of votes	275	266
Necessary to a choice	138	134

The convention adjourned without adopting a platform, but the following resolutions were adopted at a ratification meeting held in Philadelphia immediately after the convention, which was attended by most of its delegates:

1. *Resolved,* That the Whigs of the United States, here assembled by their representatives, heartily ratify the nominations of General Zachary Taylor as President and Millard Fillmore as Vice-President of the United States, and pledge themselves to their support.

2. *Resolved,* That in the choice of General Taylor as the Whig candidate for President we are glad to discover sympathy with a great popular sentiment throughout the nation—a sentiment which, having its origin in admiration of great military success, has been strengthened by the development, in every action and every word, of sound conservative opinions and of true fidelity to the great example of former days, and to the principles of the Constitution as administered by its founders.

3. *Resolved,* That General Taylor, in saying that, had he voted in 1844 he would have voted the Whig ticket, gives us the assurance—and no better is needed from a consistent and truth-speaking man—that his heart was with us at the crisis of our political destiny, when Henry Clay was our candidate, and when not only Whig principles were well defined and clearly asserted, but Whig measures depended upon success. The heart that was with us then is with us now, and we have a soldier's word of honor and a life of public and private virtue as the security.

4. *Resolved,* That we look on General Taylor's administration of the government as one conducive of peace, prosperity, and union; of peace, because no one better knows, or has greater reason to deplore, what he has seen sadly on the field of victory, the horrors of war, and especially of a foreign and aggressive war; of prosperity, now more than ever needed to relieve the nation from a burden of debt and restore industry—agricultural, manufacturing, and commercial—to its accustomed and peaceful functions and influences; of union, because we have a candidate whose very position as a Southwestern man, reared on the banks of the great stream whose tributaries, natural and artificial, embrace the whole Union, renders the protection of the interests of the whole country his first trust, and whose various duties in past life have been rendered not on the soil or under the flag of any state or section, but over the wide frontier and under the broad banner of the nation.

5. *Resolved*, That standing, as the Whig party does, on the broad and firm platform of the Constitution, braced up by all its inviolable and sacred guarantees and compromises, and cherished in the affections because protective of the interests of the people, we are proud to have as the exponent of our opinions one who is pledged to construe it by the wise and generous rules which Washington applied to it, and who has said—and no Whig desires any other assurance—that he will make Washington's administration his model.

6. *Resolved*, That as Whigs and Americans we are proud to acknowledge our gratitude for the great military services which, beginning at Palo Alto and ending at Buena Vista, first awakened the American people to a just estimate of him who is now our Whig candidate. In the discharge of a painful duty—for his march into the enemy's country was a reluctant one;—in the command of regulars at one time and volunteers at another, and of both combined; in the decisive though punctual discipline of his camp, where all respected and loved him; in the negotiations of terms for a dejected and desperate enemy; in the exigency of actual conflict when the balance was perilously doubtful—we have found him the same—brave, distinguished, and considerate: no heartless spectator of bloodshed, no trifler with human life or human happiness; and we do not know which to admire most, his heroism in withstanding the assaults of the enemy in the most hopeless fields of Buena Vista—mourning in generous sorrow over the graves of Ringgold, of Clay, of Hardin—or in giving, in the heat of battle, terms of merciful capitulation to a vanquished foe at Monterey, and not being ashamed to avow that he did it to spare women and children, helpless infancy and more helpless age, against whom no American soldier ever wars. Such a military man, whose triumphs are neither remote nor doubtful, whose virtues these trials have tested, we are proud to make our candidate.

7. *Resolved*, That in support of this nomination we ask our Whig friends throughout the nation to unite, to co-operate zealously, resolutely, with earnestness, in behalf of our candidate, whom calumny cannot reach, and with respectful demeanor to our adversaries, whose candidates have yet to prove their claims on the gratitude of the nation.

FREE-SOIL CONVENTION.

Buffalo, N. Y., August 9-10, 1848.

Chairman, CHARLES FRANCIS ADAMS,
of Massachusetts.

NOMINATED—

For President, **Martin Van Buren,**
of New York.

For Vice-President, **Charles Francis Adams,**
of Massachusetts.

[NOTE.—A prior convention was held at Utica, N. Y., on June 22, 1848, at which delegates were present from Massachusetts, New York, Ohio, and Wisconsin. Samuel Young was Chairman of this convention; and Martin Van Buren, of New York, was nominated for President, with Henry Dodge, of Wisconsin, for Vice-President. General Dodge subsequently declined.]

This was the first national convention of the Free-Soil Democrats, made up principally from the "Barnburners" and the old Liberty party. They were joined by many Democrats. The nominations were by acclamation.

The convention adopted the following platform:—

FREE-SOIL PLATFORM.

Whereas, We have assembled in convention as a union of free men, for the sake of freedom, forgetting all past political differences, in a common resolve to maintain the rights of free labor against the aggression of the slave power, and to secure free soil to a free people; and

Whereas, The political conventions recently assembled at Baltimore and Philadelphia—the one stifling the voice of a great constituency entitled to be heard in its deliberations, and the other abandoning its distinctive principles for mere availability—have dissolved the national party organization heretofore existing, by nominating for the chief magistracy of the United States, under the slaveholding dictation, candidates neither of whom can be supported by the opponents of slavery extension without a sacrifice of consistency, duty and self-respect; and

Whereas, These nominations so made furnish the occasion and demonstrate the necessity of the union of the people under the banner of free democracy, in a solemn and formal declaration of their independence of the slave power, and of their fixed determination to rescue the federal government from its control,—

1. *Resolved,* Therefore, that we, the people here assembled, remembering the example of our fathers in the days of the first Declaration of Independence, putting our trust in God for the triumph of our cause, and invoking His guidance in our endeavors to advance it, do now plant ourselves upon the national platform of freedom, in opposition to the sectional platform of slavery.

2. *Resolved,* That slavery in the several states of this Union which recognize its existence depends upon the state laws alone, which cannot be repealed or modified by the federal government, and for which laws that government is not responsible. We therefore propose no interference by Congress with slavery within the limits of any state.

3. *Resolved,* That the proviso of Jefferson, to prohibit the existence of slavery after 1800 in all the territories of the United States, southern and northern; the votes of six states and sixteen delegates in the Congress of 1784 for the proviso, to three states and seven delegates against it; the actual exclusion of slavery from the Northwestern Territory, by the Ordinance of 1787, unanimously adopted by the states in Congress, and the entire history of that period,—clearly show that it was the settled policy of the nation not to extend, nationalize, or encourage, but to limit, localize, and discourage slavery; and to this policy, which should never have been departed from, the government ought to return.

4. *Resolved,* That our fathers ordained the Constitution of the United States in order, among other great national objects, to establish justice, promote the general welfare, and secure the blessings of liberty; but expressly denied to the federal government, which they created, a constitutional power to deprive any person of life, liberty, or property, without due legal process.

5. *Resolved,* That in the judgment of this convention Congress has no more power to make a slave than to make a

king; no more power to institute or establish slavery than to institute or establish a monarchy. No such power can be found among those specifically conferred by the Constitution, or derived by just implication from them.

6. *Resolved,* That it is the duty of the federal government to relieve itself from all responsibility for the existence or continuance of slavery wherever the government possesses constitutional power to legislate on that subject, and is thus responsible for its existence.

7. *Resolved,* That the true and, in the judgment of this convention, the only safe means of preventing the extension of slavery into territory now free is to prohibit its extension in all such territory by an act of Congress.

8. *Resolved,* That we accept the issue which the slave power has forced upon us; and to their demand for more slave states and more slave territory, our calm but final answer is: No more slave states and no more slave territory. Let the soil of our extensive domain be kept free for the hardy pioneers of our own land and the oppressed and banished of other lands seeking homes of comfort and fields of enterprise in the new world.

9. *Resolved,* That the bill lately reported by the committee of eight in the Senate of the United States was no compromise, but an absolute surrender of the rights of the non-slaveholders of the states; and while we rejoice to know that a measure which, while opening the door for the introduction of slavery into the territories now free, would also have opened the door to litigation and strife among the future inhabitants thereof, to the ruin of their peace and prosperity, was defeated in the House of Representatives, its passage in hot haste by a majority, embracing several Senators who voted in open violation of the known will of their constituents, should warn the people to see to it that their representatives be not suffered to betray them. There must be no more compromises with slavery; if made, they must be repealed.

10. *Resolved,* That we demand freedom and established institutions for our brethren in Oregon now exposed to hardships, peril, and massacre, by the reckless hostility of the slave power to the establishment of free government for free territories; and not only for them, but for our brethren in California and New Mexico.

11. *Resolved,* It is due not only to this occasion, but to the whole people of the United States, that we should also declare ourselves on certain other questions of national policy; therefore,

12. *Resolved*, That we demand cheap postage for the people; a retrenchment of the expenses and patronage of the federal government; the abolition of all unnecessary offices and salaries; and the election by the people of all civil officers in the service of the government so far as the same may be practicable.

13. *Resolved*, That river and harbor improvements, when demanded by the safety and convenience of commerce with foreign nations, or among the several states, are objects of national concern, and that it is the duty of Congress, in the exercise of its constitutional power, to provide therefor.

14. *Resolved*, That the free grant to actual settlers, in consideration of the expenses they incur in making settlements in the wilderness, which are usually fully equal to their actual cost, and of the public benefits resulting therefrom, of reasonable portions of the public lands under suitable limitations, is a wise and just measure of public policy, which will promote, in various ways, the interest of all the states of this Union; and we therefore recommend it to the favorable consideration of the American people.

15. *Resolved*, That the obligations of honor and patriotism require the earliest practical payment of the national debt, and we are therefore in favor of such a tariff of duties as will raise revenue adequate to defray the expenses of the federal government, and to pay annual instalments of our debt, and the interest thereon.

16. *Resolved*, That we inscribe on our banner, "Free Soil Free Speech, Free Labor, and Free Men," and under it we will fight on, and fight forever, until a triumphant victory shall reward our exertions.

NATIVE AMERICAN CONVENTION.

Philadelphia, Pa., September, 1847.

RECOMMENDED—

For President, **Zachary Taylor,**
of Louisiana.

For Vice-President, **Henry A. S. Dearborn,**
of Massachusetts.

The convention recommended, but did not nominate, Zachary Taylor.

ABOLITIONIST CONVENTION.

New York, N. Y., November, 1847.

NOMINATED—

For President, **John P. Hale,**
of New Hampshire.

For Vice-President, **Leicester King,**
of Ohio.

Mr. Hale afterwards withdrew.

LIBERTY LEAGUE CONVENTION.

Rochester, N. Y., June 2, 1848.

NOMINATED—

For President, **Gerritt Smith,**
of New York.

For Vice-President, **Rev. Charles E. Foote,**
of Michigan.

This was an Abolition body.

INDUSTRIAL CONGRESS.

Philadelphia, Pa., June 13, 1848.

NOMINATED—

For President, **Gerritt Smith,**
of New York.

For Vice-President, **William S. Waitt,**
of Illinois.

The election occurred on November 7, 1848.

Congress in 1845 had passed an act requiring all of the presidential electors to be appointed in each state on the

Tuesday next after the first Monday in the month of November of the year in which the election was held. The electors were thus chosen for the first time under the new law.

THIRTY STATES VOTED.

POPULAR VOTE.

STATES.	Zachary Taylor, Whig.	Lewis Cass, Democrat.	Martin Van Buren, Free Soil.	Total vote.
Alabama	30,482	31,363	....	61,845
Arkansas	7,588	9,300	....	16,888
Connecticut	30,314	27,046	5,005	62,365
Delaware	6,421	5,898	80	12,399
Florida	3,116	1,847	....	4,963
Georgia	47,544	44,802	....	92,346
Illinois	53,047	56,300	15,775	125,121
Indiana	69,907	74,745	8,100	152,752
Iowa	11,084	12,093	1,126	24,303
Kentucky	67,141	49,720	....	116,861
Louisiana	18,217	15,370	....	33,587
Maine	35,125	39.880	12,096	87,101
Maryland	37,702	34,528	125	72,355
Massachusetts	61,072	35,281	38,058	134,411
Michigan	23,940	30,687	10,389	65,016
Mississippi	25,922	26,537	....	52,459
Missouri	32,671	40,077	....	72,748
New Hampshire	14.781	27,763	7,560	50,104
New Jersey	40,015	36,901	829	77,745
New York	218,603	114,318	120,510	453,431
North Carolina	43,550	34,869	....	78,419
Ohio	138,360	154,775	35,354	328 489
Pennsylvania	185,513	171,176	11,263	367,952
Rhode Island	6,779	3,646	730	11,155
*South Carolina	....	....	....	....
Tennessee	64,705	58,419	....	123,124
Texas	4.509	10,668	....	15,177
Vermont	23,122	10,948	13,837	47,907
Virginia	45,124	46,586	9	91,719
Wisconsin	13,747	15,001	10,418	39,166
Total	1,360,101	1,220,544	291,263	2,871,908

* The electors were chosen by the legislature.

ELECTORAL VOTE.

Counted on February 14, 1849.

STATES.	PRESIDENT.		VICE-PRESIDENT.		No. entitled to vote.
	Zachary Taylor, of Louisiana.	Lewis Cass, of Michigan.	Millard Fillmore, of New York.	William O. Butler, of Kentucky.	
Alabama	..	9	..	9	9
Arkansas	..	3	..	3	3
Connecticut	6	..	6	..	6
Delaware	3	..	3	..	3
Florida	3	..	3	..	3
Georgia	10	..	10	..	10
Illinois	..	9	..	9	9
Indiana	..	12	..	12	12
Iowa	..	4	..	4	4
Kentucky	12	..	12	..	12
Louisiana	6	..	6	..	6
Maine	..	9	..	9	9
Maryland	8	..	8	..	8
Massachusetts	12	..	12	..	12
Michigan	..	5	..	5	5
Mississippi	..	6	..	6	6
Missouri	..	7	..	7	7
New Hampshire	..	6	..	6	6
New Jersey	7	..	7	..	7
New York	36	..	36	..	36
North Carolina	11	..	11	..	11
Ohio	..	23	..	23	23
Pennsylvania	26	..	26	..	26
Rhode Island	4	..	4	..	4
South Carolina	..	9	..	9	9
Tennessee	13	..	13	..	13
Texas	..	4	..	4	4
Vermont	6	..	6	..	6
Virginia	..	17	..	17	17
Wisconsin	..	4	..	4	4
Total	163	127	163	127	290

Zachary Taylor was elected President and Millard Fillmore as Vice-President.

During this period Congress was divided politically as follows:

Thirty-first Congress.

Senate— 35 Democrats, 25 Whigs, 2 Free Soil ....Total, 62
House—116 Democrats, 111 Whigs .... " 227

Thirty-second Congress.

Senate— 36 Democrats, 23 Whigs, 3 Free Soil............Total, 62
House—140 Democrats, 88 Whigs, 5 Free Soil............ " 233

Election of 1852

DEMOCRATIC CONVENTION.

Baltimore, Md., June 1-6, 1852.

Chairman, JOHN W. DAVIS,
of Indiana.

NOMINATED—

For President, **Franklin Pierce,**
of New Hampshire.

For Vice-President, **William R. King,**
of Alabama.

The convention soon reached an organization, but a protracted struggle ensued for the nomination. Forty-nine ballots for President were taken, a condensed summary of which follows:

CANDIDATES.	1st.	10th.	20th.	30th.	40th.	49th.
LEWIS CASS, of Michigan	116	111	81	33	107	2
JAMES BUCHANAN, of Pennsylvania	93	86	92	83	27	..
STEPHEN A. DOUGLAS, of Illinois	20	40	64	80	33	2
WILLIAM L. MARCY, of New York	27	27	26	26	85	..
FRANKLIN PIERCE, of New Hampshire	..	..	..	..	29	282
Whole number of votes, 282. Necessary to a choice, 188.						

Scattering votes were cast for a number of others besides those given.

For Vice-President, William R. King, of Alabama, was

unanimously nominated on the second ballot. The first ballot resulted as follows:

CANDIDATES.	Votes.	CANDIDATES.	Votes.
WILLIAM R. KING, of Alabama	126	DAVID R. ATCHISON, of Missouri	25
S. U. DOWNS, of Louisiana	30	ROBERT STRANGE, of North Carolina	23
JOHN B. WELLER, of California	28	T. J. RUSK, of Texas	12
WILLIAM O. BUTLER, of Kentucky	27	JEFFERSON DAVIS, of Mississippi	2
GIDEON J. PILLOW, of Tennessee	25	HOWELL COBB, of Georgia	2

The convention adopted the following platform:—

DEMOCRATIC PLATFORM.

Resolutions 1, 2, 3, 4, 5, 6, and 7 of the platform of 1848 (see page 59) were reaffirmed, to which were added the following:

8. *Resolved,* That it is the duty of every branch of the government to enforce and practice the most rigid economy in conducting our public affairs, and that no more revenue ought to be raised than is required to defray the necessary expenses of the government and for the gradual but certain extinction of the public debt.

9. *Resolved,* That Congress has no power to charter a national bank; that we believe such an institution one of deadly hostility to the best interests of the country, dangerous to our republican institutions and the liberties of the people, and calculated to place the business of the country within the control of a concentrated money power and above the laws and the will of the people; and that the results of Democratic legislation in this and all other financial measures upon which issues have been made between the two political parties of the country have demonstrated to candid and practical men of all parties, their soundness, safety, and utility in all business pursuits.

10. *Resolved,* That the separation of the moneys of the government from banking institutions is indispensable for the safety of the funds of the government and the rights of the people.

11. *Resolved,* That the liberal principles embodied by Jeffer-

son in the Declaration of Independence and sanctioned in the Constitution, which make ours the land of liberty and the asylum of the oppressed of every nation, have ever been cardinal principles in the Democratic faith; and every attempt to abridge the privilege of becoming citizens and the owners of the soil among us ought to be resisted with the same spirit that swept the Alien and Sedition laws from our statute-books.

12. *Resolved*, That Congress has no power, under the Constitution, to interfere with or control the domestic institutions of the several states, and that such states are the sole and proper judges of everything appertaining to their own affairs not prohibited by the Constitution; that all efforts of the Abolitionists or others made to induce Congress to interfere with questions of slavery, or to take incipient steps in relation thereto, are calculated to lead to the most alarming and dangerous consequences; and that all such efforts have an inevitable tendency to diminish the happiness of the people and endanger the stability and permanency of the Union, and ought not to be countenanced by any friend of our political institutions.

13. *Resolved*, That the foregoing proposition covers, and is intended to embrace, the whole subject of slavery agitation in Congress; and therefore the Democratic party of the Union, standing on this national platform, will abide by and adhere to a faithful execution of the acts known as the "compromise" measures settled by the last Congress—"the act for reclaiming fugitives from service or labor" included; which act, being designed to carry out an express provision of the Constitution, cannot, with fidelity thereto, be repealed nor so changed as to destroy or impair its efficiency.

14. *Resolved*, That the Democratic party will resist all attempts at renewing, in Congress or out of it, the agitation of the slavery question, under whatever shape or color the attempt may be made.

(Here resolutions 13 and 14 of the platform of 1848 were inserted.)

17. *Resolved*, That the Democratic party will faithfully abide by and uphold the principles laid down in the Kentucky and Virginia resolutions of 1792 and 1798, and in the report of Mr. Madison to the Virginia Legislature in 1799; that it adopts those principles as constituting one of the main foundations of its political creed, and is resolved to carry them out in their obvious meaning and import.

18. *Resolved*, That the war with Mexico, upon all the principles of patriotism and the law of nations, was a just and necessary war on our part, in which no American citizen should have shown himself opposed to his country, and neither morally nor physically, by word or deed, given aid and comfort to the enemy.

19. *Resolved*, That we rejoice at the restoration of friendly relations with our sister republic of Mexico, and earnestly desire for her all the blessings and the prosperity which we enjoy under republican institutions; and we congratulate the American people on the results of that war, which have so manifestly justified the policy and conduct of the Democratic party and insured to the United States indemnity for the past and security for the future.

20. *Resolved*, That, in view of the condition of popular institutions in the Old World, a high and sacred duty is devolved, with increased responsibility, upon the Democracy of this country, as the party of the people, to uphold and maintain the rights of every state, and thereby the union of states, and to sustain and advance among them constitutional liberty by continuing to resist all monopolies and exclusive legislation for the benefit of the few at the expense of the many, and by a vigilant and constant adherence to those principles and compromises of the Constitution which are broad enough and strong enough to embrace and uphold the Union as it is, and the Union as it should be, in the full expansion of the energies and capacity of this great and progressive people.

WHIG CONVENTION.

Baltimore, Md., June 16–19, 1852.

Chairman, JOHN G. CHAPMAN,
of Maryland.

NOMINATED—

For President, **Winfield Scott,**
of New Jersey.

For Vice-President, **William A. Graham,**
of North Carolina.

All the states were represented at this convention.

Fifty-three ballots for President were taken, of which the following is a summary:

CANDIDATES.	1st.	10th.	30th.	40th.	50th.	53d.
MILLARD FILLMORE, of New York	133	130	128	129	124	112
WINFIELD SCOTT, of New Jersey	131	135	134	132	142	159
DANIEL WEBSTER, of Massachusetts	29	29	29	32	28	21
Whole No. of votes, 293. Necessary to a choice, 147.						

For Vice-President, William A. Graham, of North Carolina, was nominated on the second ballot.

The convention adopted the following platform:—

WHIG PLATFORM.

The Whigs of the United States, in convention assembled, adhering to the great conservative principles by which they are controlled and governed, and now as ever relying upon the intelligence of the American people, with an abiding confidence in their capacity for self-government and their devotion to the Constitution and the Union, do proclaim the following as the political sentiments and determination for the establishment and maintenance of which their national organization as a party was effected:

First. The Government of the United States is of a limited character, and is confined to the exercise of powers expressly granted by the Constitution, and such as may be necessary and proper for carrying the granted powers into full execution, and that powers not granted or necessarily implied are reserved to the states respectively and to the people.

Second. The state governments should be held secure to their reserved rights, and the general government sustained in its constitutional powers, and that the Union should be revered and watched over as the palladium of our liberties.

Third. That while struggling freedom everywhere enlists the warmest sympathy of the Whig party, we still adhere to the doctrines of the Father of his Country, as announced in his Farewell Address, of keeping ourselves free from all entangling alliances with foreign countries, and of never quitting our own to stand upon foreign grounds; that our mission as a republic is not to propagate our opinions, or impose upon other countries our forms of government by artifice or force, but to teach by example, and show by our success, moderation and justice, the blessings of self-government and the advantages of free institutions.

Fourth. That as the people make and control the government, they should obey its Constitution, laws, and treaties, as they would retain their self-respect and the respect which they claim and will enforce from foreign powers.

Fifth. Governments should be conducted on principles of the strictest economy, and revenue sufficient for the expenses thereof in time of peace ought to be derived mainly from a duty on imports, and not from direct taxes; and in laying such duties sound policy requires a just discrimination; and, when practicable, by specific duties, whereby suitable encouragement may be afforded to American industry equally to all classes and to all portions of the country.

Sixth. The Constitution vests in Congress the power to open and repair harbors and remove obstructions from navigable rivers whenever such improvements are necessary for the common defence and for the protection and facility of commerce with foreign nations or among the states, said improvements being in every instance national and general in their character.

Seventh. The federal and state governments are parts of one system, alike necessary for the common prosperity, peace, and security, and ought to be regarded alike with a cordial, habitual, and immovable attachment. Respect for the authority of each, and acquiescence in the just constitutional measures of each, are duties required by the plainest considerations of national, state, and individual welfare.

Eighth. That the series of acts of the Thirty-second Congress, the act known as the Fugitive Slave Law included, are received and acquiesced in by the Whig party of the United States as a settlement in principle and substance of the dangerous and exciting questions which they embrace, and so far as they are concerned we will maintain them and insist upon their strict enforcement until time and experience shall demonstrate the necessity for further legislation to guard against the evasion of the laws on the one hand, and the abuse of their powers on the other, not impairing their present efficiency; and we deprecate all further agitation of the question thus settled as dangerous to our peace, and will discountenance all efforts to continue or renew such agitation, whenever, wherever, or however the attempt may be made; and we will maintain the system as essential to the nationality of the Whig party and the integrity of the Union.

FREE-SOIL DEMOCRATIC CONVENTION.

Pittsburgh, Pa., August 11, 1852.

Chairman, HENRY WILSON,
of Massachusetts.

NOMINATED—

For President, **John P. Hale,**
of New Hampshire.

For Vice-President, **George W. Julian,**
of Indiana.

Nominations were made as above given, and the following platform was adopted:—

FREE-SOIL DEMOCRATIC PLATFORM.

Having assembled in national convention as the Free Democracy of the United States, united by a common resolve to maintain right against wrong, and freedom against slavery; confiding in the intelligence, patriotism, and discriminating justice of the American people; putting our trust in God for the triumph of our cause, and invoking His guidance in our endeavors to advance it, we now submit to the candid judgment of all men, the following declaration of principles and measures:

First. That governments deriving their just powers from the consent of the governed are instituted among men to secure to all those inalienable rights of life, liberty, and the pursuit of happiness with which they are endowed by their Creator, and of which none can be deprived by valid legislation, except for crime.

Second. That the true mission of American Democracy is to maintain the liberties of the people, the sovereignty of the states, and the perpetuity of the Union, by the impartial application to public affairs, without sectional discrimination, of the fundamental principles of human rights, strict justice, and an economical administration.

Third. That the federal government is one of the limited powers derived solely from the Constitution, and the grants of powers therein ought to be strictly construed by all the departments and agents of the government, and it is inexpedient and dangerous to exercise doubtful constitutional powers.

Fourth. That the Constitution of the United States, ordained to form a more perfect Union, to establish justice, and secure the blessings of liberty, expressly denies to the general government all power to deprive any person of life, liberty, or property without due process of law; and therefore the Government, having no more power to make a slave than to make a king, and no more power to establish slavery than to establish a monarchy, should at once proceed to relieve itself from all responsibility for the existence of slavery, wherever it possesses constitutional power to legislate for its extinction.

Fifth. That to the persevering and importunate demands of the slave power for more slave states, new slave territories, and the nationalization of slavery, our distinct and final answer is: No more slave states, no slave territory, no nationalized slavery, and no national legislation for the extradition of slaves.

Sixth. That slavery is a sin against God and a crime against man, which no human enactment nor usage can make right; and that Christianity, humanity, and patriotism alike demand its abolition.

Seventh. That the Fugitive Slave Act of 1850 is repugnant to the Constitution, to the principles of the common law, to the spirit of Christianity, and to the sentiments of the civilized world. We therefore deny its binding force on the American people, and demand its immediate and total repeal.

Eighth. That the doctrine that any human law is a finality, and not subject to modification or repeal, is not in accordance with the creed of the founders of our government, and is dangerous to the liberties of the people.

Ninth. That the acts of Congress known as the "compromise" measures of 1850,—by making the admission of a sovereign state contingent upon the adoption of other measures demanded by the special interests of slavery; by their omission to guarantee freedom in the free territories; by their attempt to impose unconstitutional limitations on the powers of Congress and the people to admit new states; by their provisions for the assumption of five millions of the state debt of Texas, and for the payment of five millions more, and the cession of large territory to the same state under menace, as an inducement to their relinquishment of a groundless claim; and by their invasion of the sovereignty of the states and the liberties of the people, through the enactment of an unjust, oppressive, and unconstitutional fugitive slave law,—are proved to be inconsistent with all the principles and maxims of Democracy, and wholly inadequate to the settlement of the questions of which they are claimed to be an adjustment.

Tenth. That no permanent settlement of the slavery question can be looked for except in the practical recognition of the truth that slavery is sectional and freedom national; by the total separation of the general government from slavery, and the exercise of its legitimate and constitutional influence on the side of freedom; and by leaving to the states the whole subject of slavery and the extradition of fugitives from service.

Eleventh. That all men have a natural right to a portion of the soil; and that as the use of the soil is indispensable to life, the right of all men to the soil is as sacred as their right to life itself.

Twelfth. That the public lands of the United States belong to the people, and should not be sold to individuals, nor granted to corporations, but should be held as a sacred trust for the benefit of the people, and should be granted in limited quantities, free of cost, to landless settlers.

Thirteenth. That a due regard for the federal Constitution and a sound administrative policy demand that the funds of the general government be kept separate from banking institutions; that inland and ocean postage should be reduced to the lowest possible point; that no more revenue should be raised than is required to defray the strictly necessary expenses of the public service and to pay off the public debt; and that the power and patronage of the government should be diminished by the abolition of all unnecessary offices, salaries, and privileges, and by the election by the people of all civil officers in the service of the United States, so far as may be consistent with the prompt and efficient transaction of the public business.

Fourteenth. That river and harbor improvements, when necessary to the safety and convenience of commerce with foreign nations or among the several states, are objects of national concern, and it is the duty of Congress, in the exercise of its constitutional powers, to provide for the same.

Fifteenth. That emigrants and exiles from the Old World should find a cordial welcome to homes of comfort and fields of enterprise in the New; and every attempt to abridge their privilege of becoming citizens and owners of soil among us ought to be resisted with inflexible determination.

Sixteenth. That every nation has a clear right to alter or change its own government, and to administer its own concerns in such manner as may best secure the rights and promote the happiness of the people; and foreign interference with that right is a dangerous violation of the law of nations, against which all independent governments should protest, and endeavor by all proper means to prevent; and especially is it the duty of the American government, representing the chief republic of the world, to protest against, and by all proper means to prevent, the intervention of kings and emperors against nations seeking to establish for themselves republican or constitutional governments.

Seventeenth. That the independence of Hayti ought to be recognized by our government, and our commercial relations with it placed on the footing of the most favored nations.

Eighteenth. That as, by the Constitution, "the citizens of each state shall be entitled to all the privileges and immunities of citizens of the several states," the practice of imprisoning colored seamen of other states while the vessels to which they belong lie in port, and refusing the exercise of the right to bring such cases before the Supreme Court of the United States, to test the legality of such proceedings, is a flagrant violation of the Constitution and an invasion of the rights of the citizens of other states, utterly inconsistent with the professions made by the slaveholders that they wish the provisions of the Constitution faithfully observed by every state in the Union.

Nineteenth. That we recommend the introduction into all treaties hereafter to be negotiated between the United States and foreign nations, of some provision for the amicable settlement of difficulties by a resort to decisive arbitration.

Twentieth. That the Free Democratic party is not organized to aid either the Whig or Democratic wing of the great slave-compromise party of the nation, but to defeat them both; and that, repudiating and renouncing both as hopelessly corrupt and utterly unworthy of confidence, the purpose of the Free Democracy is to take possession of the federal government and administer it for the better protection of the rights and interests of the whole people.

Twenty-first. That we inscribe on our banner Free Soil, Free Speech, Free Labor, and Free Men, and under it will fight on and fight ever until a triumphant victory shall reward our exertions.

Twenty-second. That upon this platform the convention presents to the American people as a candidate for the office of

President of the United States, John P. Hale, of New Hampshire, and as a candidate for the office of Vice-President of the United States, George W. Julian, of Indiana, and earnestly commends them to the support of all free men and all parties.

The election occurred on November 2, 1852.

THIRTY-ONE STATES VOTED.

POPULAR VOTE.

STATES.	Franklin Pierce, Democrat.	Winfield Scott, Whig.	John P. Hale, Free Soil Democrat.	Total vote.
Alabama	26,881	15,038	....	41,919
Arkansas	12,173	7,404	....	19,577
California	40,626	35,407	100	76,133
Connecticut	33,249	30,357	3,160	66,766
Delaware	6,318	6,293	62	12,673
Florida	4,318	2,875	....	7,193
Georgia	34,705	16,660	....	51,365
Illinois	80,597	64,934	9,966	155,497
Indiana	95,340	80,901	6,929	183,170
Iowa	17,763	15,856	1,604	35,223
Kentucky	53,806	57,068	265	111,139
Louisiana	18,647	17,255	....	35,902
Maine	41,609	32,543	8,030	82,182
Maryland	40,020	35,066	54	75,140
Massachusetts	44,569	52,683	28,023	125,275
Michigan	41,842	33,859	7,237	82,938
Mississippi	26,876	17,548	....	44,424
Missouri	38,353	29,984	....	68,337
New Hampshire	29,997	16,147	6,695	52,839
New Jersey	44,305	38,556	350	83,211
New York	262,083	234,882	25,329	522,294
North Carolina	39,744	39,058	59	78,861
Ohio	169,220	152,526	31,682	353,428
Pennsylvania	198,568	179,174	8,525	386,267
Rhode Island	8,735	7,626	644	17,005
* South Carolina	....	....	....	....
Tennessee	57,018	58,898	...	115,916
Texas	13,552	4,995	....	18,547
Vermont	13,044	22,173	8,621	43,838
Virginia	73,858	58,572	....	132,430
Wisconsin	31,658	22,240	8,814	64,712
Total	1,601,474	1,386,578	156,149	3,144,201

* The electors were chosen by the legislature.

ELECTORAL VOTE.

Counted on February 9, 1853.

STATES.	PRESIDENT.		VICE-PRESIDENT.		No. entitled to vote.
	Franklin Pierce, of New Hampshire.	Winfield Scott, of New Jersey.	William R. King, of Alabama.	William A. Graham, of North Carolina.	
Alabama	9	..	9	..	9
Arkansas	4	..	4	..	4
California	4	..	4	..	4
Connecticut	6	..	6	..	6
Delaware	3	..	3	..	3
Florida	3	..	3	..	3
Georgia	10	..	10	..	10
Illinois	11	..	11	..	11
Indiana	13	..	13	..	13
Iowa	4	..	4	..	4
Kentucky	..	12	..	12	12
Louisiana	6	..	6	..	6
Maine	8	..	8	..	8
Maryland	8	..	8	..	8
Massachusetts	..	13	..	13	13
Michigan	6	..	6	..	6
Mississippi	7	..	7	..	7
Missouri	9	..	9	..	9
New Hampshire	5	..	5	..	5
New Jersey	7	..	7	..	7
New York	35	..	35	..	35
North Carolina	10	..	10	..	10
Ohio	23	..	23	..	23
Pennsylvania	27	..	27	..	27
Rhode Island	4	..	4	..	4
South Carolina	8	..	8	..	8
Tennessee	..	12	..	12	12
Texas	4	..	4	..	4
Vermont	..	5	..	5	5
Virginia	15	..	15	..	15
Wisconsin	5	..	5	..	5
Total	254	42	254	42	296

Franklin Pierce was elected President and William R. King as Vice-President.

During this period Congress was divided politically as follows:

Thirty-third Congress.

Senate— 38 Democrats, 22 Whigs, 2 Free Soil ....Total, 62
House—159 Democrats, 71 Whigs, 4 Free Soil .... " 234

Thirty-fourth Congress.

Senate—42 Democrats, 15 Republicans, 5 Americans....Total, 62
House—83 Democrats, 108 Republicans, 43 Americans.... " 234

Election of 1856

Democratic National Committee:

Chairman, DAVID A. SMALLEY, of Vermont.

DEMOCRATIC CONVENTION.

Cincinnati, O., June 2–6, 1856.

Chairman, JOHN E. WARD,
of Georgia.

NOMINATED—

For President, **James Buchanan,**
of Pennsylvania.

For Vice-President, **John C. Breckinridge,**
of Kentucky.

This convention organized without opposition to the two-thirds rule. Seventeen ballots were necessary to nominate a candidate for President, of which the following is a summary:

CANDIDATES.	1st.	7th.	10th.	14th.	16th.	17th.
JAMES BUCHANAN, of Pennsylvania	135	155	147	152	168	296
FRANKLIN PIERCE, of New Hampshire	122	89	80	75	..	..
STEPHEN A. DOUGLAS, of Illinois	33	58	62	63	122	..
LEWIS CASS, of Michigan	5	5	5	5	6	..
Whole No. of votes, 296. Necessary to a choice, 198.						

For Vice-President, John C. Breckinridge, of Kentucky, was nominated on the second ballot by a unanimous vote. The following is the result of the first ballot:

CANDIDATES.	Votes.	CANDIDATES.	Votes.
JOHN A. QUITMAN, of Mississippi	59	AARON V. BROWN, of Tennessee	29
JOHN C. BRECKINRIDGE, of Kentucky	55	JAMES C. DOBBIN, of North Carolina	13
LINN BOYD, of Kentucky	33	BENJAMIN FITZPATRICK, of Alabama	11
HERSCHEL V. JOHNSON, of Georgia	31	TRUSTEN POLK, of Missouri	5
JAMES A. BAYARD, of Delaware	31	THOMAS J. RUSK, of Texas	2

The convention adopted the following platform:—

DEMOCRATIC PLATFORM.

1. *Resolved*, That the American Democracy place their trust in the intelligence, the patriotism, and the discriminating justice of the American people.

2. *Resolved*, That we regard this as a distinctive feature of our political creed, which we are proud to maintain before the world as the great moral element in a form of government springing from and upheld by the popular will; and we contrast it with the creed and practice of federalism, under whatever name or form, which seeks to palsy the will of the constituent, and which conceives no imposture too monstrous for the popular credulity.

3. *Resolved, therefore*, That, entertaining these views, the Democratic party of this Union, through their delegates assembled in a general convention of the states, coming together in a spirit of concord, of devotion to the doctrines and faith of a free and representative government, and appealing to their fellow citizens for the rectitude of their intentions, renew and reassert before the American people the declarations of principles avowed by them when, on former occasions, in general convention, they presented their candidates for the popular suffrage:

1. That the federal government is one of limited power, derived solely from the Constitution; and the grants of power made therein ought to be strictly construed by all the depart-

ments and agents of the government; and that it is inexpedient and dangerous to exercise doubtful constitutional powers.

2. That the Constitution does not confer upon the general government the power to commence and carry on a general system of internal improvements.

3. That the Constitution does not confer authority upon the federal government, directly or indirectly, to assume the debts of the several states, contracted for local and internal improvements, or other state purposes; nor would such assumption be just or expedient.

4. That justice and sound policy forbid the federal government to foster one branch of industry to the detriment of any other, or to cherish the interests of one portion to the injury of another portion of our common country; that every citizen and every section of the country has a right to demand and insist upon an equality of rights and privileges, and to complete and ample protection of person and property from domestic violence or foreign aggression.

5. That it is the duty of every branch of the government to enforce and practice the most rigid economy in conducting our public affairs, and that no more revenue ought to be raised than is required to defray the necessary expenses of the government and for the gradual but certain extinction of the public debt.

6. That the proceeds of the public lands ought to be sacredly applied to the national objects specified in the Constitution; and that we are opposed to any law for the distribution of such proceeds among the states, as alike inexpedient in policy and repugnant to the Constitution.

7. That Congress has no power to charter a national bank; that we believe such an institution one of deadly hostility to the best interests of the country, dangerous to our republican institutions and the liberties of the people, and calculated to place the business of the country within the control of a concentrated money power and above the laws and the will of the people; and that the results of Democratic legislation in this and all other financial measures upon which issues have been made between the two political parties of the country have demonstrated to candid and practical men of all parties, their soundness, safety, and utility in all business pursuits.

8. That the separation of the moneys of the government from banking institutions is indispensable for the safety of the funds of the government and the rights of the people.

9. That we are decidedly opposed to taking from the President the qualified veto power, by which he is enabled, under restrictions and responsibilities amply sufficient to guard the public interests, to suspend the passage of a bill whose merits cannot secure the approval of two thirds of the Senate and House of Representatives, until the judgment of the people can be obtained thereon, and which has saved the American people from the corrupt and tyrannical domination of the Bank of the United States and from a corrupting system of general internal improvements

10. That the liberal principles embodied by Jefferson in the Declaration of Independence, and sanctioned in the Constitution, which make ours the land of liberty and the asylum of the oppressed of every nation, have ever been cardinal principles in the Democratic faith, and every attempt to abridge the privilege of becoming citizens and the owners of soil among us ought to be resisted with the same spirit which swept the Alien and Sedition laws from our statute-books; and

Whereas, Since the foregoing declaration was uniformly adopted by our predecessors in national conventions, an adverse political and religious test has been secretly organized by a party claiming to be exclusively American, and it is proper that the American Democracy should clearly define its relation thereto, and declare its determined opposition to all secret political societies, by whatever name they may be called.

Resolved, That the foundation of this Union of States having been laid in, and its prosperity, expansion, and pre-eminent example in free government built upon, entire freedom in matters of religious concernment, and no respect of person in regard to rank or place of birth, no party can justly be deemed national, constitutional, or in accordance with American principles which bases its exclusive organization upon religious opinions and accidental birthplace. And hence a political crusade in the nineteenth century, and in the United States of America, against Catholic and foreign-born is neither justified by the past history or the future prospects of the country, nor in unison with the spirit of toleration and enlarged freedom which peculiarly distinguishes the American system of popular government.

Resolved, That we reiterate with renewed energy of purpose the well-considered declarations of former conventions upon the sectional issue of domestic slavery and concerning the reserved rights of the states:—

1. That Congress has no power under the Constitution to interfere with or control the domestic institutions of the several states, and that such states are the sole and proper judges of everything appertaining to their own affairs not prohibited by the Constitution; that all efforts of the Abolitionists, or others, made to induce Congress to interfere with questions of slavery, or to take incipient steps in relation thereto, are calculated to lead to the most alarming and dangerous consequences, and that all such efforts have an inevitable tendency to diminish the happiness of the people and endanger the stability and permanency of the Union, and ought not to be countenanced by any friend of our political institutions.

2. That the foregoing proposition covers, and was intended to embrace the whole subject of slavery agitation in Congress; and therefore the Democratic party of the Union, standing on this national platform, will abide by and adhere to a faithful execution of the acts known as the "compromise" measures, settled by the Congress of 1850; "the act for reclaiming fugitives from service or labor" included, which act, being designed to carry out an express provision of the Constitution, cannot, with fidelity thereto, be repealed or so changed as to destroy or impair its efficiency.

3. That the Democratic party will resist all attempts at renewing, in Congress or out of it, the agitation of the slavery question, under whatever shape or color the attempt may be made.

4. That the Democratic party will faithfully abide by and uphold the principles laid down in the Kentucky and Virginia resolutions of 1798, and in the report of Mr. Madison to the Virginia Legislature in 1799; that it adopts those principles as constituting one of the main foundations of its political creed, and is resolved to carry them out in their obvious meaning and import.

And that we may more distinctly meet the issue on which a sectional party, subsisting exclusively on slavery agitation, now relies to test the fidelity of the people, North and South, to the Constitution and the Union—

1. *Resolved,* That, claiming fellowship with and desiring the co-operation of all who regard the preservation of the Union under the Constitution as the paramount issue, and repudiating all sectional parties and platforms concerning domestic slavery which seek to embroil the states and incite to treason and armed resistance to law in the territories, and whose avowed

purposes, if consummated, must end in civil war and disunion, the American Democracy recognize and adopt the principles contained in the organic laws establishing the Territories of Kansas and Nebraska as embodying the only sound and safe solution of the "slavery question" upon which the great national idea of the people of this whole country can repose in its determined conservatism of the Union—NON-INTERFERENCE BY CONGRESS WITH SLAVERY IN STATE AND TERRITORY, OR IN THE DISTRICT OF COLUMBIA.

2. That was the basis of the compromises of 1850—confirmed by both the Democratic and Whig parties in national conventions, ratified by the people in the election of 1852, and rightly applied to the organization of territories in 1854.

3. That by the uniform application of this Democratic principle to the organization of territories and to the admission of new states, with or without domestic slavery, as they may elect, the equal rights of all the states will be preserved intact, the original compacts of the Constitution maintained inviolate, and the perpetuity and expansion of this Union insured to its utmost capacity of embracing, in peace and harmony, every future American state that may be constituted or annexed, with a republican form of government.

Resolved, That we recognize the right of the people of all the territories, including Kansas and Nebraska, acting through the legally and fairly expressed will of a majority of actual residents, and whenever the number of their inhabitants justifies it, to form a Constitution, with or without domestic slavery, and be admitted into the Union upon terms of perfect equality with the other states.

Resolved, finally, That in view of the condition of popular institutions in the Old World (and the dangerous tendencies of sectional agitation, combined with the attempt to enforce civil and religious disabilities against the rights of acquiring and enjoying citizenship in our own land), a high and sacred duty is devolved with increased responsibility upon the Democratic party of this country, as the party of the Union, to uphold and maintain the rights of every state, and thereby the Union of the states; and to sustain and advance among us constitutional liberty, by continuing to resist all monopolies and exclusive legislation for the benefit of the few at the expense of the many, and by a vigilant and constant adherence to those principles and compromises of the Constitution which are broad enough and strong enough to embrace and uphold the Union as it was, the Union as it is, and the Union as it shall be, in the full expansion of the energies and capacity of this great and progressive people.

1. *Resolved,* That there are questions connected with the foreign policy of this country which are inferior to no domestic question whatever. The time has come for the people of the United States to declare themselves in favor of free seas and progressive free trade throughout the world, and, by solemn manifestations, to place their moral influence at the side of their successful example.

2. *Resolved,* That our geographical and political position with reference to the other states of this continent, no less than the interest of our commerce and the development of our growing power, requires that we should hold as sacred the principles involved in the Monroe Doctrine. Their bearing and import admit of no misconstruction; they should be applied with unbending rigidity.

3. *Resolved,* That the great highway which nature, as well as the assent of the states most immediately interested in its maintenance, has marked out for a free communication between the Atlantic and the Pacific oceans, constitutes one of the most important achievements realized by the spirit of modern times and the unconquerable energy of our people. That result should be secured by a timely and efficient exertion of the control which we have the right to claim over it, and no power on earth should be suffered to impede or clog its progress by any interference with the relations it may suit our policy to establish between our government and the governments of the states within whose dominions it lies. We can, under no circumstances, surrender our preponderance in the adjustment of all questions arising out of it.

4. *Resolved,* That, in view of so commanding an interest, the people of the United States cannot but sympathize with the efforts which are being made by the people of Central America to regenerate that portion of the continent which covers the passage across the interoceanic isthmus.

5. *Resolved,* That the Democratic party will expect of the next administration that every proper effort be made to insure our ascendency in the Gulf of Mexico, and to maintain a permanent protection to the great outlets through which are emptied into its waters the products raised out of the soil and the commodities created by the industry of the people of our Western valleys and the Union at large.

Resolved, That the Democratic party recognizes the great importance, in a political and commercial point of view, of a safe and speedy communication, by military and postal roads, through our own territory between the Atlantic and Pacific coasts of this Union, and that it is the duty of the federal government to exercise promptly all its constitutional power for the attainment of that object.

Resolved, That the administration of Franklin Pierce has been true to the great interests of the country. In the face of the most determined opposition it has maintained the laws, enforced economy, fostered progress, and infused integrity and vigor into every department of the government at home. It has signally improved our treaty relations, extended the field of commercial enterprise, and vindicated the rights of American citizens abroad. It has asserted with eminent impartiality the just claims of every section, and has at all times been faithful to the Constitution. We therefore proclaim our unqualified approbation of its measures and its policy.

WHIG CONVENTION.

Baltimore, Md., September 17–18, 1856.

Chairman, EDWARD BATES,
of Missouri.

RATIFIED—

For President, **Millard Fillmore,**
of New York.

For Vice-President, **Andrew Jackson Donelson,**
of Tennessee.

The convention ratified the nominations of the American (Know-Nothing) Convention of February 22, 1856. At this convention 26 states were represented. California, Iowa, Michigan, Texas, and Wisconsin were not represented. The convention adopted the following platform:—

WHIG PLATFORM.

Resolved, That the Whigs of the United States, now here assembled, hereby declare their reverence for the Constitution of the United States, their unalterable attachment to the national Union, and a fixed determination to do all in their power to preserve them for themselves and their posterity. They have no new principles to announce, no new platform to establish; but are content to broadly rest—where their fathers rested—upon the Constitution of the United States, wishing no safer guide, no higher law.

Resolved, That we regard with the deepest interest and anxiety the present disordered condition of our national affairs—a portion of the country ravaged by civil war, large sections of our population embittered by mutual recriminations; and we distinctly trace these calamities to the culpable neglect of duty by the present national administration.

Resolved, That the government of the United States was formed by the conjunction in political unity of widespread geographical sections, materially differing, not only in climate and products, but in social and domestic institutions; and that any cause that shall permanently array the different sections of the Union in political hostility and organize parties founded only on geographical distinctions, must inevitably prove fatal to a continuance of the national Union.

Resolved, That the Whigs of the United States declare, as a fundamental article of political faith, an absolute necessity for avoiding geographical parties. The danger, so clearly discerned by the Father of his Country, has now become fearfully apparent in the agitation now convulsing the nation, and must be arrested at once if we would preserve our Constitution and our Union from dismemberment, and the name of America from being blotted out from the family of civilized nations.

Resolved, That all who revere the Constitution and the Union must look with alarm at the parties in the field in the present presidential campaign—one claiming only to represent sixteen Northern States, and the other appealing mainly to the passions and prejudices of the Southern States; that the success of either faction must add fuel to the flame which now threatens to wrap our dearest interests in a common ruin.

Resolved, That the only remedy for an evil so appalling is to support a candidate pledged to neither of the geographical sections nor arrayed in political antagonism, but holding both in a just and equal regard. We congratulate the friends of the Union that such a candidate exists in Millard Fillmore.

Resolved, That, without adopting or referring to the peculiar doctrines of the party which has already selected Mr. Fillmore as a candidate, we look to him as a well-tried and faithful friend of the Constitution and the Union, eminent alike for his wisdom and firmness; for his justice and moderation in our foreign relations; calm and pacific temperament, so well becoming the head of a great nation; for his devotion to the Constitution in its true spirit; his inflexibility in executing the laws; but, beyond all these attributes, in possessing the one transcendent merit of being a representative of neither of the two sectional parties now struggling for political supremacy.

Resolved, That in the present exigency of political affairs we are not called upon to discuss the subordinate questions of administration in the exercise of the constitutional powers of the government. It is enough to know that civil war is raging, and that the Union is in peril; and we proclaim the conviction that the restoration of Mr. Fillmore to the Presidency will furnish the best, if not the only means of restoring peace.

Republican National Committee:

Chairman, EDWIN D. MORGAN, of New York.
Secretary, N. B. JUDD, of Illinois.

REPUBLICAN CONVENTION.

Philadelphia, Pa., June 17, 1856.

Chairman pro tem., ROBERT EMMET,
of New York.

Chairman, HENRY S. LANE,
of Indiana.

NOMINATED—

For President, **John C. Fremont,**
of California.

For Vice-President, **William L. Dayton,**
of New Jersey.

This was the first National Republican Convention held. The delegates were not chosen by any settled rule. New

York with 96, Pennsylvania with 81, and Ohio with 69 votes shows the size of some of the delegations. All of the Northern States were represented, as were Delaware, Kentucky, Maryland, and Virginia.

General John C. Fremont was nominated informally on the first ballot, receiving 359 votes; 196 being cast for John McLean, of Ohio; 2 for Charles Sumner, of Massachusetts, and 1 for William H. Seward, of New York. On a formal ballot Fremont was unanimously nominated.

On an informal ballot for Vice-President, William L. Dayton, of New Jersey, received 259; Abraham Lincoln, of Illinois, 110; Nathaniel P. Banks, of Massachusetts, 46, while 12 other candidates received some votes each. On a formal ballot Dayton was unanimously nominated.

The convention adopted the following platform:—

REPUBLICAN PLATFORM.

This convention of delegates, assembled in pursuance of a call addressed to the people of the United States, without regard to past political differences or divisions, who are opposed to the repeal of the Missouri Compromise, to the policy of the present administration, to the extension of slavery into free territory, in favor of admitting Kansas as a free state, of restoring the action of the federal government to the principles of Washington and Jefferson, and who purpose to unite in presenting candidates for the offices of President and Vice-President, do resolve as follows:

Resolved, That the maintenance of the principles promulgated in the Declaration of Independence and embodied in the federal Constitution is essential to the preservation of our republican institutions, and that the federal Constitution, the rights of the states, and the union of the states, shall be preserved.

Resolved, That, with our republican fathers, we hold it to be a self-evident truth that all men are endowed with the inalienable rights to life, liberty, and the pursuit of happiness, and that the primary object and ulterior design of our federal government were to secure these rights to all persons within its exclusive jurisdiction; that, as our republican fathers, when they had abolished slavery in all our national territory, ordained that no person should be deprived of life, liberty, or property without due process of law, it becomes our duty to maintain this provision of the Constitution against all attempts to violate it for the purpose of establishing slavery in the United States, by positive legislation prohibiting its existence or extension therein; that we deny the authority of Congress, of a territorial legislature, of any individual or association of individuals, to give legal existence to slavery in any territory of the United States while the present Constitution shall be maintained.

Resolved, That the Constitution confers upon Congress sovereign power over the territories of the United States for their government, and that in the exercise of this power it is both the right and the duty of Congress to prohibit in the territories those twin relics of barbarism, polygamy, and slavery.

Resolved, That while the Constitution of the United States was ordained and established by the people "in order to form a more perfect union, establish justice, insure domestic tranquillity, provide for the common defense, promote the general welfare, and secure the blessings of liberty," and contains ample provision for the protection of the life, liberty, and property of every citizen, the dearest constitutional rights of the people of Kansas have been fraudulently and violently taken from them; their territory has been invaded by an armed force; spurious and pretended legislative, judicial, and executive officers have been set over them, by whose usurped authority, sustained by the military power of the government, tyrannical and unconstitutional laws have been enacted and enforced; the right of the people to keep and bear arms has been infringed; test oaths of an extraordinary and entangling nature have been imposed as a condition of exercising the right of suffrage and holding office; the right of an accused person to a speedy and public trial by an impartial jury has been denied; the right of the people to be secure in their persons, houses, papers, and effects, against unreasonable searches and seizures, has been violated; they have been deprived of life, liberty, and property without due process of law; that the freedom of speech and of the press has been abridged: the right to choose their representatives has been made of no effect; murders, robberies, and arsons have been instigated and encouraged, and the offenders have been allowed to go unpunished; that all these things have been done with the knowledge, sanction, and procurement of the present administration; and that for this high crime against the Constitution, the Union, and humanity, we arraign the administration, the President, his advisers, agents, supporters, apologists, and accessories, either *before* or *after* the fact, before the country and before the world; and that it is our fixed purpose to bring the actual perpetrators of these atrocious outrages, and their accomplices, to a sure and condign punishment hereafter.

Resolved, That Kansas should be immediately admitted as a state of the Union, with her present free Constitution, as at once the most effectual way of securing to her citizens the enjoyment of the rights and privileges to which they are entitled, and of ending the civil strife now raging in her territory.

Resolved, That the highwayman's plea, that "might makes right," embodied in the Ostend circular, was in every respect unworthy of American diplomacy, and would bring shame and dishonor upon any government or people that gave it their sanction.

Resolved, That a railroad to the Pacific Ocean by the most central and practicable route is imperatively demanded by the interests of the whole country, and that the federal government ought to render immediate and efficient aid in its construction; and as an auxiliary thereto, to the immediate construction of an emigrant route on the line of the railroad.

Resolved, That appropriations by Congress for the improvement of rivers and harbors of a national character, required for the accommodation and security of our existing commerce, are authorized by the Constitution and justified by the obligation of the government to protect the lives and property of its citizens.

Resolved, That we invite the affiliation and co-operation of freemen of all parties, however differing from us in other respects, in support of the principles herein declared; and, believing that the spirit of our institutions as well as the Constitution of our country, guarantees liberty of conscience and equality of rights among citizens, we oppose all legislation impairing their security.

AMERICAN (KNOW-NOTHING) CONVENTION.

Philadelphia, Pa., February 22–25, 1856.

Chairman, EPHRAIM MARSH, of New Jersey.

NOMINATED—

For President, **Millard Fillmore,** of New York.

For Vice-President, **Andrew Jackson Donelson,** of Tennessee.

Twenty-seven states were represented in the convention by 227 delegates; Georgia, Maine, South Carolina, and Vermont were not represented. A motion to proceed to nominate a candidate for President was carried by a vote of 151 to 51, whereupon nearly all the delegates from New England, Ohio, Pennsylvania, Illinois, and Iowa withdrew from the convention.

After an informal ballot had been taken, Millard Fillmore was nominated on a formal ballot as follows:

CANDIDATES.	Votes.	CANDIDATES.	Votes.
MILLARD FILLMORE, of New York	179	JOHN MCLEAN, of Ohio	13
GEORGE LAW, of New York	24	GARRETT DAVIS, of Kentucky	10
KENNETH RAYNOR, of North Carolina	14	SAMUEL HOUSTON, of Texas	3

Andrew J. Donelson was nominated for Vice-President on the first ballot, as follows:

CANDIDATES.	Votes.	CANDIDATES.	Votes.
ANDREW J. DONELSON, of Tennessee	181	KENNETH RAYNOR, of North Carolina	8
HENRY J. GARDNER, of Massachusetts	12	PERCEY WALKER, of Alabama	8

The convention adopted the following platform:—

AMERICAN PLATFORM.

1. An humble acknowledgment to the Supreme Being for His protecting care vouchsafed to our fathers in their successful revolutionary struggle, and hitherto manifested to us, their descendants, in the preservation of the liberties, the independence, and the union of these states.

2. The perpetuation of the federal Union and Constitution as the palladium of our civil and religious liberties, and the only sure bulwark of American independence.

3. Americans must rule America; and to this end native-born citizens should be selected for all state, federal, and municipal government employment, in preference to all others. Nevertheless,

4. Persons born of American parents residing temporarily abroad should be entitled to all the rights of native-born citizens.

5. No person should be selected for political station (whether of native or foreign birth) who recognizes any allegiance or obligation of any description to any foreign prince, potentate or power, or who refuses to recognize the federal and state Constitutions (each within its own sphere) as paramount to all other laws as rules of political action.

6. The unequalled recognition and maintenance of the reserved rights of the several states, and the cultivation of harmony and fraternal good-will between the citizens of the several states, and, to this end, non-interference by Congress with questions appertaining solely to the individual states, and non-intervention by each state with the affairs of any other state.

7. The recognition of the right of native-born and naturalized citizens of the United States, permanently residing in any territory thereof, to frame their constitution and laws, and to regulate their domestic and social affairs in their own mode, subject only to the provisions of the federal Constitution, with the privilege of admission into the Union whenever they have the requisite population for one representative in Congress.

Provided, That none but those who are citizens of the United States under the Constitution and laws thereof, and who have a fixed residence in any such territory, are to participate in the formation of the constitution or in the enactment of laws for said territory or state.

8. An enforcement of the principles that no state or territory ought to admit others than citizens to the right of suffrage or of holding political offices of the United States.

9. A change in the laws of naturalization, making a con-

tinued residence of twenty-one years, of all not heretofore provided for, an indispensable requisite for citizenship hereafter, and excluding all paupers or persons convicted of crime from landing upon our shores; but no interference with the vested rights of foreigners.

10. Opposition to any union between church and state; no interference with religious faith or worship; and no test oaths for office.

11. Free and thorough investigation into any and all alleged abuses of public functionaries, and a strict economy in public expenditures.

12. The maintenance and enforcement of all laws constitutionally enacted, until said laws shall be repealed or shall be declared null and void by competent judicial authority.

13. Opposition to the reckless and unwise policy of the present administration in the general management of our national affairs, and more especially as shown in removing "Americans" (by designation) and conservatives in principle, from office, and placing foreigners and ultraists in their places; as shown in a truckling subserviency to the stronger, and an insolent and cowardly bravado toward the weaker powers; as shown in re-opening sectional agitation, by the repeal of the Missouri Compromise; as shown in granting to unnaturalized foreigners the right of suffrage in Kansas and Nebraska; as shown in its vacillating course on the Kansas and Nebraska question; as shown in the corruptions which pervade some of the departments of the government; as shown in disgracing meritorious naval officers through prejudiced caprice; and as shown in the blundering mismanagement of our foreign relations.

14. Therefore, to remedy existing evils and prevent the disastrous consequences otherwise resulting therefrom, we would build up the "American Party" upon the principles hereinbefore stated.

15. That each state council shall have authority to amend their several constitutions, so as to abolish the several degrees and substitute a pledge of honor, instead of other obligations, for fellowship and admission into the party.

16. A free and open discussion of all political principles embraced in our platform.

NOTE.—The seceding delegates from this convention soon after met, and nominated John C. Fremont, of

California, for President, and William F. Johnston, of Pennsylvania, for Vice-President; but they adopted no platform.

The election occurred on November 4, 1856.

THIRTY-ONE STATES VOTED.

POPULAR VOTE.

STATES.	James Buchanan, Democrat.	John C. Fremont, Republican.	Millard Fillmore, American and Whig.	Total vote.
Alabama	46,739	....	28,552	75,291
Arkansas	21,910	....	10,787	32,697
California	53,365	20,691	36,165	110,221
Connecticut	34,995	42,715	2,615	80,325
Delaware	8,004	308	6,175	14,487
Florida	6,358	....	4,833	11,191
Georgia	56,578	....	42,228	98,806
Illinois	105,348	96,189	37,444	238,981
Indiana	118,670	94,375	22,386	235,431
Iowa	36,170	43,954	9,180	89,304
Kentucky	74,642	314	67,416	142,372
Louisiana	22,164	....	20,709	42,873
Maine	39,080	67,379	3,325	109,784
Maryland	39,115	281	47,460	86,856
Massachusetts	39,240	108,190	19,626	167,056
Michigan	52,136	71,762	1,660	125,558
Mississippi	35,446	....	24,195	59,641
Missouri	58,164	....	48,524	106,688
New Hampshire	32,789	38,345	422	71,556
New Jersey	46,943	28,338	24,115	99,396
New York	195,878	276,007	124,604	596,489
North Carolina	48,246	....	36,886	85,132
Ohio	170,874	187,497	28,126	386,497
Pennsylvania	230,710	147,510	82,175	460,395
Rhode Island	6,680	11,467	1,675	19,822
*South Carolina	....	....	....	....
Tennessee	73,638	....	66,178	139,816
Texas	31,169	....	15,639	46,808
Vermont	10,569	39,561	545	50,675
Virginia	89,706	291	60,310	150,307
Wisconsin	52,843	66,090	579	119,512
Total	1,838,169	1,341,264	874,534	4,053,967

* The electors were chosen by the legislature.

ELECTORAL VOTE.

Counted on February 11, 1857.

STATES.	PRESIDENT.			VICE-PRESIDENT.			
	James Buchanan, of Pennsylvania.	John C. Fremont, of California.	Millard Fillmore, of New York.	John C. Breckinridge, of Kentucky.	William L. Dayton, of New Jersey.	Andrew J. Donelson, of Tennessee.	No. entitled to vote.
Alabama	9	..	..	9	..	..	9
Arkansas	4	..	..	4	..	..	4
California	4	..	..	4	..	..	4
Connecticut	..	6	..	..	6	..	6
Delaware	3	..	..	3	..	..	3
Florida	3	..	..	3	..	..	3
Georgia	10	..	..	10	..	..	10
Illinois	11	..	..	11	..	..	11
Indiana	13	..	..	13	..	..	13
Iowa	..	4	..	..	4	..	4
Kentucky	12	..	..	12	..	..	12
Louisiana	6	..	..	6	..	..	6
Maine	..	8	..	..	8	..	8
Maryland	..	..	8	..	..	8	8
Massachusetts	..	13	..	..	13	..	13
Michigan	..	6	..	..	6	..	6
Mississippi	7	..	..	7	..	..	7
Missouri	9	..	..	9	..	..	9
New Hampshire	..	5	..	..	5	..	5
New Jersey	7	..	..	7	..	..	7
New York	..	35	..	..	35	..	35
North Carolina	10	..	..	10	..	..	10
Ohio	..	23	..	..	23	..	23
Pennsylvania	27	..	..	27	..	..	27
Rhode Island	..	4	..	..	4	..	4
South Carolina	8	..	..	8	..	..	8
Tennessee	12	..	..	12	..	..	12
Texas	4	..	..	4	..	..	4
Vermont	..	5	..	..	5	..	5
Virginia	15	..	..	15	..	..	15
Wisconsin	..	5	..	..	5	..	5
Total	174	114	8	174	114	8	296

James Buchanan was elected President and John C. Breckinridge as Vice-President.

During this period Congress was divided politically as follows:

Thirty-fifth Congress.

Senate— 39 Democrats, 20 Republicans, 5 Americans....Total, 64
House—131 Democrats, 92 Republicans, 14 Americans.... " 237

Thirty-sixth Congress.

Senate— 38 Democrats, 26 Republicans, 2 Americans...Total, 66
House—101 Democrats, 113 Republicans, 23 Americans... " 237

Election of 1860

Democratic National Committee:

Chairman, AUGUST BELMONT, of New York.
Secretary, FREDERICK O. PRINCE, of Massachusetts.

DEMOCRATIC CONVENTION.

Charleston, S. C., April 23, 1860.

Chairman pro tem., FRANCIS B. FLOURNOY, of Arkansas.

Chairman, CALEB CUSHING, of Massachusetts.

Every state was represented by full delegations. After being in session for 10 days and having taken 57 ballots without reaching a nomination, the convention adjourned to meet in Baltimore on June 18, 1860.

The following is a summary of the ballots taken :—

CANDIDATES.	1st.	10th.	20th.	30th.	40th.	57th.
STEPHEN A. DOUGLAS, of Illinois	145	150	150	151	151	151
R. M. T. HUNTER, of Virginia	42	39	26	25	16	16
JAMES GUTHRIE, of Kentucky	35	39	42	42	66	65
ANDREW JOHNSON, of Tennessee	12	12	12	12	..	..
DANIEL S. DICKINSON, of New York	7	4	..	13	5	4
JOSEPH LANE, of Oregon	6	5	20	7	2	14
ISAAC TOUCEY, of Connecticut	2	..	..	..	..	..
JEFFERSON DAVIS, of Mississippi	2	1	1	1	..	1
FRANKLIN PIERCE, of New Hampshire	1	..	..	..	..	..
Whole No. of votes, 303. Necessary to a choice, 202.						

On May 30 a platform was agreed to, for which see the resolutions of the Baltimore convention of 1860.

NOTE.—After the adoption of these resolutions many of the Southern delegates withdrew from the convention. These seceders met in another hall in Charleston, and organized a convention by electing Senator James A. Bayard, of Delaware, as Chairman; and, after adopting resolutions [see the Democratic Platform (*Breckinridge*), Baltimore, June 18, 1860], adjourned to meet in Richmond, Va., on June 11, 1860.

DEMOCRATIC CONVENTION, Adjourned Meeting.

Baltimore, Md., June 18-23, 1860.

Chairman, CALEB CUSHING,
of Massachusetts.

2d Chairman, GOVERNOR TOD,
of Ohio.

NOMINATED—

For President, **Stephen A. Douglas,**
of Illinois.

For Vice-President, **Herschel V. Johnson,**
of Georgia.

Three whole days were occupied in the preliminary organization; and as soon as the organization was completed, many of the Southern delegates withdrew, including the presiding officer, Mr. Cushing.

Governor Tod, of Ohio, took the chair, and then the convention proceeded to ballot for a candidate. On the second ballot Mr. Douglas was declared nominated. Here follow the ballots:

CANDIDATES.	1st.	2d.
STEPHEN A. DOUGLAS, of Illinois	173	181
JAMES GUTHRIE, of Kentucky	10	5
JOHN C. BRECKINRIDGE, of Kentucky	5	7

For Vice-President, Benjamin Fitzpatrick, of Alabama, was nominated on the first ballot. Mr. Fitzpatrick afterward declined, and the National Democratic Committee substituted Herschel V. Johnson, of Georgia.

The convention ratified the platform adopted at Charleston, S. C., on Monday, May 30, 1860, and added a further resolve, being No. 7 as herein printed. The following is the platform as agreed upon by the convention:—

DEMOCRATIC PLATFORM.

1. *Resolved,* That we, the Democracy of the Union, in convention assembled, hereby declare our affirmance of the resolutions unanimously adopted and declared as a platform of principles by the Democratic Convention at Cincinnati in the year 1856, believing that Democratic principles are unchangeable in their nature when applied to the same subject-matters; and we recommend, as the only further resolutions, the following:—Inasmuch as differences of opinion exist in the Democratic party as to the nature and extent of the powers of a territorial legislature, and as to the powers and duties of Congress, under the Constitution of the United States, over the institution of slavery within the territories,—

2. *Resolved,* That the Democratic party will abide by the decisions of the Supreme Court of the United States on the questions of constitutional law.

3. *Resolved,* That it is the duty of the United States to afford ample and complete protection to all its citizens, whether at home or abroad, and whether native or foreign.

4. *Resolved,* That one of the necessities of the age, in a military, commercial, and postal point of view, is speedy communication between the Atlantic and Pacific States; and the Democratic party pledge such constitutional government aid as will insure the construction of a railroad to the Pacific coast at the earliest practicable period.

5. *Resolved,* That the Democratic party are in favor of the acquisition of the Island of Cuba on such terms as shall be honorable to ourselves and just to Spain.

6. *Resolved,* That the enactments of state legislatures to defeat the faithful execution of the Fugitive Slave Law are hostile in character, subversive of the Constitution, and revolutionary in their effect.

7. *Resolved,* That it is in accordance with the true interpretation of the Cincinnati platform that, during the existence of the territorial governments, the measure of restriction, whatever it may be, imposed by the federal constitution on the power of the territorial legislature over the subject of the domestic relations, as the same has been, or shall hereafter be, finally determined by the Supreme Court of the United States, should be respected by all good citizens and enforced with promptness and fidelity by every branch of the general government.

(BRECKINRIDGE) DEMOCRATIC CONVENTION.

Baltimore, Md., June 18–28, 1860.

Chairman, CALEB CUSHING,
of Massachusetts.

NOMINATED—

For President, **John C. Breckinridge,**
of Kentucky.

For Vice-President, **Joseph Lane,**
of Oregon.

The nominations of Breckinridge and Lane were accomplished by bolting factions of the regular Democratic convention. The first bolt was made at Charleston, S. C., at the meeting of April 23 to May 3, 1860. The bolting faction organized by electing Senator James A. Bayard, of Delaware, Chairman. After adopting the resolutions rejected by the Charleston convention, they adjourned to meet in Richmond, Va., on June 11, 1860. On reassembling, John Erwin, of Alabama, was chosen Chairman; after which they adjourned until June 28, 1860, when the nominations of Breckinridge and Lane, previously made by the bolters at Baltimore, were ratified.

The second bolt was at Baltimore, Md., on the reassembling of the convention which had met at Charleston, S. C. The presiding officer, Caleb Cushing, with most of the Southern delegates, finding themselves in a minority, withdrew, and organized another convention, over which Mr. Cushing presided. Twenty-one states were represented, but no delegates were present from Connecticut, Illinois, Indiana, Iowa, Maine, Michigan, New Hampshire, New Jersey, Ohio, Rhode Island, South Carolina, and Wisconsin. John C. Breckinridge, of Kentucky, for President, and Joseph Lane, of Oregon, for Vice-President, were unanimously nominated.

The following platform (which had been reported by a majority of the Committee on Resolutions in the Charleston convention, and was afterward rejected) was adopted:—

(BRECKINRIDGE) DEMOCRATIC PLATFORM.

Resolved, That the platform adopted by the Democratic party at Cincinnati be affirmed, with the following explanatory resolutions:

1. That the government of a territory organized by an act of Congress is provisional and temporary, and during its existence all citizens of the United States have an equal right to settle with their property in the territory, without their rights, either of person or property, being destroyed or impaired by congressional or territorial legislation.

2. That it is the duty of the federal government, in all its departments, to protect, when necessary, the rights of persons and property in the territories, and wherever else its constitutional authority extends.

3. That when the settlers in a territory, having an adequate population, form a state constitution, the right of sovereignty commences, and, being consummated by admission into the Union, they stand on an equal footing with the people of other states; and the State thus organized ought to be admitted into the federal Union, whether its constitution prohibits or recognizes the institution of slavery.

4. That the Democratic party are in favor of the acquisition

of the Island of Cuba, on such terms as shall be honorable to ourselves and just to Spain, at the earliest practicable moment.

5. That the enactments of state legislatures to defeat the faithful execution of the Fugitive Slave Law are hostile in character, subversive of the Constitution, and revolutionary in their effect.

6. The Democracy of the United States recognize it as the imperative duty of this government to protect the naturalized citizen in all his rights, whether at home or in foreign lands, to the same extent as its native-born citizens.

Whereas, One of the greatest necessities of the age, in a political, commercial, postal, and military point of view, is a speedy communication between the Pacific and Atlantic coasts; therefore be it

Resolved, That the National Democratic Party do hereby pledge themselves to use every means in their power to secure the passage of some bill, to the extent of the constitutional authority of Congress, for the construction of a Pacific railroad from the Mississippi River to the Pacific Ocean, at the earliest practicable moment.

Republican National Committee:

Chairman, EDWIN D. MORGAN, of New York.
Secretary, EDWARD MCPHERSON, of Pennsylvania.

REPUBLICAN CONVENTION.

Chicago, Ill., May 16–18, 1860.

Chairman pro tem., DAVID WILMOT,
of Pennsylvania.

Chairman, GEORGE ASHMUN,
of Massachusetts.

NOMINATED—

For President, **Abraham Lincoln,**
of Illinois.

For Vice-President, **Hannibal Hamlin,**
of Maine.

Delegates were present from all of the free states, as also from Delaware, Kentucky, Maryland, Missouri, Texas, and Virginia, and from the Territories of Kansas, Nebraska, and the District of Columbia. Three ballots were taken, with the following result:

CANDIDATES.	1st.	2d.	3d.
WILLIAM H. SEWARD, of New York	173	184	180
ABRAHAM LINCOLN, of Illinois	102	181	231
SIMON CAMERON, of Pennsylvania	50	2	..
SALMON P. CHASE, of Ohio	49	42	24
EDWARD BATES, of Missouri	48	35	22
WILLIAM L. DAYTON, of New Jersey	14	10	..
JOHN McLEAN, of Ohio	12	8	5
JACOB COLLAMER, of Vermont	10	..	
Whole number of votes, 465. Necessary to a choice, 233.			

Then Lincoln was nominated by the quick changing of four votes from Ohio, when one delegation after another changed in his favor until 354 votes were recorded for him. On motion of Mr. W. M. Evarts, of New York, the nomination was made unanimous.

For Vice-President, Hannibal Hamlin, of Maine, was nominated on the second ballot. The following is the vote:

CANDIDATES.	1st.	2d.
HANNIBAL HAMLIN, of Maine	194	367
CASSIUS M. CLAY, of Kentucky	101	86
JOHN HICKMAN, of Pennsylvania	58	13
ANDREW H. REEDER, of Pennsylvania	51	..
NATHANIEL P. BANKS, of Massachusetts	38	..

The convention adopted the following platform:—

REPUBLICAN PLATFORM.

Resolved, That we, the delegated representatives of the Republican electors of the United States, in convention assembled, in discharge of the duty we owe to our constituents and our country, unite in the following declarations:

1. That the history of the nation during the last four years has fully established the propriety and necessity of the organization and perpetuation of the Republican party, and that the causes which called it into existence are permanent in their nature, and now, more than ever before, demand its peaceful and constitutional triumph.

2. That the maintenance of the principles promulgated in the Declaration of Independence and embodied in the federal Constitution, "That all men are created equal; that they are endowed by their Creator with certain inalienable rights; that among these are life, liberty, and the pursuit of happiness; that to secure these rights, governments are instituted among men, deriving their just powers from the consent of the governed,"—is essential to the preservation of our republican institutions; and that the federal Constitution, the rights of the states, and the union of the states must and shall be preserved.

3. That to the union of the states this nation owes its unprecedented increase in population, its surprising development of material resources, its rapid augmentation of wealth, its happiness at home and its honor abroad; and we hold in abhorrence all schemes for disunion, come from whatever source they may; and we congratulate the country that no Republican member of Congress has uttered or countenanced the threats of disunion so often made by Democratic members, without rebuke and with applause from their political associates; and we denounce those threats of disunion, in case of a popular overthrow of their ascendency, as denying the vital principles of a free government, and as an avowal of contemplated treason, which it is the imperative duty of an indignant people sternly to rebuke and forever silence.

4. That the maintenance inviolate of the rights of the states, and especially the right of each state to order and control its own domestic institutions according to its own judgment exclusively, is essential to that balance of power on which the perfection and endurance of our political fabric depends; and we denounce the lawless invasion by armed force of the soil

or any state or territory, no matter under what pretext, as among the gravest of crimes.

5. That the present Democratic administration has far exceeded our worst apprehensions, in its measureless subserviency to the exactions of a sectional interest, as especially evinced in its desperate exertions to force the infamous Lecompton constitution upon the protesting people of Kansas; in construing the personal relations between master and servant to involve an unqualified property in persons; in its attempted enforcement everywhere, on land and sea, through the intervention of Congress and of the federal courts, of the extreme pretensions of a purely local interest; and in its general and unvarying abuse of the power intrusted to it by a confiding people.

6. That the people justly view with alarm the reckless extravagance which pervades every department of the federal government; that a return to rigid economy and accountability is indispensable to arrest the systematic plunder of the public treasury by favored partisans, while the recent startling developments of frauds and corruptions at the federal metropolis show that an entire change of administration is imperatively demanded.

7. That the new dogma,—that the Constitution, of its own force, carries slavery into any or all of the territories of the United States,—is a dangerous political heresy, at variance with the explicit provisions of that instrument itself, with contemporaneous exposition, and with legislative and judicial precedent; is revolutionary in its tendency and subversive of the peace and harmony of the country.

8. That the normal condition of all the territory of the United States is that of freedom; that, as our republican fathers, when they had abolished slavery in all our national territory, ordained that "no person should be deprived of life, liberty, or property without due process of law," it becomes our duty, by legislation, whenever such legislation is necessary, to maintain this provision of the Constitution against all attempts to violate it; and we deny the authority of Congress, of a territorial legislature, or of any individuals, to give legal existence to slavery in any territory of the United States.

9. That we brand the recent reopening of the African slave trade, under the cover of our national flag, aided by perversions of judicial power, as a crime against humanity and a

burning shame to our country and age; and we call upon Congress to take prompt and efficient measures for the total and final suppression of that execrable traffic.

10. That in the recent vetoes, by their federal governors, of the acts of the legislatures of Kansas and Nebraska, prohibiting slavery in those territories, we find a practical illustration of the boasted Democratic principle of non-intervention and popular sovereignty, embodied in the Kansas-Nebraska Bill, and a demonstration of the deception and fraud involved therein.

11. That Kansas should of right be immediately admitted as a state under the constitution recently formed and adopted by her people and accepted by the House of Representatives.

12. That, while providing revenue for the support of the general government by duties upon imports, sound policy requires such an adjustment of these imposts as to encourage the development of the industrial interests of the whole country; and we commend that policy of national exchanges which secures to the workingmen liberal wages, to agriculture remunerative prices, to mechanics and manufacturers an adequate reward for their skill, labor, and enterprise, and to the nation commercial prosperity and independence.

13. That we protest against any sale or alienation to others of the public lands held by actual settlers, and against any view of the free-homestead policy which regards the settlers as paupers or suppliants for public bounty; and we demand the passage by Congress of the complete and satisfactory homestead measure which has already passed the House.

14. That the Republican party is opposed to any change in our naturalization laws, or any state legislation by which the rights of citizens hitherto accorded to immigrants from foreign lands shall be abridged or impaired; and in favor of giving a full and efficient protection to the rights of all classes of citizens, whether native or naturalized, both at home and abroad.

15. That appropriations by Congress for river and harbor improvements of a national character, required for the accommodation and security of an existing commerce, are authorized by the Constitution and justified by the obligation of government to protect the lives and property of its citizens.

16. That a railroad to the Pacific Ocean is imperatively demanded by the interests of the whole country; that the federal government ought to render immediate and efficient aid in its

construction; and that, as preliminary thereto, a daily overland mail should be promptly established.

17. Finally, having thus set forth our distinctive principles and views, we invite the co-operation of all citizens, however differing on other questions, who substantially agree with us in their affirmance and support.

CONSTITUTIONAL UNION CONVENTION.

Baltimore, Md., May 9, 1860.

Chairman, WASHINGTON HUNT,
of New York.

NOMINATED—

For President, **John Bell,**
of Tennessee.

For Vice-President, **Edward Everett,**
of Massachusetts.

This was the first and only general convention held by the party. Most of the states were represented. Two ballots were necessary to nominate. John Bell was nominated for President on the second ballot. The following is the vote:

CANDIDATES.	1st.	2d.
JOHN BELL, of Tennessee	68	138
SAMUEL HOUSTON, of Texas	57	68
JOHN J. CRITTENDEN, of Kentucky	28	8
EDWARD EVERETT, of Massachusetts	25	9
JOHN MCLEAN, of Ohio	22	..
WILLIAM A. GRAHAM, of North Carolina	22	18
WILLIAM C RIVES, of Virginia	9	5
WILLIAM L. SHARKEY, of Mississippi	6	5
WILLIAM L. GOGGIN, of Virginia	3	..

For Vice-President, Edward Everett, of Massachusetts, was nominated by a unanimous vote.

The convention adopted the following platform:—

CONSTITUTIONAL UNION PLATFORM.

Whereas, Experience has demonstrated that platforms adopted by the partisan conventions of the country have had the effect to mislead and deceive the people, and at the same time to widen the political divisions of the country, by the creation and encouragement of geographical and sectional parties; therefore

Resolved, That it is both the part of patriotism and of duty to *recognize* no political principles other than THE CONSTITUTION OF THE COUNTRY, THE UNION OF THE STATES, AND THE ENFORCEMENT OF THE LAWS; and that, as representatives of the Constitutional Union men of the country, in national convention assembled, we hereby pledge ourselves to maintain, protect, and defend, separately and unitedly, these great principles of public liberty and national safety, against all enemies, at home and abroad; believing that thereby peace may once more be restored to the country; the rights of the people and of the states re-established, and the government again placed in that condition of justice, fraternity, and equality which, under the example and Constitution of our fathers, has solemnly bound every citizen of the United States to maintain a more perfect Union, establish justice, insure domestic tranquillity, provide for common defense, promote the general welfare, and secure the blessings of liberty to ourselves and our posterity.

The election occurred on November 6, 1860.

THIRTY-THREE STATES VOTED.

POPULAR VOTE.

STATES.	Abraham Lincoln, Republican.	Stephen A. Douglas, Democrat.	John C. Breckinridge, Independent Democrat.	John Bell, Constitutional Union.	Total vote.
Alabama	....	13,651	48,831	27,825	90,307
Arkansas	....	5,227	28,732	20,094	54,053
California	39,173	38,516	34,334	6,817	118,840
Connecticut	43,692	15,522	14,641	3,291	77,146
Delaware	3,815	1,023	7,347	3,864	16,049
Florida	....	367	8,543	5,437	14,347
Georgia	...	11,590	51,889	42,886	106,365
Illinois	172,161	160,215	2,404	3,913	338,693
Indiana	139,033	115,509	12,295	5,306	272,143
Iowa	70,409	55,111	1,048	1,763	128,331
Kentucky	1,364	25,651	53,143	66,058	146,216
Louisiana	....	7,625	22,681	20,204	50,510
Maine	62,811	26,693	6,368	2,046	97,918
Maryland	2,294	5,966	42,482	41,760	92,502
Massachusetts	106,533	34,372	5,939	22,331	169,175
Michigan	88,480	65,057	805	405	154,747
Minnesota	22,069	11,920	748	62	34,799
Mississippi	....	3,283	40,797	25,040	69,120
Missouri	17,028	58,801	31,317	58,372	165,518
New Hampshire	37,519	25,881	2,112	441	65,953
New Jersey	58,324	62,801	...	....	121,125
New York	362,646	312,510	....	....	675,156
North Carolina	....	2,701	48,339	44,990	96,030
Ohio	231,610	187,232	11,405	12,194	442,441
Oregon	5,270	3,951	3,006	183	12,410
Pennsylvania	268,030	16,765	178,871	12,776	476,442
Rhode Island	12,244	7,707	....	....	19,951
*South Carolina	....	....	....	....	....
Tennessee	....	11,350	64,709	69,274	145,333
Texas	....	....	47,548	15,438	62,986
Vermont	33,808	6,849	1,969	218	42,844
Virginia	1,929	16,290	74,323	74,681	167,223
Wisconsin	86,110	65,021	888	161	152,180
Total	1,866,352	1,375,157	847,514	587,830	4,676,853

* The electors were chosen by the legislature.

ELECTORAL VOTE.

Counted on February 13, 1861.

STATES.	PRESIDENT.				VICE-PRESIDENT.				
	Abraham Lincoln, of Illinois.	John C. Breckinridge, of Kentucky.	John Bell, of Tennessee.	Stephen A. Douglas, of Illinois.	Hannibal Hamlin, of Maine.	Joseph Lane, of Oregon.	Edward Everett, of Massachusetts.	Herschel V. Johnson, of Georgia.	No. entitled to vote.
Alabama	..	9	..	..	..	9	..	..	9
Arkansas	..	4	..	..	..	4	..	..	4
California	4	..	..	..	4	..	..	..	4
Connecticut	6	..	..	..	6	..	..	..	6
Delaware	..	3	..	..	..	3	..	..	3
Florida	..	3	..	..	..	3	..	..	3
Georgia	..	10	..	..	..	10	..	..	10
Illinois	11	..	..	..	11	..	..	..	11
Indiana	13	..	..	..	13	..	..	..	13
Iowa	4	..	..	..	4	..	..	..	4
Kentucky	..	..	12	..	..	..	12	..	12
Louisiana	..	6	..	..	..	6	..	..	6
Maine	8	..	..	..	8	..	..	..	8
Maryland	..	8	..	..	..	8	..	..	8
Massachusetts	13	..	..	..	13	..	..	..	13
Michigan	6	..	..	..	6	..	..	..	6
Minnesota	4	..	..	..	4	..	..	..	4
Mississippi	..	7	..	..	..	7	..	..	7
Missouri	..	..	..	9	..	..	..	9	9
New Hampshire	5	..	..	..	5	..	..	..	5
New Jersey	4	..	..	3	4	..	..	3	7
New York	35	..	..	..	35	..	..	..	35
North Carolina	..	10	..	..	..	10	..	..	10
Ohio	23	..	..	..	23	..	..	..	23
Oregon	3	..	..	..	3	..	..	..	3
Pennsylvania	27	..	..	..	27	..	..	..	27
Rhode Island	4	..	..	..	4	..	..	..	4
South Carolina	..	8	..	..	..	8	..	..	8
Tennessee	..	..	12	..	..	..	12	..	12
Texas	..	4	..	..	..	4	..	..	4
Vermont	5	..	..	..	5	..	..	..	5
Virginia	..	..	15	..	..	..	15	..	15
Wisconsin	5	..	..	..	5	..	..	..	5
Total	180	72	39	12	180	72	39	12	303

Abraham Lincoln was elected President and Hannibal Hamlin as Vice-President.

During this period Congress was divided politically as follows:

Thirty-seventh Congress.

Senate—11 Democrats, 31 Republicans, 7 Americans, 1 vacancy ....Total, 50
House—42 Democrats, 106 Republicans, 28 Americans, 2 vacancies .... " 178

Thirty-eighth Congress.

Senate—12 Democrats, 39 Republicans ....Total, 51
House—80 Democrats, 103 Republicans .... " 183

Election of 1864

Democratic National Committee:

Chairman, AUGUST BELMONT, of New York.
Secretary, F. O. PRINCE, of Massachusetts.

DEMOCRATIC CONVENTION.

Chicago, Ill., August 29, 1864.

Chairman pro tem., WILLIAM BIGLER,
of Pennsylvania.

Chairman, HORATIO SEYMOUR,
of New York.

NOMINATED—

For President, **George B. McClellan,**
of New Jersey.

For Vice-President, **George H. Pendleton,**
of Ohio.

Twenty-three states participated in this convention. Delaware, Kentucky, Maryland, and Missouri were the only Southern States represented. One ballot was sufficient to nominate a candidate for President, George B. McClellan receiving 202½, and Horatio Seymour, 28½ votes. McClellan's nomination was, on the motion of Mr. Vallandigham, of Ohio, made unanimous.

For Vice-President, George H. Pendleton was nominated on the second ballot by a unanimous vote. The following is the result of the first ballot:

CANDIDATES.	Votes.	CANDIDATES.	Votes.
JAMES GUTHRIE, of Kentucky	65	DANIEL W. VOORHEES, of Indiana	13
GEORGE H. PENDLETON, of Ohio	55	JOHN D. CATON, of Illinois	16
LAZARUS W. POWELL, of Kentucky	32	AUGUSTUS C. DODGE, of Iowa	9
GEORGE W. CASS, of Pennsylvania	26	JOHN S. PHELPS, of Missouri	8

The convention adopted the following platform:—

DEMOCRATIC PLATFORM.

Resolved, That in the future, as in the past, we will adhere with unswerving fidelity to the Union under the Constitution as the only solid foundation of our strength, security, and happiness as a people, and as a framework of government equally conducive to the welfare and prosperity of all the States, both Northern and Southern.

Resolved, That this convention does explicitly declare, as the sense of the American people, that after four years of failure to restore the Union by the experiment of war, during which, under the pretense of a military necessity or war-power higher than the Constitution, the Constitution itself has been disregarded in every part, and public liberty and private right alike trodden down, and the material prosperity of the country essentially impaired—justice, humanity, liberty, and the public welfare demand that immediate efforts be made for a cessation of hostilities, with a view to the ultimate convention of the states, or other peaceable means, to the end that, at the earliest practicable moment, peace may be restored on the basis of the federal union of the states.

Resolved, That the direct interference of the military authorities of the United States in the recent elections held in Kentucky, Maryland, Missouri, and Delaware was a shameful violation of the Constitution, and a repetition of such acts in the approaching election will be held as revolutionary, and resisted with all the means and power under our control.

Resolved, That the aim and object of the Democratic party is to preserve the federal Union and the rights of the states unimpaired, and they hereby declare that they consider that the administrative usurpation of extraordinary and dangerous powers not granted by the Constitution—the subversion of the civil by military law in states not in insurrection; the arbitrary military arrest, imprisonment, trial, and sentence of American citizens in states where civil law exists in full force; the suppression of freedom of speech and of the press; the denial of the right of asylum; the open and avowed disregard of state rights; the employment of unusual test-oaths; and the interference with and denial of the right of the people to bear arms in their defense—is calculated to prevent a restoration of the Union and the perpetuation of a government deriving its just powers from the consent of the governed.

Resolved, That the shameful disregard of the administration to its duty in respect to our fellow citizens who now are and long have been prisoners of war and in a suffering condition, deserves the severest reprobation on the score alike of public policy and common humanity.

Resolved, That the sympathy of the Democratic party is heartily and earnestly extended to the soldiers of our army and sailors of our navy who are and have been in the field and on the sea under the flag of our country, and, in the event of its attaining power, they will receive all the care, protection, and regard that the brave soldiers and sailors of the republic have so nobly earned.

Republican National Committee:

Chairman, MARCUS L. WARD, of New Jersey.
Secretary, JOHN D. DEFREES, of Indiana.

(REGULAR) REPUBLICAN CONVENTION.

Baltimore, Md., June 7, 1864.

Chairman pro tem.,
REV. DR. ROBERT J. BRECKINRIDGE,
of Kentucky.

Chairman, WILLIAM DENNISON,
of Ohio.

NOMINATED—

For President, **Abraham Lincoln,**
of Illinois.

For Vice-President, **Andrew Johnson,**
of Tennessee.

Thirty-one states, including eight Southern States, were represented at this convention. Abraham Lincoln was nominated for President, by a unanimous vote, on the first ballot. Missouri voted for General U. S. Grant, but changed to Lincoln.

For Vice-President, Andrew Johnson, of Tennessee, was nominated on the first ballot. The vote as first cast was Johnson, 200; Hannibal Hamlin, of Maine, 150; Daniel S. Dickinson, of New York, 108; and 61 votes were scattered among seven others; but before the vote was declared, many changes were reported, leaving the final vote stand: Johnson, 494; Dickinson, 17; and Hamlin, 9.

The following is the platform as adopted:—

REPUBLICAN PLATFORM.

1. *Resolved,* That it is the highest duty of every American citizen to maintain against all their enemies, the integrity of the Union and the paramount authority of the Constitution and laws of the United States; and that, laying aside all differences of political opinion, we pledge ourselves as Union men, animated by a common sentiment and aiming at a common object, to do everything in our power to aid the government in quelling by force of arms the rebellion now raging against its authority, and in bringing to the punishment due to their crimes the rebels and traitors arrayed against it.

2. *Resolved,* That we approve the determination of the government of the United States not to compromise with rebels, or to offer them any terms of peace except such as may be based upon an unconditional surrender of their hostility and a return to their just allegiance to the Constitution and laws of the United States; and that we call upon the government to maintain this position and to prosecute the war with the utmost possible vigor, to the complete suppression of the rebellion, in full reliance upon the self-sacrificing patriotism, the heroic valor, and the undying devotion of the American people to the country and its free institutions.

3. *Resolved,* That as slavery was the cause and now constitutes the strength of this rebellion, and as it must be always and everywhere hostile to the principles of republican government, justice and the national safety demand its utter and

complete extirpation from the soil of the republic; and that while we uphold and maintain the acts and proclamations by which the government, in its own defense, has aimed a death-blow at this gigantic evil, we are in favor, furthermore, of such an amendment to the Constitution, to be made by the people in conformity with its provisions, as shall terminate and forever prohibit the existence of slavery within the limits of the jurisdiction of the United States.

4. *Resolved*, That the thanks of the American people are due to the soldiers and sailors of the army and navy who have periled their lives in defense of the country and in vindication of the honor of its flag; that the nation owes to them some permanent recognition of their patriotism and their valor, and ample and permanent provision for those of their survivors who have received disabling and honorable wounds in the service of the country; and that the memories of those who have fallen in its defense shall be held in grateful and everlasting remembrance.

5. *Resolved*, That we approve and applaud the practical wisdom, the unselfish patriotism, and the unswerving fidelity to the Constitution and the principles of American liberty with which Abraham Lincoln has discharged, under circumstances of unparalleled difficulty, the great duties and responsibilities of the presidential office; that we approve and indorse, as demanded by the emergency and essential to the preservation of the nation, and as within the provisions of the Constitution, the measures and acts which he has adopted to defend the nation against its open and secret foes; that we approve especially the proclamation of emancipation and the employment as Union soldiers of men heretofore held in slavery; and that we have full confidence in his determination to carry these and all other constitutional measures essential to the salvation of the country into full and complete effect.

6. *Resolved*, That we deem it essential to the general welfare that harmony should prevail in the national councils, and we regard as worthy of public confidence and official trust those only who cordially indorse the principles proclaimed in these resolutions, and which should characterize the administration of the government.

7. *Resolved*, That the government owes to all men employed in its armies, without regard to distinction of color, the full protection of the laws of war; and that any violation of these laws, or of the usages of civilized nations in time of war, by the rebels now in arms, should be made the subject of prompt and full redress.

8. *Resolved*, That foreign immigration, which in the past has added so much to the wealth, development of resources, and increase of power to the nation—the asylum of the oppressed of all nations—should be fostered and encouraged by a liberal and just policy.

9. *Resolved*, That we are in favor of the speedy construction of the railroad to the Pacific coast.

10. *Resolved*, That the national faith, pledged for the redemption of the public debt, must be kept inviolate, and that for this purpose we recommend economy and rigid responsibility in the public expenditures, and a vigorous and just system of taxation; and that it is the duty of every loyal state to sustain the credit and promote the use of the national currency.

11. *Resolved*, That we approve the position taken by the government, that the people of the United States can never regard with indifference the attempt of any European power to overthrow by force, or to supplant by fraud, the institutions of any republican government on the western continent; and that they will view with extreme jealousy, as menacing to the peace and independence of their own country, the efforts of any such power to obtain new footholds for monarchical governments, sustained by foreign military force, in near proximity to the United States.

(RADICAL) REPUBLICAN CONVENTION.

Cleveland, O., May 31, 1864.

Chairman, JOHN COCHRANE,
of New York.

NOMINATED—

For President, **John C. Fremont,**
of California.

For Vice-President, **John Cochrane,**
of New York.

About 350 persons attended this convention. General John C. Fremont was nominated by acclamation for President, and General John Cochrane for Vice-President. On September 21 both candidates withdrew, and the party united in support of the regular Republican nominees.

The convention adopted the following platform:—

(RADICAL) REPUBLICAN PLATFORM.

1. That the federal Union shall be preserved.

2. That the Constitution and laws of the United States must be observed and obeyed.

3. That the rebellion must be suppressed by force of arms and without compromise.

4. That the rights of free speech, free press, and *habeas corpus* be held inviolate, save in districts where martial law has been proclaimed.

5. That the rebellion has destroyed slavery; and the federal Constitution should be so amended as to prohibit its re-establishment, and to secure to all men absolute equality before the law.

6. That integrity and economy are demanded at all times in the administration of the government, and that in time of war the want of them is criminal.

7. That the right of asylum, except for crime and subject to law, is a recognized principle of American liberty; and that any violation of it cannot be overlooked and must not go unrebuked.

8. That the national policy known as the "Monroe Doctrine" has become a recognized principle; and that the establishment of any anti-republican government on this continent by any foreign power cannot be tolerated.

9. That the gratitude and support of the nation are due to the faithful soldiers and the earnest leaders of the Union Army and Navy for their heroic achievements and deathless valor in defense of our imperilled country and civil liberty.

10. That the one-term policy for the Presidency adopted by the people is strengthened by the force of the existing crisis, and should be maintained by Constitutional amendment.

11. That the Constitution should be so amended that the President and Vice-President shall be elected by a direct vote of the people.

12. That the question of the reconstruction of the rebellious states belongs to the people, through their representatives in Congress, and not to the Executive.

13. That the confiscation of the lands of the rebels and their distribution among the soldiers and actual settlers is a measure of justice.

The election occurred on November 8, 1864.

TWENTY-FIVE STATES VOTED. (War period.)

POPULAR AND ARMY VOTES.

The popular and army votes are placed side by side, as follows:

STATES.	POPULAR VOTE.		ARMY VOTE.*		Total vote.
	Abraham Lincoln, Republican.	George B. McClellan, Democrat.	Abraham Lincoln, Republican.	George B. McClellan, Democrat.	
California	62,134	43,841	2,600	237	108,812
Connecticut	44,693	42,288	..	..	86,981
Delaware	8,155	8,767	..	..	16,922
Illinois	189,487	158,349	..	..	347,836
Indiana	150,422	130,233	..	..	280,655
Iowa	87,331	49,260	15,178	1,364	153,133
Kansas	14,228	3,871	..	..	18,099
Kentucky	27,786	64,301	1,194	2,823	96,104
Maine	72,278	47,736	4,174	741	124,929
Maryland	40,153	32,739	2,800	321	76,013
Massachusetts	126,742	48,745	..	..	175,487
Michigan	85,352	67,370	9,402	2,959	165,083
Minnesota	25,060	17,375	..	..	42,435
Missouri	72,991	31,026	..	..	104,017
Nevada	9,826	6,594	..	..	16,420
New Hampshire	36,595	33,034	2,066	690	72,385
New Jersey	60,723	68,014	..	..	128,737
New York	368,726	361,986	..	..	730,712
Ohio	265,154	205,568	41,146	9,757	521,625
Oregon	9,888	8,457	..	..	18,345
Pennsylvania	296,389	276,308	26,712	12,349	611,758
Rhode Island	14,343	8,718	..	..	23,061
Vermont	42,422	13,325	243	49	56,039
West Virginia	23,223	10,457	..	..	33,680
Wisconsin	79,564	63,875	11,372	2,458	157,269
Total	2,213,665	1,802,237	116,887	33,748	4,166,537

* Provision had been made by some of the states, for taking the vote of the soldiers in the field. The army votes of Kansas and Minnesota arrived too late to be counted.

ELECTORAL VOTE.

Counted on February 8, 1865.

STATES.	PRESIDENT.		VICE-PRESIDENT.		No. entitled to vote.
	Abraham Lincoln, of Illinois.	George B. McClellan, of New Jersey.	Andrew Johnson, of Tennessee.	George H. Pendleton, of Ohio.	
California	5	..	5	..	5
Connecticut	6	..	6	..	6
Delaware	..	3	..	3	3
Illinois	16	..	16	..	16
Indiana	13	..	13	..	13
Iowa	8	..	8	..	8
Kansas	3	..	3	..	3
Kentucky	..	11	..	11	11
Maine	7	..	7	..	7
Maryland	7	..	7	..	7
Massachusetts	12	..	12	..	12
Michigan	8	..	8	..	8
Minnesota	4	..	4	..	4
Missouri	11	..	11	..	11
Nevada*	2	..	2	..	2
New Hampshire	5	..	5	..	5
New Jersey	..	7	..	7	7
New York	33	..	33	..	33
Ohio	21	..	21	..	21
Oregon	3	..	3	..	3
Pennsylvania	26	..	26	..	26
Rhode Island	4	..	4	..	4
Vermont	5	..	5	..	5
West Virginia	5	..	5	..	5
Wisconsin	8	..	8	..	8
Total	212	21	212	21	233

Abraham Lincoln was elected President and Andrew Johnson as Vice-President.

* Nevada chose three electors, one of whom died before the election.

During this period Congress was divided politically as follows:

Thirty-ninth Congress.

Senate—10 Democrats, 42 Republicans ....Total, 52
House—46 Democrats, 145 Republicans .... " 191

Fortieth Congress.

Senate—11 Democrats, 42 Republicans ....Total, 53
House—49 Democrats, 143 Republicans, 1 vacancy .... " 193

Election of 1868

Democratic National Committee:

Chairman, AUGUST BELMONT, of New York.
Secretary, F. O. PRINCE, of Massachusetts.

DEMOCRATIC CONVENTION.

New York, N. Y., July 4-11, 1868.

Chairman pro tem., JOHN M. PALMER, of Illinois.

Chairman, HORATIO SEYMOUR, of New York.

NOMINATED—

For President, **Horatio Seymour,** of New York.

For Vice-President, **Francis P. Blair, Jr.,** of Missouri.

This convention was held in Tammany Hall, New York, on Fourteenth street. The convention convened on Saturday, but balloting did not begin until Tuesday, and continued until Thursday. After twenty-one unsuccessful ballots, a stampede began on the twenty-second ballot, for Horatio Seymour, the chairman of the convention, and when the ballot was announced it was found to be a unanimous vote. The following summary will prove interesting:

CANDIDATES.	1st.	8th.	16th.	18th.	21st.	22d.
GEORGE H. PENDLETON, of Ohio	105	156½	107½	56½	..	..
ANDREW JOHNSON, of Tennessee	65	6	5½	10	5	..
WINFIELD S. HANCOCK, of Pennsylvania	33½	28	113½	144½	135½	..
SANFORD E. CHURCH, of New York	33	..	..	..	..	..
ASA PACKER, of Pennsylvania	26	26	..	..	..	..
JOEL PARKER, of New Jersey	13	7	7	3½	..	..
JAMES E. ENGLISH, of Connecticut	16	6	..	..	19	..
JAMES R. DOOLITTLE, of Wisconsin	13	12	12	12	12½	..
THOMAS A. HENDRICKS, of Indiana	2½	75	70½	87	132	..
SALMON P. CHASE, of Ohio	..	..	..	½	½	..
HORATIO SEYMOUR, of New York	..	..	..	..	..	317
Whole number of votes, 317. Necessary to a choice, 212.						

For Vice-President, Francis P. Blair, Jr., of Missouri, was nominated unanimously on the first ballot.

The convention adopted the following platform:—

DEMOCRATIC PLATFORM.

The Democratic party, in national convention assembled, reposing its trust in the intelligence, patriotism, and discriminating justice of the people, standing upon the Constitution as the foundation and limitation of the powers of the government and the guarantee of the liberties of the citizen, and recognizing the questions of slavery and secession as having been settled for all time to come by the war or the voluntary action of the Southern States in constitutional conventions assembled, and never to be renewed or reagitated,—do, with the return of peace, demand—

1. Immediate restoration of all the states to their rights in the Union under the Constitution, and of civil government to the American people.

2. Amnesty for all past political offenses, and the regulation of the elective franchise in the states by their citizens.

3. Payment of the public debt of the United States as rapidly as practicable: all moneys drawn from the people by taxation, except so much as is requisite for the necessities of the government, economically administered, being honestly applied to such payment; and where the obligations of the government do not expressly state upon their face, or the law under which they were issued does not provide that they shall be paid in coin, they ought, in right and in justice, to be paid in the lawful money of the United States.

4. Equal taxation of every species of property according to its real value, including government bonds and other public securities.

5. One currency for the government and the people, the laborer and the officeholder, the pensioner and the soldier, the producer and the bondholder.

6. Economy in the administration of the government; the reduction of the standing army and navy; the abolition of the Freedmen's Bureau and all political instrumentalities designed to secure negro supremacy; simplification of the system, and discontinuance of inquisitorial modes of assessing and collecting internal revenue, so that the burden of taxation may be equalized and lessened; the credit of the government and the currency made good; the repeal of all enactments for enrolling the state militia into national forces in time of peace; and a tariff for revenue upon foreign imports, and such equal taxation under the Internal Revenue Laws as will afford incidental protection to domestic manufactures, and as will, without impairing the revenue, impose the least burden upon, and best promote and encourage, the great industrial interests of the country.

7. Reform of abuses in the administration; the expulsion of corrupt men from office; the abrogation of useless offices; the restoration of rightful authority to, and the independence of, the executive and judicial departments of the government; the subordination of the military to the civil power, to the end that the usurpations of Congress and the despotism of the sword may cease.

8. Equal rights and protection for naturalized and native-born citizens at home and abroad; the assertion of American nationality which shall command the respect of foreign powers and furnish an example and encouragement to people struggling for national integrity, constitutional liberty, and individual rights, and the maintenance of the rights of natural-

ized citizens against the absolute doctrine of immutable allegiance, and the claims of foreign powers to punish them for alleged crime committed beyond their jurisdiction.

In demanding these measures and reforms we arraign the Radical party for its disregard of right and the unparalleled oppression and tyranny which have marked its career. After the most solemn and unanimous pledge of both Houses of Congress to prosecute the war exclusively for the maintenance of the government and the preservation of the Union under the Constitution, it has repeatedly violated that most sacred pledge under which alone was rallied that noble volunteer army which carried our flag to victory. Instead of restoring the Union, it has, so far as in its power, dissolved it, and subjected ten states, in time of profound peace, to military despotism and negro supremacy. It has nullified there the right of trial by jury; it has abolished the *habeas corpus*, that most sacred writ of liberty; it has overthrown the freedom of speech and the press; it has substituted arbitrary seizures and arrests, and military trials and secret star-chamber inquisitions for the constitutional tribunals; it has disregarded, in time of peace, the right of the people to be free from searches and seizures; it has entered the post and telegraph offices, and even the private rooms of individuals, and seized their private papers and letters without any specific charge or notice of affidavit, as required by the organic law; it has converted the American Capitol into a bastile; it has established a system of spies and official espionage to which no constitutional monarchy of Europe would now dare to resort; it has abolished the right of appeal, on important Constitutional questions, to the supreme judicial tribunals, and threatens to curtail or destroy its original jurisdiction, which is irrevocably vested by the Constitution; while the learned chief justice has been subjected to the most atrocious calumnies, merely because he would not prostitute his high office to the support of the false and partisan charges preferred against the President. Its corruption and extravagance have exceeded anything known in history, and, by its frauds and monopolies it has nearly doubled the burden of the debt created by the war. It has stripped the President of his Constitutional power of appointment, even of his own Cabinet. Under its repeated assaults the pillars of the government are rocking on their base, and should it succeed in November next, and inaugurate its President, we will meet, as a subjected and conquered people, amid the ruins of liberty and the scattered fragments of the Constitution.

And we do declare and resolve that ever since the people of the United States threw off all subjection to the British Crown the privilege and trust of suffrage have belonged to the several states, and have been granted, regulated, and controlled exclusively by the political power of each state respectively, and that any attempt by Congress, on any pretext whatever, to deprive any state of this right, or interfere with its exercise, is a flagrant usurpation of power which can find no warrant in the Constitution, and, if sanctioned by the people, will subvert our form of government, and can only end in a single, centralized, and consolidated government, in which the separate existence of the states will be entirely absorbed, and an unqualified despotism be established in place of a federal Union of co-equal states.

And that we regard the Reconstruction Acts (so-called), of Congress, as such, as usurpations, and unconstitutional, revolutionary, and void. That our soldiers and sailors, who carried the flag of our country to victory against a most gallant and determined foe, must ever be gratefully remembered, and all the guarantees given in their favor must be faithfully carried into execution.

That the public lands should be distributed as widely as possible among the people, and should be disposed of either under the Pre-emption or Homestead Laws, or sold in reasonable quantities, and to none but actual occupants, at the minimum price established by the government. When grants of the public lands may be allowed, necessary for the encouragement of important public improvements, the proceeds of the sale of such lands, and not the lands themselves, should be so applied.

That the President of the United States, Andrew Johnson, in exercising the power of his high office in resisting the aggressions of Congress upon the Constitutional rights of the states and the people, is entitled to the gratitude of the whole American people, and in behalf of the Democratic party we tender him our thanks for his patriotic efforts in that regard.

Upon this platform the Democratic party appeal to every patriot, including all the conservative element and all who desire to support the Constitution and restore the Union, forgetting all past differences of opinion, to unite with us in the present great struggle for the liberties of the people; and that to all such, to whatever party they may have heretofore belonged, we extend the right hand of fellowship, and hail all such co-operating with us as friends and brethren.

Resolved, That this convention sympathize cordially with the workingmen of the United States in their efforts to protect the rights and interests of the laboring classes of the country.

Resolved, That the thanks of the convention are tendered to Chief Justice Salmon P. Chase for the justice, dignity, and impartiality with which he presided over the court of impeachment on the trial of President Andrew Johnson.

The last two resolutions were offered by Mr. Kernan, of New York, after the nominations and immediately before the final adjournment, and were carried by acclamation.

Republican National Committee:

Chairman, WILLIAM CLAFLIN, of Massachusetts.
Secretary, JOHN D. DEFREES, of Indiana.

REPUBLICAN CONVENTION.

Chicago, Ill., May 20–22, 1868.

Chairman pro tem., CARL SCHURZ, of Missouri.

Chairman, JOSEPH R. HAWLEY, of Connecticut.

NOMINATED—

For President, **Ulysses S. Grant,** of Illinois.

For Vice-President, **Schuyler Colfax,** of Indiana.

This convention was composed of 650 delegates. General Ulysses S. Grant, of Illinois, was unanimously nominated on the first ballot, receiving 650 votes, the full vote of the convention.

For Vice-President, five ballots had been taken, when Schuyler Colfax, of Indiana, was nominated. The following is the vote in detail:

CANDIDATES.	1st.	2d.	3d.	4th.	5th.
BENJAMIN F. WADE, of Ohio	147	170	178	206	38
REUBEN E. FENTON, of New York	126	144	139	144	69
HENRY WILSON, of Massachusetts	119	114	101	87	..
SCHUYLER COLFAX, of Indiana	115	145	165	186	541
ANDREW G. CURTIN, of Pennsylvania	51	45	40	..	..
HANNIBAL HAMLIN, of Maine	28	30	25	25	..
JAMES SPEED, of Kentucky	22	..	..	..	..
JAMES HARLAN, of Iowa	16	..	..	..	..
JOHN A. J. CRESWELL, of Maryland	14	..	..	..	..
SAMUEL C. POMEROY, of Kansas	6	..	..	..	..
WILLIAM D. KELLEY, of Pennsylvania	4	..	..	..	..

The convention adopted the following platform:—

REPUBLICAN PLATFORM.

The National Republican Party of the United States, assembled in national convention in the city of Chicago, on the 21st day of May, 1868, make the following declaration of principles:—

1. We congratulate the country on the assured success of the reconstruction policy of Congress, as evinced by the adoption, in the majority of the states lately in rebellion, of Constitutions securing equal civil and political rights to all; and it is the duty of the government to sustain those institutions and to prevent the people of such states from being remitted to a state of anarchy.

2. The guaranty by Congress of equal suffrage to all loyal men at the South was demanded by every consideration of public safety, of gratitude, and of justice, and must be maintained; while the question of suffrage in all the loyal states properly belongs to the people of those states.

3. We denounce all forms of repudiation as a national crime; and the national honor requires the payment of the public

indebtedness in the uttermost good faith to all creditors at home and abroad, not only according to the letter, but the spirit of the laws under which it was contracted.

4. It is due to the labor of the nation that taxation should be equalized, and reduced as rapidly as the national faith will permit.

5. The national debt, contracted as it has been for the preservation of the Union for all time to come, should be extended over a fair period for redemption; and it is the duty of Congress to reduce the rate of interest thereon whenever it can be honestly done.

6. That the best policy to diminish our burden of debt is to so improve our credit that capitalists will seek to loan us money at lower rates of interest than we now pay, and must continue to pay, so long as repudiation, partial or total, open or covert, is threatened or suspected.

7. The government of the United States should be administered with the strictest economy; and the corruptions which have been so shamefully nursed and fostered by Andrew Johnson call loudly for radical reform.

8. We profoundly deplore the untimely and tragic death of Abraham Lincoln, and regret the accession to the Presidency of Andrew Johnson, who has acted treacherously to the people who elected him and the cause he was pledged to support; who has usurped high legislative and judicial functions; who has refused to execute the laws; who has used his high office to induce other officers to ignore and violate the laws; who has employed his executive powers to render insecure the property, the peace, the liberty and life of the citizen; who has abused the pardoning power; who has denounced the national legislature as unconstitutional; who has persistently and corruptly resisted, by every means in his power, every proper attempt at the reconstruction of the states lately in rebellion; who has perverted the public patronage into an engine of wholesale corruption; and who has been justly impeached for high crimes and misdemeanors, and properly pronounced guilty thereof by the vote of thirty-five senators.

9. The doctrine of Great Britain and other European powers, that because a man is once a subject he is always so, must be resisted at every hazard by the United States, as a relic of feudal times, not authorized by the laws of nations, and at war with our national honor and independence. Naturalized citizens are entitled to protection in all their rights of citizenship as though they were native-born; and no citizen of the

United States, native or naturalized, must be liable to arrest and imprisonment by any foreign power for acts done or words spoken in this country; and, if so arrested and imprisoned, it is the duty of the government to interfere in his behalf.

10. Of all who were faithful in the trials of the late war there were none entitled to more especial honor than the brave soldiers and seamen who endured the hardships of campaign and cruise, and imperilled their lives in the service of the country; the bounties and pensions provided by the laws for these brave defenders of the nation are obligations never to be forgotten; the widows and orphans of the gallant dead are the wards of the people—a sacred legacy bequeathed to the nation's protecting care.

11. Foreign immigration, which in the past has added so much to the wealth, development, and resources, and increase of power to this republic—the asylum of the oppressed of all nations—should be fostered and encouraged by a liberal and just policy.

12. This convention declares itself in sympathy with all oppressed people struggling for their rights.

13. That we highly commend the spirit of magnanimity and forbearance with which men who have served in the rebellion, but who now frankly and honestly co-operate with us in restoring the peace of the country and reconstructing the Southern State governments upon the basis of impartial justice and equal rights, are received back into the communion of the loyal people; and we favor the removal of the disqualifications and restrictions imposed upon the late rebels in the same measure as the spirit of disloyalty will die out, and as may be consistent with the safety of the loyal people.

14. That we recognize the great principles laid down in the immortal Declaration of Independence as the true foundation of democratic government; and we hail with gladness every effort toward making these principles a living reality on every inch of American soil.

By the admission of Nebraska the whole number of states became thirty-seven; but Mississippi, Texas, and Virginia, under an act of Congress, were debarred from choosing electors.

The election occurred on November 3, 1868.

THIRTY-FOUR STATES VOTED.

POPULAR VOTE.

STATES.	Ulysses S. Grant, Republican.	Horatio Seymour, Democrat.	Total Vote.
Alabama	76,366	72,080	148,452
Arkansas	22,152	19,078	41,230
California	54,592	54,078	108,670
Connecticut	50,641	47,600	98,241
Delaware	7,623	10,980	18,603
*Florida	..	..	..
Georgia	57,134	102,822	159,956
Illinois	250,293	199,143	449,436
Indiana	176,552	166,980	343,532
Iowa	120,399	74,040	194,439
Kansas	31,049	14,019	45,068
Kentucky	39,566	115,889	155,455
Louisiana	33,263	80,225	113,488
Maine	70,426	42,396	112,822
Maryland	30,438	62,357	92,795
Massachusetts	136,477	59,408	195,885
Michigan	128,550	97,069	225,619
Minnesota	43,542	28,072	71,614
Missouri	85,671	59,788	145,459
Nebraska	9,729	5,439	15,168
Nevada	6,480	5,218	11,698
New Hampshire	38,191	31,224	69,415
New Jersey	80,121	83,001	163,122
New York	419,883	429,883	849,766
North Carolina	96,226	84,090	180,316
Ohio	280,128	238,700	518,828
Oregon	10,961	11,125	22,086
Pennsylvania	342,280	313,382	655,662
Rhode Island	12,993	6,548	19,541
South Carolina	62,301	45,237	107,538
Tennessee	56,757	26,311	83,068
Vermont	44,167	12,045	56,212
West Virginia	29,025	20,306	49,331
Wisconsin	108,857	84,710	193,567
Total	3,012,833	2,703,249	5,716,082

* The electors were chosen by the legislature.

ELECTORAL VOTE.

Counted on February 10, 1869.

STATES.	PRESIDENT.		VICE-PRESIDENT.		No. entitled to vote.
	Ulysses S. Grant, of Illinois.	Horatio Seymour, of New York.	Schuyler Colfax, of Indiana.	Francis P. Blair, Jr., of Missouri.	
Alabama	8	..	8	..	8
Arkansas	5	..	5	..	5
California	5	..	5	..	5
Connecticut	6	..	6	..	6
Delaware	..	3	..	3	3
Florida	3	..	3	..	3
*Georgia	..	9	..	9	9
Illinois	16	..	16	..	16
Indiana	13	..	13	..	13
Iowa	8	..	8	..	8
Kansas	3	..	3	..	3
Kentucky	..	11	..	11	11
Louisiana	..	7	..	7	7
Maine	7	..	7	..	7
Maryland	..	7	..	7	7
Massachusetts	12	..	12	..	12
Michigan	8	..	8	..	8
Minnesota	4	..	4	..	4
Missouri	11	..	11	..	11
Nebraska	3	..	3	..	3
Nevada	3	..	3	..	3
New Hampshire	5	..	5	..	5
New Jersey	..	7	..	7	7
New York	..	33	..	33	33
North Carolina	9	..	9	..	9
Ohio	21	..	21	..	21
Oregon	..	3	..	3	3
Pennsylvania	26	..	26	..	26
Rhode Island	4	..	4	..	4
South Carolina	6	..	6	..	6
Tennessee	10	..	10	..	10
Vermont	5	..	5	..	5
West Virginia	5	..	5	..	5
Wisconsin	8	..	8	..	8
Total	214	80	214	80	294

* Objections were made to counting the vote of Georgia, on the ground that the vote of the electors was not given on the first Wednesday in December; that at the date of the election of the electors, that state had not

Ulysses S. Grant was elected President and Schuyler Colfax as Vice-President.

During this period Congress was divided politically as follows:

Forty-first Congress.

Senate—11 Democrats, 61 Republicans, 2 vacancies......Total, 74
House—73 Democrats, 170 Republicans .... " 243

Forty-second Congress.

Senate— 17 Democrats, 57 Republicans ....Total, 74
House—104 Democrats, 139 Republicans .... " 243

---

been admitted to representation as a state in Congress; that the state has not fulfilled, in due form, the requirements of the Reconstruction Acts, so as to entitle her to be represented as a state, and that the election held was not a free, just and fair election. The House of Representatives sustained the objections, but the Senate did not. The president of the Senate announced the vote in a similar form and under similar circumstances as was announced the vote of 1820.

Election of 1872

Democratic National Committee:

Chairman, AUGUSTUS SCHELL, of New York.
Secretary, F. O. PRINCE, of Massachusetts.

DEMOCRATIC CONVENTION.

Baltimore, Md., July 9, 1872.

Chairman pro tem., THOMAS J. RANDOLPH, of Virginia.

Chairman, JAMES R. DOOLITTLE, of Wisconsin.

NOMINATED—

For President, **Horace Greeley,** of New York.

For Vice-President, **B. Gratz Brown,** of Missouri.

The first work of the convention was the acceptance of the platform adopted by the Liberal Republicans at Cincinnati, on May 1, 1872, in the following resolution:—

We, the Democratic electors of the United States, in convention assembled, do present the following principles, already adopted at Cincinnati, as essential to just government:

[See Liberal Republican Platform of 1872.]

Horace Greeley, of New York, was then nominated on the first ballot as follows:

CANDIDATES.	Votes.	CANDIDATES.	Votes.
HORACE GREELEY, of New York	686	THOMAS F. BAYARD, of Delaware	16
JEREMIAH S. BLACK, of Pennsylvania	21	WILLIAM S. GROESBECK, of Ohio	2
		Blank ballots	7

For Vice-President, B. Gratz Brown, of Missouri, was also nominated on the first ballot, as follows:

CANDIDATES.	Votes.	CANDIDATES.	Votes.
B GRATZ BROWN, of Missouri	713	JOHN W. STEPHENSON, of Kentucky	6
		Blank ballots	13

LIBERAL REPUBLICAN CONVENTION.

Cincinnati, O., May 1, 1872.

Chairman pro tem., STANLEY MATTHEWS, of Ohio.

Chairman, CARL SCHURZ, of Missouri.

NOMINATED—

For President, **Horace Greeley**, of New York.

For Vice-President, **B. Gratz Brown**, of Missouri.

This convention assembled as a mass-meeting, no regular delegates having been chosen. Organization was effected by allowing each state such representation as would equal two delegates or votes for each representative and senator in Congress. Six ballots were taken for a President, with the result that Horace Greeley was nominated. The following is the vote in detail:

CANDIDATES.	1st.	2d.	3d.	4th.	5th.	6th.
CHARLES FRANCIS ADAMS, of Massachusetts	203	243	264	279	258	187
HORACE GREELEY, of New York	147	245	258	251	309	482
LYMAN TRUMBULL, of Illinois	110	148	156	141	81	19
B. GRATZ BROWN, of Missouri	95	2	2	2	2	..
DAVID DAVIS, of Illinois	92½	75	41	51	30	6
ANDREW G. CURTIN, of Pennsylvania	62	..	..	..	..	..
SALMON P. CHASE, of Ohio	2½	1	..	..	24	32

For Vice-President, B. Gratz Brown was nominated on the second ballot, as follows:

CANDIDATES.	1st.	2d.
B. GRATZ BROWN, of Missouri	237	435
LYMAN TRUMBULL, of Illinois	158	175
GEORGE W. JULIAN, of Indiana	134½	..
GILBERT C. WALKER, of Virginia	84½	75
CASSIUS M. CLAY, of Kentucky	34	..
JACOB D. COX, of Ohio	25	..
JOHN M. SCOVILLE, of New Jersey	12	..
THOMAS W. TIPTON, of Nebraska	8	3
JOHN M. PALMER, of Illinois	..	8

The convention adopted the following platform·

LIBERAL REPUBLICAN PLATFORM.

We, the Liberal Republicans of the United States, in national convention assembled at Cincinnati, proclaim the following principles as essential to just government:—

1. We recognize the equality of all men before the law, and hold that it is the duty of government, in its dealings with the

people, to mete out equal and exact justice to all, of whatever nativity, race, color, or persuasion, religious or political.

2. We pledge ourselves to maintain the union of these states, emancipation, and enfranchisement, and to oppose any re-opening of the questions settled by the Thirteenth, Fourteenth, and Fifteenth Amendments to the Constitution.

3. We demand the immediate and absolute removal of all disabilities imposed on account of the rebellion, which was finally subdued seven years ago, believing that universal amnesty will result in complete pacification in all sections of the country.

4. Local self-government, with impartial suffrage, will guard the rights of all citizens more securely than any centralized power. The public welfare requires the supremacy of the civil over the military authority, and freedom of persons under the protection of the *habeas corpus*. We demand for the individual the largest liberty consistent with public order; for the state self-government, and for the nation a return to the methods of peace and the constitutional limitations of power.

5. The civil service of the government has become a mere instrument of partisan tyranny and personal ambition, and an object of selfish greed. It is a scandal and reproach upon free institutions, and breeds a demoralization dangerous to the perpetuity of republican government. We therefore regard a thorough reform of the civil service as one of the most pressing necessities of the hour; that honesty, capacity, and fidelity constitute the only valid claim to public employment; that the offices of the government cease to be a matter of arbitrary favoritism and patronage, and that public station become again a post of honor. To this end it is imperatively required that no President shall be a candidate for re-election.

6. We demand a system of federal taxation which shall not unnecessarily interfere with the industry of the people, and which shall provide the means necessary to pay the expenses of the government, economically administered, the pensions, the interest on the public debt, and a moderate reduction annually of the principal thereof; and recognizing that there are in our midst honest but irreconcilable differences of opinion with regard to the respective systems of protection and free trade, we remit the discussion of the subject to the people in their congressional districts, and to the decision of the Congress thereon, wholly free from executive interference or dictation.

7. The public credit must be sacredly maintained, and we denounce repudiation in every form and guise.

8. A speedy return to specie payment is demanded alike by the highest considerations of commercial morality and honest government.

9. We remember with gratitude the heroism and sacrifices of the soldiers and sailors of the republic, and no act of ours shall ever detract from their justly earned fame or the full reward of their patriotism.

10. We are opposed to all further grants of lands to railroads or other corporations. The public domain should be held sacred to actual settlers.

11. We hold that it is the duty of the government in its intercourse with foreign nations, to cultivate the friendships of peace by treating with all on fair and equal terms, regarding it alike dishonorable either to demand what is not right or to submit to what is wrong.

12. For the promotion and success of these vital principles, and the support of the candidates nominated by this convention, we invite and cordially welcome the co-operation of all patriotic citizens, without regard to previous political affiliations.

(STRAIGHT-OUT) DEMOCRATIC CONVENTION.

Louisville, Ky., September 3, 1872.

Chairman, JAMES LYON,
of Virginia.

NOMINATED—

For President, **Charles O'Conor,**
of New York.

For Vice-President, **John Quincy Adams,**
of Massachusetts.

The convention made the above-named nominations. The nominees declined, but their declinations were not accepted.

The convention adopted the following platform:—

(STRAIGHT-OUT) DEMOCRATIC PLATFORM.

Whereas, A frequent recurrence to first principles and eternal vigilance against abuses are the wisest provisions for liberty, which is the source of progress, and fidelity to our constitutional system is the only protection for either; therefore,

Resolved, That the original basis of our whole political structure is consent in every part thereof. The people of each state voluntarily created their state, and the states voluntarily formed the Union; and each state provided by its written constitution for everything a state could do for the protection of life, liberty, and property within it; and each state, jointly with the others, provided a federal union for foreign and interstate relations.

Resolved, That all governmental powers, whether state or federal, are trust powers coming from the people of each state, and that they are limited to the written letter of the Constitution and the laws passed in pursuance of it; which powers must be exercised in the utmost good faith, the Constitution itself stating in what manner they may be altered and amended.

Resolved, That the interests of labor and capital should not be permitted to conflict, but should be harmonized by judicious legislation. While such a conflict continues, labor, which is the parent of wealth, is entitled to paramount consideration.

Resolved, That we proclaim to the world that principle is to be preferred to power; that the Democratic party is held together by the cohesion of time-honored principles, which they will never surrender in exchange for all the offices which Presidents can confer. The pangs of the minorities are doubtless excruciating; but we welcome an eternal minority, under the banner inscribed with our principles, rather than an almighty and everlasting majority purchased by their abandonment.

Resolved, That, having been betrayed at Baltimore into a false creed and a false leadership by the convention, we repudiate both, and appeal to the people to approve our platform and to rally to the fold and support the true platform and the candidates who embody it.

Resolved, That we are opposed to giving public lands to corporations, and favor their disposal to actual settlers only.

Resolved, That we favor a judicious tariff for revenue purposes only, and that we are unalterably opposed to class legislation which enriches a few at the expense of the many, under the plea of protection.

Republican National Committee:

Chairman, EDWIN D. MORGAN, of New York.
Secretary, WILLIAM E. CHANDLER, of New Hampshire.

REPUBLICAN CONVENTION.

Philadelphia, Pa., June 5-6, 1872.

Chairman pro tem., MORTON MCMICHAEL,
of Pennsylvania.

Chairman, THOMAS SETTLE,
of North Carolina.

NOMINATED—

For President, **Ulysses S. Grant,**
of Illinois.

For Vice-President, **Henry Wilson,**
of Massachusetts.

The renomination of General Grant was conceded before the convention reached a ballot, and he was nominated by a unanimous vote.

In the contest for Vice-President, Henry Wilson, of Massachusetts, received 364½ votes, and Schuyler Colfax, of Indiana, 321½.

The convention adopted the following platform:—

REPUBLICAN PLATFORM.

The Republican party of the United States, assembled in national convention in the city of Philadelphia on the 5th and 6th days of June, 1872, again declares its faith, appeals to its history, and announces its position upon the questions before the country.

1. During eleven years of supremacy it has accepted with grand courage the solemn duties of the time. It suppressed a gigantic rebellion, emancipated four millions of slaves, decreed the equal citizenship of all, and established universal suffrage. Exhibiting unparalleled magnanimity, it criminally punished

no man for political offenses, and warmly welcomed all who proved loyalty by obeying the laws and dealing justly with their neighbors. It has steadily decreased with firm hand the resultant disorders of a great war and initiated a wise and humane policy toward the Indians. The Pacific Railroad and similar vast enterprises have been generously aided and successfully conducted, the public lands freely given to actual settlers, immigration protected and encouraged, and a full acknowledgment of the naturalized citizens' rights secured from European powers. A uniform national currency has been provided, repudiation frowned down, the national credit sustained under the most extraordinary burdens, and new bonds negotiated at lower rates. The revenues have been carefully collected and honestly applied. Despite annual large reductions in the rates of taxation, the public debt has been reduced during General Grant's Presidency at the rate of a hundred millions a year; great financial crises have been avoided, and peace and plenty prevail throughout the land. Menacing foreign difficulties have been peacefully and honorably composed, and the honor and power of the nation kept in high respect throughout the world. This glorious record of the past is the party's best pledge for the future. We believe the people will not intrust the government to any party or combination of men composed chiefly of those who have resisted every step of this beneficent progress.

2. The recent amendments to the National Constitution should be cordially sustained because they are right, not merely tolerated because they are law, and should be carried out according to their spirit by appropriate legislation, the enforcement of which can safely be entrusted only to the party that secured those amendments.

3. Complete liberty and exact equality in the enjoyment of all civil, political, and public rights should be established and effectually maintained throughout the Union, by efficient and appropriate state and federal legislation. Neither the law nor its administration should admit any discrimination in respect of citizens by reason of race, creed, color, or previous condition of servitude.

4. The national government should seek to maintain honorable peace with all nations, protecting its citizens everywhere, and sympathizing with all people who strive for greater liberty.

5. Any system of the civil service under which the subordinate positions of the government are considered rewards for mere party zeal is fatally demoralizing, and we therefore favor

a reform of the system by laws which shall abolish the evils of patronage and make honesty, efficiency, and fidelity the essential qualifications for public positions, without practically creating a life-tenure of office.

6. We are opposed to further grants of the public lands to corporations and monopolies, and demand that the national domain be set apart for free homes for the people.

7. The annual revenue, after paying current expenditures, pensions, and the interest on the public debt, should furnish a moderate balance for the reduction of the principal, and that revenue, except so much as may be derived from a tax on tobacco and liquors, should be raised by duties upon importations, the details of which should be so adjusted as to aid in securing remunerative wages to labor, and promote the industries, prosperity, and growth of the whole country.

8. We hold in undying honor the soldiers and sailors whose valor saved the Union. Their pensions are a sacred debt of the nation, and the widows and orphans of those who died for their country are entitled to the care of a generous and grateful people. We favor such additional legislation as will extend the bounty of the government to all our soldiers and sailors who were honorably discharged, and who in the line of duty became disabled, without regard to the length of service or the cause of such discharge.

9. The doctrine of Great Britain and other European powers concerning allegiance—"Once a subject always a subject"—having at last, through the efforts of the Republican party, been abandoned, and the American idea of the individual's right to transfer allegiance having been accepted by European nations, it is the duty of our government to guard with jealous care the rights of adopted citizens against the assumption of unauthorized claims by their former governments, and we urge continued careful encouragement and protection of voluntary immigration.

10. The franking privilege ought to be abolished and the way prepared for a speedy reduction in the rates of postage.

11. Among the questions which press for attention is that which concerns the relations of capital and labor, and the Republican party recognizes the duty of so shaping legislation as to secure full protection and the amplest field for capital, and for labor, the creator of capital, the largest opportunities and a just share of the mutual profits of these two great servants of civilization.

12. We hold that Congress and the President have only fulfilled an imperative duty in their measures for the suppression of violent and treasonable organizations in certain lately rebellious regions, and for the protection of the ballot-box; and therefore they are entitled to the thanks of the nation.

13. We denounce repudiation of the public debt, in any form or disguise, as a national crime. We witness with pride the reduction of the principal of the debt, and of the rates of interest upon the balance, and confidently expect that our excellent national currency will be perfected by a speedy resumption of specie payment.

14. The Republican party is mindful of its obligations to the loyal women of America for their noble devotion to the cause of freedom. Their admission to wider fields of usefulness is viewed with satisfaction; and the honest demand of any class of citizens for additional rights should be treated with respectful consideration.

15. We heartily approve the action of Congress in extending amnesty to those lately in rebellion, and rejoice in the growth of peace and fraternal feeling throughout the land.

16. The Republican party proposes to respect the rights reserved by the people to themselves as carefully as the powers delegated by them to the state and to the federal government. It disapproves of the resort to unconstitutional laws for the purpose of removing evils, by interference with rights not surrendered by the people to either the state or national government.

17. It is the duty of the general government to adopt such measures as may tend to encourage and restore American commerce and ship-building.

18. We believe that the modest patriotism, the earnest purpose, the sound judgment, the practical wisdom, the incorruptible integrity, and the illustrious services of Ulysses S. Grant have commended him to the heart of the American people, and with him at our head we start to-day upon a new march to victory.

19. Henry Wilson, nominated for the Vice-Presidency, known to the whole land from the early days of the great struggle for liberty as an indefatigable laborer in all campaigns, an incorruptible legislator, and representative man of American institutions, is worthy to associate with our great leader and share the honors which we pledge our best efforts to bestow upon them.

LABOR REFORM CONVENTION.

Columbus, O., February 21–22, 1872.

Chairman, Edwin M. Chamberlin,
of Massachusetts.

Nominated—

For President, **David Davis,**
of Illinois.

For Vice-President, **Joel Parker,**
of New Jersey.

This convention was made up of representatives of the trades unions and of dissatisfied members of the old parties. Seventeen states were represented. The convention remained in session for two days. The following is the ballot by which David Davis was nominated for President:

Candidates.	Informal.	1st.	2d.	3d.
John W. Geary, of Pennsylvania	60	..	..	..
Horace H. Day, of New York	59	21	59	3
David Davis, of Illinois	47	88	93	201
Wendell Phillips, of Massachusetts	13	12	..	..
J. M. Palmer, of Illinois	8	..	..	..
Joel Parker, of New Jersey	7	7	7	..
George W. Julian, of Indiana	6	5	..	..
B. Gratz Brown, of Missouri	..	14	..	..
Horace Greeley, of New York	..	11	..	..

For Vice-President, Joel Parker was nominated on the second ballot, as follows:

CANDIDATES.	1st.	2d.
E. M. CHAMBERLIN, of Massachusetts	72	57
JOEL PARKER, of New Jersey	70	112
ALANSON M. WEST, of Mississippi	18	..
THOMAS EWING, of Ohio	31	22
W. G. BRYAN, of Tennessee	10	..

Both candidates having declined, the convention was called together again, but only a small number of the delegates attended. Charles O'Conor, of New York, was then nominated for President, but no nomination was made for Vice-President.

The first convention had adopted the following platform:—

LABOR REFORM PLATFORM.

We hold that all political power is inherent in the people, and free government is founded on their authority and established for their benefit; that all citizens are equal in political rights, entitled to the largest religious and political liberty compatible with the good order of society, as also the use and enjoyment of the fruits of their labor and talents; and no man or set of men is entitled to exclusive separable endowments and privileges, or immunities from the government, but in consideration of public services; and any laws destructive of these fundamental principles are without moral binding force, and should be repealed. And believing that all the evils resulting from unjust legislation now affecting the industrial classes can be removed by the adoption of the principles contained in the following declaration, therefore,

Resolved, That it is the duty of the government to establish a just standard of distribution of capital and labor by providing a purely national circulating medium, based on the faith and resources of the nation, issued directly to the people without the intervention of any system of banking corporations, which money shall be legal tender in the payment of all debts, public and private, and interchangeable at the option of the holder for government bonds bearing a rate of interest not to exceed 3.65 per cent, subject to future legislation by Congress.

2. That the national debt should be paid in good faith, according to the original contract, at the earliest option of the government, without mortgaging the property of the people or the future earnings of labor, to enrich a few capitalists at home and abroad.

3. That justice demands that the burdens of government should be so adjusted as to bear equally on all classes, and that the exemption from taxation of government bonds bearing extravagant rates of interest is a violation of all just principles of revenue laws.

4. That the public lands of the United States belong to the people, and should not be sold to individuals nor granted to corporations, but should be held as a sacred trust for the benefit of the people, and should be granted to landless settlers only, in amounts not exceeding one hundred and sixty acres of land.

5. That Congress should modify the tariff so as to admit free such articles of common use as we can neither produce nor grow, and lay duties for revenue mainly upon articles of luxury and upon such articles of manufacture as will, we having the raw materials, assist in further developing the resources of the country.

6. That the presence in our country of Chinese labor, imported by capitalists in large numbers, for servile use, is an evil, entailing want and its attendant train of misery and crime on all classes of the American people, and should be prohibited by legislation.

7. That we ask for the enactment of a law by which all mechanics and day laborers employed by or on behalf of the government, whether directly or indirectly, through persons, firms, or corporations contracting with the state, shall conform to the reduced standard of eight hours a day, recently adopted by Congress for national employees, and also for an amendment to the acts of incorporation for cities and towns by which all laborers and mechanics employed at their expense shall conform to the same number of hours.

8. That the enlightened spirit of the age demands the abolition of the system of contract labor in our prisons and other reformatory institutions.

9. That the protection of life, liberty, and property are the three cardinal principles of government, and the first two are

more sacred than the latter; therefore money needed for prosecuting wars should, as it is required, be assessed and collected from the wealth of the country, and not entailed as a burden on posterity.

10. That it is the duty of the government to exercise its power over railroads and telegraph corporations, that they shall not in any case be privileged to exact such rates of freight, transportation, or charges, by whatever name, as may bear unduly or unequally upon the producer or consumer.

11. That there should be such a reform in the civil service of the national government as will remove it beyond all partisan influence, and place it in the charge and under the direction of intelligent and competent business men.

12. That as both history and experience teach us that power ever seeks to perpetuate itself by every and all means, and that its prolonged possession in the hands of one person is always dangerous to the interests of a free people, and believing that the spirit of our organic laws and the stability and safety of our free institutions are best obeyed on the one hand, and secured on the other, by a regular constitutional change in the chief of the country at each election; therefore, we are in favor of limiting the occupancy of the presidential chair to one term.

13. That we are in favor of granting general amnesty and restoring the Union at once on the basis of the equality of rights and privileges to all, the impartial administration of justice being the only true bond of union to bind the states together and restore the government of the people.

14. That we demand the subjection of the military to the civil authorities, and the confinement of its operations to national purposes alone.

15. That we deem it expedient for Congress to supervise the patent laws, so as to give labor more fully the benefit of its own ideas and inventions.

16. That fitness, and not political or personal considerations, should be the only recommendation to public office, either appointive or elective, and any and all laws looking to the establishment of this principle are heartily approved.

PROHIBITION CONVENTION.

Columbus, O., February 22, 1872.

Chairman, SAMUEL CHASE,
of Ohio.

NOMINATED—

For President, **James Black,**
of Pennsylvania.

For Vice-President, **Rev. John Russell,**
of Michigan.

Nine states, with 194 delegates, were represented at this convention. The above-mentioned candidates were presented to the convention by a committee, and were nominated by acclamation.

The convention adopted the following platform:—

PROHIBITION PLATFORM.

The preamble recites that protection and allegiance are reciprocal duties; and every citizen who yields obediently to the full commands of government should be protected in all the enjoyment of personal security, personal liberty, and private property. That the traffic in intoxicating drinks greatly impairs the personal security and personal liberty of a great mass of citizens, and renders private property insecure. That all political parties are hopelessly unwilling to adopt an adequate policy on this question.

Therefore, as a national convention, we adopt the following declaration of principles:

That while we acknowledge the patriotism and profound statesmanship of those patriots who laid the foundation of this government, securing at once the rights of the states severally and their inseparable union by the federal Constitution, we would not merely garnish the sepulchres of our republican fathers, but we do hereby renew our pledges of solemn fealty to the imperishable principles of civil and religious liberty embodied in the Declaration of Independence and our federal Constitution.

That the traffic in intoxicating beverages is a dishonor to Christian civilization, a political wrong of unequalled enormity, subversive of ordinary objects of government, not capable of being regulated or restrained by any system of license whatever, and imperatively demands, for its suppression, effective legal prohibition, both by state and national legislation.

That there can be no greater peril to a nation than the existing party competition for the liquor vote; that experience shows that any party not opposed to the traffic, that will engage in this competition, will court the favor of the criminal classes, will barter away the public morals, the purity of the ballot, and every object of the government, for party success.

That, as Prohibitionists, we will individually use all efforts to persuade men from the use of intoxicating liquors; and we invite all persons to assist in this movement.

That competence, honesty, and sobriety are indispensable qualifications for holding office.

That removals from public office for mere political differences of opinion are wrong.

That fixed and moderate salaries of public officers should take the places of fees and perquisites; and that all means should be taken to prevent corruption and encourage economy.

That the President and Vice-President should be elected directly by the people.

That we are in favor of a sound national currency, adequate to the demands of business and convertible into gold and silver at the will of the holder, and the adoption of every measure compatible with justice and public safety to appreciate our present currency to the gold standard.

That the rates of ocean and inland postage, and railroad telegraph lines and water transportation, should be made as low as possible by law.

That we are opposed to all discrimination in favor of capital against labor, as well as all monopoly and class legislation.

That the removal of the burdens imposed in the traffic in intoxicating drinks will emancipate labor, and will practically promote labor reform.

That suffrage should be granted to all persons, without regard to sex.

That the fostering and extension of common schools is a primary duty of the government.

That a liberal policy should be pursued to promote foreign emigration.

The election occurred on November 5, 1872.

THIRTY-SEVEN STATES VOTED.

POPULAR VOTE.

STATES.	Ulysses S. Grant, Republican.	Horace Greeley, Democrat and Liberal Republican.	Charles O'Conor, Democrat.	Total vote.
Alabama	90,272	79,444	....	169,716
Arkansas	41,373	37,927	....	79,300
California	54,020	40,718	1,068	95,806
Connecticut	50,638	45,880	204	96,928
Delaware	11,115	10,206	487	21,808
Florida	17,763	15,427	....	33,190
Georgia	62,550	76,356	4,000	142,906
Illinois	241,944	184,938	3,058	429,940
Indiana	186,147	163,632	1,417	351,196
Iowa	131,566	71,196	2,221	204,983
Kansas	67,048	32,970	596	100,614
Kentucky	88,766	99,995	2,374	191,135
Louisiana	71,663	57,029	....	128,692
Maine	61,422	29,087	....	90,509
Maryland	66,760	67,687	19	134,466
Massachusetts	133,472	59,260	....	192,732
Michigan	138,455	78,355	2,861	220,942
Minnesota	55,117	34,423	....	89,540
Mississippi	82,175	47,288	....	129,463
Missouri	119,196	151,434	2,429	273,059
Nebraska	18,329	7,812	...	26,141
Nevada	8,413	6,236	....	14,649
New Hampshire	37,168	31,424	100	68,892
New Jersey	91,656	76,456	630	168,742
New York	440,736	387,281	1,454	829,672
North Carolina	94,769	70,094	....	164,863
Ohio	281,852	244,321	1,163	529,436
Oregon	11,819	7,730	572	20,121
Pennsylvania	349,589	212,041	....	563,260
Rhode Island	13,665	5,329	....	18,994
South Carolina	72,290	22,703	187	95,180
Tennessee	85,655	94,391	....	180,046
Texas	47,406	66,500	2,499	116,405
Vermont	41,481	10,927	593	53,001
Virginia	93,468	91,654	42	185,164
West Virginia	32,315	29,451	600	62,366
Wisconsin	104,997	86,477	834	192,308
Total	3,597,070	2,834,079	29,408	6,466,165

James Black (Prohibitionist) received 5608 votes, which is included in total vote given above.

ELECTORAL VOTE.

Counted on February 12, 1873.

STATES.	PRESIDENT.						VICE-PRESIDENT.										No. entitled to vote.
	Ulysses S. Grant, of Illinois.	Thomas A. Hendricks, of Indiana.	B. Gratz Brown, of Missouri.	Charles J. Jenkins, of Georgia.	David Davis, of Illinois.	Not counted.	Henry Wilson, of Massachusetts.	B. Gratz Brown, of Missouri.	George W. Julian, of Indiana.	Alfred H. Colquitt, of Georgia.	John M. Palmer, of Illinois.	Thomas E. Bramlette, of Kentucky.	William S. Groesbeck, of Ohio.	Willis B. Machen, of Kentucky.	Nathaniel P. Banks, of Massachusetts.	Not counted.	
Alabama	10	..	..	..	..	..	10	..	..	..	..	..	..	..	..	..	10
*Arkansas	..	..	..	..	..	6	..	..	..	..	..	..	..	..	..	6	6
California	6	..	..	..	..	..	6	..	..	..	..	..	..	..	..	..	6
Connecticut	6	..	..	..	..	..	6	..	..	..	..	..	..	..	..	..	6
Delaware	3	..	..	..	..	..	3	..	..	..	..	..	..	..	..	..	3
Florida	4	..	..	..	..	..	4	..	..	..	..	..	..	..	..	..	4
*Georgia	..	..	6	2	..	3	..	5	..	5	..	..	..	..	1	..	11
Illinois	21	..	..	..	..	..	21	..	..	..	..	..	..	..	..	..	21
Indiana	15	..	..	..	..	..	15	..	..	..	..	..	..	..	..	..	15
Iowa	11	..	..	..	..	..	11	..	..	..	..	..	..	..	..	..	11
Kansas	5	..	..	..	..	..	5	..	..	..	..	..	..	..	..	..	5
Kentucky	..	8	4	..	..	..	..	8	..	..	..	3	..	1	..	..	12
*Louisiana	..	..	..	..	..	8	..	..	..	..	..	..	..	..	..	8	8
Maine	7	..	..	..	..	..	7	..	..	..	..	..	..	..	..	..	7
Maryland	..	8	..	..	..	..	..	8	..	..	..	..	..	..	..	..	8
Massachusetts	13	..	..	..	..	..	13	..	..	..	..	..	..	..	..	..	13
Michigan	11	..	..	..	..	..	11	..	..	..	..	..	..	..	..	..	11
Minnesota	5	..	..	..	..	..	5	..	..	..	..	..	..	..	..	..	5
Mississippi	8	..	..	..	..	..	8	..	..	..	..	..	..	..	..	..	8
Missouri	..	6	8	..	1	..	..	6	5	..	3	..	1	..	..	..	15
Nebraska	3	..	..	..	..	..	3	..	..	..	..	..	..	..	..	..	3
Nevada	3	..	..	..	..	..	3	..	..	..	..	..	..	..	..	..	3
N. Hampshire	5	..	..	..	..	..	5	..	..	..	..	..	..	..	..	..	5
New Jersey	9	..	..	..	..	..	9	..	..	..	..	..	..	..	..	..	9
New York	35	..	..	..	..	..	35	..	..	..	..	..	..	..	..	..	35
North Carolina	10	..	..	..	..	..	10	..	..	..	..	..	..	..	..	..	10
Ohio	22	..	..	..	..	..	22	..	..	..	..	..	..	..	..	..	22
Oregon	3	..	..	..	..	..	3	..	..	..	..	..	..	..	..	..	3
Pennsylvania	29	..	..	..	..	..	29	..	..	..	..	..	..	..	..	..	29
Rhode Island	4	..	..	..	..	..	4	..	..	..	..	..	..	..	..	..	4
South Carolina	7	..	..	..	..	..	7	..	..	..	..	..	..	..	..	..	7
Tennessee	..	12	..	..	..	..	..	12	..	..	..	..	..	..	..	..	12
Texas	..	8	..	..	..	..	..	8	..	..	..	..	..	..	..	..	8
Vermont	5	..	..	..	..	..	5	..	..	..	..	..	..	..	..	..	5
Virginia	11	..	..	..	..	..	11	..	..	..	..	..	..	..	..	..	11
West Virginia	5	..	..	..	..	..	5	..	..	..	..	..	..	..	..	..	5
Wisconsin	10	..	..	..	..	..	10	..	..	..	..	..	..	..	..	..	10
Total	286	42	18	2	1	17	286	47	5	5	3	3	1	1	1	14	366

* Objections were made to counting the votes of Arkansas and Louisiana, as also to the three votes cast by the Georgia electors for Horace Greeley, and Congress excluded them from the count.

NOTE.—Horace Greeley died November 29, 1872, and the Democratic and Liberal electors were compelled, on their day of voting, December 4th, to vote for other persons.

Ulysses S. Grant was elected President and Henry Wilson as Vice-President.

During this period Congress was divided politically as follows:

Forty-third Congress.

Senate—19 Democrats, 54 Republicans, 1 vacancy ......Total, 74
House—88 Democrats, 203 Republicans, 1 vacancy ...... " 292

Forty-fourth Congress.

Senate— 29 Democrats, 46 Republicans, 1 vacancy ......Total, 76
House—181 Democrats, 107 Republicans, 3 Independents, 2 vacancies.. " 293

Election of 1876.

Democratic National Committee:

Chairman, ABRAM S. HEWITT, of New York.
Secretary, F. O. PRINCE, of Massachusetts.

DEMOCRATIC CONVENTION.

St. Louis, Mo., June 27–29, 1876.

Chairman pro tem., HENRY WATTERSON,
of Kentucky.

Chairman, JOHN A. MCCLERNAND,
of Illinois.

NOMINATED—

For President, **Samuel J. Tilden,**
of New York.

For Vice-President, **Thomas A. Hendricks,**
of Indiana.

The convention was divided on the report of the Committee on Resolutions, a minority report favoring a modification of the clause relating to "Specie resumption." The minority amendment was rejected by a vote of 219 to 550, and the platform was agreed to as reported, by a vote of 651 to 83. The platform is given below.

Two ballots were necessary to nominate Samuel J. Tilden, of New York, for President. The ballots resulted as follows:

CANDIDATES.	1st.	2d.
SAMUEL J. TILDEN, of New York.	417	535
THOMAS A. HENDRICKS, of INDIANA	140	60
WINFIELD S. HANCOCK, of Pennsylvania	75	59
WILLIAM ALLEN, of Ohio	56	54
THOMAS F. BAYARD, of Delaware	33	11
JOEL PARKER, of New Jersey	18	18
ALLEN G. THURMAN, of Ohio	..	7
Whole number of votes, 744. Necessary to a choice, 496.		

For Vice-President, Thomas A. Hendricks, of Indiana, was nominated by a unanimous vote, on the first ballot.

The following is the platform as adopted:—

DEMOCRATIC PLATFORM.

We, the delegates of the Democratic party of the United States, in national convention assembled, do hereby declare the administration of the federal government to be in urgent need of immediate reform; do hereby enjoin upon the nominees of this convention, and of the Democratic party in each state, a zealous effort and co-operation to this end; and do hereby appeal to our fellow-citizens of every former political connection to undertake with us this first and most pressing patriotic duty.

For the Democracy of the whole country we do here reaffirm our faith in the permanence of the federal Union, our devotion to the Constitution of the United States, with its amendments universally accepted as a final settlement of the controversies that engendered civil war, and do here record our steadfast confidence in the perpetuity of republican self-government.

In absolute acquiescence in the will of the majority, the vital principle of republics; in the supremacy of the civil over the military authority; in the total separation of church and state, for the sake alike of civil and religious freedom; in the equality of all citizens before just laws of their own enactment; in the liberty of individual conduct, unvexed by sumptuary laws; in the faithful education of the rising generation, that they may preserve, enjoy, and transmit these best conditions of human happiness and hope,—we behold the noblest products of a hundred years of changeful history; but while upholding the bond of our Union and great charter of these our rights, it behooves a free people to practice also that eternal vigilance which is the price of liberty.

Reform is necessary to rebuild and establish in the hearts of the whole people the Union eleven years ago happily rescued from the danger of a secession of states, but now to be saved from a corrupt centralism which, after inflicting upon ten states the rapacity of carpet-bag tyrannies, has honeycombed the offices of the federal government itself with incapacity, waste, and fraud; infected states and municipalities with the contagion of misrule, and locked fast the prosperity of an industrious people in the paralysis of "hard times."

Reform is necessary to establish a sound currency, restore the public credit, and maintain the national honor.

We denounce the failure, for all these eleven years of peace, to make good the promise of the legal-tender notes, which are a changing standard of value in the hands of the people, and the non-payment of which is a disregard of the plighted faith of the nation.

We denounce the improvidence which, in eleven years of peace, has taken from the people in federal taxes thirteen times the whole amount of the legal-tender notes, and squandered four times their sum in useless expense, without accumulating any reserve for their redemption.

We denounce the financial imbecility and immorality of that party which, during eleven years of peace, has made no advance toward resumption, no preparation for resumption, but instead has obstructed resumption, by wasting our resources and exhausting all our surplus income; and, while annually professing to intend a speedy return to specie payments, has annually enacted fresh hindrances thereto. As such hindrance we denounce the resumption clause of the act of 1875, and we here demand its repeal.

We demand a judicious system of preparation by public economies, by official retrenchments, and by wise finance, which shall enable the nation soon to assure the whole world of its perfect ability and its perfect readiness to meet any of its promises at the call of the creditor entitled to payment.

We believe such a system, well devised, and, above all, intrusted to competent hands for execution, creating at no time an artificial scarcity of currency, and at no time alarming the public mind into a withdrawal of that vaster machinery of credit by which ninety-five per cent of all business transactions are performed—a system open, public, and inspiring general confidence—would from the day of its adoption bring healing on its wings to all our harassed industries, set in motion the wheels of commerce, manufactures, and the mechanic arts, restore employment to labor, and renew in all its natural sources the prosperity of the people.

Reform is necessary in the sum and modes of federal taxation, to the end that capital may be set free from distrust, and labor lightly burdened.

We denounce the present tariff, levied upon nearly 4000 articles, as a masterpiece of injustice, inequality, and false pretense. It yields a dwindling, not a yearly rising revenue. It has impoverished many industries to subsidize a few. It prohibits imports that might purchase the products of American labor. It has degraded American commerce from the first to an inferior rank on the high seas. It has cut down the sales of American manufactures at home and abroad, and depleted the returns of American agriculture—an industry followed by half our people. It costs the people five times more than it produces to the treasury, obstructs the processes of production, and wastes the fruits of labor. It promotes fraud, fosters smuggling, enriches dishonest officials, and bankrupts honest merchants. We demand that all custom-house taxation shall be only for revenue.

Reform is necessary in the scale of public expense—federal, state, and municipal. Our federal taxation has swollen from sixty millions gold, in 1860, to four hundred and fifty millions currency, in 1870; our aggregate taxation from one hundred and fifty-four millions gold, in 1860, to seven hundred and thirty millions currency, in 1870; or in one decade from less than five dollars per head to more than eighteen dollars per head. Since the peace, the people have paid to their tax-gatherers more than thrice the sum of the national debt, and more than twice that sum for the federal government alone. We demand a rigorous frugality in every department and from every officer of the government.

Reform is necessary to put a stop to the profligate waste of public lands and their diversion from actual settlers by the party in power, which has squandered 200,000,000 acres upon railroads alone, and out of more than thrice that aggregate has disposed of less than a sixth directly to tillers of the soil.

Reform is necessary to correct the omissions of a Republican Congress and the errors of our treaties and our diplomacy, which have stripped our fellow-citizens of foreign birth and kindred race, recrossing the Atlantic, of the shield of American citizenship, and have exposed our brethren of the Pacific Coast to the incursions of a race not sprung from the same great parent stock, and in fact now by law denied citizenship through naturalization, as being neither accustomed to the traditions of a progressive civilization nor exercised in liberty under equal laws. We denounce the policy which thus discards the liberty-loving German and tolerates a revival of the coolie-trade in Mongolian women imported for immoral purposes, and Mongolian men held to perform servile labor contracts, and demand such modification of the treaty with the Chinese Empire, or such legislation within Constitutional limitations, as shall prevent further importation or immigration of the Mongolian race.

Reform is necessary, and can never be effected but by making it the controlling issue of the elections, and lifting it above the two false issues with which the office-holding class and the party in power seek to smother it:—

1. The false issue with which they would enkindle sectarian strife in respect to the public schools, of which the establishment and support belong exclusively to the several states, and which the Democratic party has cherished from their foundation, and is resolved to maintain without prejudice or preference for any class, sect, or creed, and without largesses from the treasury to any.

2. The false issue by which they seek to light anew the dying embers of sectional hate between kindred peoples once estranged, but now reunited in one indivisible republic and a common destiny.

Reform is necessary in the civil service. Experience proves that efficient, economical conduct of the governmental business is not possible if its civil service be subject to change at every election, be a prize fought for at the ballot-box, be a brief reward of party zeal, instead of posts of honor assigned for proved competency, and held for fidelity in the public employ; that the dispensing of patronage should neither be a tax upon the time of all our public men nor the instrument of their ambition. Here again promises falsified in the performance attest that the party in power can work out no practical or salutary reform.

Reform is necessary even more in the higher grades of the public service. President, Vice-President, judges, senators, representatives, cabinet officers,—these and all others in authority are the people's servants. Their offices are not a private perquisite; they are a public trust.

When the annals of this republic show the disgrace and censure of a Vice-President; a late Speaker of the House of Representatives marketing his rulings as a presiding officer; three senators profiting secretly by their votes as law-makers; five chairmen of the leading committees of the late House of Representatives exposed in jobbery; a late Secretary of the Treasury forcing balances in the public accounts; a late Attorney-General misappropriating public funds; a Secretary of the Navy enriched or enriching friends by percentages levied off the profits of contractors with his department; an ambassador to England censured in a dishonorable speculation; the President's private secretary barely escaping conviction upon trial for guilty complicity in frauds upon the revenue; a Secretary of War impeached for high crimes and misdemeanors—the demonstration is complete that the first step in reform must be the people's choice of honest men from another party, lest the disease of one political organization infect the body politic, and lest by making no change of men or parties we get no change of measures and no real reform.

All these abuses, wrongs, and crimes, the product of sixteen years' ascendency of the Republican party, create a necessity for reform confessed by Republicans themselves; but their reformers are voted down in convention and displaced from the cabinet. The party's mass of honest voters is powerless to resist the 80,000 office-holders, its leaders and guides.

Reform can only be had by a peaceful civic revolution. We demand a change of system, a change of administration, a change of parties, that we may have a change of measures and of men.

Resolved, That this convention, representing the Democratic party of the United States, do cordially indorse the action of the present House of Representatives in reducing and curtailing the expenses of the federal government, in cutting down salaries, extravagant appropriations, and in abolishing useless offices and places not required by the public necessities; and we shall trust to the firmness of the Democratic members of the House that no committee of conference and no misinterpretation of the rules will be allowed to defeat these wholesome measures of economy demanded by the country.

Resolved, That the soldiers and sailors of the republic, and the widows and orphans of those who have fallen in battle, have a just claim upon the care, protection, and gratitude of their fellow-citizens.

Republican National Committee:

Chairman, ZACH. CHANDLER, of Michigan.
Secretary, R. C. MCCORMICK, of Arizona.

Mr. Chandler having resigned, J. DONALD CAMERON was selected as Chairman, and THOS. B. KEOGH, of North Carolina, succeeded Mr. McCormick as Secretary.

REPUBLICAN CONVENTION.

Cincinnati, O., June 14–16, 1876.

Chairman pro tem., THEODORE M. POMEROY,
of New York.

Chairman, EDWARD MCPHERSON,
of Pennsylvania.

NOMINATED—

For President, **Rutherford B. Hayes,**
of Ohio.

For Vice-President, **William A. Wheeler,**
of New York.

The attempt to enforce the unit rule failed, the decision of the chair being sustained by a vote of 395 to 354. The vote was taken on an appeal from a decision of the chair in which he had recognized the right of four members of the Pennsylvania delegation to have their votes separately recorded. The platform as reported by the Committee on Resolutions was opposed by a minority. E. L. Pierce, of Massachusetts, moved to strike out the eleventh resolution, relating to the Chinese. The motion to strike out was lost by a vote of 215 to 532. E. J. Davis, of Texas, moved to strike out the fourth resolution and insert a clause for the immediate resumption of specie payments. This was rejected without a roll-call, and the platform was then adopted.

Seven ballots were taken for a candidate for President, when Rutherford B. Hayes was unanimously nominated. The following is the ballot in detail:

CANDIDATES.	1st.	2d.	3d.	4th.	5th.	6th.	7th.
JAMES G. BLAINE, of Maine	285	296	293	292	286	308	351
OLIVER P. MORTON, of Indiana	125	120	113	108	95	85	..
BENJAMIN H. BRISTOW, of Kentucky	113	114	121	126	114	111	21
ROSCOE CONKLING, of New York	99	93	90	84	82	81	..
RUTHERFORD B. HAYES, of Ohio	61	64	67	68	104	113	384
JOHN F. HARTRANFT, of Pennsylvania	58	63	68	71	69	50	..
MARSHALL JEWELL, of Connecticut	11	..	..	..	..	..	..
Scattering	3	4	3	5	5	5	..
Whole number of votes	754	754	755	754	755	755	756
Necessary to a choice	378	378	378	378	378	378	379

For Vice-President, William A. Wheeler, of New York, was unanimously chosen.

The following is the platform as adopted:—

Republican Platform.

When, in the economy of Providence, this land was to be purged of human slavery, and when the strength of government of the people, by the people, and for the people was to be demonstrated, the Republican party came into power. Its deeds have passed into history, and we look back to them with pride. Incited by their memories to high aims for the good of our country and mankind, and looking to the future with unfaltering courage, hope, and purpose, we, the representatives of the party, in national convention assembled, make the following declaration of principles:—

1. The United States of America is a nation, not a league. By the combined workings of the national and state governments, under their respective constitutions, the rights of every citizen are secured, at home and abroad, and the common welfare promoted.

2. The Republican party has preserved these governments to the hundredth anniversary of the nation's birth, and they are now embodiments of the great truth spoken at its cradle: "That all men are created equal; that they are endowed by their Creator with certain inalienable rights, among which are life, liberty, and the pursuit of happiness; that for the attainment of these ends governments have been instituted among men, deriving their just powers from the consent of the governed." Until these truths are cheerfully obeyed, or, if need be, vigorously enforced, the work of the Republican party is unfinished.

3. The permanent pacification of the southern section of the Union and the complete protection of all its citizens in the free enjoyment of all their rights, is a duty to which the Republican party stands sacredly pledged. The power to provide for the enforcement of the principles embodied in the recent constitutional amendments is vested by those amendments in the Congress of the United States, and we declare it to be the solemn obligation of the legislative and executive departments of the government to put into immediate and vigorous exercise all their constitutional powers for removing any just causes of discontent on the part of any class, and for securing to every American citizen complete liberty and exact equality in the exercise of all civil, political, and public rights. To this end we imperatively demand a Congress and a Chief Executive whose courage and fidelity to these duties shall not falter until these results are placed beyond dispute or recall.

4. In the first act of Congress signed by President Grant the national government assumed to remove any doubts of its purpose to discharge all just obligations to the public creditors, and "solemnly pledged its faith to make provisions, at the earliest practicable period, for the redemption of the United States notes in coin." Commercial prosperity, public morals, and the national credit demand that this promise be fulfilled by a continuous and steady progress to specie payment.

5. Under the Constitution the President and heads of departments are to make nominations for office; the Senate is to advise and consent to appointments, and the House of Representatives is to accuse and prosecute faithless officers. The best interest of the public service demands that these distinctions be respected; that Senators and Representatives who may be judges and accusers should not dictate appointments to office. The invariable rule in appointments should have reference to the honesty, fidelity, and capacity of the appointees, giving to the party in power those places where harmony and vigor of administration require its policy to be represented, but permitting all others to be filled by persons selected with sole reference to the efficiency of the public service, and the right of all citizens to share in the honor of rendering faithful service to the country.

6. We rejoice in the quickening conscience of the people concerning political affairs, and will hold all public officers to a rigid responsibility, and engage that the prosecution and punishment of all who betray official trusts shall be swift, thorough, and unsparing.

7. The public-school system of the several states is the bulwark of the American Republic, and with a view to its security and permanence we recommend an amendment to the Constitution of the United States, forbidding the application of any public funds or property for the benefit of any schools or institutions under sectarian control.

8. The revenue necessary for current expenditures and the obligations of the public debt must be largely derived from duties upon importations, which, so far as possible, should be adjusted to promote the interests of American labor and advance the prosperity of the whole country.

9. We reaffirm our opposition to further grants of the public lands to corporations and monopolies, and demand that the national domain be devoted to free homes for the people.

10. It is the imperative duty of the government so to modify

existing treaties with European governments that the same protection shall be afforded to the adopted American citizen that is given to the native-born; and that all necessary laws should be passed to protect emigrants, in the absence of power in the states for that purpose.

11. It is the immediate duty of Congress to fully investigate the effect of the immigration and importation of Mongolians upon the moral and material interests of the country.

12. The Republican party recognizes with approval the substantial advances recently made toward the establishment of equal rights for women, by the many important amendments effected by Republican legislatures, in the laws which concern the personal and property relations of wives, mothers, and widows, and by the appointment and election of women to the superintendence of education, charities, and other public trusts. The honest demands of this class of citizens for additional rights, privileges, and immunities should be treated with respectful consideration.

13. The Constitution confers upon Congress sovereign power over the territories of the United States for their government, and in the exercise of this power it is the right and duty of Congress to prohibit and extirpate, in the territories, that relic of barbarism, polygamy; and we demand such legislation as shall secure this end and the supremacy of American institutions in all the territories.

14. The pledges which the nation has given to her soldiers and sailors must be fulfilled, and a grateful people will always hold those who imperilled their lives for the country's preservation in the kindest remembrance.

15. We sincerely deprecate all sectional feeling and tendencies. We therefore note with deep solicitude that the Democratic party counts, as its chief hope of success, upon the electoral vote of a united South, secured through the efforts of those who were recently arrayed against the nation; and we invoke the earnest attention of the country to the grave truth that a success thus achieved would reopen sectional strife and imperil national honor and human rights.

16. We charge the Democratic party with being the same in character and spirit as when it sympathized with treason; with making its control of the House of Representatives the triumph and opportunity of the nation's recent foes; with reasserting and applauding in the National Capitol the sentiments of unrepentant rebellion; with sending Union soldiers to the rear

and promoting Confederate soldiers to the front; with deliberately proposing to repudiate the plighted faith of the government; with being equally false and imbecile upon the overshadowing financial question; with thwarting the ends of justice by its partisan mismanagements and obstruction; with proving itself, through the period of its ascendency in the Lower House of Congress, utterly incompetent to administer the government; and we warn the country against trusting a party thus alike unworthy, recreant, and incapable.

17. The national administration merits commendation for its honorable work in the management of domestic and foreign affairs, and President Grant deserves the continued hearty gratitude of the American people for his patriotism and his eminent services, in war and in peace.

18. We present as our candidates for President and Vice-President of the United States two distinguished statesmen, of eminent ability and character, and conspicuously fitted for those high offices, and we confidently appeal to the American people to intrust the administration of their public affairs to Rutherford B. Hayes and William A. Wheeler.

INDEPENDENT NATIONAL (Greenback) CONVENTION.

Indianapolis, Ind., May 17–18, 1876.

Chairman pro tem., IGNATIUS DONNELLY,
of Minnesota.

Chairman, THOMAS J. DURANT,
of Washington, D. C.

NOMINATED—

For President, **Peter Cooper,**
of New York.

For Vice-President, **Samuel F. Cary,**
of Ohio.

At this convention 239 delegates, from 19 states, were assembled. Peter Cooper, of New York, for President, and Newton Booth, of California, for Vice-President, were nominated by acclamation. Mr. Booth having declined, Samuel F. Cary, of Ohio, was substituted.

The convention adopted the following platform:—

INDEPENDENT NATIONAL (GREENBACK) PLATFORM.

The Independent party is called into existence by the necessities of the people, whose industries are prostrated, whose labor is deprived of its just reward by a ruinous policy which the Republican and Democratic parties refused to change; and, in view of the failure of these parties to furnish relief to the depressed industries of the country, thereby disappointing the just hopes and expectations of the suffering people, we declare our principles, and invite all independent and patriotic men to join our ranks in this movement for financial reform and industrial emancipation.

First. We demand the immediate and unconditional repeal of the Specie-Resumption Act of January 14, 1875, and the rescue of our industries from ruin and disaster resulting from its enforcement; and we call upon all patriotic men to organize in every congressional district of the country, with a view of electing representatives to Congress who will carry out the wishes of the people in this regard, and stop the present suicidal and destructive policy of contraction.

Second. We believe that a United States note, issued directly by the government, and convertible, on demand, into United States obligations, bearing a rate of interest not exceeding one cent a day on each one hundred dollars, and exchangeable for United States notes at par, will afford the best circulating medium ever devised. Such United States notes should be full legal tenders for all purposes, except for the payment of such obligations as are, by existing contracts, especially made payable in coin; and we hold that it is the duty of the government to provide such a circulating medium, and insist, in the language of Thomas Jefferson, that " bank paper must be suppressed, and the circulation restored to the nation, to whom it belongs."

Third. It is the paramount duty of the government, in all

its legislation, to keep in view the full development of all legitimate business—agricultural, mining, manufacturing, and commercial.

Fourth. We most earnestly protest against any further issue of gold bonds for sale in foreign markets, by which we would be made for a long period "hewers of wood and drawers of water" to foreigners, especially as the American people would gladly and promptly take at par all bonds the government may need to sell, providing they are made payable at the option of the holder, and bearing interest at 3.65 per cent per annum, or even a lower rate.

Fifth. We further protest against the sale of government bonds for the purpose of purchasing silver to be used as a substitute for our more convenient and less fractional currency, which, although well calculated to enrich owners of silver mines, yet in operation it will still further oppress, in taxation, an already overburdened people.

PROHIBITION CONVENTION.

Cleveland, O., May 17, 1876.

NOMINATED—

For President, **Green Clay Smith,**
of Kentucky.

For Vice-President, **G. T. Stewart,**
of Ohio.

The convention made the above-named nominations and adopted the following platform:—

PROHIBITION PLATFORM.

The Prohibition Reform party of the United States, organized in the name of the people to revive, enforce, and perpetuate in the government the doctrines of the Declaration of Independence, submit, in this centennial year of the republic, for the suffrages of all good citizens, the following platform of national reforms and measures:—

First. The legal prohibition in the District of Columbia, the territories, and in every other place subject to the laws of Congress, of the importation, exportation, manufacture, and traffic of all alcoholic beverages as high crimes against society; an amendment of the National Constitution to render these prohibitory measures universal and permanent, and the adoption of treaty stipulations with foreign powers to prevent the importation and exportation of all alcoholic beverages.

Second. The abolition of class legislation and of special privileges in the government, and the adoption of equal suffrage and eligibility to office, without distinction of race, religious creed, property, or sex.

Third. The appropriation of the public lands, in limited quantities, to actual settlers only; the reduction of the rates of inland and ocean postage, of telegraphic communication, of railroad and water transportation and travel, to the lowest practical point, by force of laws wisely and justly framed, with reference not only to the interest of capital employed, but to the higher plane of the general good.

Fourth. The suppression by law of lotteries, and gambling in gold, stocks, produce, and every form of money and property, and the penal inhibition of the use of the public mails for advertising schemes of gambling and lotteries.

Fifth. The abolition of those foul enormities, polygamy and the social evil, and the protection of purity, peace, and happiness of homes by ample and efficient legislation.

Sixth. The national observance of the Christian Sabbath, established by laws prohibiting ordinary labor and business in all departments of public service and private employment (works of necessity, charity, and religion excepted) on that day.

Seventh. The establishment, by mandatory provisions in national and state constitutions, and by all necessary legislation, of a system of free public schools, for the universal and forced education of all the youth of the land.

Eighth. The free use of the Bible, not as a ground of religious creeds, but as a text-book of the purest morality, the best liberty, and the noblest literature, in our public schools, that our children may grow up in its light, and that its spirit and principles may pervade our nation.

Ninth. The separation of the government in all its departments and institutions, including the public schools and all funds for their maintenance, from the control of every religious sect or other association, and the protection alike of all sects by equal laws, with entire freedom of religious faith and worship.

Tenth. The introduction into all treaties hereafter negotiated with foreign governments, of a provision for the amicable settlement of international difficulties by arbitration.

Eleventh. The abolition of all barbarous modes and instruments of punishment; the recognition of the laws of God and the claims of humanity in the discipline of jails and prisons, and of that higher and wiser civilization worthy of our age and nation, which regards the reform of criminals as a means for the prevention of crime.

Twelfth. The abolition of executive and legislative patronage, and the election of President, Vice-President, United States senators, and of all civil officers, so far as practicable, by the direct vote of the people.

Thirteenth. The practice of a friendly and liberal policy to immigrants from all nations, the guarantee to them of ample protection and of equal rights and privileges.

Fourteenth. The separation of the money of government from all banking institutions. The national government only should exercise the high prerogative of issuing paper money, and that should be subject to prompt redemption, on demand, in gold and silver, the only equal standards of value recognized by the civilized world.

Fifteenth. The reduction of the salaries of public officers in a just ratio with the decline of wages and market prices; the abolition of sinecures, unnecessary offices, and official fees and perquisites; the practice of strict economy in government expenses, and a free and thorough investigation into any and all alleged abuses of public trust.

AMERICAN NATIONAL CONVENTION.

NOMINATED—

For President, **James B. Walker,**

of Illinois.

For Vice-President, **Donald Kirkpatrick,**

of New York.

PLATFORM.

We hold:

1. That ours is a Christian, and not a heathen, nation, and that the God of the Christian Scriptures is the author of civil government.

2. That God requires and man needs a Sabbath.

3. That the prohibition of the importation, manufacture, and sale of intoxicating drinks as a beverage is the true policy on the temperance question.

4. The charters of all secret lodges granted by our federal and state legislatures should be withdrawn, and their oaths prohibited by law.

5. That the civil qualities secured to all American citizens by articles 13, 14, and 15 of our amended Constitution should be preserved inviolate.

6. That arbitration of differences with nations is the most direct and sure method of securing and perpetuating a permanent peace.

7. That to cultivate the intellect without improving the morals of men is to make mere adepts and experts; therefore, the Bible should be associated with books of science and literature in all our educational institutions.

8. That land and other monopolies should be discountenanced.

9. That the government should furnish the people with an ample and sound currency and a return to specie payment, as soon as practicable.

10. That the maintenance of the public credit, protection to all loyal citizens, and justice to Indians are essential to the honor and safety of our nation.

11. And, finally, we demand for the American people the abolition of electoral colleges, and a direct vote for President and Vice-President of the United States.

The election occurred on November 7, 1876.

THIRTY-EIGHT STATES VOTED.

POPULAR VOTE.

STATES.	Samuel J. Tilden, Democrat.	Rutherford B. Hayes, Republican.	Peter Cooper, Greenback.	Green C. Smith, Prohibitionist.	*Scattering.	Total vote.
Alabama	102,002	68,230	..	..	..	170,232
Arkansas	58,071	38,669	289	..	..	97,029
California	76,465	79,269	47	..	19	155,800
†Colorado	..	..	..	..	..	..
Connecticut	61,934	59,034	774	378	36	122,156
Delaware	13,381	10,752	..	..	..	24,133
‡Florida	22,923	23,849	..	..	..	46,772
Georgia	130,088	50,446	..	..	..	180,534
Illinois	258,601	278,232	17,233	141	286	554,493
Indiana	213,526	208,011	9,533	..	..	431,070
Iowa	112,099	171,327	9,001	36	..	292,463
Kansas	37,902	78,322	7,776	110	23	124,133
Kentucky	159,690	97,156	1,944	818	..	259,608
§Louisiana	70,508	75,135	..	..	..	145,643
Maine	49,823	66,300	663	..	..	116,786
Maryland	91,780	71,981	33	10	..	163,804
Massachusetts	108,777	150,063	779	84	..	259,703
Michigan	141,095	166,534	9,060	766	71	317,526
Minnesota	48,799	72,962	2,311	72	..	124,144
Mississippi	112,173	52,605	..	..	..	164,778
Missouri	203,077	145,029	3,498	64	97	351,765
Nebraska	17,554	31,916	2,320	1,599	117	53,506
Nevada	9,308	10,383	..	..	..	19,691
New Hampshire	38,509	41,539	76	..	..	80,124
New Jersey	115,962	103,517	712	43	..	220,234
New York	521,949	489,207	1,987	2,359	1,828	1,017,330
North Carolina	125,427	108,417	..	..	..	233,844
Ohio	323,182	330,698	3,057	1,636	76	658,649
Oregon	14,149	15,206	510	..	..	29,865
Pennsylvania	366,158	384,122	7,187	1,319	83	758,869
Rhode Island	10,712	15,787	68	60	..	26,627
South Carolina	90,906	91,870	..	..	..	182,776
Tennessee	133,166	89,566	..	..	..	222,732
Texas	104,755	44,800	..	..	..	149,555
Vermont	20,254	44,092	..	..	..	64,346
Virginia	139,670	95,558	..	..	..	235,228
West Virginia	56,455	42.698	1,373	..	..	100,526
Wisconsin	123,927	130,668	1,509	27	..	256,131
Total	4,284,757	4,033,950	81,740	9,522	2,636	8,412,605

*"Scattering" includes the votes of the Anti-Masonic and American Alliance tickets.

† The electors were chosen by the legislature.

‡ Returning Board's count, Nov. 28, 1876. A majority of 94 to 1197 was claimed for Tilden by the Democrats, and the opinion of the Supreme Court of Florida gave Tilden 94 majority.

§ Returning Board's count. The figures on the face of the returns, when opened by the Board, are claimed to have been: Tilden, 82,326; Hayes, 77,023. Tilden's majority, 5,303.

ELECTORAL VOTE.

As declared on March 2, 1877.

STATES.	PRESIDENT.		VICE-PRESIDENT.		
	Rutherford B. Hayes, of Ohio.	Samuel J. Tilden, of New York.	William A. Wheeler, of New York.	Thomas A. Hendricks, of Indiana.	No. entitled to vote.
Alabama	..	10	..	10	10
Arkansas	..	6	..	6	6
California	6	..	6	..	6
Colorado	3	..	3	..	3
Connecticut	..	6	..	6	6
Delaware	..	3	..	3	3
Florida	4	..	4	..	4
Georgia	..	11	..	11	11
Illinois	21	..	21	..	21
Indiana	..	15	..	15	15
Iowa	11	..	11	..	11
Kansas	5	..	5	..	5
Kentucky	..	12	..	12	12
Louisiana	8	..	8	..	8
Maine	7	..	7	..	7
Maryland	..	8	..	8	8
Massachusetts	13	..	13	..	13
Michigan	11	..	11	..	11
Minnesota	5	..	5	..	5
Mississippi	..	8	..	8	8
Missouri	..	15	..	15	15
Nebraska	3	..	3	..	3
Nevada	3	..	3	..	3
New Hampshire	5	..	5	..	5
New Jersey	..	9	..	9	9
New York	..	35	..	35	35
North Carolina	..	10	..	10	10
Ohio	22	..	22	..	22
Oregon	3	..	3	..	3
Pennsylvania	29	..	29	..	29
Rhode Island	4	..	4	..	4
South Carolina	7	..	7	..	7
Tennessee	..	12	..	12	12
Texas	..	8	..	8	8
Vermont	5	..	5	..	5
Virginia	..	11	..	11	11
West Virginia	..	5	..	5	5
Wisconsin	10	..	10	..	10
Total	185	184	185	184	369

Immediately after the election the charge of false returns was made in several states, and Congress, in consequence, passed the act approved January 29, 1877, which provided for the Electoral Commission to decide all disputed returns. The counting of the electoral vote began on February 1, 1877, and continued until a little after four o'clock in the morning of March 2, 1877.

Rutherford B. Hayes was elected President and William A. Wheeler as Vice-President.

During this period Congress was divided politically as follows:

Forty-fifth Congress.

Senate— 36 Democrats, 39 Republicans, 1 Independent. . Total, 76
House—156 Democrats, 137 Republicans . . . . " 293

Forty-sixth Congress.

Senate— 43 Democrats, 33 Republicans . . . . Total, 76
House—150 Democrats, 128 Republicans, 14 Nationals, 1 vacancy . . . . " 293

Election of 1880

Democratic National Committee:

Chairman, WM. H. BARNUM, of Connecticut.
Secretary, F. O. PRINCE, of Massachusetts.

DEMOCRATIC CONVENTION.

Cincinnati, O., June 22–24, 1880.

Chairman pro tem., GEORGE HOADLY, of Ohio.

Chairman, JOHN W. STEVENSON, of Kentucky.

NOMINATED—

For President, **Winfield S. Hancock,** of Pennsylvania.

For Vice-President, **William H. English,** of Indiana.

This convention was organized so quickly, that balloting began on the second day, when General Hancock was nominated on the second ballot, as follows:

CANDIDATES.	1st.	2d.	After changes.
WINFIELD S. HANCOCK, of Pennsylvania	171	320	705
THOMAS F. BAYARD, of Delaware	153	113	2
HENRY B. PAYNE, of Ohio	80	..	..
ALLEN G. THURMAN, of Ohio	69	50	..
STEPHEN J. FIELD, of California	65	65	..
WILLIAM R. MORRISON, of Illinois	62	..	..
THOMAS A. HENDRICKS, of Indiana	50	31	30
SAMUEL J. TILDEN, of New York	38	6	1
HORATIO SEYMOUR, of New York	38	6	1
SAMUEL J. RANDALL, of Pennsylvania	..	128	..

For Vice-President, William H. English, of Indiana, was nominated by acclamation. Richard M. Bishop, of Ohio, had been mentioned, but his name was later withdrawn.

The convention adopted the following platform:—

DEMOCRATIC PLATFORM.

The Democrats of the United States, in convention assembled, declare—

1. We pledge ourselves anew to the Constitutional doctrines and traditions of the Democratic party, as illustrated by the teachings and example of a long line of Democratic statesmen and patriots, and embodied in the platform of the last national convention of the party.

2. Opposition to centralizationism and to that dangerous spirit of encroachment which tends to consolidate the powers of all the departments in one, and thus to create, whatever be the form of government, a real despotism. No sumptuary laws; separation of church and state, for the good of each; common schools fostered and protected.

3. Home rule; honest money—the strict maintenance of the public faith—consisting of gold and silver, and paper convertible into coin on demand; the strict maintenance of the public faith, state and national, and a tariff for revenue only.

4. The subordination of the military to the civil power, and a general and thorough reform of the civil service.

5. The right to a free ballot is the right preservative of all rights, and must and shall be maintained in every part of the United States.

6. The existing Administration is the representative of conspiracy only, and its claim of right to surround the ballot-boxes with troops and deputy marshals, to intimidate and obstruct the electors, and the unprecedented use of the veto to maintain its corrupt and despotic power, insult the people and imperil their institutions.

7. We execrate the course of this administration in making places in the civil service a reward for political crime, and demand a reform by statute which shall make it forever impossible for the defeated candidate to bribe his way to the seat of the usurper by billeting villains upon the people.

8. The great fraud of 1876-77, by which, upon a false count of the electoral votes of two states, the candidate defeated at the polls was declared to be President, and, for the first time in American history, the will of the people was set aside under a threat of military violence, struck a deadly blow at our system of representative government; the Democratic party, to preserve the country from a civil war, submitted for a time in firm and patriotic faith that the people would punish this crime in 1880; this issue precedes and dwarfs every other: it imposes a more sacred duty upon the people of the Union than ever addressed the conscience of a nation of free men.

9. The resolution of Samuel J. Tilden not again to be a candidate for the exalted place to which he was elected by a majority of his countrymen, and from which he was excluded by the leaders of the Republican party, is received by the Democrats of the United States with sensibility, and they declare their confidence in his wisdom, patriotism, and integrity, unshaken by the assaults of a common enemy, and they further assure him that he is followed into the retirement he has chosen for himself by the sympathy and respect of his fellow-citizens, who regard him as one who, by elevating the standards of public morality, merits the lasting gratitude of his country and his party.

10. Free ships and a living chance for American commerce on the seas and on the land. No discrimination in favor of transportation lines, corporations, or monopolies.

11. Amendment of the Burlingame Treaty. No more Chinese

immigration, except for travel, education, and foreign commerce, and therein carefully guarded.

12. Public money and public credit for public purposes solely, and public land for actual settlers.

13. The Democratic party is the friend of labor and the laboring man, and pledges itself to protect him alike against the cormorant and the commune.

14. We congratulate the country upon the honesty and thrift of a Democratic Congress which has reduced the public expenditure $40,000,000 a year; upon the continuation of prosperity at home and the national honor abroad; and, above all, upon the promise of such a change in the administration of the government as shall insure us genuine and lasting reform in every department of the public service.

Republican National Committee:

Chairman, DWIGHT M. SABIN, of Minnesota.
Secretary, JOHN A. MARTIN, of Kansas.

REPUBLICAN CONVENTION.

Chicago, Ill., June 2–8, 1880.

Chairman pro tem. and permanent Chairman,

GEORGE F. HOAR,
of Massachusetts.

NOMINATED—

For President, **James A. Garfield,**
of Ohio.

For Vice-President, **Chester A. Arthur,**
of New York.

Three days were spent in perfecting organization. It was at this convention that the unit-rule received its death-blow. Thirty-six ballots were taken before James A. Garfield, of Ohio, was nominated for President. The following is a brief summary:

CANDIDATES.	1st.	2d.	20th.	34th.	35th.	36th.
ULYSSES S. GRANT, of Ohio	304	305	308	312	313	306
JAMES G. BLAINE, of Maine	284	282	276	278	257	42
JOHN SHERMAN, of Ohio	98	94	96	99	99	3
GEORGE F. EDMUNDS, of Vermont	34	32	31	11	11	..
E. B. WASHBURNE, of Illinois	30	31	35	30	23	5
WILLIAM WINDOM, of Minnesota	10	10	10	3	3	..
JAMES A. GARFIELD, of Ohio	..	10	1	17	50	399

Scattering votes were cast for R. B. Hayes, Benjamin Harrison, Phil. Sheridan, Roscoe Conkling, and (?) McCreary.

For Vice-President, Chester A. Arthur, of New York, was nominated on the first ballot. The following table shows for whom the votes were cast:

CANDIDATES.	Votes.	CANDIDATES.	Votes.
CHESTER A. ARTHUR, of New York	468	BLANCHE K. BRUCE, of Mississippi	8
ELIHU B. WASHBURNE, of Illinois	199	JAMES L. ALCORN, of Mississippi	4
MARSHALL JEWELL, of Connecticut	43	THOMAS SETTLE, of Florida	2
HORACE MAYNARD, of Tennessee	30	STEWART L. WOODFORD, of New York	1
EDMUND J. DAVIS, of Texas	20		

The following is the platform as adopted:—

REPUBLICAN PLATFORM.

The Republican party, in national convention assembled, at the end of twenty years since the federal government was first committed to its charge, submits to the people of the United States this brief report of its administration:—

It suppressed a rebellion which had armed nearly a million of men to subvert the national authority; it reconstructed the union of the states with freedom instead of slavery as its corner-stone; it transformed 4,000,000 human beings from the likeness of things to the rank of citizens; it relieved Congress of the infamous work of hunting fugitive slaves, and charged it to see that slavery does not exist.

It has raised the value of our paper currency from 38 per cent. to the par of gold; it has restored, upon a solid basis, payment in coin of all national obligations, and has given us a currency absolutely good and equal in every part of our extended country; it has lifted the credit of the nation from the point of where 6 per cent. bonds sold at 86 to that where 4 per cent. bonds are eagerly sought at a premium.

Under its administration railways have increased from 31,000 miles in 1860 to more than 82,000 miles in 1879.

Our foreign trade increased from $700,000,000 to $1,150,-000,000 in the same time, and our exports, which were $20,-000,000 less than our imports in 1860, were $265,000,000 more than our imports in 1879.

Without resorting to loans, it has, since the war closed, defrayed the ordinary expenses of government besides the accruing interest on the public debt, and has disbursed annually more than $30,000,000 for soldiers' and sailors' pensions. It has paid $880,000,000 of the public debt, and, by refunding the balance at lower rates, has reduced the annual interest-charge from nearly $150,000,000 to less than $89,000,000.

All the industries of the country have revived, labor is in demand, wages have increased, and throughout the entire country there is evidence of a coming prosperity greater than we have ever enjoyed.

Upon this record the Republican party asks for the continued confidence and support of the people, and this convention submits for their approval the following statement of the principles and purposes which will continue to guide and inspire its efforts:

1. We affirm that the work of the Republican party for the last twenty years has been such as to commend it to the favor

of the nation; that the fruits of the costly victories which we have achieved through immense difficulties should be preserved; that the peace regained should be cherished; that the Union should be perpetuated, and that the liberty secured to this generation should be transmitted undiminished to other generations; that the order established and the credit acquired should never be impaired; that the pensions promised should be paid; that the debt, so much reduced, should be extinguished by the full payment of every dollar thereof; that the reviving industries should be further promoted, and that the commerce, already increasing, should be steadily encouraged.

2. The Constitution of the United States is a supreme law, and not a mere contract. Out of confederated states it made a sovereign nation. Some powers are denied to the nation, while others are denied to the states; but the boundary between the powers delegated and those reserved is to be determined by the national, and not by the state tribunal.

3. The work of popular education is one left to the care of the several states, but it is the duty of the national government to aid that work to the extent of its constitutional ability. The intelligence of the nation is but the aggregate of the intelligence in the several states, and the destiny of the nation must be guided, not by the genius of any one state, but by the average genius of all.

4. The Constitution wisely forbids Congress to make any law respecting the establishment of religion, but it is idle to hope that the nation can be protected against the influence of secret sectarianism while each state is exposed to its domination. We therefore recommend that the Constitution be so amended as to lay the same prohibition upon the legislature of each state, and to forbid the appropriation of public funds to the support of sectarian schools.

5. We reaffirm the belief avowed in 1876, that the duties levied for the purpose of revenue should so discriminate as to favor American labor; that no further grants of the public domain should be made to any railway or other corporation; that, slavery having perished in the states, its twin barbarity—polygamy—must die in the territories; that everywhere the protection accorded to a citizen of American birth must be secured to citizens by American adoption; that we deem it the duty of Congress to develop and improve our seacoast and harbors, but insist that further subsidies to private persons or corporations must cease; that the obligations of the republic

to the men who preserved its integrity in the day of battle are undiminished by the lapse of fifteen years since their final victory—to do them honor is and shall forever be the grateful privilege and sacred duty of the American people.

6. Since the authority to regulate immigration and intercourse between the United States and foreign nations rests with the Congress of the United States and the treaty-making power, the Republican party, regarding the unrestricted immigration of Chinese as a matter of grave concernment under the exercise of both these powers, would limit and restrict that immigration by the enactment of such just, humane, and reasonable laws and treaties as will produce that result.

7. That the purity and patriotism which characterized the earlier career of Rutherford B. Hayes in peace and war, and which guided the thoughts of our immediate predecessors to him for a presidential candidate, have continued to inspire him in his career as Chief Executive; and that history will accord to his administration the honors which are due to an efficient, just, and courteous discharge of the public business, and will honor his vetoes interposed between the people and attempted partisan laws.

8. We charge upon the Democratic party the habitual sacrifice of patriotism and justice to a supreme and insatiable lust for office and patronage; that to obtain possession of the national government and control of the place, they have obstructed all efforts to promote the purity and to conserve the freedom of the suffrage, and have devised fraudulent ballots and invented fraudulent certification of returns; have labored to unseat lawfully elected members of Congress, to secure at all hazards the vote of a majority of the states in the House of Representatives; have endeavored to occupy by force and fraud the places of trust given to others by the people of Maine, rescued by the courage and action of Maine's patriotic sons; have, by methods vicious in principle and tyrannical in practice, attached partisan legislation to appropriation bills upon whose passage the very movement of the government depended; have crushed the rights of the individual; have advocated the principles and sought the favor of the rebellion against the nation, and have endeavored to obliterate the sacred memories and to overcome its inestimably valuable results of nationality, personal freedom, and individual equality.

The equal, steady, and complete enforcement of the laws and the protection of all our citizens in the enjoyment of all the privileges and immunities guaranteed by the Constitution, are the first duties of the nation.

The dangers of a "Solid South" can only be averted by a faithful performance of every promise which the nation has made to the citizen. The execution of the laws, and the punishment of all those who violate them, are the only safe methods by which an enduring peace can be secured and genuine prosperity established throughout the South. Whatever promises the nation makes the nation must perform. A nation cannot with safety relegate this duty to the states. The "Solid South" must be divided by the peaceful agencies of the ballot, and all honest opinions must there find free expression. To this end the honest voter must be protected against terrorism, violence, or fraud.

And we affirm it to be the duty and the purpose of the Republican party to use all legitimate means to restore all the states of this Union to the most perfect harmony which may be possible, and we submit to the practical, sensible people of these United States to say whether it would not be dangerous to the dearest interests of our country at this time to surrender the administration of the national government to a party which seeks to overthrow the existing policy under which we are so prosperous, and thus bring distrust and confusion where there is now order, confidence, and hope.

9. The Republican party, adhering to the principles affirmed by its last national convention of respect for the constitutional rules governing appointments to office, adopts the declaration of President Hayes that the reform of the civil service should be thorough, radical, and complete. To this end it demands the co-operation of the legislative with the executive departments of the government, and that Congress shall so legislate that fitness, ascertained by proper practical tests, shall admit to the public service.

GREENBACK CONVENTION.

Chicago, Ill., June 9–11, 1880.

Chairman pro tem.,
REV. GILBERT DE LA MATYR,
of Indiana.

Chairman, RICHARD TREVELLICK,
of Michigan.

NOMINATED—

For President, **James B. Weaver,**
of Iowa.

For Vice-President, **B. J. Chambers,**
of Texas.

At this convention James B. Weaver, of Iowa, was nominated for President on the first ballot:—

CANDIDATES.	Votes.	CANDIDATES.	Votes.
JAMES B. WEAVER, of Iowa	224½	SOLON CHASE, of Maine	89
HENDRICK B. WRIGHT, of Pennsylvania	126½	EDWARD P. ALLIS, of Wisconsin	41
STEPHEN D. DILLAYE, of New York	119	ALEXANDER CAMPBELL, of Illinois	21
BENJAMIN F. BUTLER, of Massachusetts	95		

Mr. Weaver's nomination was afterward made unanimous.

On a vote for a candidate for Vice-President, B. J. Chambers, of Texas, received 403 votes, and Alanson M. West, of Mississippi, 311; whereupon Mr. Chambers was unanimously nominated.

The convention adopted the following platform:—

GREENBACK PLATFORM.

First. That the right to make and issue money is a sovereign power, to be maintained by the people for their common benefit. The delegation of this right to corporations is a surrender of the central attribute of sovereignty, void of constitutional sanction, and conferring upon a subordinate and irresponsible power an absolute dominion over industry and commerce. All money, whether metallic or paper, should be issued, and its volume controlled, by the government, and not by or through banking corporations; and, when so issued, should be a full legal tender for all debts, public and private.

Second. That the bonds of the United States should not be refunded, but paid as rapidly as practicable, according to contract. To enable the government to meet these obligations, legal-tender currency should be substituted for the notes of the national banks, the national banking system abolished, and the unlimited coinage of silver, as well as gold, established by law.

Third. That labor should be so protected by national and state authority as to equalize its burdens and insure a just distribution of its results. The eight-hour law of Congress should be enforced; the sanitary condition of industrial establishments placed under rigid control; the competition of contract convict labor abolished; a bureau of labor statistics established; factories, mines, and workshops inspected; the employment of children under fourteen years of age forbidden; and wages paid in cash.

Fourth. Slavery being simply cheap labor, and cheap labor being simply slavery, the importation and presence of Chinese serfs necessarily tends to brutalize and degrade American labor; therefore immediate steps should be taken to abrogate the Burlingame Treaty.

Fifth. Railroad land grants forfeited by reason of non-fulfillment of contract should be immediately reclaimed by the government; and henceforth the public domain reserved exclusively as homes for actual settlers.

Sixth. It is the duty of Congress to regulate interstate commerce. All lines of communication and transportation should be brought under such legislative control as shall secure moderate, fair, and uniform rates for passenger and freight traffic.

Seventh. We denounce as destructive to property and dangerous to liberty, the action of the old parties in fostering and sustaining gigantic land, railroad, and money corporations, and monopolies invested with and exercising powers belonging to the government, and yet not responsible to it for the manner of their exercise.

Eighth. That the Constitution, in giving Congress the power to borrow money, to declare war, to raise and support armies, to provide and maintain a navy, never intended that the men who loaned their money for an interest consideration should be preferred to the soldiers and sailors who perilled their lives and shed their blood on land and sea in defense of their country; and we condemn the cruel class-legislation of the Republican party, which, while professing great gratitude to the soldier, has most unjustly discriminated against him and in favor of the bondholder.

Ninth. All property should bear its just proportion of taxation, and we demand a graduated income tax.

Tenth. We denounce as dangerous the efforts everywhere manifest to restrict the right of suffrage.

Eleventh. We are opposed to an increase of the standing army in time of peace, and the insidious scheme to establish an enormous military power under the guise of militia laws.

Twelfth. We demand absolute democratic rules for the government of Congress, placing all representatives of the people upon an equal footing, and taking away from committees a veto power greater than that of the President.

Thirteenth. We demand a government of the people, by the people, and for the people, instead of a government of the bondholder, by the bondholder, and for the bondholder; and we denounce every attempt to stir up sectional strife as an effort to conceal monstrous crimes against the people.

Fourteenth. In the furtherance of these ends we ask the co-operation of all fair-minded people. We have no quarrel with individuals, wage no war on classes, but only against vicious institutions. We are not content to endure further discipline from our present actual rulers, who, having dominion over money, over transportation, over land and labor, over the press and the machinery of government, wield unwarrantable power over our institutions and over our life and property.

Fifteenth. That every citizen of due age, sound mind, and not a felon, be fully enfranchised, and that this resolution be referred to the states, with recommendation for their favorable consideration.

PROHIBITION CONVENTION.

Cleveland, O., June 17, 1880.

Chairman, REV. DR. MINER,

of Massachusetts.

NOMINATED—

For President, **Neal Dow,**

of Maine.

For Vice-President, **A. M. Thompson,**

of Ohio.

Only twelve states were represented, by 142 delegates, Neal Dow, of Maine, was nominated for President and A. M. Thompson, of Ohio, for Vice-President.

The convention adopted the following platform:—

PROHIBITION PLATFORM.

The Prohibition Reform party of the United States, organized in the name of the people, to revive, enforce, and perpetuate in the government the doctrines of the Declaration of Independence, submit, for the suffrage of all good citizens, the following platform of national reforms and measures.

In the examination and discussion of the temperance question, it has been proven, and is an accepted truth, that alcoholic drinks, whether fermented, brewed, or distilled, are poisonous to the healthy human body, the drinking of which is not only needless but hurtful, necessarily tending to form intemperate habits, increasing greatly the number, severity, and fatal termination of diseases, weakening and deranging the intellect, polluting the affections, hardening the heart, and corrupting the morals; depriving many of reason and still more of its healthful exercise, and annually bringing down large numbers to untimely graves; producing in the children of many who drink, a predisposition to intemperance, insanity, and various bodily and mental diseases; causing diminution of strength, feebleness of vision, fickleness of purpose, and premature old age, and inducing, in all future generations, deterioration of moral and physical character. Alcoholic drinks are thus the implacable foe of man as an individual.

First. The legalized importation, manufacture, and sale of intoxicating drinks ministers to their use, and teaches the erroneous and destructive sentiment that such use is right, thus tending to produce and perpetuate the above-mentioned evils.

Second. To the home it is an enemy—proving itself to be a disturber and destroyer of its peace, prosperity, and happiness; taking from it the earnings of the husband; depriving the dependent wife and children of essential food, clothing, and education; bringing into it profanity, abuse, and violence; setting at naught the vows of the marriage altar; breaking up the family and sundering the children from the parents, and thus destroying one of the most beneficent institutions of our

Creator; and removing the sure foundation of good government, national prosperity, and welfare.

Third. To the community it is equally an enemy—producing vice, demoralization, and wickedness; its places of sale being resorts of gaming, lewdness, and debauchery, and the hiding-place of those who prey upon society; counteracting the efficacy of religious effort, and of all means of intellectual elevation, moral purity, social happiness, and the eternal good of mankind, without rendering any counteracting or compensating benefits; being in its influence and effect evil and only evil, and that continually.

Fourth. To the state it is equally an enemy—legislative inquiries, judicial investigations, and official reports of all penal, reformatory, and dependent institutions showing that the manufacture and sale of such beverages is the promoting cause of intemperance, crime, and pauperism, and of demands upon public and private charity, imposing the larger part of taxation, paralyzing thrift, industry, manufactures, and commercial life, which, but for it, would be unnecessary; disturbing the peace of streets and highways; filling prisons and poor-houses; corrupting politics, legislation, and the execution of the laws; shortening lives; diminishing wealth, industry, and productive power in manufactures and art; and is manifestly unjust as well as injurious to the community upon which it is imposed, and is contrary to all just views of civil liberty, as well as a violation of the fundamental maxim of our common law, to use your own property or liberty so as not to injure others.

Fifth. It is neither right nor politic for the state to afford legal protection to any traffic or any system which tends to waste the resources, to corrupt the social habits, and to destroy the health and lives of the people; that the importation, manufacture, and sale of intoxicating beverages is proven to be inimical to the true interest of the individual home, community, and state, and destructive to the order and welfare of society, and ought, therefore, to be classed among crimes to be prohibited.

Sixth. In this time of profound peace at home and abroad, the entire separation of the general government from the drink traffic, and its prohibition in the District of Columbia, territories, and in all places and ways over which, under the Constitution, Congress has control and power, is a political issue of the first importance to the peace and prosperity of the nation. There can be no stable peace and protection to personal liberty, life, or property until secured by national or state constitutional provisions, enforced by adequate laws.

Seventh. All legitimate industries require deliverance from the taxation and loss which the liquor traffic imposes upon them, and financial or other legislation could not accomplish so much to increase production and cause a demand for labor—and, as a result, for the comforts of living—as the suppression of this traffic would bring to thousands of homes, as one of its blessings.

Eighth. The administration of the government and the execution of the laws are through political parties; and we arraign the Republican party, which has been in continuous power in the nation for twenty years, as being false to duty, as false to loudly proclaimed principles of equal justice to all and special favors to none, and of protection to the weak and dependent; insensible to the mischief which the trade in liquor has constantly inflicted upon industry, trade, commerce, and the social happiness of the people; that 5652 distilleries, 3830 breweries, and 175,266 places for the sale of these poisonous liquors, involving an annual waste to the nation of one million five hundred thousand dollars and the sacrifice of one hundred thousand lives, have, under its legislation, grown up and been fostered as a legitimate source of revenue; that during its history six territories have been organized and five states been admitted into the Union, with constitutions provided and approved by Congress, but the prohibition of this debasing and destructive traffic has not been provided for, nor even the people given, at the time of admission, power to forbid it in any one of them. Its history further shows that not in a single instance has an original prohibitory law been passed by any state that was controlled by it, while in four states so governed the laws found on its advent to power have been repealed. At its national convention in 1872 it declared, as part of its party faith, that "it disapproves of the resort to unconstitutional laws for the purpose of removing evils, by interference with rights not surrendered by the people to either the state or national government," which, the author of this plank says, was adopted by the platform committee with the full and implicit understanding that its purpose was the discountenancing of all so-called Temperance, Prohibitory and Sunday laws.

Ninth. We arraign also the Democratic party as unfaithful, and unworthy of reliance on this question; for, although not clothed with power, but occupying the relation of an opposition party during twenty years past, strong in numbers and organization, it has allied itself with liquor traffickers, and become, in all the states of the Union, their special political defenders, and in its national convention in 1876, as an article of its political faith, declared against prohibition and just laws in restraint of the trade in drink, by saying it was opposed to what it was pleased to call "all sumptuary laws." The National party has been dumb on this question.

Tenth. Drink-traffickers, having the history and experience of all ages, climes, and conditions of men, declaring their business destructive of all good—finding no support in the Bible, morals, or reason—appeal to misapplied law for their justification, and intrench themselves behind the evil elements of political party for defense, and thus party tactics and party inertia become battling forces protecting this evil.

Eleventh. In view of the foregoing facts and history, we cordially invite all voters, without regard to former party affiliations, to unite with us in the use of the ballot for the abolition of the drinking system under the authority of our national and state governments. We also demand, as a right, that women, having the privilege of citizens in other respects, be clothed with the ballot for their protection and as a rightful means for the proper settlement of the liquor question.

Twelfth. To remove the apprehension of some who allege that a loss of public revenue would follow the suppression of a direct trade, we confidently point to the experience of governments abroad and at home, which shows that thrift and revenue from the consumption of legitimate manufactures and commerce have so largely followed the abolition of drink as to fully supply all loss of liquor-taxes.

Thirteenth. We recognize the good providence of Almighty God, Who has preserved and prospered us as a nation; and, asking for His Spirit to guide us to ultimate success, we all look for it, relying upon His omnipotent arm.

The election occurred on November 2, 1880.

THIRTY-EIGHT STATES VOTED.

POPULAR VOTE.

STATES.	James A. Garfield, Republican.	Winfield S. Hancock, Democrat.	James B. Weaver, Greenbacker.	Neal Dow, Prohibitionist.	Total vote.
Alabama	56,221	91,185	4,642	....	152,048
Arkansas	42,436	60,775	4,079	....	107,290
California	80,348	80,426	3,392	....	164,166
Colorado	27,450	24,647	1,435	...	53,532
Connecticut	67,071	64,415	868	409	132,763
Delaware	14,133	15,275	120	....	29,528
Florida	23,654	27,964	....	....	51,618
Georgia	54,086	102,470	969	....	157,525
Illinois	318,037	277,321	26,358	443	622,159
Indiana	232,164	225,522	12,986	....	470,672
Iowa	183,927	105,845	32,701	592	323,065
Kansas	121,549	59,801	19,851	25	201,226
Kentucky	106,306	149,068	11,499	258	267,131
Louisiana	* 38,637	65,067	439	....	104,143
Maine	74,039	† 65,171	4,408	93	143,711
Maryland	78,515	93,706	818	...	173,039
Massachusetts	165,205	111,960	4,548	682	282,395
Michigan	185,341	131,597	34,895	942	352,775
Minnesota	93,903	53,315	3,267	286	150,771
Mississippi	34,854	75,750	5,797	....	116,401
Missouri	153,567	208,609	35,135	....	397,311
Nebraska	54,979	28,523	3,950	....	87,452
Nevada	8,732	9,613	....	....	18,345
New Hampshire	44,852	40,794	528	180	86,354
New Jersey	120,555	122,565	2,617	191	245,928
New York	555,544	534,511	12,373	1,517	1,103,945
North Carolina	115,874	124,208	1,126	....	241,208
Ohio	375,048	340,821	6,456	2,616	724,941
Oregon	20,619	19,948	249	....	40,816
Pennsylvania	444,704	407,428	20,668	1,939	874,739
Rhode Island	18,195	10,779	236	20	29,230
South Carolina	58,071	112,312	566	....	170,949
Tennessee	107,677	128,191	5,917	43	241,828
Texas	57,893	156,428	27,405	....	241,726
Vermont	45,567	18,316	1,215	....	65,098
Virginia	84,020	‡ 128,586	....	....	212,606
West Virginia	46,243	57,391	9,079	....	112,713
Wisconsin	144,400	114,649	7,986	69	267,104
Total	4,454,416	4,444,952	308,578	10,305	9,218,251

* Two Republican tickets were voted for.

† Votes for a fusion electoral ticket, made up of three Democrats and four Greenbackers. A "straight" Greenback ticket was also voted for.

‡ Two Democratic tickets were voted for in Virginia. The regular ticket received 96,912, and was successful; the "Readjusters" polled 31,674 votes.

ELECTORAL VOTE.

Counted on February 9, 1881.

STATES.	PRESIDENT.		VICE-PRESIDENT.		Number entitled to vote.
	James A. Garfield, of Ohio.	Winfield S. Hancock, of Pennsylvania.	Chester A. Arthur, of New York.	William H. English, of Indiana.	
Alabama	..	10	..	10	10
Arkansas	..	6	..	6	6
California	1	5	1	5	6
Colorado	3	..	3	..	3
Connecticut	6	..	6	..	6
Delaware	..	3	..	3	3
Florida	..	4	..	4	4
Georgia	..	11	..	11	11
Illinois	21	..	21	..	21
Indiana	15	..	15	..	15
Iowa	11	..	11	..	11
Kansas	5	..	5	..	5
Kentucky	..	12	..	12	12
Louisiana	..	8	..	8	8
Maine	7	..	7	..	7
Maryland	..	8	..	8	8
Massachusetts	13	..	13	..	13
Michigan	11	..	11	..	11
Minnesota	5	..	5	..	5
Mississippi	..	8	..	8	8
Missouri	..	15	..	15	15
Nebraska	3	..	3	..	3
Nevada	..	3	..	3	3
New Hampshire	5	..	5	..	5
New Jersey	..	9	..	9	9
New York	35	..	35	..	35
North Carolina	..	10	..	10	10
Ohio	22	..	22	..	22
Oregon	3	..	3	..	3
Pennsylvania	29	..	29	..	29
Rhode Island	4	..	4	..	4
South Carolina	..	7	..	7	7
Tennessee	..	12	..	12	12
Texas	..	8	..	8	8
Vermont	5	..	5	..	5
Virginia	..	11	..	11	11
West Virginia	..	5	..	5	5
Wisconsin	10	..	10	..	10
Total	214	155	214	155	369

James A. Garfield was elected President and Chester A. Arthur as Vice-President.

During this period Congress was divided politically as follows:

Forty-seventh Congress.

Senate— 37 Democrats, 37 Republicans, 1 Independent, 1 Readjuster..Total, 76
House—130 Democrats, 152 Republicans, 9 Nationals, 2 Readjusters.. " 293

Forty-eighth Congress.

Senate— 36 Democrats, 40 Republicans................Total, 76
House—200 Democrats, 119 Republicans, 4 Independents, 2 Nationals.. " 325

Election of 1884

Democratic National Committee:

Chairman, WM. H. BARNUM, of Connecticut.
Secretary, F. O. PRINCE, of Massachusetts.

DEMOCRATIC CONVENTION.

Chicago, Ill., July 8–11, 1884.

Chairman pro tem., RICHARD B. HUBBARD, of Texas.

Chairman, WILLIAM F. VILAS, of Wisconsin.

NOMINATED—

For President, **Grover Cleveland**, of New York.

For Vice-President, **Thomas A. Hendricks**, of Indiana.

At this convention an attempt to break down the unit-rule was made by the Tammany opposition to Grover Cleveland, but it met with defeat.

Two ballots were necessary to effect the nomination of Grover Cleveland, of New York, as President. The following table gives the ballots in detail:

CANDIDATES	1st.	2d.
GROVER CLEVELAND, of New York	392	684
THOMAS F. BAYARD, of Delaware	168	81
ALLEN G. THURMAN, of Ohio	88	4
SAMUEL J. RANDALL, of Pennsylvania	78	4
THOMAS A. HENDRICKS, of Indiana	1	45
JOSEPH E. MCDONALD, of Indiana	56	1
JOHN G. CARLISLE, of Kentucky	27	..
ROSWELL P. FLOWER, of New York	4	..
GEORGE HOADLY, of Ohio	3	..
SAMUEL J. TILDEN, of New York	1	..

For Vice-President, John C. Black, of Illinois; William S. Rosecrans, of California, and George W. Glick, of Kansas, were named as candidates, but were all withdrawn, and Thomas A. Hendricks, of Indiana, was unanimously chosen on the first ballot.

The following is the platform as adopted:—

DEMOCRATIC PLATFORM.

The Democratic party of the Union, through its representatives in national convention assembled, recognizes that, as the nation grows older, new issues are born of time and progress, and old issues perish. But the fundamental principles of the Democracy, approved by the united voice of the people, remain and will ever remain as the best and only security for the continuance of free government. The preservation of personal rights; the equality of all citizens before the law; the reserved rights of the states, and the supremacy of the federal government within the limits of the Constitution, will ever form the true basis of our liberties, and can never be surrendered without destroying that balance of rights and powers which enables a continent to be developed in peace, and social order to be maintained by means of local self-government. But it is indispensable for the practical application and enforcement of these fundamental principles, that the government should not always be controlled by one political party. Frequent change of administration is as necessary as constant recurrence to the popular will. Otherwise, abuses grow, and the government, instead of being carried on for the general welfare, becomes an instrumentality for imposing heavy burdens on the many who are governed, for the benefit of the few who govern. Public servants thus become arbitrary rulers. This is now the condition of the country; hence a change is demanded.

The Republican party, so far as principle is concerned, is a reminiscence. In practice it is an organization for enriching those who control its machinery. The frauds and jobbery which have been brought to light in every department of the government are sufficient to have called for reform within the Republican party; yet those in authority, made reckless by the long possession of power, have succumbed to its corrupting influence and have placed in nomination a ticket against which the independent portion of the party are in open revolt. Therefore, a change is demanded. Such a change was alike necessary in 1876, but the will of the people was then defeated by a fraud which can never be forgotten nor condoned. Again, in 1880, the change demanded by the people was defeated by the lavish use of money contributed by unscrupulous contractors and shameless jobbers, who had bargained for unlawful profits or high office. The Republican party, during its legal, its stolen, and its bought tenures of power, has steadily decayed in moral character and political capacity. Its platform-promises are now a list of its past failures. It demands the restoration of our navy: it has squandered hundreds of millions to create a navy that does not exist. It calls upon Congress to remove the burdens under which American shipping has been depressed: it imposed and has continued those burdens. It professes a policy of reserving the public lands for small holdings by actual settlers: it has given away the people's heritage till now a few railroads and non-resident aliens, individual and corporate, possess a larger area than that of all our farms between the two seas. It professes a preference for free institutions: it organized and tried to legalize a control of state elections by federal troops. It professes a desire to elevate labor: it has subjected American workingmen to the competition of convict and imported contract labor. It professes gratitude to all who were disabled or died in the war, leaving widows and orphans: it left to a Democratic

House of Representatives the first effort to equalize both bounties and pensions. It proffers a pledge to correct the irregularities of our tariff: it created and has continued them. Its own tariff commission confessed the needs of more than twenty per cent. reduction: its Congress gave a reduction of less than four per cent. It professes the protection of American manufactures: it has subjected them to an increasing flood of manufactured goods and a hopeless competition with manufacturing nations, not one of which taxes raw materials. It professes to protect all American industries: it has impoverished many, to subsidize a few. It professes the protection of American labor: it has depleted the returns of American agriculture and industry, followed by half of our people. It professes the equality of all men before the law, attempting to fix the status of colored citizens: the acts of its Congress were overset by the decisions of its courts. It "accepts anew the duty of leading in the work of progress and reform": its caught criminals are permitted to escape through contrived delays or actual connivance in the prosecution. Honeycombed with corruption, outbreaking exposures no longer shock its moral sense. Its honest members, its independent journals no longer maintain a successful contest for authority in its councils or a veto upon bad nominations. That change is necessary is proved by an existing surplus of more than $100,000,000, which has yearly been collected from a suffering people. Unnecessary taxation is unjust taxation. We denounce the Republican party for having failed to relieve the people from crushing war-taxes, which have paralyzed business, crippled industry, and deprived labor of employment and of just reward.

The Democracy pledges itself to purify the administration from corruption, to restore economy, to revive respect for law, and to reduce taxation to the lowest limit consistent with due regard to the preservation of the faith of the nation to its creditors and pensioners. Knowing full well, however, that legislation affecting the operations of the people should be cautious and conservative in method, not in advance of public opinion, but responsive to its demands, the Democratic party is pledged to revise the tariff in a spirit of fairness to all interests. But, in making reduction in taxes, it is not proposed to injure any domestic industries, but rather to promote their healthy growth. From the foundation of this government, taxes collected at the custom-house have been the chief source of federal revenue. Such they must continue to be. Moreover, many industries have come to rely upon legislation for successful continuance, so that any change of law must be at every step regardful of the labor and capital thus involved. The process of reform must be subject in the execution to this plain dictate of justice: all taxation shall be limited to the requirements of economical government. The necessary reduction and taxation can and must be effected without depriving American labor of the ability to compete successfully with foreign labor, and without imposing lower rates of duty than will be ample to cover any increased cost of production which may exist in consequence of the higher rate of wages prevailing in this country. Sufficient revenue to pay all the expenses of the federal government, economically administered, including pensions, interest and principal of the public debt, can be got under our present system of taxation from the custom-house taxes on fewer imported articles, bearing heaviest on articles of luxury and bearing lightest on articles of necessity. We therefore denounce the abuses of the existing tariff, and, subject to the preceding limitations, we demand that federal taxation shall be exclusively for public purposes, and shall not exceed the needs of the government, economically administered.

The system of direct taxation known as the "internal revenue" is a war-tax, and, so long as the law continues, the money derived therefrom should be sacredly devoted to the relief of the people from the remaining burdens of the war, and be made a fund to defray the expense of the care and comfort of worthy soldiers disabled in line of duty in the wars of the republic, and for the payment of such pensions as Congress may from time to time grant to such soldiers, a like fund for the sailors having already been provided; and any surplus should be paid into the Treasury.

We favor an American continental policy based upon more intimate commercial and political relations with the fifteen sister republics of North, Central, and South America, but entangling alliances with none.

We believe in honest money, the gold and silver coinage of the Constitution, and a circulating medium convertible into such money without loss.

Asserting the equality of all men before the law, we hold that it is the duty of the government in its dealings with the people to mete out equal and exact justice to all citizens, of whatever nativity, race, color, or persuasion, religious or political.

We believe in a free ballot and a fair count, and we recall to the memory of the people the noble struggle of the Democrats in the Forty-fifth and Forty-sixth Congresses, by which a reluctant Republican opposition was compelled to assent to legislation making everywhere illegal the presence of troops at the polls, as the conclusive proof that a Democratic administration will preserve liberty with order.

The selection of federal officers for the territories should be restricted to citizens previously resident therein.

We oppose sumptuary laws, which vex the citizen and interfere with individual liberty.

We favor honest civil-service reform and a compensation of all United States officers by fixed salaries; the separation of church and state, and the diffusion of free education by common schools, so that every child in the land may be taught the rights and duties of citizenship.

While we favor all legislation which will tend to the equitable distribution of property, to the prevention of monopoly, and to the strict enforcement of individual rights against corporate abuses, we hold that the welfare of society depends upon a scrupulous regard for the right of property as defined by law.

We believe that labor is best rewarded where it is freest and most enlightened. It should therefore be fostered and cherished. We favor the repeal of all laws restricting the free action of labor, and the enactment of laws by which labor organizations may be incorporated, and of all such legislation as will tend to enlighten the people as to the true relations of capital and labor.

We believe that the public land ought, as far as possible, to be kept as homesteads for actual settlers; that all unearned lands heretofore improvidently granted to railroad corporations by the action of the Republican party should be restored to the public domain, and that no more grants of land shall be made to corporations, or be allowed to fall into the ownership of alien absentees.

We are opposed to all propositions which, upon any pretext, would convert the general government into a machine for collecting taxes, to be distributed among the states, or the citizens thereof.

In reaffirming the declaration of the Democratic platform of 1856, that the liberal principles embodied by Jefferson in the Declaration of Independence, and sanctioned in the Constitution, which makes ours the land of liberty and the asylum of the oppressed of every nation, have ever been cardinal principles in the Democratic faith, we nevertheless do not sanction the importation of foreign labor or the admission of servile races, unfitted by habits, training, religion, or kindred, for absorption into the great body of our people, or for the citizenship which our laws confer. American civilization demands that against the immigration or importation of Mongolians to these shores our gates be closed.

The Democratic party insists that it is the duty of the government to protect with equal fidelity and vigilance the rights of its citizens, native and naturalized, at home and abroad, and to the end that this protection may be assured, United States papers of naturalization, issued by courts of competent jurisdiction, must be respected by the executive and legislative departments of our own government and by all foreign powers. It is an imperative duty of this government to efficiently protect all the rights of persons and property of every American citizen in foreign lands, and demand and enforce full reparation for any invasion thereof. An American citizen is only responsible to his own government for any act done in his own country or under her flag, and can only be tried therefor on her own soil and according to her laws; and no power exists in this government to expatriate an American citizen to be tried in any foreign land for any such act.

This country has never had a well-defined and executed foreign policy, save under Democratic administration. That policy has ever been in regard to foreign nations, so long as they do not act detrimental to the interests of the country or hurtful to our citizens, to let them alone; that as a result of this policy we recall the acquisition of Louisiana, Florida, California, and of the adjacent Mexican territory, by purchase alone, and contrast these grand acquisitions of Democratic statesmanship with the purchase of Alaska, the sole fruit of a Republican administration of nearly a quarter of a century.

The federal government should care for and improve the Mississippi River and other great waterways of the republic, so as to secure for the interior states easy and cheap transportation to tide-water.

Under a long period of Democratic rule and policy our merchant marine was fast overtaking, and on the point of outstripping, that of Great Britain. Under twenty years of Republican rule and policy our commerce has been left to British bottoms, and the American flag has almost been swept off the high seas. Instead of the Republican party's British policy, we demand for the people of the United States an American policy. Under Democratic rule and policy our merchants and sailors, flying the Stars and Stripes in every port, successfully searched out a market for the varied products of American industry: under a quarter of a century of Republican rule and policy—despite our manifest advantage over all other nations in high-paid labor, favorable climate, and teeming soils; despite freedom of trade among all these United States; despite their population by the foremost races of men, and an annual immigration of the young, thrifty, and adventurous of all nations; despite our freedom here from the inherited burdens of life and industry in the Old World monarchies, their costly war navies, their vast tax-consuming, non-producing standing armies; despite twenty years of peace—that Republican rule and policy have managed to surrender to Great Britain, along with our commerce, the control of the markets of the world. Instead of the Republican party's British policy, we demand, in behalf of the American Democracy, an American policy. Instead of the Republican party's discredited scheme and false pretense of friendship for American labor, expressed by imposing taxes, we demand, in behalf of the Democracy, freedom for American labor, by reducing taxes, to the end that these United States may compete with unhindered powers for the primacy among nations in all the arts of peace and fruits of liberty.

With profound regret, we have been apprised by the venerable statesman through whose person was struck that blow at the vital principle of republics—acquiescence in the will of the majority—that he cannot permit us again to place in his hands the leadership of the Democratic hosts, for the reason that the achievement of reform in the administration of the federal government is an undertaking now too heavy for his age and failing strength. Rejoicing that his life has been prolonged until the general judgment of our fellow-countrymen is united in the wish that that wrong were righted in his person, for the Democracy of the United States we offer to him, in his withdrawal from public cares, not only our respectful sympathy and esteem, but also that best homage of freemen—the pledge of our devotion to the principles and the cause now inseparable in the history of this republic from the labors and the name of Samuel J. Tilden.

With this statement of the hopes, principles, and purposes of the Democratic party, the great issue of reform and change in administration is submitted to the people, in calm confidence that the popular voice will pronounce in favor of new men and new and more favorable conditions for the growth of industry, the extension of trade, the employment and due reward of labor and of capital, and the general welfare of the whole country.

Republican National Committee:

Chairman, B. F. JONES, of Pennsylvania.
Secretary, SAMUEL FESSENDEN, of Connecticut.

REPUBLICAN CONVENTION.

Chicago, Ill., June 3–6, 1884.

Chairman pro tem., JOHN R. LYNCH,
of Mississippi.

Chairman, JOHN B. HENDERSON,
of Missouri.

NOMINATED—

For President, **James G. Blaine,**
of Maine.

For Vice-President, **John A. Logan,**
of Illinois.

When the convention met there was a contest for the temporary chairmanship, which resulted in the selection of John R. Lynch, of Mississippi, a distinguished colored man, by 431 votes, against 387 given for Powell Clayton, of Arkansas. At this convention an important rule was adopted, excluding all office-holders as members of the national committee, and for allowing more freedom in the selection of delegates to future conventions. As a candidate for President, James G. Blaine, of Maine, was nominated on the fourth ballot, as follows:

CANDIDATES.	1st.	2d.	3d.	4th.
JAMES G. BLAINE, of Maine	334½	349	375	541
CHESTER A. ARTHUR, of New York	278	276	274	207
GEORGE F. EDMUNDS, of Vermont	93	85	69	41
JOHN A. LOGAN, of Illinois	63½	61	53	7
JOHN SHERMAN, of Ohio	30	28	25	..
JOSEPH R. HAWLEY, of Connecticut	13	13	13	15
ROBERT T. LINCOLN, of Illinois	4	4	8	2
WILLIAM T. SHERMAN, of Missouri	2	2	2	..

Mr. Blaine's nomination was afterward made unanimous.

For Vice-President, John A. Logan, of Illinois, was nominated by 779 votes; Lucius Fairchild, of Wisconsin, received 7, and Walter Q. Gresham, of Indiana, 6.

The convention adopted the following platform:—

REPUBLICAN PLATFORM.

The Republicans of the United States, in national convention assembled, renew their allegiance to the principles upon which they have triumphed in six successive Presidential elections, and congratulate the American people on the attainment of so many results in legislation and administration, by which the Republican party has, after saving the Union, done so much to render its institutions just, equal, and beneficent, the safeguard of liberty and the embodiment of the best thought and highest purpose of our citizens.

The Republican party has gained its strength by quick and faithful response to the demands of the people for the freedom and equality of all men; for a united nation, assuring the rights of all citizens; for the elevation of labor; for an honest currency; for purity in legislation, and for integrity and accountability in all departments of the government, and it accepts anew the duty of leading in the work of progress and reform.

We lament the death of President Garfield, whose sound statesmanship, long conspicuous in Congress, gave promise of a strong and successful administration—a promise fully realized during the short period of his office as President of the United States. His distinguished services in war and peace have endeared him to the hearts of the American people.

In the administration of President Arthur we recognize a wise, conservative, and patriotic policy, under which the country has been blessed with remarkable prosperity, and we believe his eminent services are entitled to and will receive the hearty approval of every citizen.

It is the first duty of a good government to protect the rights and promote the interests of its own people.

The largest diversity of industry is most productive of general prosperity, and of the comfort and independence of the people.

We therefore demand that the imposition of duties on foreign imports shall be made, not "for revenue only," but that in raising the requisite revenues for the government such duties shall be so levied as to afford security to our diversified industries and protection to the rights and wages of the laborer, to the end that active and intelligent labor, as well as capital, may have its just reward, and the laboring man his full share in the national prosperity.

Against the so-called economic system of the Democratic party, which would degrade our labor to the foreign standard, we enter our earnest protest.

The Democratic party has failed completely to relieve the people of the burden of unnecessary taxation, by a wise reduction of the surplus.

The Republican party pledges itself to correct the inequalities of the tariff and to reduce the surplus, not by the vicious and indiscriminate process of horizontal reduction, but by such methods as will relieve the tax-payer without injuring the laborer or the great productive interests of the country.

We recognize the importance of sheep-husbandry in the United States, the serious depression which it is now experiencing, and the danger threatening its future prosperity; and we therefore respect the demands of the representatives of this important agricultural interest for a readjustment of duties upon foreign wool, in order that such industry shall have full and adequate protection.

We have always recommended the best money known to the civilized world; and we urge that efforts should be made to unite all commercial nations in the establishment of an international standard, which shall fix for all the relative value of gold and silver coinage.

The regulation of commerce with foreign nations and between the states is one of the most important prerogatives of the general government; and the Republican party distinctly announces its purpose to support such legislation as will fully and efficiently carry out the constitutional power of Congress over interstate commerce.

The principle of public regulation of railway corporations is a wise and salutary one for the protection of all classes of the people; and we favor legislation that shall prevent unjust discrimination and excessive charges for transportation, and that shall secure to the people and the railways alike the fair and equal protection of the laws.

We favor the establishment of a national bureau of labor; the enforcement of the eight-hour law; a wise and judicious system of general legislation by adequate appropriation from the national revenues, wherever the same is needed. We believe that everywhere the protection to a citizen of American birth must be secured to citizens by American adoption; and we favor the settlement of national differences by international arbitration.

The Republican party, having its birth in a hatred of slave labor and a desire that all men may be truly free and equal, is unalterably opposed to placing our workingmen in competition with any form of servile labor, whether at home or abroad. In this spirit we denounce the importation of contract labor, whether from Europe or Asia, as an offense against the spirit of American institutions; and we pledge ourselves to sustain the present law restricting Chinese immigration, and to provide such further legislation as is necessary to carry out its purposes.

Reform of the civil service, auspiciously begun under Republican administration, should be completed by the further extension of the reform system, already established by law, to all the grades of the service to which it is applicable. The spirit and purpose of the reform should be observed in all executive appointments, and all laws at variance with the objects of existing reform legislation should be repealed, to the end that the dangers to free institutions which lurk in the power of official patronage may be wisely and effectively avoided.

The public lands are a heritage of the people of the United States, and should be reserved as far as possible for small holdings by actual settlers. We are opposed to the acquisition of large tracts of these lands by corporations or individuals, especially where such holdings are in the hands of non-residents or aliens, and we will endeavor to obtain such legislation as will tend to correct this evil. We demand of Congress the speedy forfeiture of all land-grants which have lapsed by reason of non-compliance with acts of incorporation, in all cases where there has been no attempt in good faith to perform the conditions of such grants.

The grateful thanks of the American people are due to the Union soldiers and sailors of the late war; and the Republican party stands pledged to suitable pensions for all who were disabled, and for the widows and orphans of those who died in the war. The Republican party also pledges itself to the repeal of the limitations contained in the Arrears Act of 1879, so that all invalid soldiers shall share alike, and their pensions begin with the date of disability or discharge, and not with the date of application.

The Republican party favors a policy which shall keep us from entangling alliances with foreign nations, and which gives us the right to expect that foreign nations shall refrain from meddling in American affairs—a policy which seeks peace and trade with all powers, but especially with those of the Western Hemisphere.

We demand the restoration of our navy to its old-time strength and efficiency, that it may in any sea protect the rights of American citizens and the interests of American commerce; and we call upon Congress to remove the burdens under which American shipping has been depressed, so that it may again be true that we have a commerce which leaves no sea unexplored, and a navy which takes no law from superior force.

Resolved, That appointments by the President to offices in the territories should be made from the *bona fide* citizens and residents of the territories wherein they are to serve.

Resolved, That it is the duty of Congress to enact such laws as shall promptly and effectually suppress the system of polygamy within our territories, and divorce the political from the ecclesiastical power of the so-called Mormon Church; and that the laws so enacted should be rigidly enforced by the civil authorities, if possible, and by the military, if need be.

The people of the United States, in their organized capacity, constitute a nation, and not an American federacy of states. The national government is supreme within the sphere of its national duties; but the states have reserved rights which should be faithfully maintained. Each should be guarded with jealous care, so that the harmony of our system of government may be preserved and the Union kept inviolate.

The perpetuity of our institutions rests upon the maintenance of a free ballot, an honest count, and correct returns. We denounce the fraud and violence practised by the Democracy in Southern States, by which the will of a voter is defeated, as dangerous to the preservation of free institutions; and we solemnly arraign the Democratic party as being the guilty recipient of the fruits of such fraud and violence.

We extend to the Republicans of the South, regardless of their former party affiliations, our cordial sympathy, and pledge to them our most earnest efforts to promote the passage of such legislation as will secure to every citizen, of whatever race and color, the full and complete recognition, possession, and exercise of all civil and political rights.

GREENBACK NATIONAL CONVENTION.

Indianapolis, Ind., May 28–29, 1884.

Chairman pro tem., JOHN TYLER,
of Florida.

Chairman, JAMES B. WEAVER,
of Iowa.

NOMINATED—

For President, **Benjamin F. Butler,**
of Massachusetts.

For Vice-President, **Alanson M. West,**
of Mississippi.

Gen. Benjamin F. Butler, of Massachusetts, was nominated for President on the first ballot, receiving 322 votes out of a total of 425. Jesse Harper, of Illinois; Solon Chase, of Maine; Edward P. Allis, of Wisconsin, and David Davis, of Illinois, were also voted for.

For Vice-President, Gen. Alanson M. West, of Mississippi, was nominated by acclamation.

The convention adopted the following platform:—

GREENBACK PLATFORM.

1. That we hold the late decision of the Supreme Court on the legal-tender question to be a full vindication of the theory which our party has always advocated on the right and authority of Congress over the issue of legal-tender notes, and we hereby pledge ourselves to uphold said decision, and to defend the Constitution against alterations or amendments intended to deprive the people of any rights or privileges conferred by that instrument. We demand the issue of such money in sufficient quantities to supply the actual demands of trade and commerce, in accordance with the increase of population and the development of our industries. We demand the substitution of greenbacks for national-bank notes, and the prompt payment of the public debt. We want that money which saved our country in time of war and which has given it prosperity and happiness in peace. We condemn the retirement of the fractional currency and the small denominations of greenbacks, and demand their restoration. We demand the issue of the hoards of money now locked up in the United States Treasury, by applying them to the payment of the public debt now due.

2. We denounce as dangerous to our republican institutions, those methods and policies of the Democratic and Republican parties which have sanctioned or permitted the establishment of land, railroad, money, and other gigantic monopolies; and we demand such governmental action as may be necessary to take from such monopolies the power they have so corruptly and unjustly usurped, and restore them to the people, to whom they belong.

3. The public lands being the natural inheritance of the people, we denounce that policy which has granted to corporations vast tracts of land, and we demand that immediate and vigorous measures be taken to reclaim from such corporations, for the people's use and benefit, all such land-grants as have

been forfeited by reason of non-fulfilment of contract, or that may have been wrongfully acquired by corrupt legislation, and that such reclaimed lands and other public domain be henceforth held as a sacred trust, to be granted only to actual settlers in limited quantities; and we also demand that the alien ownership of land, individual or corporate, shall be prohibited.

4. We demand Congressional regulations of interstate commerce, we denounce "pooling," stock-watering, and discrimination in rates and charges, and demand that Congress shall correct these abuses, even, if necessary, by the construction of national railroads. We also demand the establishment of a government postal-telegraph system.

5. All private property, all forms of money and obligations to pay money, should bear their just proportion of the taxes. We demand a graduated income-tax.

6. We demand the amelioration of the condition of labor by enforcing the sanitary laws in industrial establishments, by the abolition of the convict labor system, by a rigid inspection of mines and factories, by a reduction of the hours of labor in industrial establishments, by fostering educational institutions, and by abolishing child labor.

7. We condemn all importations of contract labor, made with a view of reducing to starvation wages the workingmen of this country, and demand laws for its prevention.

8. We insist upon a constitutional amendment reducing the terms of United States Senators.

9. We demand such rules for the government of Congress as shall place all representatives of the people upon an equal footing, and take away from committees a veto-power greater than that of the President.

10. The question as to the amount of duties to be levied upon various articles of import has been agitated and quarreled over, and has divided communities for nearly a hundred years. It is not now and never will be settled unless by the abolition of indirect taxation. It is a convenient issue—always raised when the people are excited over abuses in their midst. While we favor a wise revision of the tariff laws, with a view to raising a revenue from the luxuries rather than necessaries, we insist that as an economic question its importance is insignificant as compared with financial issues; for, whereas we have suffered our worst panics under low and also under high tariff, we have never suffered from a panic or seen our factories or workshops closed while the volume of money in

circulation was adequate to the needs of commerce. Give our farmers and manufacturers money as cheap as you now give it to our bankers, and they can pay high wages to labor and compete with all the world.

11. For the purpose of testing the sense of the people upon the subject, we are in favor of submitting to the people an amendment to the Constitution in favor of suffrage, regardless of sex, and also on the subject of the liquor-traffic.

12. All disabled soldiers of the late war should be equitably pensioned, and we denounce the policy of keeping a small army of office-holders, whose only business is to prevent, on technical grounds, deserving soldiers from obtaining justice from the government they helped to save.

13. As our name indicates, we are a National Party, knowing no East, no West, no North, no South. Having no sectional prejudices, we can properly place in nomination for the high offices of state, as candidates, men from any section of the Union.

14. We appeal to all people who believe in our principles, to aid us by voice, pen, and votes.

AMERICAN PROHIBITION NATIONAL CONVENTION.

Chicago, Ill., June 19, 1884.

Chairman, J. L. BARLOW,
of Connecticut.

NOMINATED—

For President, **Samuel C. Pomeroy,**
of Kansas.

For Vice-President, **John A. Conant,**
of Connecticut.

This was not a representative body, but rather a mass convention of the whole party. They made the above-mentioned nominations and adopted the following platform:—

American Prohibition National Platform.

We hold:

1. That ours is a Christian, and not a heathen nation, and that the God of the Christian Scriptures is the author of civil government.

2. That the Bible should be associated with books of science and literature in all our educational institutions.

3. That God requires and man needs a Sabbath.

4. That we demand the prohibition of the importation, manufacture, and sale of intoxicating drinks.

5. That the charters of all secret lodges granted by our federal and state legislatures should be withdrawn and their oaths prohibited by law.

6. We are opposed to putting prison labor, or depreciated contract labor from foreign countries, in competition with free labor, to benefit manufacturers, corporations, and speculators.

7. We are in favor of a thorough revision and enforcement of the law concerning patents and inventions, for the prevention and punishment of frauds either upon inventors or the general public.

8. We hold to and will vote for woman suffrage.

9. We hold that the civil equality secured to all American citizens by Articles 13, 14, and 15 of our amended national Constitution should be preserved inviolate, and the same equality should be extended to Indians and Chinamen.

10. That international differences should be settled by arbitration.

11. That land and other monopolies should be discouraged.

12. That the general government should furnish the people with an ample and sound currency.

13. That it should be the settled policy of the government to reduce the tariffs and taxes as rapidly as the necessities of revenue and vested business interests will allow.

14. That polygamy should be immediately suppressed by law, and that the Republican party is censurable for its long neglect of its duty in respect to this evil.

15. And, finally, we demand for the American people the abolition of electoral colleges, and a direct vote for President and Vice-President of the United States.

NATIONAL PROHIBITION CONVENTION.

Pittsburgh, Pa., July 23, 1884.

Chairman pro tem., WILLIAM DANIEL,
of Maryland.

Chairman, SAMUEL DICKIE,
of Michigan.

NOMINATED—

For President, **John P. St. John,**
of Kansas.

For Vice-President, **William Daniel,**
of Maryland.

The convention adopted a platform and unanimously nominated the candidates above mentioned. The following is the platform as adopted:—

NATIONAL PROHIBITION PLATFORM.

The Prohibition Home Protection party, in national convention assembled, acknowledge Almighty God as the rightful Sovereign of all men, from Whom the first powers of government are derived, and to Whose laws human enactments should conform; and that peace, prosperity, and happiness only can come to the people when the laws of their national and state governments are in accord with the Divine Will.

That the importation, manufacture, supply, and sale of alcoholic beverages, created and maintained by the laws of the national and state governments, during the entire history of such laws is everywhere shown to be the promoting cause of intemperance, with resulting crime and pauperism; making large demands upon public and private charity; imposing large and unjust taxation and public burdens for penal and sheltering institutions upon thrift, industry, manufactures, and commerce; endangering the public peace; causing desecration of the Sabbath; corrupting our politics, legislation, and administration of the laws; shortening lives, impairing health, and diminishing productive industry; causing education to be neglected and despised; nullifying the teachings of the Bible, the church, and the school, the standards and guides of our fathers and their children in the founding and growth, under God, of our widely extended country; and while imperilling the perpetuity of our civil and religious liberty, are baleful fruits by which we know that these laws are alike contrary to God's laws and contravene our happiness; and we call upon our fellow citizens to aid in the repeal of these laws and in the legal suppression of this baneful liquor-traffic.

The fact that during the twenty-four years in which the Republican party has controlled the general government and that of many of the states, no effort has been made to change this policy; that territories have been created from the national domain and governments for them established, and states from them admitted into the Union, in no instance in either of which has this traffic been forbidden, or the people of these territories or states been permitted to prohibit it; that there are now over two hundred thousand distilleries, breweries, wholesale and retail dealers in these drinks, holding certificates and claiming the authority of government for the continuation of a business which is so destructive to the moral and material welfare of the people; together with the fact that they have turned a deaf ear to remonstrance and petition for the correction of this abuse of civil government,—is conclusive that the Republican party is insensible to or impotent for the redress of those wrongs, and should no longer be intrusted with the powers and responsibilities of government; that, although this party in its late national convention was silent on the liquor question, not so its candidates, Messrs. Blaine and Logan. Within the year past Mr. Blaine has publicly recommended that the revenues derived from the liquor-traffic shall be distributed among the states, and Senator Logan has by a bill proposed to devote these revenues to the support of the schools. Thus both virtually recommend the perpetuation of the traffic, and that the state and its citizens shall become partners in the liquor crime.

The fact that the Democratic party has in its national deliverance of party policy arrayed itself on the side of the drink-makers and sellers, by declaring against the policy of prohibition of such traffic under the false name of "Sumptuary Laws," and, when in power in some of the states, in refusing remedial legislation, and in Congress of refusing to permit the creation of a board of inquiry to investigate and report upon the effects of this traffic, proves that the Democratic party should not be intrusted with power or place.

That there can be no greater peril to the nation than the existing competition of the Republican and Democratic parties for the liquor vote, experience shows that any party not openly opposed to the traffic will engage in this competition, will court the favor of the criminal classes, will barter away the public morals, the purity of the ballot, and every trust and object of good government for party success; and patriots and good citizens should find in this practice sufficient cause for immediate withdrawal from all connection with their party.

That we favor reforms in the administration of the government; in the abolition of all sinecures, useless offices and officers; in the election of the post-office officials of the government, instead of appointment by the President; that competency, honesty, and sobriety are essential qualifications for holding civil office; and we oppose the removal of such persons from mere administrative offices, except so far as it may be absolutely necessary to secure effectiveness to the vital issues on which the general administration of the government has been intrusted to a party; that the collection of revenues from alcohol, liquors, and tobacco should be abolished, as the vices of men are not a proper subject for taxation; that revenues for customs duties should be levied for the support of the government, economically administered; and, when so levied, the fostering of American labor, manufactures, and industries should constantly be held in view; that the public land should be held for homes for the people, and not for gifts to corporations, or to be held in large bodies for speculation upon the needs of actual settlers.

That all money, coin, and paper, shall be made, issued, and regulated by the general government, and shall be a legal tender for all debts, public and private.

That grateful care and support should be given to our soldiers and sailors, their dependent widows and orphans, disabled in the service of the country.

That we repudiate as un-American, contrary to and subversive of the principles of the Declaration of Independence, from which our government has grown to be the government of fifty-five millions of people, and a recognized power among the nations, that any person or people shall or may be excluded from residence or citizenship with all others who may desire the benefits which our institutions confer upon the oppressed of all nations.

That while there are important reforms that are demanded for purity of administration and the welfare of the people, their importance sinks into insignificance when compared with the reform of the drink-traffic, which annually wastes $800,-000,000 of the wealth created by toil and thrift, and drags down thousands of families from comfort to poverty; which fills jails, penitentiaries, insane asylums, hospitals, and institutions for dependency; which destroys the health, saps industry, and causes loss of life and property to thousands in the land; lowers intellectual and physical vigor, dulls the cunning hand of the artisan, is the chief cause of bankruptcy, insolvency and loss in trade, and by its corrupting power endangers the perpetuity of free institutions.

That Congress should exercise its undoubted power, and prohibit the manufacture and sale of intoxicating beverages in the District of Columbia, the territories of the United States, in all places over which the government has exclusive jurisdiction; that hereafter no state shall be admitted into the Union until its constitution shall expressly prohibit polygamy and the manufacture and sale of intoxicating beverages.

We earnestly call the attention of the laborer and the mechanic, the miner and manufacturer, and ask investigation of the baneful effects upon labor and industry caused by the needless liquor business, which will be found the robber who lessens wages and profits, the destroyer of the happiness and family welfare of the laboring man; and that labor and all legitimate industry demand deliverance from the taxation and loss which this traffic imposes; and that no tariff or other legislation can so healthily stimulate production, or increase a demand for capital and labor, or produce so much of comfort and content, as the suppressing of this traffic would bring to the laboring man, mechanic, or employer of labor, throughout our land.

That the activity and co-operation of the women of America for the promotion of temperance has, in all the history of the past, been a strength and encouragement, which we gratefully acknowledge and record. In the later and present phase of the movement for the prohibition of the licensed traffic by the abolition of the drink saloon, the purity of purpose and method, the earnestness, zeal, intelligence and devotion, of the mothers and daughters of the Woman's Christian Temperance Union, has been eminently blessed by God. Kansas and Iowa have been given her as "sheaves of rejoicing," and the education and arousing of the public mind, and the demand for constitutional amendment now prevailing, are largely the fruit of her prayers and labors, and we rejoice to have our Christian women unite with us in sharing the labor that shall bring the abolition of this traffic to the polls. She shall join in the grand "Praise God, from Whom all blessings flow," when by law our boys and friends shall be free from legal drink and temptation.

That we believe in the civil and political equality of the sexes, and that the ballot in the hand of woman is a right for her protection, and would prove a powerful ally for the abolition of the drink saloon, the execution of law, the promotion of reform in civil affairs, and the removal of corruption in public life; and thus believing, we relegate the practical outworking of this reform to the discretion of the Prohibition party in the several states, according to the condition of public sentiment in those states. That, gratefully, we acknowledge and praise God for the presence of His Spirit, guiding our counsels and granting the success which has been vouchsafed in the progress of temperance reform; and, looking to Him from Whom all wisdom and help come, we ask the voters of the United States to make the principles of the above declaration a ruling principle in the government of the nation and of the states.

Resolved, That henceforth the Prohibition Home Protection party shall be called by the name of "The Prohibition Party."

ANTI-MONOPOLY CONVENTION.

Chicago, Ill., May 14, 1884.

Chairman pro tem., ALSON J. STREETER, of Illinois.

Chairman, JOHN F. HENRY.

NOMINATED—

For President, **Benjamin F. Butler**, of Massachusetts.

For Vice-President, **Alanson M. West**, of Mississippi.

Representatives from seventeen states and the District of Columbia participated in the proceedings of this convention. General Benjamin F. Butler, of Massachusetts, was nominated as a candidate for President on the first ballot; but no candidate for Vice-President was presented, and so the national committee afterward named General Alanson M. West, of Mississippi.

The following platform was adopted:—

ANTI-MONOPOLY PLATFORM.

The Anti-Monopoly organization of the United States, in convention assembled, declares:—

1. That labor and capital should be allies; and we demand justice for both, by protecting the rights of all against privileges for the few.

2. That corporations, the creatures of law, should be controlled by law.

3. That we propose the greatest reduction practicable in public expenses.

4. That in the enactment and vigorous execution of just laws, equality of rights, equality of burdens, equality of privileges, and equality of powers in all citizens will be secured. To this end, we declare:—

5. That it is the duty of the government to immediately exercise its constitutional prerogative to regulate commerce among the states. The great instruments by which this commerce is carried on are transportation, money, and the transmission of intelligence. They are now mercilessly controlled by giant monopolies, to the impoverishment of labor, the crushing out of healthful competition, and the destruction of business security. We hold it, therefore, to be the imperative and immediate duty of Congress, to pass all needful laws for the control and regulation of those great agents of commerce, in accordance with the oft-repeated decisions of the Supreme Court of the United States.

6. That these monopolies, which have exacted from enterprise such heavy tribute, have also inflicted countless wrongs

upon the toiling millions of the United States; and no system of reform should commend itself to the support of the people which does not protect the man who earns his bread by the sweat of his face. Bureaus of labor-statistics must be established, both state and national; arbitration take the place of brute force in the settlement of disputes between employer and employed; the national eight-hour law be honestly enforced; the importation of foreign labor under contract be made illegal; and whatever practical reforms may be necessary for the protection of united labor must be granted, to the end that unto the toiler shall be given that proportion of the profits of the thing or value created which his labor bears to the cost of production.

7. That we approve and favor the passage of an interstate commerce bill. Navigable waters should be improved by the government, and be free.

8. We demand the payment of the bonded debt as it falls due; the election of United States Senators by the direct vote of the people of their respective states; a graduated income-tax; and a tariff, which is a tax upon the people, that shall be so levied as to bear as lightly as possible upon necessaries. We denounce the present tariff as being largely in the interest of monopoly, and demand that it be speedily and radically reformed in the interest of labor, instead of capital.

9. That no further grants of public lands shall be made to corporations. All enactments granting lands to corporations should be strictly construed; and all land-grants should be forfeited, where the terms upon which the grants were made have not been strictly complied with. The lands must be held for homes for actual settlers, and must not be subject to purchase or control by non-resident foreigners or other speculators.

10. That we deprecate the discrimination of American legislation against the greatest of American industries—agriculture—by which it has been deprived of nearly all beneficial legislation, while forced to bear the brunt of taxation; and we demand for it the fostering care of government, and the just recognition of its importance in the development and advancement of our land; and we appeal to the American farmer to co-operate with us in our endeavors to advance the national interests of the country and the overthrow of monopoly in every shape, whenever and wherever found.

EQUAL (OR WOMAN'S) RIGHTS CONVENTION.

San Francisco, Cal., September 20, 1884.

Chairman, MRS. MARIETTA L. STOW,
of California.

NOMINATED—

For President, **Mrs. Belva A. Lockwood,**
of District of Columbia.

For Vice-President, **Mrs. Marietta L. Stow,**
of California.

The convention made the above-named nominations and adopted the following platform:—

EQUAL RIGHTS PLATFORM.

1. We pledge ourselves, if elected to power, so far as in us lies to do equal and exact justice to every class of our citizens, without distinction of color, sex, or nationality.

2. We shall recommend that the laws of the several states be so amended that women will be recognized as voters, and their property-rights made equal with that of the male population, to the end that they may become self-supporting rather than a dependent class.

3. It will be our earnest endeavor to revive the now lagging industries of the country by encouraging and strengthening our commercial relations with other countries, especially with the Central and South American States, whose wealth of productions are now largely diverted to England and other European countries, for lack of well-established steamship lines and railroad communications between these countries and our own; encourage exports by an effort to create a demand for our home productions; and to this end we deem that a moderate tariff—sufficient to protect the laboring classes, but not so high as to keep our goods out of the market—as most likely to conserve the best interests of our whole people. That is to

say, we shall avoid as much as possible a high protective tariff on the one hand, and free trade on the other. We shall also endeavor, by all laudable means, to increase the wages of laboring men and women. Our protective system will be most earnestly exerted to protect the commonwealth of the country from venality and corruption in high places.

4. It will be our earnest effort to see that the solemn contract made with the soldiers of the country on enlistment into the United States service—viz.: that if disabled therein they should be pensioned—strictly carried out; and that without unnecessary expense and delay to them; and a re-enactment of the Arrears Act.

5. We shall discountenance by every legal means the liquor-traffic, because its tendency is to demoralize the youth of the land, to lower the standard of morality among the people; and we do not believe that the revenue derived from it would feed and clothe the paupers that it makes, and the money expended on its account in the courts, workhouses, and prisons.

6. We believe that the only solution of the Indian question is, to break up all of their small principalities and chieftainships, that have ever presented the anomaly of small kingdoms scattered through a republic, and ever liable to break out in some unexpected locality, and which have been hitherto maintained at such great expense to the government, and treat the Indian like a rational human being, as we have the negro—make him a citizen, amenable to the laws, and let him manage his own private affairs.

7. That it is but just that every protection granted to citizens of the United States by birth should also be secured to the citizens of the United States by adoption.

8. We shall continue gradually to pay the public debt and to refund the balance, but not in such manner as to curtail the circulating medium of the country, so as to embarrass trade; but pledge ourselves that every dollar shall be paid in good time.

9. We oppose monopoly, the tendency of which is to make the rich richer, and the poor poorer, as opposed to the genius and welfare of republican institutions.

10. We shall endeavor to aid in every laudable way the work of educating the masses of the people, not only in book knowledge, but in physical, moral, and social culture, in such a manner as will tend to elevate the standard of American man-

hood and womanhood—that the individual may receive the highest possible development.

11. We recommend a uniform system of laws for the several states as desirable, as far as practicable; and especially the laws relating to the descent of property, marriage and divorce, and the limitation of contracts.

12. We will endeavor to maintain the peaceable relations which now exist between the various sections of our vast country, and strive to enter into a compact of peace with the other American as well as the European nations, in order that the peace which we now enjoy may become perpetual. We believe that war is a relic of barbarism belonging to the past, and should only be resorted to in the direst extremity.

13. That the dangers of a solid South or a solid North shall be averted by a strict regard to the interests of every section of the country, a fair distribution of public offices, and such a distribution of the public funds, for the increase of the facilities of inter-commercial relations, as will restore the South to her former industrial prestige, develop the exhaustless resources of the West, foster the iron, coal, and woolen interests of the Middle States, and revive the manufactures of the East.

14. We shall foster civil service, believing that a true civil-service reform, honestly and candidly administered, will lift us out of the imputation of having become a nation of office-seekers, and have a tendency to develop in candidates for office an earnest desire to make themselves worthy and capable of performing the duties of the office that they desire to fill; and, in order to make the reform a permanent one, recommend that it be engrafted into the Constitution of the United States.

15. It will be the policy of the Equal Rights party to see that the residue of the public domain is parceled out to actual settlers only, that the honest yeomanry of the land, and especially those who have fought to preserve it, shall enjoy its benefits.

The election occurred on November 4, 1884.

THIRTY-EIGHT STATES VOTED.

POPULAR VOTE.

STATES.	Grover Cleveland, Democrat.	James G. Blaine, Republican.	Benjamin F. Butler, Greenbacker.	John P. St. John, Prohibitionist.	Total vote.
Alabama	93,951	59,591	873	612	155,027
Arkansas	72,927	50,895	1,847	....	125,669
California	89,288	102,416	2,017	2,920	196,641
Colorado	27,723	36,290	1,953	761	66,727
Connecticut	67,199	65,923	1,688	2,305	137,115
Delaware	16,964	12,951	6	55	29,976
Florida	31,766	28,031	....	72	59,869
Georgia	94,667	48,603	145	195	143,610
Illinois	312,355	337,474	10,910	12,074	672,813
Indiana	244,990	238,463	8,293	3,028	494,774
Iowa	177,316	197,089	....	1,472	375,877
Kansas	90,132	154,406	16,341	4,495	265,374
Kentucky	152,961	118,122	1,691	3,139	275,913
Louisiana	62,540	46,347	....	....	108,887
Maine	52,140	72,209	3,953	2,160	130,462
Maryland	96,932	85,699	531	2,794	185,956
Massachusetts	122,481	146,724	24,433	10,026	303,664
Michigan	149,835	192,669	42,243	18,403	403,150
Minnesota	70,144	111,923	3,583	4,684	190,334
Mississippi	76,510	43,509	....	....	120,019
Missouri	235,988	202,929	....	2,153	441,070
Nebraska	54,391	79,912	....	2,899	137,202
Nevada	5,578	7,193	26	....	12,797
New Hampshire	39,183	43,249	552	1,571	84,555
New Jersey	127,798	123,440	3,496	6,159	260,893
New York	563,154	562,005	16,994	25,016	1,167,169
North Carolina	142,952	125,068	....	454	268,474
Ohio	368,280	400,082	5,179	11,069	784,610
Oregon	24,604	26,860	726	492	52,682
Pennsylvania	392,785	473,804	16,992	15,283	898,864
Rhode Island	12,391	19,030	422	928	32,771
South Carolina	69,890	21,733	....	....	91,623
Tennessee	133,258	124,078	957	1,131	259,424
Texas	225,309	93,141	3,321	3,534	325,305
Vermont	17,331	39,514	785	1,752	59,382
Virginia	185,497	139,356	....	138	324,991
West Virginia	67,317	63,096	810	939	132,162
Wisconsin	146,459	161,157	4,598	7,656	319,870
Total	4,914,986	4,854,981	175,365	150,369	10,095,701

ELECTORAL VOTE.

Counted on February 11, 1885.

STATES.	PRESIDENT.		VICE-PRESIDENT.		Number entitled to vote.
	Grover Cleveland, of New York.	James G. Blaine, of Maine.	Thomas A. Hendricks, of Indiana.	John A. Logan, of Illinois.	
Alabama	10	..	10	..	10
Arkansas	7	..	7	..	7
California	..	8	..	8	8
Colorado	..	3	..	3	3
Connecticut	6	..	6	..	6
Delaware	3	..	3	..	3
Florida	4	..	4	..	4
Georgia	12	..	12	..	12
Illinois	..	22	..	22	22
Indiana	15	..	15	..	15
Iowa	..	13	..	13	13
Kansas	..	9	..	9	9
Kentucky	13	..	13	..	13
Louisiana	8	..	8	..	8
Maine	..	6	..	6	6
Maryland	8	..	8	..	8
Massachusetts	..	14	..	14	14
Michigan	..	13	..	13	13
Minnesota	..	7	..	7	7
Mississippi	9	..	9	..	9
Missouri	16	..	16	..	16
Nebraska	..	5	..	5	5
Nevada	..	3	..	3	3
New Hampshire	..	4	..	4	4
New Jersey	9	..	9	..	9
New York	36	..	36	..	36
North Carolina	11	..	11	..	11
Ohio	..	23	..	23	23
Oregon	..	3	..	3	3
Pennsylvania	..	30	..	30	30
Rhode Island	..	4	..	4	4
South Carolina	9	..	9	..	9
Tennessee	12	..	12	..	12
Texas	13	..	13	..	13
Vermont	..	4	..	4	4
Virginia	12	..	12	..	12
West Virginia	6	..	6	..	6
Wisconsin	..	11	..	11	11
Total	219	182	219	182	401

Grover Cleveland was elected President and Thomas A. Hendricks as Vice-President.

During this period Congress was divided politically as follows:

Forty-ninth Congress.

Senate— 34 Democrats, 41 Republicans, 1 vacancy .....Total, 76
House—182 Democrats, 140 Republicans, 2 Nationals, 1 vacancy .... " 325

Fiftieth Congress.

Senate— 37 Democrats, 39 Republicans ....Total, 76
House—170 Democrats, 151 Republicans, 1 Independent, 3 Laborites .... " 325

Election of 1888

Democratic National Committee:

Chairman, CALVIN S. BRICE, of Ohio.
Secretary, SIMON P. SHEERIN, of Indiana.

DEMOCRATIC CONVENTION.

St. Louis, Mo., June 5, 1888.

Chairman pro tem., S. M. WHITE, of California.

Chairman, PATRICK A. COLLINS, of Massachusetts.

NOMINATED—

For President, **Grover Cleveland,** of New York.

For Vice-President, **Allen G. Thurman,** of Ohio.

Forty-eight years had passed since a candidate for President had been nominated by a Democratic convention by acclamation. At this convention Grover Cleveland was nominated for a second term, by resolution, without opposition.

For Vice-President, Allen G. Thurman, of Ohio, was nominated on the first ballot, receiving 690 votes. Votes were also cast for Isaac P. Gray, of Indiana (105), and for John C. Black, of Illinois (25).

The convention adopted the following platform:—

DEMOCRATIC PLATFORM.

The Democratic party of the United States, in national convention assembled, renews the pledge of its fidelity to Democratic faith, and reaffirms the platform adopted by its representatives at the convention of 1884, and indorses the views expressed by President Cleveland in his last earnest message to Congress as the correct interpretation of that platform upon the question of tariff reduction; and also indorses the efforts of our Democratic representatives in Congress to secure a reduction of excessive taxation.

MAINTENANCE OF THE UNION.

Chief among its principles of party faith are the maintenance of an indissoluble union of free and indestructible states, now about to enter upon its second century of unexampled progress and renown; devotion to a plan of government regulated by a written constitution, strictly specifying every granted power and expressly reserving to the states or people the entire ungranted residue of power; the encouragement of a jealous popular vigilance, directed to all who have been chosen for brief terms to enact and execute the laws, and are charged with the duty of preserving peace, insuring equality, and establishing justice.

PLEDGES REDEEMED.

The Democratic party welcomes an exacting scrutiny of the administration of the executive power, which four years ago was committed to its trust in the selection of Grover Cleveland as President of the United States; but it challenges the most searching scrutiny concerning its fidelity and devotion to the pledges which then invited the suffrages of the people. During a most critical period of our financial affairs, resulting from over-taxation, the anomalous condition of our currency, and a public debt unmatured, it has, by the adoption of a wise and conservative course, not only averted disaster, but greatly promoted the prosperity of the people.

HOMES FOR THE PEOPLE.

It has reversed the improvident and unwise policy of the Republican party touching the public domain, and has reclaimed from corporations and syndicates, alien and domestic, and restored to the people, nearly 100,000,000 acres of valuable land, to be sacredly held as homesteads for our citizens.

PENSIONS FOR THE SOLDIERS.

While carefully guarding the interests of the taxpayers and conforming strictly to the principles of justice and equity, it has paid out more for pensions and bounties to the soldiers and sailors of the republic than was ever paid before during an equal period.

FOREIGN POLICY.

It has adopted and consistently pursued a firm and prudent foreign policy, preserving peace with all nations, while scrupulously maintaining all the rights and interests of our own government and people, at home and abroad. The exclusion from our shores of Chinese laborers has been effectually secured under the provisions of a treaty, the operation of which has been postponed by the action of a Republican majority in the Senate.

CIVIL-SERVICE REFORM.

Honest reform in the civil service has been inaugurated and maintained by President Cleveland, and he has brought the public service to the highest standard of efficiency, not only by rule and precept, but by the example of his own untiring and unselfish administration of public affairs.

RIGHTS OF THE PEOPLE.

In every branch and department of the government under Democratic control, the rights and the welfare of all the people have been guarded and defended; every public interest has been protected, and the equality of all our citizens before the law, without regard to race or color, has been steadfastly maintained. Upon its record, thus exhibited, and upon the pledge of a continuance to the people of these benefits, the Democracy invokes a renewal of popular trust by the re-election of a Chief Magistrate who has been faithful, able, and prudent. We invoke, in addition to that trust, the transfer also to the Democracy of the entire legislative power.

TAXATION.

The Republican party, controlling the Senate and resisting in both Houses of Congress a reformation of unjust and unequal tax laws which have outlasted the necessities of war, and are now undermining the abundance of a long peace, denies to the people equality before the law and the fairness and the justice which are their right. Thus the cry of American labor for a better share in the rewards of industry is stifled with false pretenses, enterprise is fettered and bound down to home markets, capital is discouraged with doubt, and unequal, unjust laws can neither be properly amended nor repealed. The Democratic party will continue, with all the power confided to it, the struggle to reform these laws in accordance with the pledges of its last platform, indorsed at the ballot-box by the suffrages of the people.

Of all the industrious freemen of our land, the immense majority, including every tiller of the soil, gain no advantage from excessive tax laws, but the price of nearly everything they buy is increased by the favoritism of an unequal system of tax legislation. All unnecessary taxation is unjust taxation. It is repugnant to the creed of Democracy that by such taxation the cost of the necessaries of life should be unjustifiably increased to all our people. Judged by Democratic principles, the interests of the people are betrayed when, by unnecessary taxation, trusts and combinations are permitted to exist, which, while unduly enriching the few that combine, rob the body of our citizens by depriving them of the benefits of natural competition.

NATIONAL SURPLUS.

Every Democratic rule of governmental action is violated when, through unnecessary taxation, a vast sum of money, far beyond the needs of an economical administration, is drawn from the people and the channels of trade and accumulated as a demoralizing surplus in the National Treasury. The money now lying idle in the general treasury, resulting from superfluous taxation, amounts to more than one hundred and twenty-five millions, and the surplus collected is reaching the sum of more than sixty millions annually. Debauched by this immense temptation, the remedy of the Republican party is to meet and exhaust, by extravagant appropriations and expenses, whether constitutional or not, the accumulation of extravagant taxation. The Democratic policy is to enforce frugality in public expense and to abolish unnecessary taxation.

TARIFF REFORM.

Our established domestic industries and enterprises should not and need not be endangered by the reduction and correction of the burdens of taxation. On the contrary, a fair and careful revision of our tax laws, with due allowance for the difference between the wages of American and foreign labor, most promote and encourage every branch of such industries and enterprises, by giving them assurance of an extended market and steady and continuous operations. In the interests of American labor, which should in no event be neglected, the revision of our tax laws contemplated by the Democratic party should promote the advantage of such labor, by cheapening the cost of necessaries of life in the home of every workingman, and at the same time securing to him steady and remunerative employment. Upon this question of tariff reform, so closely concerning every phase of our national life, and upon every question involved in the problem of good government, the Democratic party submits its principles and professions to the intelligent suffrages of the American people.

REDUCTION OF REVENUE.

Resolution presented by Mr. Scott, of Pennsylvania:

Resolved, That this convention hereby indorses and recommends the early passage of the bill for the reduction of the revenue now pending in the House of Representatives.

ADMITTANCE OF TERRITORIES.

Resolution presented by Mr. Lehmann, of Iowa:

Resolved, That a just and liberal policy should be pursued in reference to the territories; that right of self-government is inherent in the people and guaranteed under the Constitution; that the Territories of Washington, Dakota, Montana, and New Mexico are, by virtue of population and development, entitled to admission into the Union as states, and we unqualifiedly condemn the course of the Republican party in refusing statehood and self-government to their people.

FOREIGN SELF-GOVERNMENT.

Resolution presented by ex-Governor Leon Abbett, of New Jersey:

Resolved, That we express our cordial sympathy with the struggling people of all nations in their efforts to secure for themselves the inestimable blessings of self-government and civil and religious liberty, and we especially declare our sympathy with the efforts of those noble patriots who, led by Gladstone and Parnell, have conducted their grand and peaceful contest for home rule in Ireland.

Republican National Committee:

Chairman, M. S. QUAY, of Pennsylvania.
Secretary, J. SLOAT FASSETT, of New York.

In 1891 Mr. Quay resigned, and JAMES S. CLARKSON, of Iowa, was chosen Chairman.

REPUBLICAN CONVENTION.

Chicago, Ill., June 19, 1888.

Chairman pro tem., JOHN M. THURSTON,
of Nebraska.

Chairman, M. M. ESTEE,
of California.

NOMINATED—

For President, **Benjamin Harrison,**
of Indiana.

For Vice-President, **Levi P. Morton,**
of New York.

The session of this convention was one of the longest in the history of the country having lasted for six days. From among the large number of candidates for President, Benjamin Harrison was chosen on the eighth ballot. The following is the vote in detail:

CANDIDATES.	1st.	2d.	3d.	4th.	5th.	6th.	7th.	8th.
JOHN SHERMAN, of Ohio	229	249	244	235	224	244	231	118
WALTER Q. GRESHAM, of Indiana	111	108	123	98	87	91	91	59
CHAUNCEY M. DEPEW, of New York	99	99	91	..	..	..	..	..
RUSSEL A. ALGER, of Michigan	84	116	122	135	142	137	120	100
BENJAMIN HARRISON, of Indiana	80	91	94	217	213	231	278	544
WILLIAM B. ALLISON, of Iowa	72	75	88	88	99	73	76	..
JAMES G. BLAINE, of Maine	35	33	35	42	48	40	15	5
JOHN J. INGALLS, of Kansas	28	16	..	..	..	..	..	..
JEREMIAH M. RUSK, of Wisconsin	25	20	16	..	..	..	..	..
WILLIAM W. PHELPS, of New Jersey	25	18	5	..	..	..	..	..
E. H. FITLER, of Pennsylvania	24	..	..	..	..	..	..	..
JOSEPH R. HAWLEY, of Connecticut	13	..	..	..	..	..	..	..
ROBERT T. LINCOLN, of Illinois	3	2	2	1	..	..	2	..
WILLIAM MCKINLEY, JR., of Ohio	2	3	8	11	14	12	16	4
SAMUEL F. MILLER, of Iowa	..	..	2	..	..	..	..	..
FREDERICK DOUGLASS, of District of Columbia	..	..	..	1	..	..	..	..
JOSEPH B. FORAKER, of Ohio	..	..	..	1	..	1	1	..
FREDERICK D. GRANT, of New York	..	..	..	..	..	1	..	..
CREED HAYMOND, of California	..	..	..	..	..	..	1	..
Whole number of votes	830	830	830	829	827	830	831	830
Necessary to a choice	416	416	416	415	414	416	416	416

For Vice-President, Levi P. Morton, of New York, was nominated on the first ballot, receiving 591 votes. Votes were also cast for other candidates, as follows: William Walter Phelps, of New Jersey, 119; William O. Bradley, of Kentucky, 103; Blanche K. Bruce, of Mississippi, 11; and Walter F. Thomas, of Texas, 1.

The following is the platform as adopted:—

REPUBLICAN PLATFORM.

The Republicans of the United States, assembled by their delegates in national convention, pause on the threshold of their proceedings to honor the memory of their first great leader, the immortal champion of liberty and the rights of the people—Abraham Lincoln;—and to cover also with wreaths of imperishable remembrance and gratitude the heroic names of our later leaders, who have more recently been called away from our councils—Grant, Garfield, Arthur, Logan, Conkling. May their memories be faithfully cherished. We also recall, with our greetings and with prayer for his recovery, the name of one of our living heroes, whose memory will be treasured in the history both of Republicans and of the republic—the name of that noble soldier and favorite child of victory, Philip H. Sheridan.

In the spirit of those great leaders, and of our own devotion to human liberty, and with that hostility to all forms of despotism and oppression which is the fundamental idea of the Republican party, we send fraternal congratulations to our fellow-Americans of Brazil upon their great act of emancipation, which completed the abolition of slavery throughout the two American continents. We earnestly hope that we may soon congratulate our fellow-citizens of Irish birth upon the peaceful recovery of home rule for Ireland.

FREE SUFFRAGE.

We reaffirm our unswerving devotion to the national Constitution and to the indissoluble union of the states; to the autonomy reserved to the states under the Constitution; to the personal rights and liberties of citizens in all the states and territories in the Union, and especially to the supreme and sovereign right of every lawful citizen, rich or poor, native or foreign-born, white or black, to cast one free ballot in public elections and to have that ballot duly counted. We hold the free and honest popular ballot and the just and equal representation of all the people to be the foundation of our republican government, and demand effective legislation to secure the integrity and purity of elections, which are the fountains of all public authority. We charge that the present administration and the Democratic majority in Congress owe their existence to the suppression of the ballot by a criminal nullification of the Constitution and laws of the United States.

PROTECTION TO AMERICAN INDUSTRIES.

We are uncompromisingly in favor of the American system of protection; we protest against its destruction as proposed by the President and his party. They serve the interests of Europe; we will support the interests of America. We accept the issue and confidently appeal to the people for their judgment. The protective system must be maintained. Its abandonment has always been followed by general disaster to all interests, except those of the usurer and the sheriff. We denounce the Mills bill as destructive to the general business, the labor, and the farming interests of the country, and we heartily indorse the consistent and patriotic action of the Republican representatives in Congress in opposing its passage.

DUTIES ON WOOL.

We condemn the proposition of the Democratic party to place wool on the free list, and we insist that the duties thereon shall be adjusted and maintained so as to furnish full and adequate protection to that industry.

THE INTERNAL REVENUE.

The Republican party would effect all needed reduction of the national revenue by repealing the taxes upon tobacco, which are an annoyance and burden to agriculture, and the tax upon spirits used in the arts and for mechanical purposes, and by such revision of the tariff laws as will tend to check imports of such articles as are produced by our people, the production of which gives employment to our labor, and release from import duties those articles of foreign production (except luxuries) the like of which cannot be produced at home. If there shall still remain a larger revenue than is requisite for the wants of the government, we favor the entire repeal of internal taxes rather than the surrender of any part of our protective system, at the joint behests of the whiskey trusts and the agents of foreign manufacturers.

FOREIGN CONTRACT LABOR.

We declare our hostility to the introduction into this country of foreign contract labor and of Chinese labor, alien to our civilization and our Constitution, and we demand the rigid enforcement of the existing laws against it, and favor such immediate legislation as will exclude such labor from our shores.

COMBINATIONS OF CAPITAL.

We declare our opposition to all combinations of capital, organized in trusts or otherwise, to control arbitrarily the condition of trade among our citizens; and we recommend to Congress and the state legislatures, in their respective jurisdictions, such legislation as will prevent the execution of all schemes to oppress the people by undue charges on their supplies, or by unjust rates for the transportation of their products to market. We approve the legislation by Congress to prevent alike unjust burdens and unfair discriminations between the states.

HOMES FOR THE PEOPLE.

We reaffirm the policy of appropriating the public lands of the United States to be homesteads for American citizens and settlers, not aliens, which the Republican party established in 1862, against the persistent opposition of the Democrats in Congress, and which has brought our great Western domain into such magnificent development. The restoration of unearned railroad land-grants to the public domain for the use of actual settlers, which was begun under the administration of President Arthur, should be continued. We deny that the Democratic party has ever restored one acre to the people, but declare that by the joint action of the Republicans and Democrats about 50,000,000 of acres of unearned lands originally granted for the construction of railroads have been restored to the public domain, in pursuance of the conditions inserted by the Republican party in the original grants. We charge the Democratic administration with failure to execute the laws securing to settlers title to their homesteads, and with using appropriations made for that purpose to harass innocent settlers with spies and prosecutions, under the false pretense of exposing frauds and vindicating the law.

HOME RULE IN TERRITORIES.

The government by Congress of the territories is based upon necessity only, to the end that they may become states in the Union; therefore, whenever the conditions of population, material resources, public intelligence and morality are such as to insure a stable local government therein, the people of such territories should be permitted, as a right inherent in them, the right to form for themselves constitutions and state governments, and be admitted into the Union. Pending the preparation for statehood, all officers thereof should be selected from the *bona fide* residents and citizens of the territory wherein they are to serve.

ADMITTANCE OF SOUTH DAKOTA.

South Dakota should of right be immediately admitted as a state in the Union, under the constitution framed and adopted by her people, and we heartily indorse the action of the Republican Senate in twice passing bills for her admission. The refusal of the Democratic House of Representatives, for partisan purposes, to favorably consider these bills, is a willful violation of the sacred American principle of local self-government, and merits the condemnation of all just men. The pending bills in the Senate for acts to enable the people of Washington, North Dakota, and Montana Territories to form constitutions and establish state governments should be passed without unnecessary delay. The Republican party pledges itself to do all in its power to facilitate the admission of the Territories of New Mexico, Wyoming, Idaho, and Arizona to the enjoyment of self-government as state—such of them as are now qualified as soon as possible, and the others as soon as they may become so.

MORMONISM.

The political power of the Mormon Church in the territories as exercised in the past is a menace to free institutions, a danger no longer to be suffered. Therefore we pledge the Republican party to appropriate legislation asserting the sovereignty of the nation in all territories where the same is questioned, and in furtherance of that end to place upon the statute-books legislation stringent enough to divorce the political from the ecclesiastical power, and thus stamp out the attendant wickedness of polygamy.

BIMETALLISM.

The Republican party is in favor of the use of both gold and silver as money, and condemns the policy of the Democratic administration in its efforts to demonetize silver.

REDUCTION OF LETTER POSTAGE.

We demand the reduction of letter postage to one cent per ounce.

FREE SCHOOLS.

In a Republic like ours, where the citizen is the sovereign and the official the servant, where no power is exercised except by the will of the people, it is important that the sovereign—

the people—should possess intelligence. The free school is the promoter of that intelligence which is to preserve us a free nation; therefore the state or nation, or both combined, should support free institutions of learning sufficient to afford to every child growing up in the land the opportunity of a good common-school education.

ARMY AND NAVY FORTIFICATIONS.

We earnestly recommend that prompt action be taken by Congress in the enactment of such legislation as will best secure the rehabilitation of our American merchant marine, and we protest against the passage by Congress of a free-ship bill, as calculated to work injustice to labor by lessening the wages of those engaged in preparing materials as well as those directly employed in our shipyards. We demand appropriations for the early rebuilding of our navy; for the construction of coast fortifications and modern ordnance, and other approved modern means of defense for the protection of our defenseless harbors and cities; for the payment of just pensions to our soldiers; for the necessary works of national importance in the improvement of harbors and the channels of internal, coastwise, and foreign commerce; for the encouragement of the shipping interests of the Atlantic, Gulf and Pacific States, as well as for the payment of the maturing public debt. This policy will give employment to our labor, activity to our various industries, increase the security of our country, promote trade, open new and direct markets for our produce, and cheapen the cost of transportation. We affirm this to be far better for our country than the Democratic policy of loaning the government's money, without interest, to "pet banks."

THE MONROE DOCTRINE.

The conduct of foreign affairs by the present administration has been distinguished by its inefficiency and its cowardice. Having withdrawn from the Senate all pending treaties effected by Republican administrations for the removal of foreign burdens and restrictions upon our commerce and for its extension into better markets, it has neither effected nor proposed any others in their stead. Professing adherence to the Monroe doctrine, it has seen, with idle complacency, the extension of foreign influence in Central America and of foreign trade everywhere among our neighbors. It has refused to charter, sanction, or encourage any American organization for constructing the Nicaragua Canal, a work of vital importance to the maintenance of the Monroe doctrine, and of our national influence in Central and South America, and necessary for the development of trade with our Pacific territory, with South America, and with the islands and farther coasts of the Pacific Ocean.

PROTECTION OF OUR FISHERIES.

We arraign the present Democratic administration for its weak and unpatriotic treatment of the fisheries question, and its pusillanimous surrender of the essential privileges to which our fishing vessels are entitled in Canadian ports under the treaty of 1818, the reciprocal maritime legislation of 1830, and the comity of nations, and which Canadian fishing vessels receive in the ports of the United States. We condemn the policy of the present administration and the Democratic majority in Congress toward our fisheries as unfriendly and conspicuously unpatriotic, and as tending to destroy a valuable national industry and an indispensable resource of defense against a foreign enemy. The name of American applies alike to all citizens of the republic, and imposes upon all alike the same obligation of obedience to the laws. At the same time that citizenship is and must be the panoply and safeguard of him who wears it, and protect him, whether high or low, rich or poor, in all his civil rights. It should and must afford him protection at home, and follow and protect him abroad, in whatever land he may be, on a lawful errand.

CIVIL-SERVICE REFORM.

The men who abandoned the Republican party in 1884 and continue to adhere to the Democratic party have deserted not only the cause of honest government, of sound finance, of freedom, of purity of the ballot, but especially have deserted the cause of reform in the civil service. We will not fail to keep our pledges because they have broken theirs, or because their candidate has broken his. We therefore repeat our declaration of 1884, to wit: "The reform of the civil service, auspiciously begun under the Republican administration, should be completed by the further extension of the reform system, already established by law, to all the grades of the service to which it is applicable. The spirit and purpose of the reform should be observed in all executive appointments, and all laws at variance with the object of existing reform legislation should be repealed, to the end that the dangers to free institutions which lurk in the power of official patronage may be wisely and effectively avoided.

PENSIONS FOR THE SOLDIERS.

The gratitude of the nation to the defenders of the Union cannot be measured by laws. The legislation of Congress should conform to the pledge made by a loyal people, and be so enlarged and extended as to provide against the possibility that any man who honorably wore the Federal uniform should become the inmate of an almshouse, or dependent upon private charity. In the presence of an overflowing treasury, it would be a public scandal to do less for those whose valorous service preserved the government. We denounce the hostile spirit of President Cleveland in his numerous vetoes of measures for pension relief, and the action of the Democratic House of Representatives in refusing even a consideration of general pension legislation.

In support of the principles herewith enunciated, we invite the co-operation of patriotic men of all parties, and especially of all workingmen, whose prosperity is seriously threatened by the free-trade policy of the present administration.

RESOLUTION RELATING TO PROHIBITION.

Offered by Mr. Boutelle, of Maine:

The first concern of all good government is the virtue and sobriety of the people and the purity of their homes. The Republican party cordially sympathizes with all wise and well-directed efforts for the promotion of temperance and morality.

PROHIBITION CONVENTION.

Indianapolis, Ind., May 20, 1888.

Chairman pro tem., REV. H. A. DELANO,
of Connecticut.

Chairman, JOHN P. ST. JOHN,
of Kansas.

NOMINATED—

For President, **Clinton B. Fisk,**
of New Jersey.

For Vice-President, **John A. Brooks,**
of Missouri.

It was estimated that there were at least 4000 members of the party present at this convention, not including the 1029 delegates, representing nearly all the states. The convention nominated the above-named candidates unanimously and by acclamation, and adopted the following platform:—

PROHIBITION PLATFORM.

Preamble: The Prohibition party, in national convention assembled, acknowledging Almighty God as the source of all power in government, do hereby declare:

1. That the manufacture, importation, exportation, transportation, and sale of alcoholic beverages should be made public crimes, and prohibited as such.

2. That such prohibition must be secured through amendments of our national and state constitutions, enforced by adequate laws adequately supported by administrative authority; and to this end the organization of the Prohibition party is imperatively demanded in state and nation.

3. That any form of license, taxation, or regulation of the liquor traffic is contrary to good government; that any party which supports regulation, license, or taxation enters into alliance with such traffic and becomes the actual foe of the state's welfare; and that we arraign the Republican and Democratic parties for their persistent attitude in favor of the licensed iniquity, whereby they oppose the demand of the people for prohibition, and, through open complicity with the liquor crime, defeat the enforcement of law.

INTERNAL-REVENUE SYSTEM.

4. For the immediate abolition of the internal-revenue system, whereby our national government is deriving support from our greatest national vice.

IMPORT DUTIES.

5. That, an adequate public revenue being necessary, it may be properly raised by import duties, imposed on such articles of import as will give protection both to the manufacturing employer and producing laborer against the competition of the world; but import duties should be so reduced that no surplus shall be accumulated in the treasury; and that the burdens of taxation shall be removed from foods, clothing, and other comforts and necessaries of life.

RIGHT OF SUFFRAGE.

6. That the right of suffrage rests on no mere accident of race, color, sex, or nationality; and that where, from any cause, it has been withheld from citizens who are of suitable age and mentally and morally qualified for the exercise of an intelligent ballot, it should be restored by the people through the legislatures of the several states, on such educational basis as they may deem wise.

CIVIL SERVICE.

7. That civil-service appointments for all civil offices, chiefly clerical in their duties, should be based upon moral, intellectual, and physical qualifications, and not upon party service or party necessity.

MARRIAGE LAWS.

8. For the abolition of polygamy and the establishment of uniform laws governing marriage and divorce.

MONOPOLIES.

9. For prohibiting all combinations of capital to control and to increase the cost of products for popular consumption.

OBSERVATION OF SABBATH.

10. For the preservation and defense of the Sabbath as a civil institution, without oppressing any who religiously observe the same on any other than the first day of the week.

ARBITRATION.

11. That arbitration is the Christian, wise, and economic method of settling national differences, and the same method should, by judicious legislation, be applied to the settlement of disputes between large bodies of employees and their employers.

LABOR REFORM.

That the abolition of the saloon would remove burdens, moral, physical, pecuniary, and social, which now oppress labor and rob it of its earnings, and would prove to be a wise and successful way of promoting labor reform; and we invite labor and capital to unite with us for the accomplishment thereof. That monopoly in land is a wrong to the people, and the public land should be reserved to actual settlers; and that men and women should receive equal wages for equal work.

LAWS OF IMMIGRATION.

12. That our immigration laws should be so enforced as to prevent the introduction into our country of all convicts, inmates of other dependent institutions, and all others physically incapacitated for self-support; and that no person should have the ballot in any state who is not a citizen of the United States.

PROHIBITION AS A NATIONAL ISSUE.

Recognizing and declaring that prohibition of the liquor traffic has become the dominant issue in national politics, we invite to full party fellowship all who on this one dominant issue are with us agreed, in the full belief that this party can and will remove sectional differences, promote national unity, and insure the best welfare of our entire land.

UNION LABOR CONVENTION.

Cincinnati, O., May 15, 1888.

Chairman pro tem., S. F. NORTON,
of Chicago.

Chairman, JOHN SEITZ.

NOMINATED—

For President, **Alson J. Streeter,**
of Illinois.

For Vice-President, **Samuel Evans,**
of Texas.

Twenty states were represented at this convention by about 220 delegates. Alson J. Streeter, of Illinois, was nominated for President by acclamation.

For Vice-President, Samuel Evans, of Texas, was nominated on the first ballot, receiving 124 votes; 44 were cast for T. P. Rynders, of Pennsylvania, and 32 for Charles R. Cunningham, of Arkansas.

The following platform was adopted:

UNION LABOR PLATFORM.

General discontent prevails on the part of the wealth-producers. Farmers are suffering from a poverty which has forced most of them to mortgage their estates, and the prices of products are so low as to offer no relief except through bankruptcy, and laborers are sinking into greater dependence. Strikes are resorted to without relief, because of the inability of employers in many cases to pay living wages, while more and more are driven into the street. Business men find collections almost impossible, and meantime hundreds of millions of the idle public money, which is needed for relief, is locked up in the United States Treasury or placed, without interest, in favored banks, in grim mockery of distress. Land-monopoly flourishes as never before, and more owners of the soil are daily becoming tenants. Great transportation corporations still succeed in extorting their profits on watered stock through unjust charges. The United States Senate has become an open scandal, its membership being purchased by the rich in open defiance of the popular will. Various efforts are made to squander the public money, which are designed to empty the treasury without paying the public debt. Under these and other alarming conditions, we appeal to the people of our country to come out of old party organizations, whose indifference to the public welfare is responsible for this distress, and aid the Union Labor party to repeal existing class legislation and relieve the distress of our industries, by establishing the following principles:—

LAND.

While we believe that the proper solution of the financial question will greatly relieve those now in danger of losing their homes by mortgages and foreclosures, and enable all industrious persons to secure a home as the highest result of civilization, we oppose land-monopoly in every form, demand the forfeiture of unearned grants, the limitation of land-ownership, and such other legislation as will stop speculations in land and holding it unused from those whose necessities require it.

We believe the earth was made for the people, and not to enable an idle aristocracy to subsist through rents upon the toil of the industrious, and that corners in land are as bad as corners in food, and that those who are not residents or citizens should not be allowed to own lands in the United

States. A homestead should be exempt, to a limited extent, from execution or taxation.

TRANSPORTATION.

The means of communication and transportation shall be owned by the people, as is the United States postal service.

MONEY.

The establishment of a national monetary system in the interest of the producer, instead of the speculator and usurer, by which the circulating medium, in necessary quantity and full legal tender, shall be issued directly to the people, without the intervention of banks, or loaned to citizens upon land security at a low rate of interest, to relieve them from extortions of usury and enable them to control the money-supply. Postal savings-banks should be established. While we have free coinage of gold, we should have free coinage of silver. We demand the immediate application of all the money in the United States Treasury to the payment of the bonded debt, and condemn the further issue of interest-bearing bonds, either by the national government or by states, territories, or municipalities.

LABOR.

Arbitration should take the place of strikes and other injurious methods of settling labor disputes. The letting of convict labor to contractors should be prohibited, the contract system be abolished in public works, the hours of labor in industrial establishments be reduced, commensurate with the increased production by labor-saving machinery, employees protected from bodily injury, equal pay for equal work for both sexes, and labor, agricultural, and co-operative associations be fostered and encouraged by law. The foundation of a republic is in the intelligence of its citizens, and children who are driven into workshops, mines, and factories are deprived of the education which should be secured to all by proper legislation.

PENSIONS.

We demand the passage of a service-pension bill to every honorably discharged soldier and sailor of the United States.

INCOME-TAX.

A graduated income-tax is the most equitable system of taxation, placing the burden of government on those who can best afford to pay, instead of laying it on the farmers and producers, and exempting millionaire bondholders and corporations.

UNITED STATES SENATE.

We demand a constitutional amendment making United States senators elective by a direct vote of the people.

CONTRACT LABOR.

We demand the strict enforcement of laws prohibiting the importation of subjects of foreign countries under contract.

CHINESE.

We demand the passage and enforcement of such legislation as will absolutely exclude the Chinese from the United States.

WOMAN SUFFRAGE.

The right to vote is inherent in citizenship, irrespective of sex, and is properly within the province of state legislation.

PARAMOUNT ISSUES.

The paramount issues to be solved in the interests of humanity are the abolition of usury, monopoly, and trusts, and we denounce the Democratic and Republican parties for creating and perpetuating these monstrous evils.

UNITED LABOR CONVENTION.

Cincinnati, O., May 15, 1888.

Chairman, WILLIAM B. OGDEN,
of Kentucky.

NOMINATED—

For President, **Robert H. Cowdrey,**
of Illinois.

For Vice-President, **W. H. T. Wakefield,**
of Kansas.

The number in attendance was small, and it was rather a conference than a convention. A platform was adopted and the above-mentioned nominations were made. The following is the platform as adopted:—

UNITED LABOR PLATFORM.

We, the delegates of the United Labor party of the United States, in national convention assembled, hold that the corruptions of government and the impoverishment of the masses result from neglect of the self-evident truths proclaimed by the founders of this republic—that all men are created equal and are endowed with inalienable rights. We aim at the abolition of the system which compels men to pay their fellow-creatures for the use of the common bounties of nature, and permits monopolizers to deprive labor of natural opportunities for employment.

FARMING LANDS.

We see access to farming land denied to labor except on payment of exorbitant rent or the acceptance of mortgage burdens, and labor, thus forbidden to employ itself, driven into the cities. We see the wage-workers of the cities subjected to this unnatural competition and forced to pay an exorbitant share of their scanty earnings for cramped and unhealthful lodgings. We see the same intense competition condemning the great majority of business and professional men to a bitter and often unavailing struggle to avoid bankruptcy, and that, while the price of all that labor produces ever falls, the price of land ever rises. We trace these evils to a fundamental wrong—the making of the land on which all must live the exclusive property of but a portion of the community. To this denial of natural rights are due want of employment, low wages, business depressions, that intense competition which makes it so difficult for the majority of men to get a comfortable living, and that wrongful distribution of wealth which is producing the millionaire on one side and the tramp on the other.

TAXATION OF LAND.

To give all men an interest in the land of their country; to enable all to share in the benefits of social growth and improvement; to prevent the shutting out of labor from employment by the monopolization of natural opportunities; to do away with the one-sided competition which cuts down wages to starvation rates; to restore life to business and prevent periodical depressions; to do away with that monstrous injustice which deprives producers of the fruits of their toil, while idlers grow rich; to prevent the conflicts which are arraying class against class, and which are fraught with menacing dangers to society,—we propose so to change the existing system of taxation that no one shall be taxed on the wealth he produces, nor any one suffered to appropriate wealth he does not produce, by taking to himself the increasing values which the growth of society adds to land. What we propose is not the disturbing of any man in his holding or title, but, by taxation of land according to its value and not according to its area, to devote to common use and benefit those values which arise not from the exertion of the individual, but from the growth of society, and to abolish all taxes on industry and its products. This increased taxation of land values must, while relieving the working farmer and small homestead-owner of the undue burdens now imposed upon them, make it unprofitable to hold land for speculation, and thus throw open abundant opportunities for the employment of labor and the building up of homes.

A CHANNEL FOR THE SURPLUS.

We would do away with the present unjust and wasteful system of finance, which piles up hundreds of millions of dollars in treasury vaults while we are paying interest on an enormous debt; and we would establish in its stead a monetary system in which a legal tender circulating medium should be issued by the government without the intervention of banks.

GOVERNMENT RAILROADS AND TELEGRAPHS.

We wish to abolish the present unjust and wasteful system of ownership of railroads and telegraphs by private corporations—a system which, while failing to supply adequately public needs, impoverishes the farmer, oppresses the manufacturer, hampers the merchant, impedes travel and communication, and builds up enormous fortunes and corrupting monopolies that are becoming more powerful than the government itself. For this system we would substitute government ownership and control for the benefit of the whole people instead of private profit.

MEASURES OF RELIEF.

While declaring the foregoing to be the fundamental principles and aims of the United Labor party, and while conscious that no reform can give effectual and permanent relief to labor that does not involve the legal recognition of equal rights to natural opportunities, we, nevertheless, as measures of relief from some of the evil effects of ignoring those rights, favor such legislation as may tend to reduce the hours of labor, to prevent the employment of children of tender years, to avoid the competition of convict labor with honest industry, to secure the sanitary inspection of tenements, factories, and mines, and to put an end to the abuse of conspiracy laws.

OUR COURT LAWS AND EXPENSES.

We desire also to so simplify the procedure of our courts and diminish the expense of legal proceedings, that the poor may therein be placed on an equality with the rich, and the long delays which now result in scandalous miscarriages of justice may be prevented.

THE AUSTRALIAN VOTING SYSTEM.

Since the ballot is the only means by which, in our republic, the redress of political and social grievances is to be sought, we especially and emphatically declare for the adoption of what is known as the Australian system of voting, in order that the effectual secrecy of the ballot, and the relief of candidates for public office from the heavy expenses now imposed upon them, may prevent bribery and intimidation, do away with practical discriminations in favor of the rich and unscrupulous, and lessen the pernicious influence of money in politics.

CORRUPTION OF POLITICAL PARTIES.

We denounce the Democratic and Republican parties as hopelessly and shamelessly corrupt, and, by reason of their affiliation with monopolies, equally unworthy of the suffrages of those who do not live upon public plunder; we therefore require of those who would act with us that they sever all connection with both.

In support of these aims, we solicit the co-operation of all patriotic citizens who, sick of the degradation of politics desire by constitutional methods to establish justice, to preserve liberty, to extend the spirit of fraternity, and to elevate humanity.

AMERICAN CONVENTION.

Washington, D. C., August 14, 1888.

NOMINATED—

For President, **James Langdon Curtis,**
of New York.

For Vice-President, **James R. Greer,**
of Tennessee.

This convention was composed of 126 delegates, of whom 65 were from New York and 15 from California. On the second day of the convention there was a contest over the apportionment of votes, and all the members except those from California and New York seceded, and held a convention of their own; but the seceders made no nominations. The delegates from California and New York then adopted a platform and made the above-named nominations. Mr. Greer subsequently declined the nomination.

The following is the platform adopted:—

AMERICAN PLATFORM.

Resolved, That all law-abiding citizens of the United States of America, whether native or foreign born, are politically equals (except as provided by the Constitution), and all are entitled to, and should receive, the full protection of the laws.

Resolved, That the Constitution of the United States should be so amended as to prohibit the federal and state governments from conferring upon any person the right to vote unless such person be a citizen of the United States.

Resolved, That we are in favor of fostering and encouraging American industries of every class and kind, and declare that the assumed issue "Protection" *vs.* "Free Trade" is a fraud and a snare. The best "protection" is that which protects the labor and life blood of the republic from the degrading competition with and contamination by imported foreigners; and the most dangerous "free trade" is that in paupers, criminals, communists, and anarchists, in which the balance has always been against the United States.

Whereas, One of the greatest evils of unrestricted foreign immigration is the reduction of the wages of the American working-man and working-woman to the level of the underfed and underpaid labor of foreign countries; therefore

Resolved, That we demand that no immigrant shall be admitted into the United States without a passport obtained from the American consul at the port from which he sails; that no passport shall be issued to any pauper, criminal, or insane person, or to any person who, in the judgment of the consul, is not likely to become a desirable citizen of the United States; and that for each immigrant passport there shall be collected by the consul issuing the same the sum of one hundred dollars, to be by him paid into the treasury of the United States.

Resolved, That the present naturalization laws of the United States shall be unconditionally repealed.

Resolved, That the soil of America should belong to Americans; that no alien non-resident should be permitted to own real estate in the United States; and that the realty possessions of the resident alien should be limited in value and area.

Resolved, That no flag shall float on any public buildings—municipal, state, or national—in the United States, except the municipal, state, or national flag of the United States—the flag of the stars and stripes.

Resolved, That we reassert the American principles of absolute freedom of religious worship and belief, the permanent separation of church and state; and we oppose the appropriation of public money or property to any church, or institution administered by the church. We maintain that all church property should be subject to taxation.

EQUAL RIGHTS CONVENTION.

Des Moines, Iowa, May 15, 1888.

Chairman, MRS. NETTIE SANDFORD CHAPIN,
of Iowa.

NOMINATED—

For President, **Mrs. Belva A. Lockwood,**
of the District of Columbia.

For Vice-President, **Alfred H. Love,**
of Pennsylvania.

The convention was not largely attended; proxy ballots were used. Mrs. Belva A. Lockwood, of the District of Columbia, and Alfred H. Love, of Pennsylvania, were nominated for President and Vice-President respectively, each receiving 310 votes.

The convention adopted a platform favoring woman suffrage, pensions for all needy soldiers and sailors, protective tariff with free sugar and lumber, the repeal of the tax on whisky and tobacco, and opposition to unrestricted immigration.

The election occurred on November 6, 1888.

THIRTY-EIGHT STATES VOTED.

POPULAR VOTE.

STATES.	Benjamin Harrison, Republican.	Grover Cleveland, Democrat.	Clinton B. Fisk, Prohibitionist.	Alson J. Streeter, Union Labor.	Total vote.
Alabama	56,197	117,320	583	....	174,100
Arkansas	58,752	85,962	641	10,613	155,968
*California	124,816	117,729	5,761	....	248,306
Colorado	50,774	37,567	2,191	1,266	91,798
Connecticut	74,584	74,920	4,234	240	153,978
Delaware	12,973	16,414	400	....	29,787
Florida	26,657	39,561	423	....	66,641
Georgia	40,496	100,499	1,808	136	142,939
†Illinois	370,473	348,278	21,695	7,090	747,536
Indiana	263,361	261,013	9,881	2,694	536,949
Iowa	211,598	179,887	3,550	9,105	404,140
Kansas	182,934	103,744	6,768	37,726	331,172
Kentucky	155,134	183,800	5,225	622	344,781
Louisiana	30,484	85,032	160	39	115,715
Maine	73,734	50,481	2,691	1,344	128,250
Maryland	99,986	106,168	4,767	....	210,921
Massachusetts	183,892	151,856	8,701	....	344,449
Michigan	236,370	213,459	20,942	4,541	475,312
Minnesota	142,492	104,385	15,311	1,094	263,282
Mississippi	30,096	85,471	218	22	115,807
Missouri	236,257	261,974	4,539	18,632	521,402
Nebraska	108,425	80,552	9,429	4,226	202,632
Nevada	7,229	5,362	41	....	12,632
New Hampshire	45,728	43,458	1,593	13	90,792
New Jersey	144,344	151,493	7,904	....	303,741
‡New York	648,759	635,757	30,231	626	1,315,373
North Carolina	134,784	147,902	2,787	32	285,505
Ohio	416,054	396,455	24,356	3,496	840,361
Oregon	33,291	26,522	1,677	363	61,853
Pennsylvania	526,091	446,633	20,947	3,873	997,544
Rhode Island	21,968	17,530	1,250	18	40,766
South Carolina	13,736	65,825	....	....	79,561
Tennessee	138,988	158,779	5,969	48	303,784
Texas	88,422	234,883	4,749	29,459	357,513
Vermont	45,192	16,785	1,460	....	63,437
Virginia	150,438	151,977	1,678	....	304,093
West Virginia	77,791	79,664	669	1,064	159,188
Wisconsin	176,553	155,232	14,277	8,552	354,614
Total	5,439,853	5,540,329	249,506	146,934	11,376,622

* 1,591 for Curtis, American.

† 150 for Cowdrey, United Labor.

‡ 2,268 for Cowdrey.

ELECTORAL VOTE.

Counted on February 13, 1889.

STATES.	PRESIDENT.		VICE-PRESIDENT.		Number entitled to vote.
	Benjamin Harrison, of Indiana.	Grover Cleveland, of New York.	Levi P. Morton, of New York.	Allen G. Thurman, of Ohio.	
Alabama	..	10	..	10	10
Arkansas	..	7	..	7	7
California	8	..	8	..	8
Colorado	3	..	3	..	3
Connecticut	..	6	..	6	6
Delaware	..	3	..	3	3
Florida	..	4	..	4	4
Georgia	..	12	..	12	12
Illinois	22	..	22	..	22
Indiana	15	..	15	..	15
Iowa	13	..	13	..	13
Kansas	9	..	9	..	9
Kentucky	..	13	..	13	13
Louisiana	..	8	..	8	8
Maine	6	..	6	..	6
Maryland	..	8	..	8	8
Massachusetts	14	..	14	..	14
Michigan	13	..	13	..	13
Minnesota	7	..	7	..	7
Mississippi	..	9	..	9	9
Missouri	..	16	..	16	16
Nebraska	5	..	5	..	5
Nevada	3	..	3	..	3
New Hampshire	4	..	4	..	4
New Jersey	..	9	..	9	9
New York	36	..	36	..	36
North Carolina	..	11	..	11	11
Ohio	23	..	23	..	23
Oregon	3	..	3	..	3
Pennsylvania	30	..	30	..	30
Rhode Island	4	..	4	..	4
South Carolina	..	9	..	9	9
Tennessee	..	12	..	12	12
Texas	..	13	..	13	13
Vermont	4	..	4	..	4
Virginia	..	12	..	12	12
West Virginia	..	6	..	6	6
Wisconsin	11	..	11	..	11
Total	233	168	233	168	401

The count of electoral votes took place under the act of February 3, 1887, and it is the first in the history of the government under the Constitution which was regulated by a general law, not requiring previous concurrent action by the two Houses of Congress for the time being.

Benjamin Harrison was elected President and Levi P. Morton as Vice-President.

During this period Congress was divided politically as follows:—

Fifty-first Congress.

Senate— 37 Democrats, 47 Republicans ....Total, 84
House—156 Democrats, 173 Republicans, 1 Independent.. " 330

Fifty-second Congress.

Senate— 39 Democrats, 47 Republicans, 2 Alliance......Total, 88
House—231 Democrats, 88 Republicans, 14 Populists..... " 333

Election of 1892

Democratic National Committee:

Chairman, WM. F. HARRITY, of Pennsylvania.
Secretary, S. P. SHEERIN, of Indiana.

DEMOCRATIC CONVENTION.

Chicago, Ill., June 21, 1892.

Chairman pro tem., WILLIAM C. OWENS, of Kentucky.

Chairman, WILLIAM L. WILSON, of West Virginia.

NOMINATED—

For President, **Grover Cleveland,** of New York.

For Vice-President, **Adlai E. Stevenson,** of Illinois.

There was a prolonged struggle at this convention over the tariff plank of the platform as reported by the Committee on Resolutions, and the one printed herein was substituted, and finally adopted. After the adoption of the platform, the convention proceeded to nominate a candidate for President, and Grover Cleveland, of New York, was nominated on the first ballot. The following table gives the result of the vote:

CANDIDATES.	Votes.	CANDIDATES.	Votes.
GROVER CLEVELAND, of New York	617⅓	WILLIAM R. MORRISON, of Illinois	3
DAVID B. HILL, of New York	114	JAMES E. CAMPBELL, of Ohio	2
HORACE BOIES, of Iowa	103	WILLIAM C. WHITNEY, of New York	1
ARTHUR P. GORMAN, of Maryland	36⅙	WILLIAM E. RUSSELL, of Massachusetts	1
ADLAI STEVENSON, of Illinois	16⅔	ROBERT E. PATTISON, of Pennsylvania	1
JOHN G. CARLISLE, of Kentucky	14	Whole number of votes, 909⅙ Necessary to a choice, 607	

But one ballot was taken for a candidate for Vice-President, which resulted as follows:

CANDIDATES.	Votes.	CANDIDATES.	Votes.
ADLAI E. STEVENSON, of Illinois	402	BOURKE COCKRAN, of New York	5
ISAAC P. GRAY, of Indiana	343	LAMBERT TREE, of Illinois	1
ALLEN B. MORSE, of Michigan	86	HORACE BOIES, of Iowa	1
JOHN L. MITCHELL, of Wisconsin	45		
HENRY WATTERSON, of Kentucky	26	Whole number of votes, 909 Necessary to a choice, 606	

A motion was then made and adopted that Adlai E. Stevenson, of Illinois, be the candidate for Vice-President.

The platform adopted by the convention follows:—

DEMOCRATIC PLATFORM.

SECTION 1. The representatives of the Democratic party of the United States, in national convention assembled, do reaffirm their allegiance to the principles of the party as formulated by Jefferson and exemplified by the long and illustrious line of his successors in Democratic leadership, from Madison to Cleveland; we believe the public welfare demands that these principles be applied to the conduct of the federal government, through the accession to power of the party that advocates them; and we solemnly declare that the need of a return to these fundamental principles of a free popular government, based on home rule and individual liberty, was never more urgent than now, when the tendency to centralize all power at the federal capital has become a menace to the reserved rights of the states that strikes at the very roots of our government, under the Constitution, as framed by the fathers of the republic.

FEDERAL CONTROL OF ELECTIONS.

SECTION 2. We warn the people of our common country, jealous for the preservation of their free institutions, that the policy of federal control of elections, to which the Republican party has committed itself, is fraught with the gravest dangers, scarcely less momentous than would result from a revolution practically establishing monarchy on the ruins of the republic. It strikes at the North as well as at the South, and injures the colored citizens even more than the white. It means a horde of deputy marshals at every polling place, armed with federal power; returning boards appointed and controlled by federal authority; the outrage of the electoral rights of the people in the several states; the subjugation of the colored people to the control of the party in power, and the reviving of race antagonisms now happily abated, of the utmost peril to the safety and happiness of all—a measure deliberately and justly described by a leading Republican senator as "the most infamous bill that ever crossed the threshold of the Senate." Such a policy, if sanctioned by law, would mean the dominance of a self-perpetuating oligarchy of office-holders, and the party first intrusted with its machinery could be dislodged from power only by an appeal to the reserved rights of the people to resist oppression, which is inherent in all self-governing communities. Two years ago this revolutionary policy was emphatically condemned by the people at the polls; but, in contempt of that verdict, the Republican party has defiantly declared, in its latest authoritative utterance, that its success in the coming elections will mean the enactment of the Force Bill and the usurpation of despotic control over elections in all the states.

Believing that the preservation of republican government in the United States is dependent upon the defeat of this policy of legalized force and fraud, we invite the support of all citizens who desire to see the Constitution maintained in its integrity, with the laws pursuant thereto, which have given our country a hundred years of unexampled prosperity; and we pledge the Democratic party, if it be intrusted with power, not only to the defeat of the Force Bill, but also to relentless opposition to the Republican policy of profligate expenditure, which, in the short space of two years, has squandered an enormous surplus and emptied an overflowing treasury, after piling new burdens of taxation upon the already overtaxed labor of the country.

TARIFF LEGISLATION.

SECTION 3. We denounce Republican protection as a fraud—a robbery of the great majority of the American people for the benefit of the few. We declare it to be a fundamental principle of the Democratic party that the federal government has no constitutional power to impose and collect tariff duties, except for the purposes of revenue only, and we demand that the collection of such taxes shall be limited to the necessities of the government when honestly and economically administered.

We denounce the McKinley tariff law enacted by the Fifty-first Congress as the culminating atrocity of class-legislation; we indorse the efforts made by the Democrats of the present Congress to modify its most oppressive features in the direction of free raw materials and cheaper manufactured goods that enter into general consumption, and we promise its repeal as one of the beneficent results that will follow the action of the people in intrusting power to the Democratic party. Since the McKinley tariff went into operation there have been ten reductions of the wages of the laboring man to one increase. We deny that there has been any increase of prosperity to the country since that tariff went into operation, and we point to the dullness and distress, to the wage-reductions and strikes in the iron trade, as the best possible evidence that no such prosperity has resulted from the McKinley Act.

We call the attention of thoughtful Americans to the fact that, after thirty years of restrictive taxes against the importation of foreign wealth in exchange for our agricultural surplus, the homes and farms of the country have become burdened with a real estate mortgage debt of over two thousand five hundred million dollars, exclusive of all other forms of indebtedness; that in one of the chief agricultural states of the West there appears a real estate mortgage debt averaging $165 per capita of the total population, and that similar conditions and tendencies are shown to exist in the other agricultural-exporting states. We denounce a policy which fosters no industry so much as it does that of the sheriff.

RECIPROCITY.

SECTION 4. Trade-interchange on the basis of reciprocal advantages to the countries participating is a time-honored doctrine of the Democratic faith, but we denounce the sham reciprocity which juggles with the people's desire for enlarged foreign markets and freer exchanges, by pretending to establish closer trade relations for a country whose articles of export are almost exclusively agricultural products, with other countries that are also agricultural, while erecting a custom-house barrier of prohibitive tariff taxes against the richest countries of the world, that stand ready to take our entire surplus of products, and to exchange therefor commodities which are necessaries and comforts of life among our own people.

TRUSTS AND COMBINATIONS.

SECTION 5. We recognize in the trusts and combinations, which are designed to enable capital to secure more than its just share of the joint product of capital and labor, a natural consequence of the prohibitive taxes which prevent the free competition which is the life of honest trade; but we believe their worst evils can be abated by law, and we demand the rigid enforcement of the laws made to prevent and control them, together with such further legislation in restraint of their abuses as experience may show to be necessary.

PUBLIC LAND.

SECTION 6. The Republican party, while professing a policy of reserving the public land for small holdings by actual settlers, has given away the people's heritage, till now a few railroads and non-resident aliens, individual and corporate, possess a larger area than that of all our farms between the two seas. The last Democratic administration reversed the improvident and unwise policy of the Republican party touching the public domain, and reclaimed from corporations and syndicates, alien and domestic, and restored to the people, nearly 100,000,000 acres of valuable land, to be sacredly held as homesteads for our citizens, and we pledge ourselves to continue this policy until every acre of land so unlawfully held shall be reclaimed and restored to the people.

GOLD AND SILVER.

SECTION 7. We denounce the Republican legislation known as the Sherman Act of 1890 as a cowardly makeshift, fraught with possibilities of danger in the future which should make all of its supporters, as well as its author, anxious for its speedy repeal. We hold to the use of both gold and silver as the standard money of the country, and to the coinage of both gold and silver without discriminating against either metal or charge for mintage; but the dollar unit of coinage of both metals must be of equal intrinsic and exchangeable value, or be adjusted through international agreement or by such safeguards of legislation as shall insure the maintenance of the parity of the two metals and the equal power of every dollar, at all times, in the markets and in the payment of debts; and we demand that all paper currency shall be kept at par with and redeemable in such coin. We insist upon this policy as especially necessary for the protection of the farmers and laboring classes, the first and most defenseless victims of unstable money and a fluctuating currency.

TAX ON STATE BANKS.

SECTION 8. We recommend that the prohibitory 10 per cent. tax on state bank issues be repealed.

CIVIL SERVICE.

SECTION 9. Public office is a public trust. We reaffirm the declaration of the Democratic National Convention of 1876 for the reform of the civil service, and we call for the honest enforcement of all laws regulating the same. The nomination of a President, as in the recent Republican convention, by delegations composed largely of his appointees, holding office at his pleasure, is a scandalous satire upon free popular institutions, and a startling illustration of the methods by which a President may gratify his ambition. We denounce a policy under which federal office-holders usurp control of party conventions in the states, and we pledge the Democratic party to the reform of these and all other abuses which threaten individual liberty and local self-government.

FOREIGN POLICY.

SECTION 10. The Democratic party is the only party that has ever given the country a foreign policy consistent and vigorous, compelling respect abroad and inspiring confidence at home. While avoiding entangling alliances, it has aimed to cultivate friendly relations with other nations, and especially with our neighbors on the American continent, whose destiny is closely linked with our own, and we view with alarm the tendency to a policy of irritation and bluster, which is liable at any time to confront us with the alternative of humiliation or war. We favor the maintenance of a navy strong enough for all purposes of national defense, and to properly maintain the honor and dignity of the country abroad.

SYMPATHY FOR THE OPPRESSED.

SECTION 11. This country has always been the refuge of the oppressed from every land—exiles for conscience' sake—and, in the spirit of the founders of our government, we condemn the oppression practised by the Russian Government upon its Lutheran and Jewish subjects, and we call upon our National Government, in the interest of justice and humanity, by all just and proper means, to use its prompt and best efforts to bring about a cessation of these cruel persecutions in the dominions of the Czar, and to secure to the oppressed equal rights. We tender our profound and earnest sympathy to those lovers of freedom who are struggling for home rule and the great cause of local self-government in Ireland.

IMMIGRATION.

SECTION 12. We heartily approve all legitimate efforts to prevent the United States from being used as the dumping ground for the known criminals and professional paupers of Europe, and we demand the rigid enforcement of the laws against Chinese immigration, or the importation of foreign labor and lessen its wages; but we condemn and denounce any and all attempts to restrict the immigration of the industrious and worthy of foreign lands.

PENSIONS.

SECTION 13. This convention hereby renews the expression of appreciation of the patriotism of the soldiers and sailors of the Union in the war for its preservation, and we favor just and liberal pensions for all disabled Union soldiers, their widows and dependents; but we demand that the work of the Pension Office shall be done industriously, impartially, and honestly. We denounce the present administration of that office as incompetent, corrupt, disgraceful, and dishonest.

WATERWAYS.

SECTION 14. The federal government shall care for and improve the Mississippi River and other great waterways of the republic, so as to secure for the interior states easy and cheap transportation to the tide-water. When any waterway of the public is of sufficient importance to demand the aid of the government, such aid should be extended with a definite plan of continuous work until permanent improvement is secured.

NICARAGUA CANAL.

SECTION 15. For purposes of national defense and the promotion of commerce between the states, we recognize the early construction of the Nicaragua canal and its protection against foreign control as of great importance to the United States.

WORLD'S FAIR.

SECTION 16. Recognizing the World's Columbian Exposition as a national undertaking of vast importance, in which the general government has invited the co-operation of all the powers of the world, and appreciating the acceptance by many of such powers of the invitation so extended, and the broadest liberal efforts being made by them to contribute to the grandeur of the undertaking, we are of the opinion that Congress should make such necessary financial provision as shall be requisite to the maintenance of the national honor and public faith.

EDUCATION.

SECTION 17. Popular education being the only safe basis of popular suffrage, we recommend to the several states most liberal appropriations for the public schools. Free common schools are the nursery of good government, and they have always received the fostering care of the Democratic party, which favors every means of increasing intelligence. Freedom of education being an essential of civil and religious liberty as well as a necessity for the development of intelligence, must not be interfered with under any pretext whatever. We are opposed to state interference with parental rights and rights of conscience in the education of children as an infringement of the fundamental Democratic doctrine that the largest individual liberty consistent with the rights of others insures the highest type of American citizenship and the best government.

ADMISSION OF TERRITORIES.

SECTION 18. We approve the action of the present House of Representatives in passing bills for the admission into the Union as states of the Territories of New Mexico and Arizona, and we favor the early admission of all the territories having necessary population and resources to admit them to statehood; and while they remain territories, we hold that the officials appointed to administer the government of any territory, together with the Districts of Columbia and Alaska, should be *bona fide* residents of the territory or district in which their duties are to be performed. The Democratic party believes in home rule and the control of their own affairs by the people of the vicinage.

PROTECTION OF RAILROAD EMPLOYEES.

SECTION 19. We favor legislation by Congress and state legislatures to protect the lives and limbs of railway employees and those of other hazardous transportation companies, and denounce the inactivity of the Republican party, and particularly the Republican Senate, for causing the defeat of measures beneficial and protective to this class of wage-workers.

SWEATING SYSTEM.

SECTION 20. We are in favor of the enactment by the states of laws for abolishing the notorious sweating system; for abolishing contract convict labor, and for prohibiting the employment in factories of children under 15 years of age.

SUMPTUARY LAWS.

SECTION 21. We are opposed to all sumptuary laws as an interference with the individual rights of the citizen.

CHANGES ASKED.

SECTION 22. Upon this statement of principles and policies the Democratic party asks the intelligent judgment of the American people. It asks a change of administration and a change of party, in order that there may be a change of system and a change of methods, thus assuring the maintenance unimpaired of institutions under which the republic has grown great and powerful.

Republican National Committee:

Chairman, THOMAS H. CARTER, of Montana.
Secretary, LOUIS E. MCCOMAS, of Maryland.

Mr. McComas having been appointed to a judgeship in the District of Columbia, JOSEPH H. MANLEY, of Maine, succeeded him.

REPUBLICAN CONVENTION.

Minneapolis, Minn., June 7–10, 1892.

Chairman pro tem., J. SLOAT FASSETT,
of New York.

Chairman, WILLIAM MCKINLEY, JR.,
of Ohio.

NOMINATED—

For President, **Benjamin Harrison,**
of Indiana.

For Vice-President, **Whitelaw Reid,**
of New York.

On the first ballot for a candidate for President, Benjamin Harrison, of Indiana, was nominated for a second term. The vote stood as follows:

CANDIDATES.	Votes.	CANDIDATES.	Votes.
BENJAMIN HARRISON, of Indiana	$535\frac{1}{6}$	THOMAS B. REED, of Maine	4
JAMES G. BLAINE, of Maine	$182\frac{5}{6}$	ROBERT T. LINCOLN, of Illinois	1
WILLIAM MCKINLEY, JR., of Ohio	182	Whole number of votes	905
		Necessary to a choice	453

For Vice-President, Whitelaw Reid, of New York, was nominated by acclamation.

The platform of the Tenth National Republican Convention, at Minneapolis, adopted June 9, 1892, is as follows:—

REPUBLICAN PLATFORM.

The representatives of the Republicans of the United States, assembled in general convention on the shores of the Mississippi River, the everlasting bond of an indestructible republic, whose most glorious chapter of history is the record of the Republican party, congratulate their countrymen on the majestic march of the nation under the banners inscribed with the principles of our platform of 1888, vindicated by victory at the polls and prosperity in our fields, workshops and mines, and make the following declaration of principles:—

THE PRINCIPLE OF PROTECTION.

We reaffirm the American doctrine of protection. We call attention to its growth abroad. We maintain that the prosperous condition of our country is largely due to the wise revenue legislation of the last Republican Congress. We believe that all articles which cannot be produced in the United States, except luxuries, should be admitted free of duty, and that on all imports coming into competition with the products of American labor there should be levied duties equal to the difference between wages abroad and at home.

We assert that the prices of manufactured articles of general consumption have been reduced under the operations of the Tariff Act of 1890.

We denounce the efforts of the Democratic majority of the House of Representatives to destroy our tariff laws piecemeal, as manifested by their attacks upon wool, lead, and lead ores, the chief products of a number of states, and we ask the people for their judgment thereon.

TRIUMPH OF RECIPROCITY.

We point to the success of the Republican policy of reciprocity, under which our export trade has vastly increased and new and enlarged markets have been opened for the products of our farms and workshops. We remind the people of the bitter opposition of the Democratic party to this practical business measure, and claim that, executed by a Republican administration, our present laws will eventually give us control of the trade of the world.

FREE AND SAFE COINAGE OF GOLD AND SILVER.

The American people, from tradition and interest, favor bimetallism, and the Republican party demands the use of both gold and silver as standard money, with such restrictions and under such provisions, to be determined by legislation, as will secure the maintenance of the parity of values of the two metals, so that the purchasing and debt-paying power of the dollar, whether of silver, gold, or paper, shall be at all times equal. The interests of the producers of the country, its farmers and its workingmen, demand that every dollar, paper, or coin, issued by the government shall be as good as any other.

We commend the wise and patriotic steps already taken by our government to secure an international conference to adopt such measures as will insure a parity of value between gold and silver for use as money throughout the world.

FREEDOM OF THE BALLOT.

We demand that every citizen of the United States shall be allowed to cast one free and unrestricted ballot in all public elections, and that such ballot shall be counted and returned as cast; that such laws shall be enacted and enforced as will secure to every citizen, be he rich or poor, native or foreign-born, white or black, this sovereign right, guaranteed by the Constitution. The free and honest popular ballot, the just and equal representation of all the people, as well as their just and equal protection under the laws, are the foundation of our republican institutions, and the party will never relax its efforts until the integrity of the ballot and the purity of elections shall be fully guaranteed and protected in every state.

OUTRAGES IN THE SOUTH.

We denounce the continued inhuman outrages perpetrated upon American citizens for political reasons in certain Southern States of the Union.

EXTENSION OF FOREIGN COMMERCE.

We favor the extension of our foreign commerce, the restoration of our mercantile marine by home-built ships, and the creation of a navy for the protection of our national interests and the honor of our flag; the maintenance of the most friendly relations with all foreign powers, entangling alliances with none, and the protection of the rights of our fishermen.

MONROE DOCTRINE.

We reaffirm our approval of the Monroe doctrine, and believe in the achievement of the manifest destiny of the republic in its broadest sense.

RESTRICTION OF IMMIGRATION.

We favor the enactment of more stringent laws and regulations for the restriction of criminal, pauper, and contract immigration.

EMPLOYEES OF RAILROADS.

We favor efficient legislation by Congress to protect the life and limbs of employees of transportation companies engaged in carrying on interstate commerce, and recommend legislation by the respective states that will protect employees engaged in state commerce, in mining and manufacturing.

CHAMPIONING THE OPPRESSED.

The Republican party has always been the champion of the oppressed and recognizes the dignity of manhood, irrespective of faith, color, or nationality. It sympathizes with the cause of home rule in Ireland, and protests against the persecution of the Jews in Russia.

FREEDOM OF THOUGHT AND SPEECH.

The ultimate reliance of free popular government is the intelligence of the people and the maintenance of freedom among all men. We therefore declare anew our devotion to liberty of thought and conscience, of speech and press, and approve all agencies and instrumentalities which contribute to the education of the children of the land; but while insisting upon the fullest measure of religious liberty, we are opposed to any union of church and state.

TRUSTS CONDEMNED.

We reaffirm our opposition, declared in the Republican platform of 1888, to all combinations of capital, organized in trusts or otherwise, to control arbitrarily the condition of trade among our citizens. We heartily indorse the action already taken upon this subject, and ask for such further legislation as may be required to remedy any defects in existing laws and to render their enforcement more complete and effective.

FREE-DELIVERY SERVICE.

We approve the policy of extending to towns, villages, and rural communities the advantages of the free-delivery service now enjoyed by the larger cities of the country, and reaffirm the declaration contained in the Republican platform of 1888, pledging the reduction of letter postage to one cent at the earliest possible moment consistent with the maintenance of the Postoffice Department and the highest class of postal service.

SPIRIT OF CIVIL-SERVICE REFORM.

We commend the spirit and evidence of reform in the civil service, and the wise and consistent enforcement by the Republican party of the laws regulating the same.

THE NICARAGUA CANAL.

The construction of the Nicaragua Canal is of the highest importance to the American people, both as a measure of defense and to build up and maintain American commerce, and it should be controlled by the United States Government.

TERRITORIES.

We favor the admission of the remaining territories at the earliest practicable day, having due regard to the interests of the people of the territories and of the United States.

FEDERAL TERRITORIAL OFFICERS.

All the federal officers appointed for the territories should be selected from *bona fide* residents thereof, and the right of self-government should be accorded as far as practicable.

ARID LANDS.

We favor cession, subject to the homestead laws, of the arid public lands to the states and territories in which they lie, under such congressional restrictions as to disposition, reclamation, and occupancy by settlers as will secure the maximum benefits to the people.

THE COLUMBIAN EXPOSITION.

The World's Columbian Exposition is a great national undertaking, and Congress should promptly enact such reasonable legislation in aid thereof as will insure a discharging of the expense and obligations incident thereto and the attainment of results commensurate with the dignity and progress of the nation.

SYMPATHY FOR TEMPERANCE.

We sympathize with all wise and legitimate efforts to lessen and prevent the evils of intemperance and promote morality.

PLEDGES TO THE VETERANS.

Ever mindful of the services and sacrifices of the men who saved the life of the nation, we pledge anew to the veteran soldiers of the republic a watchful care and a just recognition of their claims upon a grateful people.

HARRISON'S ADMINISTRATION COMMENDED.

We commend the able, patriotic, and thoroughly American administration of President Harrison. Under it the country has enjoyed remarkable prosperity, and the dignity and honor of the nation, at home and abroad, have been faithfully maintained, and we offer the record of pledges kept as a guarantee of faithful performance in the future.

PROHIBITION CONVENTION.

Cincinnati, O., June 29, 1892.

Chairman pro tem., JOHN P. ST. JOHN, of Kansas.

Chairman, ELI RITTER, of Indiana.

NOMINATED—

For President, **John Bidwell,** of California.

For Vice-President, **J. B. Cranfill,** of Texas.

John Bidwell, of California, was nominated for President by the following vote:

CANDIDATES.	Votes.	CANDIDATES.	Votes.
JOHN BIDWELL, of California	590	W. JENNINGS DEMOREST, of New York	139
GIDEON T. STEWART, of Ohio	179	H. CLAY BASCOM, of New York	3
		Whole number of votes	911
		Necessary to a choice	456

As a candidate for Vice-President, J. B. Cranfill, of Texas, was chosen by the following vote:

CANDIDATES.	Votes.	CANDIDATES.	Votes.
J. B. CRANFILL, of Texas	417	THOMAS R. CARSKADON, of West Virginia	19
JOSHUA LEVERING, of Maryland	351		
W. W. SATTERLY, of Minnesota	26	Whole number of votes	811
		Necessary to choice	406

The convention adopted the following platform:—

PROHIBITION PLATFORM.

The Prohibition party, in national convention assembled, acknowledging Almighty God as the Source of all true government, and His Law as the standard to which all human enactments must conform to secure the blessings of peace and prosperity, presents the following declaration of principles:—

LIQUOR TRAFFIC.

1. The liquor traffic is a foe to civilization, the arch enemy of popular government, and a public nuisance. It is the citadel of the forces that corrupt politics, promote poverty and crime, degrade the nation's home-life, thwart the will of the people, and deliver our country into the hands of rapacious class interests. All laws that, under the guise of regulation, legalize and protect this traffic, or make the government share its ill-gotten gains, are " vicious in principle and powerless as a remedy."

We declare anew for the entire suppression of the manufacture, sale, importation, exportation, and transportation of alcoholic liquors as a beverage by federal and state legislation, and the full powers of the government should be exerted to secure this result. Any party that fails to recognize the dominant nature of this issue in American politics is undeserving of the support of the people.

SUFFRAGE.

2. No citizen should be denied the right to vote on account of sex, and equal labor should receive equal wages, without regard to sex.

MONEY.

3. The money of the country should consist of gold, silver, and paper, and be issued by the general government only in sufficient quantities to meet the demands of business and give full opportunity for the employment of labor. To this end an increase in the volume of money is demanded, and no individual or corporation should be allowed to make any profit through its issue. It should be made a legal tender for the payment of all debts, public and private. Its volume should be fixed at a definite sum per capita, and made to increase with our increase in population.

TARIFF.

4. Tariff should be levied only as a defense against the foreign governments which levy tariff upon or bar out our pro-

ducts from their markets, revenue being incidental. The residue of means necessary to an economical administration of the government should be raised by levying a burden on what the people possess instead of upon what they consume.

GOVERNMENTAL CONTROL.

5. Railroad, telegraph, and other public corporations should be controlled by the government in the interest of the people, and no higher charges allowed than are necessary to give fair interest on the capital actually invested.

IMMIGRATION.

6. Foreign immigration has become a burden upon industry, one of the factors in depressing wages and causing discontent; therefore our immigration laws should be revised and strictly enforced. The time of residence for naturalization should be extended, and no naturalized person should be allowed to vote until one year after he becomes a citizen.

ALIEN OWNERSHIP.

7. Non-resident aliens should not be allowed to acquire land in this country, and we favor the limitation of individual and corporate ownership of land. All unearned grants of land to railroad companies or other corporations should be reclaimed.

MOB LAWS.

8. Years of inaction and treachery on the part of the Republican and Democratic parties have resulted in the present reign of mob law, and we demand that every citizen be protected in the right of trial by constitutional tribunals.

SABBATH.

9. All men should be protected by law in their right to one day's rest in seven.

ARBITRATION.

10. Arbitration is the wisest and most economical and humane method of settling national differences.

MARGINS, TRUSTS, AND COMBINES.

11. Speculation in margins, the cornering of grain, money, and products, and the formation of pools, trusts, and combinations for the arbitrary advancement of prices should be suppressed.

PENSIONS.

12. We pledge that the Prohibition party, if elected to power, will ever grant just pensions to disabled veterans of the Union Army and Navy, their widows and orphans.

PUBLIC SCHOOLS.

13. We stand unequivocally for the American public school, and are opposed to any appropriation of any public moneys for sectarian schools. We declare that only by united support of such common schools, taught in the English language, can we hope to become and remain a homogeneous and harmonious people.

NATIONAL ISSUES.

14. We arraign the Republican and Democratic parties as false to the standards reared by their founders; as faithless to the principles of the illustrious leaders of the past to whom they do homage with the lips; as recreant to the "higher law," which is as inflexible in political affairs as in personal life, and as no longer embodying the aspirations of the American people or inviting the confidence of enlightened progressive patriotism. Their protest against the admission of "moral issues" into politics is a confession of their own moral degeneracy. The declaration of an eminent authority that municipal misrule is "the one conspicuous failure of American politics" follows as a natural consequence of such degeneracy, and it is true alike of cities under Republican and Democratic control. Each accuses the other of extravagance in congressional appropriations, and both are alike guilty; both protest, when out of power, against the infraction of the civil-service laws, and each, when in power, violates those laws in letter and spirit; each professes fealty to the interests of the toiling masses, but both covertly truckle to the money power in their administration of public affairs. Even the tariff issue, as represented in the Democratic Mills Bill and the Republican McKinley Bill, is no longer treated by them as an issue upon great and divergent principles of government, but is a mere catering to different sectional and class interests. The attempt in many states to wrest the Australian ballot system from its true purpose, and to so deform it as to render it extremely difficult for new parties to exercise the rights of suffrage, is an outrage upon popular government. The competition of both parties for the vote of the slums, and their assiduous courting of the liquor power and subserviency to the money

power, have resulted in placing those powers in the position of practical arbiters of the destinies of the nation. We renew our protest against these perilous tendencies, and invite all citizens to join us in the upbuilding of a party that has shown in five national campaigns that it prefers temporary defeat to an abandonment of the claims of justice, sobriety, personal rights, and the protection of American homes.

PARTY FELLOWSHIP.

15. Recognizing and declaring that prohibition of the liquor-traffic has become the dominant issue in national politics, we invite to full party fellowship all those who on this one dominant issue are with us agreed, in the full belief that this party can and will remove sectional differences, promote national unity, and insure the best welfare of our entire land.

WORLD'S FAIR.

Resolved, That we favor a liberal appropriation by the federal government for the World's Columbian Exposition, but only on the condition that the sale of intoxicating liquors on the grounds be prohibited and that the Exposition be kept closed on Sundays.

FARMERS' ALLIANCE CONVENTION.

Ocala, Fla., December, 1890.

The Farmers' Alliance Convention which met in St. Louis, Mo., in December, 1889, adopted a plan of Confederation with the Knights of Labor and exchanged friendly greetings with the Greenback party and the Single Tax party. The convention at Ocala was the first meeting under this confederation of party factions, and it is noted here as of especial interest. No candidates were chosen, but the following platform, generally known as the "Ocala Platform," was adopted:—

FARMERS' ALLIANCE PLATFORM.

1. We demand the abolition of national banks, and the substitution of legal tender treasury notes in lieu of national bank notes, issued in sufficient volume to do the business of

the country on a cash system, regulating the amount needed on a *per capita* basis as the business interests of the country expand; and that all money issued by the government shall be legal tender in payment of all debts, both public and private.

2. We demand that Congress shall pass such laws as shall eventually prevent the dealing in futures of all agricultural and mechanical productions, preserving a stringent system of procedure in trials, and imposing such penalties as shall secure the most perfect compliance with the law.

3. We demand the free and unlimited coinage of silver.

4. We demand the passage of laws prohibiting the alien ownership of land, and that Congress take early steps to devise some plan to obtain all lands now owned by aliens and foreign syndicates, and that all lands now held by railroads and other corporations in excess of such as are actually used and needed by them be reclaimed by the government and held for actual settlers.

5. Believing in the doctrine of equal rights to all and special privileges to none, we demand that taxation, national or state, shall not be used to build up one interest or class at the expense of another. We believe that the money of the country should be kept as much as possible in the hands of the people; and hence we demand that all revenues—national, state, or county—shall be limited to the necessary expenses of the government, economically and honestly administered.

6. We demand that Congress issue a sufficient amount of fractional paper currency to facilitate exchange through the medium of the United States mail.

NATIONAL PEOPLE'S CONVENTION.

Omaha, Neb., July 2-5, 1892.

Chairman pro tem., C. H. ELLINGTON,
of Georgia.

Chairman, H. L. LOUCKS,
of South Dakota.

NOMINATED—

For President, **James B. Weaver,**
of Iowa.

For Vice-President, **James G. Field,**
of Virginia.

This was the first national convention of the party, and the representation, in consequence, was very irregular. Both James B. Weaver, of Iowa, and James G. Field, of Virginia, candidates for President and Vice-President respectively, were nominated on the first ballot, by large majorities, as will be seen from the following tables:

CANDIDATES FOR PRESIDENT.	Votes.
JAMES B. WEAVER, of Iowa	995
JAMES H. KYLE, of South Dakota	265
MANN PAGE, of Virginia	1
LELAND STANFORD, of California	1
—— NORTON,	1
Whole number of votes, 1263.	
Necessary to a choice, 632.	

CANDIDATES FOR VICE-PRESIDENT.	Votes.
JAMES G. FIELD, of Virginia	733
BEN. S. TERRELL, of Texas	554
Whole number of votes, 1287	
Necessary to a choice, 644	

The convention adopted the following platform:—

NATIONAL PEOPLE'S PLATFORM.

Assembled upon the 116th anniversary of the Declaration of Independence, the People's party of America, in their first national convention, invoking upon their action the blessing of Almighty God, puts forth, in the name and on behalf of the people of this country, the following preamble and declaration of principles:

The conditions which surround us best justify our co-operation: we meet in the midst of a nation brought to the verge of moral, political, and material ruin. Corruption dominates the ballot-box, the legislatures, the Congress, and touches even the ermine of the bench. The people are demoralized; most of the states have been compelled to isolate the voters at the polling places to prevent universal intimidation or bribery. The newspapers are largely subsidized or muzzled, public opinion silenced, business prostrated, our homes covered with mortgages, labor impoverished, and the land concentrating in the hands of the capitalists. The urban workmen are denied the right of organization for self-protection; imported pauperized labor beats down their wages, a hireling standing army, unrecognized by our laws, is established to shoot them down, and they are rapidly degenerating into European conditions. The fruits of the toil of millions are boldly stolen to build up colossal fortunes for a few, unprecedented in the history of mankind; and the possessors of these, in turn, despise the republic and endanger liberty. From the same prolific womb of governmental injustice we breed the two great classes—tramps and millionaires.

The national power to create money is appropriated to enrich bondholders; a vast public debt payable in legal-tender currency has been funded into gold-bearing bonds, thereby adding millions to the burdens of the people.

Silver, which has been accepted as coin since the dawn of history, has been demonetized, to add to the purchasing power of gold by decreasing the value of all forms of property as well as human labor, and the supply of currency is purposely abridged to fatten usurers, bankrupt enterprise, and enslave industry. A vast conspiracy against mankind has been organized on two continents, and it is rapidly taking possession of the world. If not met and overthrown at once, it forebodes terrible social convulsions, the destruction of civilization or the establishment of an absolute despotism.

We have witnessed for more than a quarter of a century the struggles of the two great political parties for power and plunder, while grievous wrongs have been inflicted upon the suffering people. We charge that the controlling influences dominating both these parties have permitted the existing dreadful conditions to develop without serious effort to prevent or restrain them. Neither do they now promise us any substantial reform. They have agreed together to ignore, in the coming campaign, every issue but one. They propose to drown the outcries of a plundered people with the uproar of a sham battle over the tariff, so that capitalists, corporations, national banks, rings, trusts, watered stock, the demonetization of silver, and the oppressions of the usurers may all be lost sight of. They propose to sacrifice our homes, lives, and children on the altar of Mammon; to destroy the multitude in order to secure corruption funds from the millionaires.

Assembled on the anniversary of the birthday of the nation, and filled with the spirit of the grand general chief who established our independence, we seek to restore the government of the republic to the hands of "the plain people," with whose class it originated. We assert our purposes to be identical with the purposes of the National Constitution, "to form a more perfect union and establish justice, insure domestic tranquillity, provide for the common defense, promote the general welfare, and secure the blessings of liberty for ourselves and our posterity."

We declare that this republic can only endure as a free government while built upon the love of the whole people for each other and for the nation; that it cannot be pinned together by bayonets; that the civil war is over, and that every passion and resentment which grew out of it must die with it, and that we must be in fact, as we are in name, one united brotherhood.

Our country finds itself confronted by conditions for which there is no precedent in the history of the world. Our annual agricultural productions amount to billions of dollars in value, which must within a few weeks or months be exchanged for billions of dollars of commodities consumed in their production; the existing currency supply is wholly inadequate to make this exchange. The results are falling prices, the formation of combines and rings, the impoverishment of the producing class. We pledge ourselves that, if given power, we will labor to correct these evils by wise and reasonable legislation in accordance with the terms of our platform.

We believe that the powers of government—in other words, of the people—should be expanded (as in the case of the postal service) as rapidly and as far as the good sense of an intelligent people and the teachings of experience shall justify, to the end that oppression, injustice, and poverty shall eventually cease in the land.

While our sympathies as a party of reform are naturally upon the side of every proposition which will tend to make men intelligent, virtuous, and temperate, we nevertheless regard these questions, important as they are, as secondary to the great issues now pressing for solution, and upon which not only our individual prosperity, but the very existence of free institutions depend; and we ask all men to first help us to determine whether we are to have a republic to administer, before we differ as to the conditions upon which it is to be administered, believing that the forces of reform this day organized will never cease to move forward until every wrong is righted and equal rights and equal privileges securely established for all the men and women of this country. We declare, therefore—

UNION OF THE PEOPLE.

1. That the union of the labor forces of the United States this day consummated shall be permanent and perpetual: may its spirit enter into all hearts for the salvation of the republic and the uplifting of mankind!

2. Wealth belongs to him who creates it, and every dollar taken from industry without an equivalent is robbery. "If any will not work, neither shall he eat." The interests of rural and civic labor are the same; their enemies are identical.

3. We believe that the time has come when the railroad corporations will either own the people or the people must own the railroads; and should the government enter upon the work of owning and managing all railroads, we should favor an amendment to the Constitution by which all persons engaged in the government service shall be placed under a civil-service regulation of the most rigid character, so as to prevent the increase of the power of the national administration by the use of such additional government employees.

THE QUESTION OF FINANCE.

We demand a national currency, safe, sound, and flexible, issued by the general government only, a full legal tender for all debts, public and private, and that without the use of banking corporations; a just, equitable, and efficient means of distribution direct to the people, at a tax not to exceed two per cent. per annum, to be provided as set forth in the sub-treasury plan of the Farmers' Alliance, or a better system; also, by payments in discharge of its obligations for public improvements.

We demand free and unlimited coinage of silver and gold at the present legal ratio of sixteen to one.

We demand that the amount of circulating medium be speedily increased to not less than $50 per capita.

We demand a graduated income-tax.

We believe that the money of the country should be kept as much as possible in the hands of the people; and hence we demand that all state and national issues shall be limited to the necessary expenses of the government, economically and honestly administered.

We demand that postal savings-banks be established by the

government for the safe deposit of the earnings of the people and to facilitate exchange.

CONTROL OF TRANSPORTATION.

Transportation being a means of exchange and a public necessity, the government should own and operate the railroads in the interest of the people.

The telegraph and telephone, like the post-office system, being a necessity for the transmission of news, should be owned and operated by the government in the interest of the people.

RECLAIMING THE LAND.

The land, including all the natural sources of wealth, is the heritage of the people, and should not be monopolized for speculative purposes, and alien ownership of land should be prohibited. All land now held by railroads and other corporations in excess of their actual needs, and all lands now owned by aliens, should be reclaimed by the government and held for actual settlers only.

Resolved, 1. That we demand a free ballot and a fair count in all elections, and pledge ourselves to secure it to every legal voter, without federal intervention, through the adoption by the states of the unperverted Australian secret ballot system.

Resolved, 2. That the revenue derived from a graduated income-tax should be applied to the reduction of the burdens of taxation now levied upon the domestic industries of this country.

Resolved, 3. That we pledge our support to fair and liberal pensions to ex-Union soldiers and sailors.

Resolved, 4. That we condemn the fallacy of protecting American labor under the present system, which opens our ports to the pauper and criminal classes of the world and crowds out our wage-earners, and we denounce the present ineffective law against contract labor, and demand the further restriction of undesirable immigration.

Resolved, 5. That we cordially sympathize with the efforts of organized workingmen to shorten the hours of labor, and demand a rigid enforcement of the existing eight-hour law on government work, and ask that a penalty clause be added to the said law.

Resolved, 6. That we regard the maintenance of a large standing army of mercenaries, known as the Pinkerton system, as a menace to our liberties, and we demand its abolition; and we condemn the recent invasion of the Territory of Wyoming by the hired assassins of plutocracy, assisted by federal officers.

Resolved, 7. That we commend to the thoughtful consideration of the people and the reform press, the legislative system known as the initiative and referendum.

Resolved, 8. That we favor a constitutional provision limiting the office of President and Vice-President to one term, and providing for the election of senators of the United States by a direct vote of the people.

Resolved, 9. That we oppose any subsidy or national aid to any private corporation for any purpose.

SOCIALIST-LABOR CONVENTION.

New York, N. Y., August 28, 1892.

NOMINATED—

For President, **Simon Wing,**
of Massachusetts.

For Vice-President, **Charles H. Matchett,**
of New York.

At this convention, nominations were made as above given, and the following platform was adopted:—

SOCIALIST-LABOR PLATFORM.

Social Demands:—1. Reduction of the hours of labor in proportion to the progress of production.

2. The United States shall obtain possession of the railroads, canals, telegraphs, telephones, and all other means of public transportation and communication.

3. The municipalities to obtain possession of the local railroads, ferries, waterworks, gasworks, electric plants, and all industries requiring municipal franchises.

4. The public lands to be declared inalienable. Revocation of all land-grants to corporations or individuals, the conditions of which have not been complied with.

5. Legal incorporation by the states of local trade-unions which have no national organization.

6. The United States to have the exclusive right to issue money.

7. Congressional legislation providing for the scientific management of forests and waterways, and prohibiting the waste of the natural resources of the country.

8. Inventions to be free to all; the inventors to be remunerated by the nation.

9. Progressive income-tax and tax on inheritances; the smaller incomes to be exempt.

10. School education of all children under fourteen years of age to be compulsory, gratuitous, and accessible to all by public assistance in meals, clothing, books, etc., where necessary.

11. Repeal of all pauper, tramp, conspiracy, and sumptuary laws. Unabridged right of combination.

12. Official statistics concerning the condition of labor. Prohibition of the employment of children of school age, and of the employment of female labor in occupations detrimental to health or morality. Abolition of the convict labor contract system.

13. All wages to be paid in lawful money of the United States. Equalization of women's wages with those of men where equal service is performed.

14. Laws for the protection of life and limb in all occupations, and an efficient employers' liability law.

Political Demands:—1. The people to have the right to propose laws and to vote upon all measures of importance, according to the referendum principle.

2. Abolition of the Presidency, Vice-Presidency, and Senate of the United States. An Executive Board to be established, whose members are to be elected, and may at any time be recalled, by the House of Representatives, as the only legislative body. The states and municipalities to adopt corresponding amendments to their constitutions and statutes.

3. Municipal self-government.

4. Direct vote and secret ballots in all elections. Universal and equal right of suffrage, without regard to color, creed, or sex. Election days to be legal holidays. The principle of minority representation to be introduced.

5. All public officers to be subject to recall by their respective constituencies.

6. Uniform civil and criminal law throughout the United States. Administration of justice to be free of charge. Abolition of capital punishment.

The election occurred on November 8, 1892.

FORTY-FOUR STATES VOTED, six new states having been admitted since the previous election—Idaho, Montana, North and South Dakota, Washington, and Wyoming.

POPULAR VOTE.

STATES.	Grover Cleveland, Democrat.	Benjamin Harrison, Republican.	James B. Weaver, Populist.	John Bidwell, Prohibitionist.	Total vote.*
Alabama	138,138	9,197	85,181	239	232,755
Arkansas	87,834	46,884	11,831	113	146,662
California	118,293	118,149	25,352	8,129	269,923
Colorado	....	38,620	53,584	1,638	93,842
Connecticut	82,395	77,025	806	4,025	164,251
Delaware	18,581	18,083	13	565	37,242
Florida	30,143	....	4,843	475	35,461
Georgia	129,361	48,305	42,937	988	221,591
Idaho	....	8,599	10,520	288	19,407
Illinois	426,281	399,288	22,207	25,870	873,646
Indiana	262,740	255,615	22,208	13,050	553,613
Iowa	196,367	219,795	20,595	6,402	443,159
Kansas	....	157,237	163,111	4,539	324,887
Kentucky	175,461	135,441	23,500	6,442	340,844
Louisiana	87,922	13,282	13,281	....	114,485
Maine	48,044	62,923	2,381	3,062	116,410
Maryland	113,866	92,736	796	5,877	213,275
Massachusetts	176,813	202,814	3,210	7,539	390,376
Michigan	202,296	222,708	19,892	14,069	458,965
Minnesota	100,920	122,823	29,313	12,182	265,238
Mississippi	40,237	1,406	10,256	910	52,809
Missouri	268,398	226,918	41,213	4,331	540,860
Montana	17,581	18,851	7,334	549	44,315
Nebraska	24,943	87,227	83,134	4,902	200,206
Nevada	714	2,811	7,264	89	10,878
New Hampshire	42,081	45,658	292	1,297	89,328
New Jersey	171,042	156,068	969	8,131	336,210
New York	654,868	609,350	16,429	38,190	1,318,837
North Carolina	132,951	100,342	44,736	2,636	280,665
North Dakota	....	17,519	17,700	899	36,118
Ohio	404,115	405,187	14,850	26,012	850,164
Oregon	14,243	35,002	26,965	2,281	78,491
Pennsylvania	452,264	516,011	8,714	25,123	1,002,112
Rhode Island	24,335	26,972	228	1,654	53,189
South Carolina	54,692	13,345	2,407	....	70,444
South Dakota	9,081	34,888	26,544	....	70,513
Tennessee	138,874	100,331	23,477	4,851	267,533
Texas	239,148	81,444	99,688	2,165	422,445
Vermont	16,325	37,992	43	1,415	55,775
Virginia	163,977	113,262	12,275	2,738	292,252
Washington	29,802	36,460	19,165	2,542	87,969
West Virginia	84,467	80,293	4,166	2,145	171,071
Wisconsin	177,335	170,791	9,909	13,132	371,167
Wyoming	....	8,454	7,722	530	16,706
Total	5,556,928	5,176,106	1,041,021	262,034	12,036,089

* Simon Wing, the Socialist-Labor candidate, polled a total of 21,164 votes, which is included in the total vote.

ELECTORAL VOTE.

Counted on February 8, 1893.

STATES.	PRESIDENT.			VICE-PRESIDENT.			
	Grover Cleveland, of New York.	Benjamin Harrison, of Indiana.	James B. Weaver, of Iowa.	Adlai E. Stevenson, of Illinois.	Whitelaw Reid, of New York.	James G. Field, of Virginia.	No. entitled to vote.
Alabama	11	..	..	11	..	..	11
Arkansas	8	..	..	8	..	..	8
California	8	1	..	8	1	..	9
Colorado	..	..	4	..	..	4	4
Connecticut	6	..	..	6	..	..	6
Delaware	3	..	..	3	..	..	3
Florida	4	..	..	4	..	..	4
Georgia	13	..	..	13	..	..	13
Idaho	..	..	3	..	..	3	3
Illinois	24	..	..	24	..	..	24
Indiana	15	..	..	15	..	..	15
Iowa	..	13	..	..	13	..	13
Kansas	..	..	10	..	..	10	10
Kentucky	13	..	..	13	..	..	13
Louisiana	8	..	..	8	..	..	8
Maine	..	6	..	..	6	..	6
Maryland	8	..	..	8	..	..	8
Massachusetts	..	15	..	..	15	..	15
Michigan	5	9	..	5	9	..	14
Minnesota	..	9	..	..	9	..	9
Mississippi	9	..	..	9	..	..	9
Missouri	17	..	..	17	..	..	17
Montana	..	3	..	..	3	..	3
Nebraska	..	8	..	..	8	..	8
Nevada	..	..	3	..	..	3	3
New Hampshire	..	4	..	..	4	..	4
New Jersey	10	..	..	10	..	..	10
New York	36	..	..	36	..	..	36
North Carolina	11	..	..	11	..	..	11
North Dakota	1	1	1	1	1	1	3
Ohio	1	22	..	1	22	..	23
Oregon	..	3	1	..	3	1	4
Pennsylvania	..	32	..	..	32	..	32
Rhode Island	..	4	..	..	4	..	4
South Carolina	9	..	..	9	..	..	9
South Dakota	..	4	..	..	4	..	4
Tennessee	12	..	..	12	..	..	12
Texas	15	..	..	15	..	..	15
Vermont	..	4	..	..	4	..	4
Virginia	12	..	..	12	..	..	12
Washington	..	4	..	..	4	..	4
West Virginia	6	..	..	6	..	..	6
Wisconsin	12	..	..	12	..	..	12
Wyoming	..	3	..	..	3	..	3
Total	277	145	22	277	145	22	444

Grover Cleveland was elected President and Adlai E. Stevenson as Vice-President.

During this period Congress was divided politically as follows:

Fifty-third Congress.

Senate—44 Democrats, 38 Republicans, 1 Independent, 2 Alliance, 3 vacancies ....Total, 88
House—220 Democrats, 128 Republicans, 8 Populists .... " 356

Fifty-fourth Congress.

Senate—39 Democrats, 44 Republicans, 6 Alliance, 1 vacancy ....Total, 90
House—104 Democrats, 245 Republicans, 1 Silverite, 7 Populists .... " 357

Election of 1896

Democratic National Committee:
Chairman, JAMES K. JONES, of Arkansas.
Secretary, CHARLES A. WALSH, of Iowa.

DEMOCRATIC CONVENTION.

Chicago, Ill., July 7, 1896.

Chairman pro tem., JOHN W. DANIEL,
of Virginia.

Chairman, STEPHEN M. WHITE,
of California.

NOMINATED—

For President, **William J. Bryan,**
of Nebraska.

For Vice-President, **Arthur Sewall,**
of Maine.

There were 930 delegates present at this convention. A spirited contest took place for the temporary chairmanship of the convention, which resulted as above stated. There was much discussion occasioned by the financial plank of the platform, and many motions to amend were made; but the platform was finally adopted as at first reported, by the vote of 628 to 301. William J. Bryan, of Nebraska, was nominated for President on the fifth ballot. This was accomplished by 78 delegates transferring their votes to Mr. Bryan after the roll-call was completed, but before the result was announced. The following is the vote in detail:

CANDIDATES.	1st.	2d.	3d.	4th.	5th.
WILLIAM J. BRYAN, of Nebraska	119	190	219	280	500
RICHARD P. BLAND, of Missouri	235	283	291	241	106
ROBERT E. PATTISON, of Pennsylvania	95	100	97	97	95
HORACE BOIES, of Iowa	85	41	36	33	26
JOSEPH S. C. BLACKBURN, of Kentucky	83	41	27	27	..
JOSEPH R. McLEAN, of Ohio	54	53	54	46	..
CLAUDE MATTHEWS, of Indiana	37	33	34	36	31
BENJAMIN R. TILLMAN, of South Carolina	17	..	..	..	..
SYLVESTER PENNOYER, of Oregon	8	8	..	..	..
HENRY M. TELLER, of Colorado	8	8	..	..	..
ADLAI E. STEVENSON, of Illinois	7	10	9	8	8
WILLIAM E. RUSSELL, of Massachusetts	2	..	..	..	..
JAMES E. CAMPBELL, of Ohio	1	..	..	..	..
DAVID B. HILL, of New York	1	1	1	1	1
DAVID TURPIE, of Indiana	..	..	..	..	1
Not voting	178	162	162	162	162
Whole number of votes	752	768	768	769	768
Necessary to a choice	502	512	512	513	512

For Vice-President, Arthur Sewall, of Maine, was nominated on the fifth ballot, as follows:

CANDIDATES.	1st.	2d.	3d.	4th.	5th.
ARTHUR SEWALL, of Maine	100	37	97	261	568
JOSEPH C. SIBLEY, of Pennsylvania	163	113	50	..	..
JOSEPH R. McLEAN, of Ohio	111	158	210	296	32
GEORGE F. WILLIAMS, of Massachusetts	76	16	15	9	9
RICHARD P. BLAND, of Missouri	62	294	255	..	..
WALTER A. CLARK, of North Carolina	50	22	22	46	22
JOHN R. WILLIAMS, of Illinois	22	13	..	..	..
WILLIAM F. HARRITY, of Pennsylvania	21	21	19	11	11
HORACE BOIES, of Iowa	20	..	..	..	..
JOSEPH S. C. BLACKBURN, of Kentucky	20	..	..	..	..
JOHN W. DANIEL, of Virginia	11	1	6	54	36
JAMES H. LEWIS, of Washington	11	..	..	..	..
ROBERT E. PATTISON, of Pennsylvania	..	1	1	1	1
HENRY M. TELLER, of Colorado	1	..	..	..	..
STEPHEN M. WHITE, of California	1	..	..	..	..
GEORGE W. FITHIAN, of Illinois	1	..	..	..	..
Not voting	260	255	255	253	251
Whole number of votes	670	675	675	677	679
Necessary to a choice	447	450	450	452	453

The convention adopted the following platform:—

DEMOCRATIC PLATFORM.

We, the Democrats of the United States, in national convention assembled, do reaffirm our allegiance to those great essential principles of justice and liberty upon which our institutions are founded, and which the Democratic party has advocated from Jefferson's time to our own—freedom of speech, freedom of the press, freedom of conscience, the preservation of personal rights, the equality of all citizens before the law, and the faithful observance of constitutional limitations.

During all these years the Democratic party has resisted the tendency of selfish interests to the centralization of governmental power, and steadfastly maintained the integrity of the dual system of government established by the founders of this republic of republics. Under its guidance and teachings the great principle of local self-government has found its best expression in the maintenance of the rights of the states and in its assertion of the necessity of confining the general government to the exercise of the powers granted by the Constitution of the United States.

The Constitution of the United States guarantees to every citizen the rights of civil and religious liberty. The Democratic party has always been the exponent of political liberty and religious freedom, and it renews its obligations and reaffirms its devotion to these fundamental principles of the Constitution.

THE MONEY PLANK.

Recognizing that the money question is paramount to all others at this time, we invite attention to the fact that the federal Constitution named silver and gold together as the money metals of the United States, and that the first coinage law passed by Congress under the Constitution made the silver dollar the monetary unit and admitted gold to free coinage at a ratio based upon the silver-dollar unit.

We declare that the act of 1873 demonetizing silver without the knowledge or approval of the American people, has resulted in the appreciation of gold and a corresponding fall in the prices of commodities produced by the people; a heavy increase in the burden of taxation and of all debts, public and private; the enrichment of the money-lending class at home and abroad; the prostration of industry and impoverishment of the people.

We are unalterably opposed to monometallism, which has locked fast the prosperity of an industrial people in the paralysis of hard times. Gold monometallism is a British policy, and its adoption has brought other nations into financial servitude to London. It is not only un-American but anti-American, and it can be fastened on the United States only by the stifling of that spirit and love of liberty which proclaimed our political independence in 1776 and won it in the War of the Revolution.

We demand the free and unlimited coinage of both silver and gold at the present legal ratio of 16 to 1, without waiting for the aid or consent of any other nation. We demand that the standard silver dollar shall be a full legal tender, equally with gold, for all debts, public and private, and we favor such legislation as will prevent for the future the demonetization of any kind of legal-tender money by private contract.

We are opposed to the policy and practice of surrendering to the holders of the obligations of the United States the option reserved by law to the government of redeeming such obligations in either silver coin or gold coin.

INTEREST-BEARING BONDS.

We are opposed to the issuing of interest-bearing bonds of the United States in time of peace, and condemn the trafficking with banking syndicates, which, in exchange for bonds and at an enormous profit to themselves, supply the federal treasury with gold to maintain the policy of gold monometallism.

AGAINST NATIONAL BANKS.

Congress alone has the power to coin and issue money, and President Jackson declared that this power could not be delegated to corporations or individuals. We therefore denounce the issuance of notes intended to circulate as money by national banks as in derogation of the Constitution, and we demand that all paper which is made a legal tender for public and private debts, or which is receivable for dues to the United States, shall be issued by the government of the United States, and shall be redeemable in coin.

TARIFF RESOLUTION.

We hold that tariff duties should be levied for purposes of revenue, such duties to be so adjusted as to operate equally throughout the country, and not discriminate between class or section, and that taxation should be limited by the needs of the government, honestly and economically administered. We denounce as disturbing to business the Republican threat to restore the McKinley law, which has twice been condemned by the people in national elections, and which, enacted under the false plea of protection to home industry, proved a prolific breeder of trusts and monopolies, enriched the few at the expense of the many, restricted trade, and deprived the producers of the great American staples of access to their natural markets.

Until the money question is settled we are opposed to any agitation for further changes in our tariff laws, except such as are necessary to meet the deficit in revenue caused by the adverse decision of the Supreme Court on the income-tax.

But for this decision by the Supreme Court, there would be no deficit in the revenue under the law passed by a Democratic Congress in strict pursuance of the uniform decisions of that court for nearly 100 years, that court having in that decision sustained constitutional objections to its enactment, which had previously been overruled by the ablest judges who have ever sat on that bench. We declare that it is the duty of Congress to use all the constitutional power which remains after that decision, or which may come from its reversal by the court as it may hereafter be constituted, so that the burdens of taxation may be equally and impartially laid, to the end that wealth may bear its due proportion of the expense of the government.

IMMIGRATION AND ARBITRATION.

We hold that the most efficient way of protecting American labor is to prevent the importation of foreign pauper labor to compete with it in the home market, and that the value of the home market to our American farmers and artisans is greatly reduced by a vicious monetary system which depresses the prices of their products below the cost of production, and thus deprives them of the means of purchasing the products of our home manufactories; and as labor creates the wealth of the country, we demand the passage of such laws as may be necessary to protect it in all its rights.

We are in favor of the arbitration of differences between employers engaged in interstate commerce and their employees, and recommend such legislation as is necessary to carry out this principle.

TRUSTS AND POOLS.

The absorption of wealth by the few, the consolidation of our leading railroad systems, and the formation of trusts and pools require a stricter control by the federal government of those arteries of commerce. We demand the enlargement of the powers of the Interstate Commerce Commission, and such restriction and guarantees in the control of railroads as will protect the people from robbery and oppression.

DECLARE FOR ECONOMY.

We denounce the profligate waste of the money wrung from the people by oppressive taxation, and the lavish appropriations of recent Republican Congresses, which have kept taxes high, while the labor that pays them is unemployed, and the products of the people's toil are depressed in price till they no longer repay the cost of production. We demand a return to that simplicity and economy which befits a democratic government, and a reduction in the number of useless offices, the salaries of which drain the substance of the people.

FEDERAL INTERFERENCE IN LOCAL AFFAIRS.

We denounce arbitrary interference by federal authorities in local affairs as a violation of the Constitution of the United States and a crime against free institutions, and we especially object to government by injunction as a new and highly dangerous form of oppression by which federal judges, in contempt of the laws of the states and rights of citizens, become at once legislators, judges, and executioners; and we approve the bill passed at the last session of the United States Senate, and now pending in the House of Representatives, relative to contempts in federal courts, and providing for trials by jury in certain cases of contempt.

PACIFIC RAILROAD.

No discrimination should be indulged in by the government of the United States in favor of any of its debtors. We approve of the refusal of the Fifty-third Congress to pass the Pacific Railroad Funding bill, and denounce the effort of the present Republican Congress to enact a similar measure.

PENSIONS.

Recognizing the just claims of deserving Union soldiers, we heartily indorse the rule of the present Commissioner of Pensions, that no names shall be arbitrarily dropped from the pension roll; and the fact of enlistment and service should be deemed conclusive evidence against disease and disability before enlistment.

ADMISSION OF TERRITORIES.

We favor the admission of the Territories of New Mexico, Arizona, and Oklahoma into the Union as States, and we favor the early admission of all the territories having the necessary population and resources to entitle them to statehood, and, while they remain territories, we hold that the officials appointed to administer the government of any territory, together with the District of Columbia and Alaska, should be *bona fide* residents of the territory or district in which their duties are to be performed. The Democratic party believes in home rule, and that all public lands of the United States should be appropriated to the establishment of free homes for American citizens.

We recommend that the Territory of Alaska be granted a delegate in Congress, and that the general land and timber laws of the United States be extended to said territory.

SYMPATHY FOR CUBA.

The Monroe doctrine, as originally declared, and as interpreted by succeeding Presidents, is a permanent part of the foreign policy of the United States, and must at all times be maintained.

We extend our sympathy to the people of Cuba in their heroic struggle for liberty and independence.

CIVIL-SERVICE LAWS.

We are opposed to life tenure in the public service, except as provided in the Constitution. We favor appointments based on merit, fixed terms of office, and such an administration of the civil-service laws as will afford equal opportunities to all citizens of ascertained fitness.

THIRD-TERM RESOLUTION.

We declare it to be the unwritten law of this republic, established by custom and usage of 100 years, and sanctioned by the examples of the greatest and wisest of those who founded and have maintained our government, that no man should be eligible for a third term of the presidential office.

IMPROVEMENT OF WATERWAYS.

The federal government should care for and improve the Mississippi River and other great waterways of the republic, so as to secure for the interior states easy and cheap transportation to tidewater. When any waterway of the republic is of sufficient importance to demand aid of the government, such aid should be extended upon a definite plan of continuous work until permanent improvement is secured.

CONCLUSION.

Confiding in the justice of our cause and the necessity of its success at the polls, we submit the foregoing declaration of principles and purposes to the considerate judgment of the American people. We invite the support of all citizens who approve them and who desire to have them made effective through legislation for the relief of the people and the restoration of the country's prosperity.

Republican National Committee:

Chairman, MARCUS A. HANNA, of Ohio.
Secretary, WM. M. OSBORN, of Massachusetts.

Mr. Osborn having resigned, CHARLES DICK, of Ohio, was chosen secretary.

REPUBLICAN CONVENTION.

St. Louis, Mo., June 16, 1896.

Chairman pro tem., CHARLES W. FAIRBANKS, of Indiana.

Chairman, JOHN M. THURSTON, of Nebraska.

NOMINATED—

For President, **William McKinley,** of Ohio.

For Vice-President, **Garret A. Hobart,** of New Jersey.

After the platform had been adopted by the convention, thirty-four members who had protested against the financial plank without avail, solemnly withdrew from the convention. William McKinley, of Ohio, was chosen as the candidate for President on the first ballot, as is shown in the following table:

CANDIDATES.	Votes.	CANDIDATES.	Votes.
WILLIAM MCKINLEY, of Ohio	661½	LEVI P. MORTON, of New York	58
THOMAS B. REED, of Maine	84½	WILLIAM B. ALLISON, of Iowa	35½
MATTHEW S. QUAY, of Pennsylvania	61½	J. DONALD CAMERON, of Pennsylvania	1
		Blank	4

As the candidate for Vice-President, Garret A. Hobart, of New Jersey, was also chosen on the first ballot, as is shown below:

CANDIDATES.	Votes.	CANDIDATES.	Votes.
GARRET A. HOBART, of New Jersey	535½	CHAUNCEY M. DEPEW, of New York...........	3
HENRY CLAY EVANS, of Tennessee............	277½	JOHN M. THURSTON, of Nebraska...	2
MORGAN G. BULKELEY, of Connecticut..........	39	FREDERICK D. GRANT, of New York...........	2
JAMES A. WALKER, of Virginia..............	24	LEVI P. MORTON, of New York...........	1
CHARLES W. LIPPITT, of Rhode Island.........	8	Whole number of votes, 895	
THOMAS B. REED, of Maine...	3	Necessary to a choice, 448	

The convention adopted the following as the platform:—

REPUBLICAN PLATFORM.

The Republicans of the United States, assembled by their representatives in national convention, appealing for the popular and historical justification of their claims to the matchless achievements of the thirty years of Republican rule, earnestly and confidently address themselves to the awakened intelligence, experience, and conscience of their countrymen in the following declaration of facts and principles:

For the first time since the Civil War the American people have witnessed the calamitous consequences of full and unrestricted Democratic control of the government. It has been a record of unparalleled incapacity, dishonor, and disaster. In administrative management it has ruthlessly sacrificed indispensable revenue, entailed an unceasing deficit, eked out ordinary current expenses with borrowed money, piled up the public debt by $262,000,000 in time of peace, forced an adverse balance of trade, kept a perpetual menace hanging over the redemption fund, pawned American credit to alien syndicates, and reversed all the measures and results of successful Republican rule.

In the broad effect of its policy it has precipitated panic, blighted industry and trade with prolonged depression, closed factories, reduced work and wages, halted enterprise, and crippled American production while stimulating foreign production for the American market. Every consideration of public safety and individual interest demands that the government shall be rescued from the hands of those who have shown themselves incapable to conduct it without disaster at home and dishonor abroad, and shall be restored to the party which for thirty years administered it with unequaled success and prosperity, and in this connection we heartily indorse the wisdom, the patriotism, and the success of the administration of President Harrison.

TARIFF.

We renew and emphasize our allegiance to the policy of protection as the bulwark of American industrial independence and the foundation of American development and prosperity. This true American policy taxes foreign products and encourages home industry; it puts the burden of revenue on foreign goods; it secures the American market for the American producer; it upholds the American standard of wages for the American workingman; it puts the factory by the side of the farm, and makes the American farmer less dependent on foreign demand and price; it diffuses general thrift, and founds the strength of all on the strength of each. In its reasonable application it is just, fair, and impartial; equally opposed to foreign control and domestic monopoly, to sectional discrimination and individual favoritism.

We denounce the present Democratic tariff as sectional, injurious to the public credit, and destructive to business enterprise. We demand such an equitable tariff on foreign imports which come into competition with American products as will not only furnish adequate revenue for the necessary expenses of the government, but will protect American labor from degradation to the wage level of other lands. We are not pledged to any particular schedules. The question of rates is a practical question to be governed by the conditions of time and of production: the ruling and uncompromising principle is the protection and development of American labor and industry. The country demands a right settlement, and then it wants rest.

RECIPROCITY.

We believe the repeal of the reciprocity arrangements negotiated by the last Republican administration was a national calamity, and we demand their renewal and extension on such terms as will equalize our trade with other nations, remove the restrictions which now obstruct the sale of American products in the ports of other countries, and secure enlarged markets for the products of our farms, forests, and factories.

Protection and reciprocity are twin measures of Republican policy and go hand in hand. Democratic rule has recklessly struck down both, and both must be re-established. Protection for what we produce; free admission for the necessaries of life which we do not produce; reciprocity agreements of mutual interests which gain open markets for us in return for our open market to others. Protection builds up domestic industry and trade, and secures our own market for ourselves; reciprocity builds up foreign trade, and finds an outlet for our surplus.

SUGAR.

We condemn the present administration for not keeping faith with the sugar-producers of this country. The Republican party favors such protection as will lead to the production on American soil of all the sugar which the American people use, and for which they pay other countries more than $100,000,000 annually.

WOOL AND WOOLENS.

To all our products—to those of the mine and the fields as well as to those of the shop and the factory; to hemp, to wool, the product of the great industry of sheep husbandry, as well as to the finished woolens of the mills—we promise the most ample protection.

MERCHANT MARINE.

We favor restoring the American policy of discriminating duties for the upbuilding of our merchant marine and the protection of our shipping in the foreign carrying trade, so that American ships—the product of American labor, employed in American shipyards, sailing under the Stars and Stripes, and manned, officered, and owned by Americans—may regain the carrying of our foreign commerce.

FINANCE.

The Republican party is unreservedly for sound money. It caused the enactment of the law providing for the resumption of specie payments in 1879; since then every dollar has been as good as gold.

We are unalterably opposed to every measure calculated to debase our currency or impair the credit of our country. We are, therefore, opposed to the free coinage of silver except by international agreement with the leading commercial nations of the world, which we pledge ourselves to promote, and until such agreement can be obtained, the existing gold standard must be preserved. All our silver and paper currency must be maintained at parity with gold, and we favor all measures designed to maintain inviolably the obligations of the United States and all our money, whether coin or paper, at the present standard, the standard of the most enlightened nations of the earth.

PENSIONS.

The veterans of the Union Army deserve and should receive fair treatment and generous recognition. Whenever practicable, they should be given the preference in the matter of employment, and they are entitled to the enactment of such laws as are best calculated to secure the fulfilment of the pledges made to them in the dark days of the country's peril. We denounce the practice in the Pension Bureau, so recklessly and unjustly carried on by the present administration, of reducing pensions and arbitrarily dropping names from the rolls, as deserving the severest condemnation of the American people.

FOREIGN RELATIONS.

Our foreign policy should be at all times firm, vigorous, and dignified, and all our interests in the Western Hemisphere carefully watched and guarded. The Hawaiian Islands should be controlled by the United States, and no foreign power should be permitted to interfere with them; the Nicaragua Canal should be built, owned, and operated by the United States; and by the purchase of the Danish islands we should secure a proper and much needed naval station in the West Indies.

ARMENIAN MASSACRES.

The massacres in Armenia have aroused the deep sympathy and just indignation of the American people, and we believe that the United States should exercise all the influence it can properly exert to bring these atrocities to an end. In Turkey, American residents have been exposed to the gravest dangers and American property destroyed. There and everywhere American citizens and American property must be absolutely protected at all hazards and at any cost.

MONROE DOCTRINE.

We reassert the Monroe doctrine in its full extent, and we reaffirm the right of the United States to give the doctrine effect by responding to the appeal of any American state for friendly intervention in case of European encroachment. We have not interfered and shall not interfere with the existing possessions of any European power in this hemisphere, but these possessions must not on any pretext be extended. We hopefully look forward to the eventual withdrawal of the European powers from this hemisphere, and to the ultimate union of all English-speaking parts of the continent by the free consent of its inhabitants.

CUBA.

From the hour of achieving their own independence, the people of the United States have regarded with sympathy the struggles of other American peoples to free themselves from European domination. We watch with deep and abiding interest the heroic battle of the Cuban patriots against cruelty and oppression, and our best hopes go out for the full success of their determined contest for liberty.

The Government of Spain having lost control of Cuba and being unable to protect the property or lives of resident American citizens or to comply with its treaty obligations, we believe that the Government of the United States should actively use its influence and good offices to restore peace and give independence to the island.

THE NAVY.

The peace and security of the republic and the maintenance of its rightful influence among the nations of the earth demand a naval power commensurate with its position and responsibility. We therefore favor the continued enlargement of the navy and a complete system of harbor and seacoast defenses.

FOREIGN IMMIGRATION.

For the protection of the quality of our American citizenship and of the wages of our workingmen against the fatal competition of low-priced labor, we demand that the immigration laws be thoroughly enforced, and so extended as to exclude from entrance to the United States those who can neither read nor write.

CIVIL SERVICE.

The civil-service law was placed on the statute-book by the Republican party, which has always sustained it, and we renew our repeated declarations that it shall be thoroughly and honestly enforced, and extended wherever practicable.

FREE BALLOT.

We demand that every citizen of the United States shall be allowed to cast one free and unrestricted ballot, and that such ballot shall be counted and returned as cast.

LYNCHINGS.

We proclaim our unqualified condemnation of the uncivilized and barbarous practice well known as lynching, or killing of human beings suspected or charged with crime, without process of law.

NATIONAL ARBITRATION.

We favor the creation of a national board of arbitration to settle and adjust differences which may arise between employers and employees engaged in interstate commerce.

HOMESTEADS.

We believe in an immediate return to the free-homestead policy of the Republican party, and urge the passage by Congress of a satisfactory free-homestead measure such as has already passed the House and is now pending in the Senate.

TERRITORIES.

We favor the admission of the remaining territories at the earliest practicable date, having due regard to the interests of the people of the territories and of the United States. All the federal officers appointed for the territories should be selected from *bona fide* residents thereof, and the right of self-government should be accorded as far as practicable.

ALASKA.

We believe the citizens of Alaska should have representation in the Congress of the United States, to the end that needful legislation may be intelligently enacted.

TEMPERANCE.

We sympathize with all wise and legitimate efforts to lessen and prevent the evils of intemperance and promote morality.

RIGHTS OF WOMEN.

The Republican party is mindful of the rights and interests of women. Protection of American industries includes equal opportunities, equal pay for equal work, and protection to the home. We favor the admission of women to wider spheres of usefulness, and welcome their co-operation in rescuing the country from Democratic and Populist mismanagement and misrule.

Such are the principles and policies of the Republican party. By these principles we will abide and these policies we will put into execution. We ask for them the considerate judgment of the American people. Confident alike in the history of our great party and in the justice of our cause, we present our platform and our candidates in the full assurance that the election will bring victory to the Republican party and prosperity to the people of the United States.

PEOPLE'S PARTY CONVENTION.

St. Louis, Mo., July 22, 1896.

Chairman pro tem., MARION C. BUTLER,
of North Carolina.

Chairman, WILLIAM V. ALLEN,
of Nebraska.

NOMINATED—

For President, **William J. Bryan,**
of Nebraska.

For Vice-President, **Thomas E. Watson,**
of Georgia.

The number of delegates was determined by the strength of the party in state elections. This was different from the custom prevailing in the older parties.

The convention reversed the usual order of proceedings at National Conventions, and nominated the candidate for Vice-President first. Thomas E. Watson, of Georgia, was nominated on the first ballot, receiving 469½ votes; Arthur Sewall, of Maine, received 257½ votes. Votes were also cast for Harry Skinner, of North Carolina; Frank Burkett, of Mississippi; A. L. Mimms, of Tennessee; and Mann Page, of Virginia.

William J. Bryan, of Nebraska, was nominated for President, the ballot resulting as follows:

CANDIDATES.	Votes.	CANDIDATES.	Votes.
WILLIAM J. BRYAN, of Nebraska............	1042	IGNATIUS DONNELLY, of Minnesota...........	3
S. F. NORTON, of Illinois	321	J. S. COXEY, of Ohio	1
EUGENE V. DEBS, of Indiana..............	8	Whole number of votes, 1375	
		Necessary to a choice, 688	

The convention adopted the following platform:

PEOPLE'S PARTY PLATFORM.

The People's party, assembled in national convention, reaffirms its allegiance to the principles declared by the founders of the republic, and also to the fundamental principles of just government as enunciated in the platform of the party in 1892.

We recognize that through the connivance of the present and preceding administrations the country has reached a crisis in its national life, as predicted in our declaration four years ago, and that prompt and patriotic action is the supreme duty of the hour.

We realize that, while we have political independence, our financial and industrial independence is yet to be attained by restoring to our country the constitutional control and exercise of the functions necessary to a people's government, which functions have been basely surrendered by our public servants to corporate monopolies. The influence of European moneychangers has been more potent in shaping legislation than the voice of the American people. Executive power and patronage have been used to corrupt our legislatures and defeat the will of the people, and plutocracy has been enthroned upon the ruins of democracy.

To restore the government intended by the fathers, and for the welfare and prosperity of this and future generations, we demand the establishment of an economic and financial system which shall make us masters of our own affairs and independent of European control, by the adoption of the following declaration of principles:—

AS TO MONEY, BONDS, AND INCOME-TAX.

1. We demand a national money, safe and sound, issued by the general government only, without the intervention of banks of issue, to be a full legal tender for all debts, public and private, and a just, equitable, and efficient means of distribution direct to the people and through the lawful disbursements of the government.

2. We demand the free and unrestricted coinage of silver and gold at the present legal ratio of 16 to 1, without waiting for the consent of foreign nations.

3. We demand that the volume of circulating medium be speedily increased to an amount sufficient to meet the demands of the business population of this country, and to restore the just level of prices of labor and production.

4. We denounce the sale of bonds and the increase of the public interest-bearing bond debt made by the present administration as unnecessary and without authority of law, and that no more bonds be issued except by specific act of Congress.

5. We demand such legal legislation as will prevent the demonetization of the lawful money of the United States by private contract.

6. We demand that the government, in payment of its obligations, shall use its option as to the kind of lawful money in which they are to be paid, and we denounce the present and preceding administrations for surrendering this option to the holders of government obligations.

7. We demand a graduated income-tax, to the end that aggregated wealth shall bear its just proportion of taxation, and we denounce the recent decision of the Supreme Court relative to the income-tax law as a misinterpretation of the Constitution and an invasion of the rightful powers of Congress over the subject of taxation.

8. We demand that postal savings-banks be established by the government for the safe deposit of the savings of the people and to facilitate exchange.

GOVERNMENT OWNERSHIP OF RAILROADS AND TELEGRAPH.

1. Transportation being a means of exchange and a public necessity, the government should own and operate the railroads in the interest of the people and on a non-partisan basis,

to the end that all may be accorded the same treatment in transportation, and that the tyranny and political power now exercised by the great railroad corporations, which result in the impairment, if not the destruction, of the political rights and personal liberties of the citizens, may be destroyed. Such ownership is to be accomplished gradually, in a manner consistent with sound public policy.

2. The interest of the United States in the public highways, built with public moneys, and the proceeds of extensive grants of land to the Pacific railroads should never be alienated, mortgaged, or sold, but guarded and protected for the general welfare, as provided by the laws organizing such railroads. The foreclosure of existing liens of the United States on these roads should at once follow default in the payment of the debt of the companies, and at the foreclosure sales of said roads the government shall purchase the same, if it become necessary to protect its interests therein, or if they can be purchased at a reasonable price; and the government shall operate said railroads as public highways, for the benefit of the whole and not in the interest of the few, under suitable provisions for protection of life and property, giving to all transportation interests equal privileges and equal rates for fares and freight.

3. We denounce the present infamous schemes for refunding these debts, and demand that the laws now applicable thereto be executed and administered according to their true intent and spirit.

4. The telegraph, like the post-office system, being a necessity for the transmission of news, should be owned and operated by the government in the interest of the people.

LAND, HOMES AND PACIFIC RAILROAD GRANTS.

1. The true policy demands that the national and state legislation shall be such as will ultimately enable every prudent and industrious citizen to secure a home, and therefore the land should not be monopolized for speculative purposes. All lands now held by railroads and other corporations in excess of their actual needs should, by lawful means, be reclaimed by the government and held for actual settlers only, and private land monopoly, as well as alien ownership, should be prohibited.

2. We condemn the frauds by which the land-grants to the Pacific railroad companies have, through the connivance of the Interior Department, robbed multitudes of *bona fide* settlers of their homes and miners of their claims, and we demand legislation by Congress which will enforce the exemption of mineral land from such grants after as well as before the patent.

3. We demand that *bona fide* settlers on all public lands be granted free homes, as provided in the national homestead law, and that no exception be made in the case of Indian reservations when opened for settlement, and that all lands not now patented come under this demand.

DIRECT LEGISLATION AND GENERAL PLANKS.

We favor a system of direct legislation through the initiative and referendum, under proper constitutional safeguards.

We demand the election of President, Vice-President, and United States senators by a direct vote of the people.

We tender to the patriotic people of Cuba our deepest sympathy in their heroic struggle for political freedom and independence, and we believe the time has come when the United States, the great republic of the world, should recognize that Cuba is and of right ought to be a free and independent state.

We favor home rule in the territories and the District of Columbia, and the early admission of the territories as states.

All public salaries should be made to correspond to the price of labor and its products.

In times of great industrial depression, idle labor should be employed on public works as far as practicable.

The arbitrary course of the courts in assuming to imprison citizens for indirect contempt and ruling by injunction should be prevented by proper legislation.

We favor just pensions for our disabled Union soldiers.

Believing that the elective franchise and an untrammeled ballot are essential to a government of, for, and by the people, the People's party condemns the wholesale system of disfranchisement adopted in some states, as unrepublican and undemocratic, and we declare it to be the duty of the several state legislatures to take such action as will secure a full, free, and fair ballot and an honest count.

FINANCIAL QUESTION "THE PRESSING ISSUE."

While the foregoing propositions constitute the platform upon which our party stands, and for the vindication of which its organization will be maintained, we recognize that the great and pressing issue of the pending campaign, upon which the present presidential election will turn, is the financial question, and upon this great and specific issue between the parties we cordially invite the aid and co-operation of all organizations and citizens agreeing with us upon this vital question.

SILVER PARTY CONVENTION.

St. Louis, Mo., July 22, 1896.

Chairman pro tem., FRANK G. NEWLANDS,
of Nevada.

Chairman, WILLIAM P. ST. JOHN,
of New York.

NOMINATED—

For President, **William J. Bryan,**
of Nebraska.

For Vice-President, **Arthur Sewall,**
of Maine.

The convention, by acclamation, endorsed the candidates nominated by the Democratic Convention at Chicago, namely, William J. Bryan for President, and Arthur Sewall for Vice-President.

The following is the platform adopted:—

SILVER PARTY PLATFORM.

The National Silver party, in convention assembled, hereby adopts the following declaration of principles:—

First. The paramount issue at this time in the United States is indisputably the money question. It is between the gold standard, gold bonds, and bank currency on the one side, and the bimetallic standard, no bonds, and government currency on the other.

On this issue we declare ourselves to be in favor of a distinctively American financial system. We are unalterably opposed to the single gold standard, and demand the immediate return to the constitutional standard of gold and silver, by the restoration by this government, independently of any foreign power, of the unrestricted coinage of both gold and silver into standard money at the ratio of 16 to 1, and upon terms of exact equality, as they existed prior to 1873; the silver coin to be a full legal tender equally with gold for all debts and dues, private and public, and we favor such legislation as will prevent for the future the demonetization of any kind of legal-tender money by private contract.

We hold that the power to control and regulate a paper currency is inseparable from the power to coin money, and hence that all currency intended to circulate as money should be issued, and its volume controlled, by the general government only, and should be at legal tender.

We are unalterably opposed to the issue by the United States of interest-bearing bonds in time of peace, and we denounce as a blunder worse than a crime the present treasury policy, concurred in by a Republican House, of plunging the country in debt by hundreds of millions in the vain attempt to maintain the gold standard by borrowing gold, and we demand the payment of all coin obligations of the United States as provided by existing laws, in either gold or silver coin, at the option of the government, and not at the option of the creditor.

The demonetization of silver in 1873 enormously increased

the demand for gold, enhancing its purchasing power and lowering all prices measured by that standard; and since that unjust and indefensible act the prices of American products have fallen, upon an average, nearly 50 per cent., carrying down with them proportionately the money value of all other forms of property. Such fall of prices has destroyed the profits of legitimate industry, injuring the producer for the benefit of the non-producer, increasing the burden of the debtor, swelling the gains of the creditor, paralyzing the productive energies of the American people, relegating to idleness vast numbers of willing workers, sending the shadows of despair into the home of the honest toiler, filling the land with tramps and paupers, and building up colossal fortunes at the money centers.

In the effort to maintain the gold standard the country has within the last two years, in a time of profound peace and plenty, been loaded down with $262,000,000 of additional interest-bearing debt, under such circumstances as to allow a syndicate of native and foreign bankers to realize a net profit of millions on a single deal.

It stands confessed that the gold standard can only be upheld by so depleting our paper currency as to force the prices of our products below the European, and even below the Asiatic level, to enable us to sell in foreign markets, thus aggravating the very evils our people so bitterly complain of, degrading American labor, and striking at the foundations of our civilization itself.

The advocates of the gold standard persistently claim that the cause of our distress is overproduction; that we have produced so much that it has made us poor—which implies that the true remedy is to close the factory, abandon the farm, and throw a multitude of people out of employment, a doctrine that leaves us unnerved and disheartened, and absolutely without hope for the future.

We affirm it to be unquestioned that there can be no such economic paradox as overproduction and at the same time tens of thousands of our fellow-citizens remaining half-clothed and half-fed, and piteously clamoring for the common necessities of life.

Second. That over and above all other questions of policy, we are in favor of restoring to the people of the United States the time-honored money of the Constitution—gold and silver; not one, but both—the money of Washington, and Hamilton, and Jefferson, and Monroe, and Jackson, and Lincoln, to the end that the American people may receive honest pay for an honest product; that the American debtor may pay his just obligations in an honest standard, and not in a dishonest and unsound standard, appreciated 100 per cent. in purchasing power, and no appreciation in debt-paying power; and to the end, further, that silver-standard countries may be deprived of the unjust advantage they now enjoy, in the difference in exchange between gold and silver—an advantage which tariff legislation alone cannot overcome.

We therefore confidently appeal to the people of the United States to leave in abeyance for the moment all other questions, however important and even momentous they may appear—to sunder, if need be, all former party ties and affiliations—and unite in one supreme effort to free themselves and their children from the domination of the money power—a power more destructive than any which has ever been fastened upon the civilized men of any race or in any age. And upon the consummation of our desires and efforts we invoke the aid of all patriotic American citizens, and the gracious favor of Divine Providence.

Inasmuch as the patriotic majority of the Chicago Convention embodied in the financial plank of its platform the principles enunciated in the platform of the American Bimetallic party, promulgated at Washington, D. C., January 22, 1896, and herein reiterated, which is not only the paramount but the only real issue in the pending campaign, therefore, recognizing that their nominees embody these patriotic principles, we recommend that this convention nominate William J. Bryan, of Nebraska, for President, and Arthur Sewall, of Maine, for Vice-President.

NATIONAL DEMOCRATIC CONVENTION.

Indianapolis, Ind., September 2, 1896.

Chairman pro tem., ROSWELL P. FLOWER,
of New York.

Chairman, DONELSON CAFFERY,
of Louisiana.

NOMINATED—

For President, **John M. Palmer,**
of Illinois.

For Vice-President, **Simon Bolivar Buckner,**
of Kentucky.

There were present at this convention, 888 delegates, representing forty-one states and three territories—Idaho, Nevada, Utah, and Wyoming having no delegates present. The delegates represented that wing of the Democratic party which refused to accept the platform adopted at the Chicago convention. They adopted the name of "National Democratic Party." Candidates were chosen as follows:—For President, John M. Palmer, of Illinois, was nominated on the first ballot, receiving 769½ votes, as against 118½ votes cast for Edward S. Bragg, of Wisconsin. For Vice-President, Simon Bolivar Buckner, of Kentucky, was nominated by acclamation.

The convention unanimously adopted the following platform:—

NATIONAL DEMOCRATIC PLATFORM.

This convention has assembled to uphold the principles upon which depend the honor and welfare of the American people, in order that Democrats throughout the Union may unite their patriotic efforts to avert disaster from their country and ruin from their party.

The Democratic party is pledged to equal and exact justice to all men, of every creed and condition; to the largest freedom of the individual consistent with good government; to the preservation of the federal government in its constitutional vigor, and to the support of the states in all their just rights; to economy in the public expenditures; to the maintenance of the public faith and sound money; and it is opposed to paternalism and all class-legislation.

The declarations of the Chicago convention attack individual freedom, the right to private contract, the independence of the judiciary, and the authority of the President to enforce federal laws. They advocate a reckless attempt to increase the price of silver by legislation, to the debasement of our monetary standard, and threaten unlimited issues of paper money by the government. They abandon for Republican allies the Democratic cause of tariff reform, to court the favor of protectionists to their fiscal heresy.

In view of these and other grave departures from Democratic principles, we cannot support the candidates of that convention nor be bound by its acts. The Democratic party has survived defeats, but could not survive a victory won in behalf of the doctrine and policy proclaimed in its name at Chicago.

The conditions, however, which made possible such utterances from a national convention are the direct result of class-legislation by the Republican party. It still proclaims, as it has for years, the power and duty of government to raise and maintain prices by law, and it proposes no remedy for existing evils, except oppressive and unjust taxation.

TARIFF.

The National Democracy here convened therefore renews its declaration of faith in Democratic principles, especially as applicable to the conditions of the times. Taxation—tariff, excise, or direct—is rightfully imposed only for public purposes, and not for private gain. Its amount is justly measured by public expenditures, which should be limited by scrupulous economy. The sum derived by the treasury from tariff and excise levies is affected by the state of trade and volume of consumption. The amount required by the treasury is determined by the appropriations made by Congress. The demand of the Republican party for an increase in tariff taxation has its pretext in the deficiency of the revenue, which has its causes in the stagnation of trade and reduced consumption, due entirely to the loss of confidence that has followed the Populist threat of free coinage and depreciation of our money, and the Republican practice of extravagant appropriations beyond the needs of good government.

We arraign and condemn the Populistic conventions of Chicago and St. Louis for their co-operation with the Republican party in creating these conditions, which are pleaded in justification of a heavy increase of the burdens of the people by a further resort to protection. We therefore denounce protection and its ally, free coinage of silver, as schemes for the personal profit of a few at the expense of the masses, and oppose the two parties which stand for these schemes as hostile to the people of the republic, whose food and shelter, comfort and prosperity are attacked by higher taxes and depreciated money. In fine, we reaffirm the historic Democratic doctrine of tariff for revenue only.

THE SHIPPING INTERESTS.

We demand that henceforth modern and liberal policies toward American shipping shall take the place of our imitation of the restricted statutes of the eighteenth century, which have been abandoned by every maritime power but the United States, and which, to the nation's humiliation, have driven American capital and enterprise to the use of alien flags and alien crews, have made the Stars and Stripes an almost unknown emblem in foreign ports, and have virtually extinguished the race of American seamen. We oppose the pretense that discriminating duties wil promote shipping: that scheme is an invitation to commercial warfare upon the United States, un-American in the light of our great commercial treaties, offering no gain whatever to American shipping, while greatly increasing ocean freights on our agricultural and manufactured products.

MONEY.

The experience of mankind has shown that, by reason of their natural qualities, gold is the necessary money of the large affairs of commerce and business, while silver is conveniently adapted to minor transactions, and the most beneficial use of both together can be insured only by the adoption of the former as a standard of monetary measure, and the maintenance of silver at a parity with gold by its limited coinage under suitable safeguards of law. Thus the largest possible enjoyment of both metals is gained, with a value universally accepted throughout the world, which constitutes the only practical bimetallic currency, assuring the most stable standard, and especially the best and safest money for all who earn their livelihood by labor or the produce of husbandry. They cannot suffer when paid in the best money known to man, but are the peculiar and most defenseless victims of a debased and fluctuating currency, which offers continual profits to the money-changer at their cost.

Realizing these truths, demonstrated by long and public inconvenience and loss, the Democratic party, in the interests of the masses and of equal justice to all, practically established by the legislation of 1834 and 1853 the gold standard of monetary measurement, and likewise entirely divorced the government from banking and currency issues. To this long-established Democratic policy we adhere, and insist upon the maintenance of the gold standard, and of the parity therewith of every dollar issued by the government, and are firmly opposed to the free and unlimited coinage of silver and to the compulsory purchase of silver bullion. But we denounce, also, the further maintenance of the present costly patchwork system of national paper currency as a constant source of injury and peril. We assert the necessity of such intelligent currency reform as will confine the government to its legitimate functions, completely separated from the banking business, and afford to all sections of our country uniform, safe, and elastic bank currency under governmental supervision, measured in volume by the needs of business.

CLEVELAND.

The fidelity, patriotism, and courage with which President Cleveland has fulfilled his great public trust; the high character of his administration, its wisdom and energy in the maintenance of civil order and the enforcement of the laws, its equal regard for the rights of every class and every section, its firm and dignified conduct of foreign affairs, and its sturdy persistence in upholding the credit and honor of the nation,—are fully recognized by the Democratic party and will secure to him a place in history beside the Fathers of the republic.

CIVIL SERVICE.

We also commend the administration for the great progress made in the reform of the public service, and we indorse its efforts to extend the merit system still further. We demand that no backward step be taken, but that the reform be supported and advanced until the un-Democratic spoils system of appointments shall be eradicated.

ECONOMY.

We demand strict economy in the appropriations and in the administration of the government.

ARBITRATION.

We favor arbitration for the settlement of international disputes.

PENSIONS.

We favor a liberal policy of pensions to deserving soldiers and sailors of the United States.

SUPREME COURT.

The Supreme Court of the United States was wisely established by the framers of our Constitution as one of the three co-ordinate branches of the government. Its independence and authority to interpret the law of the land without fear or favor must be maintained. We condemn all efforts to degrade that tribunal or impair the confidence and respect which it has deservedly held.

The Democratic party ever has maintained, and ever will maintain, the supremacy of law, the independence of its judicial administration, the inviolability of contracts, and the obligations of all good citizens to resist every illegal trust, combination, or attempt against the just rights of property and the good order of society, in which are bound up the peace and happiness of our people.

Believing these principles to be essential to the well-being of the republic, we submit them to the consideration of the American people.

PROHIBITION CONVENTION.

Pittsburgh, Pa., May 27, 1896.

Chairman pro tem., A. A. Stevens, of Pennsylvania.

Chairman, Oliver W. Stewart, of Illinois.

Nominated—

For President, **Joshua Levering**, of Maryland.

For Vice-President, **Hale Johnson**, of Illinois.

This convention met at Pittsburg on May 27, 1896, and after much contention over the adoption of the platform, split, and nominated two tickets. The faction which bolted the convention adopted the name of "National Party." The Prohibition nominees were Joshua Levering, of Maryland, for President, who was chosen by acclamation, and Hale Johnson, of Illinois, for Vice-President, who received 309 votes to 132 cast for T. C. Hughes, of Arizona.

The following is the platform adopted by this convention:—

PROHIBITION PLATFORM.

We, the members of the Prohibition party, in national convention assembled, renewing our declaration of allegiance to Almighty God as the Rightful Ruler of the universe, lay down the following as our declaration of political purpose:

The Prohibition party, in national convention assembled, declares its firm conviction that the manufacture, exportation, importation, and sale of alcoholic beverages has produced such social, commercial, industrial, and political wrongs, and is now so threatening the perpetuity of all our social and political institutions, that the suppression of the same, by a national party organized therefor, is the greatest object to be accomplished by the voters of our country, and is of such importance that it, of right, ought to control the political actions of all our patriotic citizens until such suppression is accomplished.

The urgency of this course demands the union, without further delay, of all citizens who desire the prohibition of the liquor traffic; therefore, be it

Resolved, That we favor the legal prohibition by state and national legislation of the manufacture, importation, and sale of alcoholic beverages. That we declare our purpose to organize and unite all the friends of prohibition into one party, and in order to accomplish this end we deem it of right to leave every Prohibitionist the freedom of his own convictions upon all other political questions, and trust our representatives to take such action upon other political questions as the changes occasioned by prohibition and the welfare of the whole people shall demand.

NATIONAL PARTY CONVENTION.

Pittsburgh, Pa., May 28, 1896.

Chairman, A. L. MOORE,
of Michigan.

NOMINATED—

For President, **Rev. Charles E. Bentley,**
of Nebraska.

For Vice-President, **James H. Southgate,**
of North Carolina.

This convention was composed of 299 delegates who had seceded from the Prohibition Convention. Twenty-seven states were represented. The convention adopted a platform, and nominated, by acclamation, the Rev. Charles E. Bentley, of Nebraska, as their candidate for President, and James H. Southgate, of North Carolina, for Vice-President.

The following is the platform adopted:—

NATIONAL PARTY PLATFORM.

The National party, recognizing God as the Author of all just power in government, presents the following declaration of principles, which it pledges itself to enact into effective legislation, when given the power to do so:—

1. The suppression of the manufacture and sale, importation, exportation, and transportation of intoxicating liquors for beverage purposes. We utterly reject all plans for regulating or compromising with this traffic, whether such plans be called local option, taxation, license, or public control. The sale of liquors for medicinal and other legitimate uses should be conducted by the state, without profit, and with such regulations as will prevent fraud or evasion.

2. No citizen should be denied the right to vote on account of sex.

3. All money should be issued by the general government only, and without the intervention of any private citizen, corporation, or banking institution. It should be based upon the wealth, stability, and integrity of the nation. It should be a full legal tender for all debts, public and private, and should be of sufficient volume to meet the demands of the legitimate business interests of the country. For the purpose of honestly liquidating our outstanding coin obligations, we favor the free and unlimited coinage of both silver and gold, at the ratio 16 to 1, without consulting any other nation.

4. Land is the common heritage of the people and should be preserved from monopoly and speculation. All unearned grants of land subject to forfeiture should be reclaimed by the government, and no portion of the public domain should hereafter be granted except to actual settlers, continuous use being essential to tenure.

5. Railroads, telegraphs, and other natural monopolies should be owned and operated by the government, giving to the people the benefit of service at actual cost.

6. The national Constitution should be so amended as to allow the national revenues to be raised by equitable adjustment of taxation on the properties and incomes of the people, and import duties should be levied as a means of securing equitable commercial relations with other nations.

7. The contract convict labor system, through which speculators are enriched at the expense of the state, should be abolished.

8. All citizens should be protected by law in their right to one day of rest in seven, without oppressing any who conscientiously observe any other than the first day of the week.

9. American public schools, taught in the English language, should be maintained, and no public funds should be appropriated for sectarian institutions.

10. The President, Vice-President, and United States senators should be elected by direct vote of the people.

11. Ex-soldiers and sailors of the United States army and navy, their widows and minor children, should receive liberal pensions, granted on disability and term of service, not merely as a debt of gratitude, but for service rendered in the preservation of the Union.

12. Our immigration laws should be so revised as to exclude paupers and criminals. None but citizens of the United States should be allowed to vote in any state, and naturalized citizens should not vote until one year after naturalization papers have been issued.

13. The initiative and referendum, and proportional representation, should be adopted.

14. Having herein presented our principles and purposes, we invite the co-operation and support of all citizens who are with us substantially agreed.

SOCIALIST-LABOR CONVENTION.

New York, N. Y., July 6, 1896.

Chairman, WILLIAM WATKINS,
of Ohio.

NOMINATED—

For President, **Charles H. Matchett,**
of New York.

For Vice-President, **Matthew Maguire,**
of New Jersey.

The convention of this party met at the place and time above stated, and nominated Charles H. Matchett, of New York, for President, and Matthew Maguire, of New Jersey, for Vice-President. The convention remained in session for six days.

The following is the platform adopted:—

SOCIALIST-LABOR PLATFORM.

The Socialist-Labor party of the United States, in convention assembled, reasserts the inalienable right of all men to life, liberty, and the pursuit of happiness.

With the founders of the American republic, we hold that the purpose of government is to secure every citizen in the enjoyment of this right; but, in the light of our social conditions, we hold, furthermore, that no such right can be exercised under a system of economic inequality, essentially destructive of life, of liberty, and of happiness.

With the founders of this republic, we hold that the true theory of politics is that the machinery of government must be owned and controlled by the whole people; but in the light of our industrial development we hold, furthermore, that the true theory of economics is that the machinery of production must likewise belong to the people in common.

To the obvious fact that our despotic system of economics is the direct opposite of our democratic system of politics, can plainly be traced the existence of a privileged class, the corruption of government by that class, the alienation of public property, public franchises, and public functions to that class, and the abject dependence of the mightiest of nations upon that class.

Again, through the perversion of democracy to the ends of plutocracy, .abor is robbed of the wealth which it alone produces, is denied the means of self-employment, and, by compulsory idleness in wage slavery, is even deprived of the necessaries of life. Human power and natural forces are thus wasted, that the plutocracy may rule. Ignorance and misery, with all their concomitant evils, are perpetuated, that the people may be kept in bondage. Science and invention are diverted from their humane purpose, to the enslavement of women and children.

Against such a system the Socialist-Labor party once more enters its protest. Once more it reiterates its fundamental declaration, that private property in the natural sources of production and in the instruments of labor is the obvious cause of all economic servitude and political dependence.

The time is fast coming when, in the natural course of social evolution, this system, through the destructive action of its failures and crises on one hand, and the constructive tendencies of its trusts and other capitalistic combinations on the other hand, shall have worked out its own downfall.

We therefore call upon the wage-workers of the United States, and upon all other honest citizens, to organize under the banner of the Socialist-Labor party into a class-conscious body, aware of its rights and determined to conquer them by taking possession of the public powers, so that, held together by an indomitable spirit of solidarity under the most trying conditions of the present class struggle, we may put a summary end to that barbarous struggle by the abolition of classes, the restoration of the land and of all the means of production, transportation, and distribution to the people as a collective body, and the substitution of the co-operative commonwealth for the present state of planless production, industrial war, and social disorder, a commonwealth in which every worker shall have the free exercise and full benefit of his faculties, multiplied by all modern factors of civilization.

GENERAL DEMANDS.

With a view to immediate improvement in the condition of labor, we present the following demands:

1. Reduction of the hours of labor in proportion to the progress of production.

2. The United States shall obtain possession of the railroads, canals, telegraphs, telephones, and all other means of public transportation and communication; the employees to operate the same co-operatively, under control of the federal government, and to elect their own superior officers, but no employee shall be discharged for political reasons.

3. The municipalities shall obtain possession of the local railroads, ferries, waterworks, gasworks, electric plants, and all industries requiring municipal franchises; the employees to operate the same co-operatively, under control of the municipal administration, and to elect their own superior officers, but no employee shall be discharged for political reasons.

4. The public lands to be declared inalienable. Revocation of all land-grants to corporations or individuals, the conditions of which have not been complied with.

5. The United States to have the exclusive right to issue money.

6. Congressional legislation providing for the scientific management of forests and waterways, and prohibiting the waste of the natural resources of the country.

7. Inventions to be free to all; the inventors to be remunerated by the nation.

8. Progressive income-tax and tax on inheritances; the smaller incomes to be exempt.

9. School education of all children under fourteen years of age to be compulsory, gratuitous and accessible to all by public assistance in meals, clothing, books, etc., where necessary.

10. Repeal of all pauper, tramp, conspiracy, and sumptuary laws. Unabridged right of combination.

11. Prohibition of the employment of children of school age and of female labor in occupations detrimental to health or morality. Abolition of the convict labor contract system.

12. Employment of the unemployed by the public authorities (county, city, state, or nation).

13. All wages to be paid in lawful money of the United States. Equalization of women's wages to those of men where equal service is performed.

14. Laws for the protection of life and limb in all occupations, and an efficient employers' liability law.

15. The people to have the right to propose laws and to vote upon all measures of importance, according to the referendum principle.

16. Abolition of the veto power of the executive (national, state, or municipal), wherever it exists.

17. Abolition of the United States Senate and all upper legislative chambers.

18. Municipal self-government.

19. Direct vote and secret ballots in all elections. Universal and equal right of suffrage, without regard to color, creed, or sex. Election days to be legal holidays. The principle of proportional representation to be introduced.

20. All public officers to be subject to recall by their respective constituencies.

21. Uniform civil and criminal law throughout the United States. Administration of justice to be free of charge. Abolition of capital punishment.

The election occurred on November 6, 1896.

FORTY-FIVE STATES VOTED, Utah having been admitted to statehood since the previous election.

POPUL

STATES.	William McKinley, Republican.	William J. Bryan, Democrat.	William J. Bryan, Populist.
Alabama	54,737	107,137	24,089
Arkansas	37,512	110,103	...
California	146,170	121,629	21,744
Colorado	26,271	158,674	2,389
Connecticut	110,285	56,740	....
Delaware	16,804	13,424	....
Florida	11,288	30,683	2,053
Georgia	60,091	94,232	....
Idaho	6,324	23,192	....
Illinois	607,130	464,523	1,090
Indiana	323,754	305,753	....
Iowa	289,293	223,741	....
Kansas	159,345	126,660	46,194
Kentucky	218,171	217,890	....
Louisiana	22,037	77,175	....
Maine	80,465	32,201	2,48
Maryland	136,959	104,735	....
Massachusetts	278,976	90,530	15,18
Michigan	293,582	236,714	....
Minnesota	193,501	139,626	....
Mississippi	5,130	56,363	7,51
Missouri	304,940	363,667	....
Montana	10,494	42,537	....
Nebraska	103,064	115,999	....
Nevada	1,938	7,802	57
New Hampshire	57,444	21,271	37
New Jersey	221,367	133,675	....
New York	819,838	551,396	....
North Carolina	155,222	174,488	....
North Dakota	26,335	20,686	....
Ohio	525,991	474,882	26,01
Oregon	48,779	46,662	....
Pennsylvania	728,300	422,054	11,17
Rhode Island	36,437	14,459	....
South Carolina	9,281	58,798	....
South Dakota	41,042	41,225	....
Tennessee	148,773	163,651	4,52
Texas	167,520	290,862	79,57
Utah	13,491	64,607	....
Vermont	51,127	10,179	45
Virginia	135,368	154,709	....
Washington	39,153	51,646	....
West Virginia	105,368	94,480	....
Wisconsin	268,135	165,523	....
Wyoming	10,072	10,369	28
Total	7,107,304	6,287,352	245,72

NOTE.—There was fusion on the electoral ticket of the Democrat and Populists—and in some states there was fusion on the electora ticket of the Democrats and Silver Republicans—in the followin states: Arkansas, Colorado, Connecticut, Idaho, Illinois, Iowa, Kan sas, Kentucky, Louisiana, Michigan, Minnesota, Missouri, Montana Nebraska, New Jersey, North Carolina, North Dakota, Ohio, Oregon Pennsylvania, South Dakota, Utah, Washington, West Virgini Wisconsin and Wyoming. In some of the states, like Illinois an Kansas, there were Bryan-Watson tickets run by Middle-of-the-roa Populists.

'OTE.

oshua vering, ibitionist	Charles E. Bentley, National.	Charles H. Matchett, Socialist-Labor.	John M. Palmer, Gold Democrat.	Total vote.
2,147	....	....	6,462	194,572
889	893	....	....	149,397
2,573	1,046	1,611	1,730	296,503
1,717	386	159	....	189,596
1,808	....	1,223	4,234	174,290
355	....	....	877	31,460
654	....	....	1,778	46,456
5,613	....	....	2,708	162,644
197	....	....	....	29,713
9,796	793	1,147	6,390	1,090,869
3,056	2,268	329	2,145	637,305
3,192	352	453	4,516	521,547
1,611	620	....	1,209	335,639
4,781	....	....	5,019	445,861
....	....	....	1,834	101,046
1,570	....	....	1,870	118,593
5,918	136	587	2,507	250,842
2,998	....	2,114	11,749	401,568
5,025	1,995	....	6,879	544,195
4,365	....	915	3,230	341,637
485	....	....	1,071	70,566
2,196	293	595	2,355	674,046
186	....	....	....	53,217
1,243	797	183	5,885	224,171
....	....	....	....	10,315
779	49	228	3,520	83,670
5,614	....	3,985	6,373	371,014
6,052	....	17,667	18,950	1,423,903
675	247	....	....	330,632
358	....	....	....	47,379
5,068	2,716	....	1,875	1,036,547
919	....	....	977	97,337
9,274	870	1,683	11,000	1,194,335
1,160	....	558	1,166	53,780
....	....	....	828	68,907
683	....	....	....	82,950
3,098	....	....	1,951	321,998
1,786	....	....	5,046	544,786
....	....	....	21	78,119
733	....	....	1,331	63,828
2,350	....	108	2,129	294,664
968	148	....	1,668	93,583
,216	....	....	675	201,739
,509	346	....	4,584	446,097
136	....	....	....	20,863
,753	13,955	33,545	133,542	13,952,179

has been impossible to separate the Populist from the Democratic in the states in which there was a fusion of those parties. In some e states, like Illinois, in which the two parties voted for the same ors but upon separate tickets, county officers, in making returns e secretaries of state, have combined the votes on electors, and it possible to say how the vote should be divided. In such cases the classed under the head "Bryan, Populist" is no indication of the gth of the People's party, while at the same time it gives too large e to the Democrats. There is no way of giving, even approxi- ly, the vote of the two parties on presidential electors.

ELECTORAL VOTE.

Counted on February 10, 1897.

STATES.	PRESIDENT.		VICE-PRESIDENT.			No. entitled to vote.
	William McKinley, of Ohio.	William J. Bryan, of Nebraska.	Garret A. Hobart, of New Jersey.	Arthur Sewall, of Maine.	Thomas E. Watson, of Georgia.	
Alabama	..	11	..	11	..	11
Arkansas	..	8	..	5	3	8
California	8	1	8	1	..	9
Colorado	..	4	..	4	..	4
Connecticut	6	..	6	..	..	6
Delaware	3	..	3	..	..	3
Florida	..	4	..	4	..	4
Georgia	..	13	..	13	..	13
Idaho	..	3	..	3	..	3
Illinois	24	..	24	..	..	24
Indiana	15	..	15	..	..	15
Iowa	13	..	13	..	..	13
Kansas	..	10	..	10	..	10
Kentucky	12	1	12	1	..	13
Louisiana	..	8	..	4	4	8
Maine	6	..	6	..	..	6
Maryland	8	..	8	..	..	8
Massachusetts	15	..	15	..	..	15
Michigan	14	..	14	..	..	14
Minnesota	9	..	9	..	..	9
Mississippi	..	9	..	9	..	9
Missouri	..	17	..	13	4	17
Montana	..	3	..	2	1	3
Nebraska	..	8	..	4	4	8
Nevada	..	3	..	3	..	3
New Hampshire	4	..	4	..	..	4
New Jersey	10	..	10	..	..	10
New York	36	..	36	..	..	36
North Carolina	..	11	..	6	5	11
North Dakota	3	..	3	..	..	3
Ohio	23	..	23	..	..	23
Oregon	4	..	4	..	..	4
Pennsylvania	32	..	32	..	..	32
Rhode Island	4	..	4	..	..	4
South Carolina	..	9	..	9	..	9
South Dakota	..	4	..	2	2	4
Tennessee	..	12	..	12	..	12
Texas	..	15	..	15	..	15
Utah	..	3	..	2	1	3
Vermont	4	..	4	..	..	4
Virginia	..	12	..	12	..	12
Washington	..	4	.	2	2	4
West Virginia	6	..	6	..	..	6
Wisconsin	12	..	12	..	..	12
Wyoming	..	3	..	2	1	3
Total	271	176	271	149	27	447

William McKinley was elected President and Garret A. Hobart as Vice-President.

During this period Congress was divided politically as follows:

Fifty-fifth Congress.

Senate—34 Democrats, 44 Republicans, 5 Populists, 6 Silver Republicans, 1 Independent ....Total, 90
House—121 Democrats, 203 Republicans, 21 Populists, 3 Silverites, 4 Independents, 5 vacancies .... " 357

Fifty-sixth Congress.

Senate—26 Democrats, 51 Republicans, 5 Populists, 4 Silverites, 4 vacancies ....Total, 90
House—161 Democrats, 185 Republicans, 5 Populists, 3 Silverites, 3 vacancies............................ " 357

Election of 1900

Democratic National Committee:

Chairman, JAMES K. JONES, of Arkansas.
Secretary, CHARLES A. WALSH, of Iowa.

DEMOCRATIC CONVENTION.

Kansas City, Mo., July 4–6, 1900.

Chairman pro tem., CHARLES S. THOMAS, of Colorado.

Chairman, JAMES D. RICHARDSON, of Tennessee.

NOMINATED—

For President, **William J. Bryan,** of Nebraska.

For Vice-President, **Adlai E. Stevenson,** of Illinois.

This convention consisted of 936 delegates, including six from Hawaii. Two of the delegates from Utah were women. The proceedings on the opening day included the reading of the Declaration of Independence. William J. Bryan, of Nebraska, was unanimously nominated for President on the first ballot.

But one ballot was taken for a candidate for Vice-President, resulting as follows:

CANDIDATES.	Votes.	CANDIDATES.	Votes.
ADLAI E. STEVENSON, of Illinois	559½	JOHN WALTER SMITH, of Maryland	16
DAVID B. HILL, of New York	200	ELLIOTT DANFORTH, of New York	1
CHARLES A. TOWNE, of Minnesota	89½	JAMES S. HOGG, of Texas	1
A. W. PATRICK, of Ohio	46	Whole number of votes, 936	
JULIAN S. CARR, of North Carolina	23	Necessary to a choice, 624	

Before the result of the ballot was announced, changes were made to Stevenson until every vote was recorded in his favor.

The construction of the platform was under discussion for two days by the Committee on Resolutions. A plank declaring for the free coinage of silver at the ratio of 16 to 1 was adopted by a vote of 26 to 24. The convention, without debate and without a dissenting voice, adopted by acclamation the platform as reported by the committee, as follows:—

DEMOCRATIC PLATFORM.

We, the representatives of the Democratic party of the United States, assembled in national convention, on the anniversary of the adoption of the Declaration of Independence, do reaffirm our faith in that immortal proclamation of the inalienable rights of man and our allegiance to the Constitution framed in harmony therewith by the Fathers of the Republic. We hold with the United States Supreme Court, that the Declaration of Independence is the spirit of our government, of which the Constitution is the form and letter.

THE ORIGIN AND POWERS OF GOVERNMENT.

We declare again that all governments instituted among men derive their just powers from the consent of the governed; that any government not based upon the consent of the governed is a tyranny, and that to impose upon any people a government of force is to substitute the methods of imperialism for those of a republic. We hold that the Constitution follows the flag, and denounce the doctrine that an Executive or Congress deriving their existence and their powers from the Constitution can exercise lawful authority beyond it or in violation of it.

We assert that no nation can long endure half republic and half empire, and we warn the American people that imperialism abroad will lead quickly and inevitably to despotism at home.

TAXATION OF PORTO RICO.

Believing in these fundamental principles, we denounce the Porto Rican law, enacted by a Republican Congress against the protest and opposition of the Democratic minority, as a bold and open violation of the nation's organic law and a flagrant breach of the national good faith. It imposes upon the people of Porto Rico a government without their consent and taxation without representation. It dishonors the American people by repudiating a solemn pledge made in their behalf by the commanding general of our army, which the Porto Ricans welcomed to a peaceful and unresisted occupation of their land. It doomed to poverty and distress a people whose helplessness appeals with peculiar force to our justice and magnanimity.

In this, the first act of its imperialistic programme, the Republican party seeks to commit the United States to a colonial policy inconsistent with republican institutions and condemned by the Supreme Court in numerous decisions.

PLEDGE TO CUBA.

We demand the prompt and honest fulfillment of our pledge to the Cuban people and the world, that the United States has no disposition or intention to exercise sovereignty, jurisdiction, or control over the Island of Cuba except for its pacification. The war ended nearly two years ago, profound peace reigns over all the island, and still the administration keeps the government of the island from its people, while Republican carpet-bag officials plunder its revenues and exploit the colonial theory, to the disgrace of the American people.

THE PHILIPPINES.

We condemn and denounce the Philippine policy of the present administration. It has involved the republic in unnecessary war, sacrificed the lives of many of our noblest sons, and placed the United States, previously known and applauded throughout the world as the champion of freedom, in the false and un-American position of crushing with military force the efforts of our former allies to achieve liberty and self-government. The Filipinos cannot be citizens without endangering our civilization; they cannot be subjects without imperiling our form of government; and as we are not willing to surrender our civilization nor to convert the republic into an empire, we favor an immediate declaration of the nation's purpose to give the Filipinos, first, a stable form of government; second, independence; and third, protection from outside interference, such as has been given for nearly a century to the republics of Central and South America.

The greedy commercialism which dictated the Philippine policy of the Republican administration attempts to justify it with the plea that it will pay; but even this sordid and unworthy plea fails when brought to the test of facts. The war of criminal aggression against the Filipinos, entailing an annual expense of many millions, has already cost more than any possible profit that could accrue from the entire Philippine trade for years to come. Furthermore, when trade is extended at the expense of liberty, the price is always too high.

LEGITIMATE EXPANSION.

We are not opposed to territorial expansion when it takes in desirable territory which can be erected into states in the Union, and whose people are willing and fit to become American citizens. We favor expansion by every peaceful and legitimate means. But we are unalterably opposed to seizing or purchasing distant islands to be governed outside the Constitution, and whose people can never become citizens.

We are in favor of extending the republic's influence among the nations, but believe that that influence should be extended not by force and violence, but through the persuasive power of a high and honorable example.

THE PARAMOUNT ISSUE.

The importance of other questions now pending before the American people is no wise diminished and the Democratic party takes no backward step from its position on them, but the burning issue of imperialism growing out of the Spanish war involves the very existence of the republic and the destruction of our free institutions. We regard it as the paramount issue of the campaign.

THE MONROE DOCTRINE.

The declaration in the Republican platform adopted at the Philadelphia Convention, held in June, 1900, that the Republican party " steadfastly adheres to the policy announced in the Monroe doctrine " is manifestly insincere and deceptive. This profession is contradicted by the avowed policy of that party, in opposition to the spirit of the Monroe doctrine, to acquire and hold sovereignty over large areas of territory and large numbers of people in the Eastern Hemisphere. We insist on the strict maintenance of the Monroe doctrine in all its integrity, both in letter and in spirit, as necessary to prevent the extension of European authority on this continent and as essential to our supremacy in American affairs. At the same time we declare that no American people shall ever be held by force in unwilling subjection to European authority.

MILITARISM OPPOSED.

We oppose militarism. It means conquest abroad and intimidation and oppression at home. It means the strong arm which has ever been fatal to free institutions. It is what millions of our citizens have fled from in Europe. It will impose upon our peace-loving people a large standing army and unnecessary burden of taxation, and will be a constant menace to their liberties. A small standing army and a well-disciplined state militia are amply sufficient in time of peace. This republic has no place for a vast military service and conscription.

THE NATIONAL GUARD.

In time of danger the volunteer soldier is his country's best defender. The National Guard of the United States should ever be cherished in the patriotic hearts of a free people. Such organizations are ever an element of strength and safety. For the first time in our history and coeval with the Philippine conquest has there been a wholesale departure from our time-honored and approved system of volunteer organization. We denounce it as un-American, undemocratic, and unrepublican, and as a subversion of the ancient and fixed principles of a free people.

TRUSTS.

Private monopolies are indefensible and intolerable. They destroy competition, control the price of all material and of the finished product, thus robbing both producer and consumer. They lessen the employment of labor and arbitrarily fix the terms and conditions thereof, and deprive individual energy and small capital of their opportunity for betterment. They are the most efficient means yet devised for appropriating the fruits of industry to the benefit of the few at the expense of the many, and, unless their insatiate greed is checked, all wealth will be aggregated in a few hands and the republic destroyed.

The dishonest paltering with the trust evil by the Republican party in state and national platforms is conclusive proof of the truth of the charge that trusts are the legitimate product of Republican policies, that they are fostered by Republican laws, and that they are protected by the Republican administration for campaign subscriptions and political support.

We pledge the Democratic party to an unceasing warfare in nation, state, and city against private monopoly in every form. Existing laws against trusts must be enforced and more stringent ones must be enacted, providing for publicity as to the affairs of corporations engaged in interstate commerce, requiring all corporations to show, before doing business outside the state of their origin, that they have no water in their stock and that they have not attempted, and are not attempting, to monopolize any branch of business or the production of any articles of merchandise; and the whole constitutional power of Congress over interstate commerce, the mails, and all modes of interstate communication shall be exercised by the enactment of comprehensive laws upon the subject of trusts.

THE FREE LIST AS A REMEDY.

Tariff laws should be amended by putting the products of trusts upon the free list, to prevent monopoly under the plea of protection.

REPUBLICAN INSINCERITY IN TRUST-LEGISLATION.

The failure of the present Republican administration, with an absolute control over all the branches of the national government, to enact any legislation designed to prevent or even curtail the absorbing power of trusts and illegal combinations, or to enforce the anti-trust laws already on the statute books, proves the insincerity of the high-sounding phrases of the Republican platform.

CORPORATE INTERFERENCE IN GOVERNMENT.

Corporations should be protected in all their rights and their legitimate interests should be respected, but any attempt by corporations to interfere with the public affairs of the people, or to control the sovereignty which creates them, should be forbidden under such penalties as will make such attempts impossible.

THE DINGLEY TARIFF LAW.

We condemn the Dingley Tariff Law as a trust-breeding measure, skillfully devised to give the few favors which they do not deserve and to place upon the many burdens which they should not bear.

INTERSTATE COMMERCE COMMISSION.

We favor such an enlargement of the scope of the Interstate Commerce Law as will enable the commission to protect individuals and communities from discriminations, and the public from unjust and unfair transportation rates.

THE SILVER DECLARATION.

We reaffirm and indorse the principles of the National Democratic platform adopted at Chicago in 1896, and we reiterate the demand of that platform for an American financial system, made by the American people for themselves, which shall restore and maintain a bimetallic price-level, and as part of such system the immediate restoration of the free and unlimited coinage of silver and gold at the present legal ratio of 16 to 1, without waiting for the aid or consent of any other nation.

THE CURRENCY BILL DENOUNCED.

We denounce the Currency Bill enacted at the last session of Congress as a step forward in the Republican policy which aims to discredit the sovereign right of the national government to issue all money, whether coin or paper, and to bestow upon national banks the power to issue and control the volume of paper money for their own benefit. A permanent national bank currency, secured by government bonds, must have a permanent debt to rest upon, and if the bank currency is to increase, the debt must also increase. The Republican currency scheme is therefore a scheme for fastening upon the taxpayers a perpetual and growing debt.

We are opposed to this private corporation paper circulated as money, but without legal-tender qualities, and demand the retirement of the national bank notes as fast as government paper or silver certificates can be substituted for them.

POPULAR ELECTION OF SENATORS.

We favor an amendment to the Federal Constitution providing for election of United States senators by the direct vote of the people, and we favor direct legislation wherever practicable.

INJUNCTIONS, BLACKLIST, AND ARBITRATION.

We are opposed to government by injunction; we denounce the blacklist, and favor arbitration as a means of settling disputes between corporations and their employees.

A DEPARTMENT OF LABOR.

In the interest of American labor and the uplifting of the workingman, as the cornerstone of the prosperity of our country, we recommend that Congress create a Department of Labor, in charge of a secretary with a seat in the cabinet, believing that the elevation of the American laborer will bring with it increased protection and increased prosperity to our country at home and to our commerce abroad.

LIBERAL PENSIONS.

We are proud of the courage and fidelity of the American soldiers and sailors in all our wars; we favor liberal pensions to them and their dependents, and we reiterate the position taken in the Chicago platform in 1896, that the fact of enlistment and service shall be deemed conclusive evidence against disease and disability before enlistment.

FOR THE NICARAGUAN CANAL.

We favor the immediate construction, ownership, and control of the Nicaraguan canal by the United States, and we denounce the insincerity of the plank in the Republican platform for an isthmian canal in face of the failure of the Republican majority on this subject to pass such a bill in Congress.

HAY-PAUNCEFOTE TREATY.

We condemn the Hay-Pauncefote treaty as a surrender of American rights and interests not to be tolerated by the American people.

NEW STATES AND TERRITORIES.

We denounce the failure of the Republican party to carry out its pledges to grant statehood to the territories of Arizona, New Mexico, and Oklahoma. We promise the people of those territories immediate statehood, and home-rule during their condition as territories, and we favor home-rule and a territorial form of government for Alaska and Porto Rico.

ARID LANDS.

We favor an intelligent system of improving the arid lands of the West, storing the waters for purposes of irrigation, and the holding of such lands for actual settlers.

CHINESE EXCLUSION.

We favor the continuance and strict enforcement of the Chinese Exclusion Law, and its application to the same classes of all Asiatic races.

ALLIANCES OPPOSED.

Jefferson said: "Peace, commerce, and honest friendship with all nations; entangling alliances with none." We approve this wholesome doctrine, and earnestly protest against the Republican departure which has involved us in so-called world-politics, including the diplomacy of Europe and the intrigue and land-grabbing of Asia. We especially condemn the ill-concealed Republican alliance with England, which must mean discrimination against other friendly nations, and which has already stifled the nation's voice, while liberty is being strangled in Africa.

SYMPATHY FOR THE BOERS.

Believing in the principles of self-government, and rejecting, as did our forefathers, the claim of monarchy, we view with indignation the purpose of England to overwhelm with force the South African republics. Speaking as we do for the entire American nation, except its Republican officeholders, and for all freemen everywhere, we extend our sympathies to the heroic burghers in their unequal struggle to maintain their liberty and independence.

REPUBLICAN EXTRAVAGANCE DENOUNCED.

We denounce the lavish appropriations of recent Republican Congresses, which have kept taxes high and which threaten the perpetuation of the oppressive war levies. We oppose the accumulation of a surplus, to be squandered in such barefaced frauds upon the taxpayers as the Shipping Subsidy Bill, which, under the false pretense of prospering American shipbuilding, would put unearned millions into the pockets of favorite contributors to the Republican campaign fund. We favor the reduction and speedy repeal of the war taxes, and a return to the time-honored Democratic policy of strict economy in governmental expenditures.

OUR INSTITUTIONS IMPERILED.

Believing that our most cherished institutions are in great peril, that the very existence of our constitutional republic is at stake, and that the decision now to be rendered will determine whether our children are to enjoy the blessed privileges of free government, which have made the United States great, prosperous, and honored, we earnestly ask for the foregoing declaration of principles the hearty support of the liberty-loving American people, regardless of previous party affiliations.

Republican National Committee:

Chairman, MARCUS A. HANNA, of Ohio.
Secretary, PERRY S. HEATH, of Indiana.

REPUBLICAN CONVENTION.

Philadelphia, Pa., June 19–21, 1900.

Chairman pro tem., EDWARD O. WOLCOTT, of Colorado.

Chairman, HENRY CABOT LODGE, of Massachusetts.

NOMINATED—

For President, **William McKinley,** of Ohio.

For Vice-President, **Theodore Roosevelt,** of New York.

This convention was composed of 924 delegates, including two from Hawaii. William McKinley was unanimously renominated for President on the first ballot.

For Vice-President, Theodore Roosevelt, of New York, was unanimously nominated on the first ballot, receiving 923 votes, one less than the full number, he having refrained from voting.

At this convention but one candidate was presented for each office.

The platform adopted by the Twelfth Republican National Convention, on June 20, 1900, is as follows:—

REPUBLICAN PLATFORM.

The Republicans of the United States, through their chosen representatives met in national convention, looking back upon an unsurpassed record of achievement and looking forward into a great field of duty and opportunity, and appealing to the judgment of their countrymen, make these declarations:

EXPECTATIONS FULFILLED.

The expectation in which the American people, turning from the Democratic party, intrusted power four years ago to a Republican Chief Magistrate and a Republican Congress, has been met and satisfied. When the people then assembled at the polls, after a term of Democratic legislation and administration, business was dead, industry paralyzed, and the national credit disastrously impaired. The country's capital was hidden away and its labor distressed and unemployed. The Democrats had no other plan with which to improve the ruinous conditions which they had themselves produced than to coin silver at the ratio of 16 to 1.

PROMISE OF PROSPERITY REDEEMED.

The Republican party, denouncing this plan as sure to produce conditions even worse than those from which relief was sought, promised to restore prosperity by means of two legislative measures: a protective tariff and a law making gold the standard of value. The people by great majorities issued to the Republican party a commission to enact these laws. The commission has been executed, and the Republican promise is redeemed.

Prosperity more general and more abundant than we have ever known has followed these enactments. There is no longer controversy as to the value of any government obligations.

Every American dollar is a gold dollar or its assured equivalent, and American credit stands higher than that of any nation. Capital is fully employed, and labor everywhere is profitably occupied.

GROWTH OF EXPORT TRADE.

No single fact can more strikingly tell the story of what Republican government means to the country than this, that while during the whole period of one hundred and seven years, from 1790 to 1897, there was an excess of exports over imports of only $383,028,497, there has been in the short three years of the present Republican administration an excess of exports over imports in the enormous sum of $1,483,537,094.

THE WAR WITH SPAIN.

And while the American people, sustained by this Republican legislation, have been achieving these splendid triumphs in their business and commerce, they have conducted and in victory concluded a war for liberty and human rights. No thought of national aggrandizement tarnished the high purpose with which American standards were unfurled. It was a war unsought and patiently resisted, but when it came, the American government was ready. Its fleets were cleared for action; its armies were in the field, and the quick and signal triumph of its forces on land and sea bore equal tribute to the courage of American soldiers and sailors, and to the skill and foresight of Republican statesmanship. To ten millions of the human race there was given "a new birth of freedom," and to the American people a new and noble responsibility.

MCKINLEY'S ADMINISTRATION INDORSED.

We indorse the administration of William McKinley. Its acts have been established in wisdom and in patriotism, and at home and abroad it has distinctly elevated and extended the influence of the American nation. Walking untried paths and facing unforeseen responsibilities, President McKinley has been in every situation the true American patriot and the upright statesman, clear in vision, strong in judgment, firm in action, always inspiring and deserving the confidence of his countrymen.

DEMOCRATIC INCAPACITY A MENACE TO PROSPERITY.

In asking the American people to indorse this Republican record and to renew their commission to the Republican party, we remind them of the fact that the menace to their prosperity has always resided in Democratic principles, and no less in the general incapacity of the Democratic party to conduct public affairs. The prime essential of business prosperity is public confidence in the good sense of the government and in its ability to deal intelligently with each new problem of administration and legislation. That confidence the Democratic party has never earned. It is hopelessly inadequate, and the country's prosperity, when Democratic success at the polls is announced, halts and ceases in mere anticipation of Democratic blunders and failures.

MONETARY LEGISLATION.

We renew our allegiance to the principle of the gold standard and declare our confidence in the wisdom of the legislation of the Fifty-sixth Congress, by which the parity of all our money and the stability of our currency upon a gold basis has been secured. We recognize that interest rates are a potent factor in production and business activity, and for the purpose of further equalizing and of further lowering the rates of interest, we favor such monetary legislation as will enable the varying needs of the season and of all sections to be promptly met, in order that trade may be evenly sustained, labor steadily employed, and commerce enlarged. The volume of money in circulation was never so great per capita as it is to-day.

FREE COINAGE OF SILVER OPPOSED.

We declare our steadfast opposition to the free and unlimited coinage of silver. No measure to that end could be considered which was without the support of the leading commercial countries of the world. However firmly Republican legislation may seem to have secured the country against the peril of base and discredited currency, the election of a Democratic President could not fail to impair the country's credit and to bring once more into question the intention of the American people to maintain upon the gold standard the parity of their money circulation. The Democratic party must be convinced that the American people will never tolerate the Chicago platform.

TRUSTS.

We recognize the necessity and propriety of the honest cooperation of capital to meet new business conditions, and especially to extend our rapidly increasing foreign trade; but we condemn all conspiracies and combinations intended to restrict business, to create monopolies, to limit production, or to control prices, and favor such legislation as will effectively restrain and prevent all such abuses, protect and promote competition, and secure the rights of producers, laborers, and all who are engaged in industry and commerce.

PROTECTION POLICY REAFFIRMED.

We renew our faith in the policy of protection to American labor. In that policy our industries have been established, diversified, and maintained. By protecting the home market, competition has been stimulated and production cheapened. Opportunity to the inventive genius of our people has been secured and wages in every department of labor maintained at high rates—higher now than ever before, and always distinguishing our working-people in their better conditions of life from those of any competing country. Enjoying the blessings of the American common school, secure in the right of self-government, and protected in the occupancy of their own markets, their constantly increasing knowledge and skill have enabled them to finally enter the markets of the world.

RECIPROCITY FAVORED.

We favor the associated policy of reciprocity, so directed as to open our markets on favorable terms for what we do not ourselves produce, in return for free foreign markets.

RESTRICTION OF IMMIGRATION, AND OTHER LABOR-LEGISLATION.

In the further interest of American workmen we favor a more effective restriction of the immigration of cheap labor from foreign lands, the extension of opportunities of education for working-children, the raising of the age limit for child-labor, the protection of free labor as against contract convict labor, and an effective system of labor insurance.

SHIPPING.

Our present dependence upon foreign shipping for nine-tenths of our foreign-carrying trade is a great loss to the industry of this country. It is also a serious danger to our trade, for its sudden withdrawal in the event of European war would seriously cripple our expanding foreign commerce. The national defense and naval efficiency of this country, moreover, supply a compelling reason for legislation which will enable us to recover our former place among the trade carrying fleets of the world.

DEBT TO SOLDIERS AND SAILORS.

The nation owes a debt of profound gratitude to the soldiers and sailors who have fought its battles, and it is the government's duty to provide for the survivors and for the widows and orphans of those who have fallen in the country's wars. The pension laws, founded on this just sentiment, should be liberally administered, and preference should be given, wherever practicable, with respect to employment in the public service, to soldiers and sailors and to their widows and orphans.

THE CIVIL SERVICE.

We commend the policy of the Republican party in maintaining the efficiency of the civil service. The administration has acted wisely in its effort to secure for public service in Cuba, Porto Rico, Hawaii, and the Philippine Islands, only those whose fitness has been determined by training and experience. We believe that employment in the public service in these territories should be confined, as far as practicable, to their inhabitants.

THE RACE QUESTION.

It was the plain purpose of the Fifteenth Amendment to the Constitution, to prevent discrimination on account of race or color in regulating the elective franchise. Devices of state governments, whether by statutory or constitutional enactment, to avoid the purpose of this amendment are revolutionary and should be condemned.

PUBLIC ROADS.

Public movements looking to a permanent improvement of the roads and highways of the country meet with our cordial approval, and we recommend this subject to the earnest consideration of the people and of the legislatures of the several states.

RURAL FREE DELIVERY.

We favor the extension of the rural free-delivery service wherever its extension may be justified.

LAND-LEGISLATION.

In further pursuance of the constant policy of the Republican party to provide free homes on the public domain, we recommend adequate national legislation to reclaim the arid lands of the United States, reserving control of the distribution of water for irrigation to the respective states and territories.

NEW STATES PROPOSED.

We favor home-rule for, and the early admission to statehood of, the territories of New Mexico, Arizona, and Oklahoma.

REDUCTION OF WAR TAXES.

The Dingley Act, amended to provide sufficient revenue for the conduct of the war, has so well performed its work that it has been possible to reduce the war debt in the sum of $40,000,000. So ample are the government's revenues and so great is the public confidence in the integrity of its obligations, that its newly funded 2 per cent. bonds sell at a premium. The country is now justified in expecting, and it will be the policy of the Republican party to bring about, a reduction of the war taxes.

ISTHMIAN CANAL AND NEW MARKETS.

We favor the construction, ownership, control, and protection of an isthmian canal by the government of the United States. New markets are necessary for the increasing surplus of our farm products. Every effort should be made to open and obtain new markets, especially in the Orient, and the administration is to be warmly commended for its successful efforts to commit all trading and colonizing nations to the policy of the open door in China.

DEPARTMENT OF COMMERCE.

In the interest of our expanding commerce we recommend that Congress create a Department of Commerce and Industries, in the charge of a secretary with a seat in the cabinet. The United States consular system should be reorganized under the supervision of this new department, upon such a basis of appointment and tenure as will render it still more serviceable to the nation's increasing trade.

PROTECTION OF CITIZENS.

The American Government must protect the person and property of every citizen wherever they are wrongfully violated or placed in peril.

SERVICES OF WOMEN.

We congratulate the women of America upon their splendid record of public service in the Volunteer Aid Association and as nurses in camp and hospital during the recent campaigns of our armies in the East and West Indies, and we appreciate their faithful co-operation in all works of education and industry.

FOREIGN AFFAIRS. SAMOAN AND HAWAIIAN ISLANDS.

President McKinley has conducted the foreign affairs of the United States with distinguished credit to the American people. In releasing us from the vexatious conditions of a European alliance for the government of Samoa, his course is especially to be commended. By securing to our undivided control the most important island of the Samoan group and the best harbor in the Southern Pacific, every American interest has been safeguarded.

We approve the annexation of the Hawaiian Islands to the United States.

THE HAGUE CONFERENCE. THE MONROE DOCTRINE. THE SOUTH AFRICAN WAR.

We commend the part taken by our government in the Peace Conference at The Hague. We assert our steadfast adherence to the policy announced in the Monroe doctrine. The provisions of The Hague convention were wisely regarded when President McKinley tendered his friendly offices in the interest of peace between Great Britain and the South African Republic. While the American Government must continue the policy prescribed by Washington, affirmed by every succeeding President, and imposed upon us by The Hague Treaty, of non-intervention in European controversies, the American people earnestly hope that a way may soon be found, honorable alike to both contending parties, to terminate the strife between them.

SOVEREIGNTY IN NEW POSSESSIONS.

In accepting, by the Treaty of Paris, the just responsibility of our victories in the Spanish war, the President and the Senate won the undoubted approval of the American people. No other course was possible than to destroy Spain's sovereignty throughout the West Indies and in the Philippine Islands. That course created our responsibility before the world and with the unorganized population whom our intervention had freed from Spain, to provide for the maintenance of law and order, and for the establishment of good government, and for the performance of international obligations.

Our authority could not be less than our responsibility, and wherever sovereign rights were extended it became the high duty of the government to maintain its authority, to put down armed insurrection, and to confer the blessings of liberty and civilization upon all the rescued peoples.

The largest measure of self-government consistent with their welfare and our duties shall be secured to them by law.

INDEPENDENCE OF CUBA.

To Cuba, independence and self-government were assured in the same voice by which war was declared, and to the letter this pledge shall be performed.

INVOKES THE JUDGMENT OF THE PEOPLE.

The Republican party, upon its history and upon this declaration of its principles and policies, confidently invokes the considerate and approving judgment of the American people.

People's Party National Committee:

Chairman, MARION C. BUTLER, of North Carolina.
Secretary, A. J. EDGERTON, of Colorado.

PEOPLE'S PARTY CONVENTION.

Sioux Falls, S. D., May 9–10, 1900.

Chairman pro tem., P. M. RINGDALE,
of Minnesota.

Chairman, THOMAS M. PATTERSON,
of Colorado.

NOMINATED—

For President, **William J. Bryan,**
of Nebraska.

For Vice-President, **Adlai E. Stevenson,**
of Illinois.

The nomination of William J. Bryan for President was made by acclamation; this having been a foregone conclusion, the question of the nomination of a candidate for Vice-President gave rise to a spirited contest, the friends of Mr. Bryan leading the fight against it; but after a warm struggle it was carried, and then Charles A. Towne was nominated by acclamation. Mr. Towne withdrew on August 7th and the national committee of the party, at a meeting held in Chicago on August 27th, selected Adlai E. Stevenson in his place.

The convention comprised 856 delegates, some being women. Not all of the states and territories were represented. The delegates present were permitted to cast the entire number of votes to which their states were entitled.

The following platform was adopted:—

PEOPLE'S PARTY PLATFORM.

The People's party of the United States, in convention assembled, congratulating its supporters on the wide extension of its principles in all directions, does hereby reaffirm its adherence to the fundamental principles proclaimed in its two prior platforms and calls upon all who desire to avert the subversion of free institutions by corporate and imperialistic power to unite with it in bringing the government back to the ideals of Washington, Jefferson, Jackson, and Lincoln.

It extends to its allies in the struggle for financial and economic freedom assurances of its loyalty to the principles which animate the allied forces and the promise of honest and hearty co-operation in every effort for their success.

To the people of the United States we offer the following platform as the expression of our unalterable convictions:

THE GOLD STANDARD ACT, BONDS, CURRENCY AND BANKS.

Resolved, That we denounce the act of March 14, 1900, as the culmination of a long series of conspiracies to deprive the people of their constitutional rights over the money of the nation, and relegate to a gigantic money trust the control of the purse, and hence of the people.

We denounce this act, first, for making all money obligations, domestic and foreign, payable in gold coin or its equivalent, thus enormously increasing the burdens of the debtors and enriching the creditors.

Second. For refunding "coin bonds" not to mature for

years into long-time gold bonds, so as to make their payment improbable and our debt perpetual.

Third. For taking from the treasury over $50,000,000 in a time of war, and presenting it at a premium to bondholders, to accomplish the refunding of bonds not due.

Fourth. For doubling the capital of bankers by returning to them the face value of their bonds in current money notes, so that they may draw one interest from the government and another from the people.

Fifth. For allowing banks to expand and contract their circulation at pleasure, thus controlling prices of all products.

Sixth. For authorizing the Secretary of the Treasury to issue new gold bonds to an unlimited amount whenever he deems it necessary to replenish the gold hoard, thus enabling usurers to secure more bonds and more bank currency, by drawing gold from the treasury, thereby creating an "endless chain" for perpetually adding to a perpetual debt.

Seventh. For striking down the greenback in order to force the people to borrow $346,000,000 more from the banks, at an annual cost of over $20,000,000.

While barring out the money of the Constitution, this law opens the printing mints of the treasury to the free coinage of bank paper money, to enrich the few and impoverish the many.

We pledge anew the People's party never to cease the agitation until this eighth financial conspiracy is blotted from the statute-books, the Lincoln greenback restored, the bonds all paid, and all corporation money forever retired.

FREE COINAGE OF SILVER.

We reaffirm the demand for the reopening of the mints of the United States to the free and unlimited coinage of silver and gold at the present legal ratio of 16 to 1, the immediate increase in the volume of silver coins and certificates thus created to be substituted, dollar for dollar, for the bank notes issued by private corporations under special privilege granted by law of March 14, 1900, and prior national banking laws, the remaining portion of the bank notes to be replaced with full legal-tender government paper money, and its volume so controlled as to maintain at all times a stable money market and a stable price-level.

INCOME-TAX.

We demand a graduated income and inheritance tax, to the end that aggregated wealth shall bear its just proportion of taxation.

POSTAL SAVINGS-BANKS.

We demand that postal savings-banks be established by the government for the safe deposit of the savings of the people and to facilitate exchange.

LAND MONOPOLY AND HOMESTEADS.

With Thomas Jefferson, we declare the land, including all natural sources of wealth, the inalienable heritage of the people. Government should so act as to secure homes for the people, and prevent land monopoly. The original homestead policy should be enforced, and future settlers upon the public domain should be entitled to a free homestead, while all who have paid an acreage price to the government under existing laws should have their homestead rights restored.

GOVERNMENT OWNERSHIP OF RAILROADS.

Transportation, being a means of exchange and a public necessity, the government should own and operate the railroads in the interest of the people, and on a non-partisan basis, to the end that all may be accorded the same treatment in transportation, and that the extortion, tyranny, and political power now exercised by the great railroad corporations, which result in the impairment, if not the destruction, of the political rights and personal liberties of the citizen, may be destroyed. Such ownership is to be accomplished in a manner consistent with sound public policy.

TRUSTS. THE INITIATIVE AND REFERENDUM.

Trusts, the overshadowing evil of the age, are the result and culmination of the private ownership and control of the three great instruments of commerce—money, transportation, and the means of transmission of information—which instruments of commerce are public functions, and which our forefathers declared in the Constitution should be controlled by the people through their Congress for the public welfare. The one remedy for the trusts is that the ownership and control be assumed and exercised by the people. We further demand that all tariffs on goods controlled by a trust shall be abolished.

To cope with the trust evil, the people must act directly, without the intervention of representatives, who may be controlled or influenced. We therefore demand direct legislation, giving the people the law-making and veto power under the initiative and referendum. A majority of the people can never be corruptly influenced.

WAR POLICY CONDEMNED.

Applauding the valor of our army and navy in the Spanish war, we denounce the conduct of the administration in changing a war of humanity into a war of conquest. The action of the administration in the Philippines is in conflict with all the precedents of our national life; at war with the Declaration of Independence, the Constitution, and the plain precepts of humanity. Murder and arson have been our response to the appeals of the people who asked only to establish a free government in their own land. We demand a stoppage of this war of extermination by the assurance to the Philippines of independence and protection under a stable government of their own creation.

LEVYING OF CUSTOMS DUTIES IN PORTO RICO.

The Declaration of Independence, the Constitution, and the American flag are one and inseparable. The island of Porto Rico is a part of the territory of the United States, and by levying special and extraordinary customs duties on the commerce of that island, the administration has violated the Constitution, abandoned the fundamental principles of American liberty, and has striven to give the lie to the contention of our forefathers, that there should be no taxation without representation.

IMPERIALISM AND MILITARISM.

Out of the imperialism which would force an undesired domination on the people of the Philippines, springs the un-American cry for a large standing army. Nothing in the character or purposes of our people justifies us in ignoring the plain lesson of history and putting our liberties in jeopardy by assuming the burden of militarism, which is crushing the people of the Old World. We denounce the administration for its sinister efforts to substitute a standing army for the citizen soldiery, which is the best safeguard of the republic.

SYMPATHY FOR THE BOERS.

We extend to the brave Boers of South Africa our sympathy and moral support in their patriotic struggle for the right of self-government, and we are unalterably opposed to any alliance, open or covert, between the United States and any other nation that will tend to the destruction of human liberty.

IMPERIALISM IN IDAHO.

A further manifestation of imperialism is to be found in the mining districts of Idaho. In the Cœur d'Alene soldiers have been used to overawe miners striving for a greater measure of industrial independence. We denounce the state government of Idaho and the federal government for employing the military arm of the government to abridge the civil rights of the people, and to enforce an infamous permit system which denies to laborers their inherent liberty and compels them to forswear their manhood and their right before being permitted to seek employment.

MONGOLIAN AND MALAYAN IMMIGRATION.

The importation of Japanese and other laborers under contract to serve monopolistic corporations is a notorious and flagrant violation of the immigration laws. We demand that the federal government take cognizance of this menacing evil and repress it under existing laws. We further pledge ourselves to strive for the enactment of more stringent laws for the exclusion of Mongolian and Malayan immigration.

FOR MUNICIPAL OWNERSHIP.

We indorse municipal ownership of public utilities, and declare that the advantages which have accrued to the public under that system would be multiplied a hundredfold by its extension to natural interstate monopolies.

INJUNCTIONS IN LABOR TROUBLES.

We denounce the practice of issuing injunctions in cases of dispute between employers and employees, making criminal, acts by organizations which are not criminal when performed by individuals, and demand legislation to restrain the evil.

FOR DIRECT VOTE OF THE PEOPLE.

We demand that United States Senators and all other officials, as far as practicable, be elected by direct vote of the people.

COERCION AND INTIMIDATION.

Believing that the elective franchise and untrammeled ballot are essential to a government of, for, and by the people, the People's party condemns the wholesale system of disfranchisement by coercion and intimidation adopted in some states as unrepublican and undemocratic, and we declare it to be the duty of the several state legislatures to take such action as will secure a full, free, and fair ballot and an honest count.

HOME-RULE FOR TERRITORIES.

We favor home-rule in the territories and the District of Columbia, and the early admission of the territories as states.

PENSION ADMINISTRATION.

We denounce the expensive red-tape system, political favoritism, cruel and unnecessary delay, and criminal evasion of the statutes in the management of the pension office, and demand the simple and honest execution of the law, and the fulfillment by the nation of its pledges of service pension to all its honorably discharged veterans.

People's Party (Middle-of-the-Road) National Committee:

Chairman, J. A. PARKER, of Kentucky.
Secretary,

PEOPLE'S PARTY (Middle-of-the-Road) CONVENTION.

Cincinnati, O., May 9–10, 1900.

Chairman pro tem., M. W. HOWARD,
of Alabama.

Chairman, W. L. PEEK,
of Georgia.

NOMINATED—

For President, **Wharton Barker,**
of Pennsylvania.

For Vice-President, **Ignatius Donnelly,**
of Minnesota.

This convention represented that faction of the People's party which was opposed to fusion and bolted at the convention of 1896, at St. Louis. The term "middle-of-the-road" is taken from the adjuration of Milton Park, of Texas, who led the bolt, to "Keep in the middle of the road." Wharton Barker was nominated for President on the second ballot. The following is the vote in detail:

CANDIDATES.	1st.	2d.
M. W. HOWARD, of Alabama	$326\frac{6}{10}$	336
WHARTON BARKER, of Pennsylvania	$314\frac{4}{10}$	370
IGNATIUS DONNELLY, of Minnesota	70	7
S. F. NORTON of Illinois	3	2
Whole number of votes	714	715
Necessary to a choice	358	358

For Vice-President, Ignatius Donnelly, of Minnesota, was unanimously nominated.

The convention also elected J A. Parker, of Kentucky, as chairman of the National Committee, instead of permitting the committee to choose its leader.

The convention adopted the following platform:—

PEOPLE'S PARTY (MIDDLE-OF-THE-ROAD) PLATFORM.

The People's party of the United States, assembled in national convention this 10th day of May, 1900, affirming our unshaken belief in the cardinal tenets of the People's party as set forth in the Omaha platform, and pledging ourselves anew to continued advocacy of those grand principles of human liberty until right shall triumph over might and love over greed, do adopt and proclaim this declaration of faith:

THE INITIATIVE AND REFERENDUM.

First. We demand the initiative and referendum, and the imperative mandate for such changes of existing fundamental and statute law as will enable the people in their sovereign capacity to propose and compel the enactment of such laws as they desire, to reject such as they deem injurious to their interests, and to recall unfaithful public servants.

PUBLIC OWNERSHIP OF RAILROADS, TELEGRAPH, ETC.

Second. We demand the public ownership and operation of those means of communication, transportation and production which the people may elect, such as railroads, telegraph and telephone lines, coal mines, etc.

AGAINST ALIEN AND SPECULATIVE OWNERSHIP OF LAND.

Third. The land, including all natural sources of wealth, is a heritage of the people and should not be monopolized for speculative purposes, and alien ownership of land should be prohibited. All land now held by railroads and other corporations in excess of their actual needs, and all lands now owned by aliens, should be reclaimed by the government and held for actual settlers only.

FOR PAPER MONEY AND FREE COINAGE OF SILVER.

Fourth. A scientific and absolute paper money, based upon the entire wealth and population of the nation, not redeemable in any specific commodity, but made a full legal tender for all debts and receivable for all taxes and public dues, and issued by the government only, without the intervention of banks, and in sufficient quantity to meet the demands of commerce, is the best currency that can be devised; but until such a financial system is secured, which we shall press for adoption, we favor the free and unlimited coinage of both silver and gold at the legal ratio of 16 to 1.

FOR A GRADUATED INCOME-TAX.

Fifth. We demand the levy and collection of a graduated tax on incomes and inheritances, and a constitutional amendment to secure the same, if necessary.

FOR DIRECT VOTE OF THE PEOPLE.

Sixth. We demand the election of President, Vice-President, federal judges, and United States Senators by direct vote of the people.

TRUSTS AND THE OLD PARTIES.

Seventh. We are opposed to trusts, and declare the contention between the old parties on the monopoly question is a sham battle, and that no solution of this mighty problem is possible without the adoption of the principles of public ownership of public utilities.

Silver Republican National Committee:

Chairman, D. C. TILLOTSON, of Kansas.
Secretary, E. C. CORSER, of Minnesota.

SILVER REPUBLICAN CONVENTION.

Kansas City, Mo., July 4-6, 1900.

Chairman pro tem., HENRY M. TELLER, of Colorado.

Chairman, L. W. BROWN, of Ohio.

NOMINATED—

For President, **William J. Bryan**, of Nebraska.

For Vice-President, **Adlai E. Stevenson**, of Illinois.

This convention was composed of about 1200 delegates and visitors, representing twenty-four states and territories. Only seven states east of the Mississippi River were represented. The Declaration of Independence was read on July 4. William J. Bryan was nominated for President by acclamation. No nomination was made for Vice-President, the National Committee of the party being empowered to determine upon a candidate. This committee, at a meeting held on July 7, at Kansas City, indorsed the nomination of Adlai E. Stevenson, the Democratic candidate.

The following platform was adopted:—

SILVER REPUBLICAN PLATFORM.

We, the Silver Republican party, in national convention assembled, declare these as our principles and invite the co-operation of all who agree therewith:

PRINCIPLES OF THE FOREFATHERS.

We recognize that the principles set forth in the Declaration of American Independence are fundamental and everlastingly true in their application to governments among men. We believe the patriotic words of Washington's farewell to be the words of soberness and wisdom, inspired by the spirit of right and truth. We treasure the words of Jefferson as priceless gems of American statesmanship. We hold in sacred remembrance the broad philanthropy and patriotism of Lincoln, who was the great interpreter of American history and the great apostle of human rights and of industrial freedom; and we declare, as was declared by the convention that nominated the great emancipator, that the maintenance of the principles promulgated in the Declaration of Independence and embodied in the Federal Constitution—" that all men are created equal; that they are endowed by their Creator with certain inalienable rights; that among these are life, liberty, and the pursuit of happiness; that to secure these rights governments are instituted among men, deriving their just powers from the consent of the governed "—is essential to the preservation of our republican institutions.

PRINCIPLE OF BIMETALLISM.

We declare our adherence to the principle of bimetallism as the right basis of a monetary system under our national Constitution—a principle that found place repeatedly in Republican platforms, from the demonetization of silver in 1873 to the St. Louis Republican Convention in 1896. Since that convention a Republican Congress and a Republican President, at the dictation of the trusts and money power, have passed and approved a currency bill which in itself is a repudiation of the doctrine of bimetallism advocated theretofore by the President and every great leader of his party.

EFFECT OF THE CURRENCY LAW.

This currency law destroys the full money power of the silver dollar, provides for the payment of all government obligations and the redemption of all forms of paper money in gold alone; retires the time-honored and patriotic greenbacks, constituting one-sixth of the money in circulation, and surrenders to banking corporations a sovereign function of issuing all paper money, thus enabling these corporations to control the prices of labor and property by increasing or diminishing the volume of money in circulation, and thus giving the banks power to create panics and bring disaster upon business enterprises.

The provisions of this currency law making the bonded debt of the republic payable in gold alone, change contracts between the government and the bondholders to the advantage of the latter, and are in direct opposition to the declaration of the Matthews resolution passed by Congress in 1878, for which resolution the present Republican President, then a member of Congress, voted, as did also all leading Republicans, both in the House and Senate.

FOR REPEAL OF PRESENT CURRENCY LAW AND ENACTMENT OF NEW LAW.

We declare it to be our intention to lend our efforts to the repeal of this currency law, which not only repudiates the ancient and time-honored principles of the American people before the Constitution was adopted, but is violative of the principles of the Constitution itself; and we shall not cease our efforts until there has been established in its place a monetary system based upon the free and unlimited coinage of silver and gold into money at the present legal ratio of 16 to 1 by the independent action of the United States, under which system all paper money shall be issued by the government, and all such money coined or issued shall be a full legal tender in payment of all debts, public and private, without exception.

INCOME-TAX.

We are in favor of a graduated tax upon incomes, and, if necessary to accomplish this, we favor an amendment to the Constitution.

POPULAR ELECTION OF SENATORS.

We believe that United States Senators ought to be elected by a direct vote of the people, and we favor such amendment of the Constitution and such legislation as may be necessary to that end.

THE MERIT SYSTEM.

We favor the maintenance and the extension, wherever practicable, of the merit system in the public service, appointments to be made according to fitness, competitively ascertained, and public servants to be retained in office only so long as shall be compatible with the efficiency of the service.

TRUSTS.

Combinations, trusts, and monopolies contrived and arranged for the purpose of controlling the prices and quantity of articles supplied to the public are unjust, unlawful, and oppressive. Not only do these unlawful conspiracies fix the prices of commodities in many cases, but they invade every branch of the state and national government with their polluting influence, and control the actions of their employees and dependents in private life, until their influence actually imperils society and the liberty of the citizen. We declare against them. We demand the most stringent laws for their destruction, the most severe punishment of their promoters and maintainers, and the energetic enforcement of such laws by the courts.

MONROE DOCTRINE AND NICARAGUAN CANAL.

We believe the Monroe doctrine to be sound in principle and a wise national policy, and we demand a firm adherence thereto. We condemn acts inconsistent with it and that tend to make us parties to the interests and to involve us in the controversies of European nations, and to recognition, by pending treaty, of the right of England to be considered in the construction of an inter-oceanic canal. We favor the speedy construction of the Nicaraguan canal, to be built, owned, and defended by the Government of the United States.

ALIEN OWNERSHIP OF LAND AND FRANCHISES.

We observe with anxiety and regard with disapproval the increasing ownership of American lands by aliens, and their growing control over international transportation, natural resources, and public utilities. We demand legislation to protect our public domain, our natural resources, our franchises, and our internal commerce, and to keep them free and maintain their independence of all foreign monopolies, institutions, and influences, and we declare our opposition to the leasing of the public lands of the United States, whereby corporations and syndicates will be able to secure control thereof and thus monopolize the public domain, the heritage of the people.

DIRECT LEGISLATION.

We are in favor of the principles of direct legislation.

PENSIONS.

In view of the great sacrifice made and patriotic services rendered, we are in favor of liberal pensions to deserving soldiers, their widows, orphans and other dependents. We believe that enlistment and service should be accepted as conclusive proof that the soldier was free from disease and disability at the time of his enlistment. We condemn the present administration of the pension laws.

SYMPATHY FOR THE BOERS.

We tender to the patriotic people of the South African republic our sympathy and express our admiration for them in their heroic attempts to preserve their political freedom and maintain their national independence. We declare the destruction of those republics and the subjugation of their people to be a crime against civilization. We believe this sympathy should have been voiced by the American Congress, as was done in the case of the French, the Greeks, the Hungarians, the Polanders, the Armenians, and the Cubans, and as the traditions of this country would have dictated.

PORTO RICAN TARIFF LAW.

We declare the Porto Rican Tariff Law to be not only a serious but a dangerous departure from the principles of our form of government. We believe in a republican form of government, and are opposed to monarchy and to the whole theory of imperialistic control.

THE PHILIPPINES.

We believe in self-government— a government by consent of the governed—and are unalterably opposed to a government based upon force. It is clear and certain that the inhabitants of the Philippine archipelago cannot be made citizens of the United States without endangering our civilization. We are therefore in favor of applying to the Philippine archipelago the principle we are solemnly and publicly pledged to observe in the case of Cuba.

WAR-TAXES.

There being no longer any necessity for collecting war-taxes, we demand the repeal of the war-taxes levied to carry on the war with Spain.

ADMISSION OF TERRITORIES.

We favor the immediate admission into the Union of States the Territories of Arizona, New Mexico, and Oklahoma.

PLEDGES TO CUBA.

We demand that our nation's promises to Cuba shall be fulfilled in every particular.

ARID LANDS.

We believe the national government should lend every aid, encouragement, and assistance toward the reclamation of the arid lands of the United States, and to that end we are in favor of a comprehensive survey thereof and an immediate ascertainment of the water-supply available for such reclamation, and we believe it to be the duty of the general government to provide for the construction of storage reservoirs and irrigation works, so that the water-supply of the arid region may be utilized to the greatest possible extent in the interests of the people, while preserving all rights of the state.

OWNERSHIP OF PUBLIC UTILITIES.

Transportation is a public necessity, and the means of and methods of it are matters of public concern. Railway companies exercise a power over industries, business, and commerce which they ought not to do, and should be made to serve the public interests without making unreasonable charges or unjust discrimination. We observe with satisfaction the growing sentiment among the people in favor of the public ownership and operation of public utilities.

WHEN WAR IS JUSTIFIED AND WHEN IMMORAL.

Peace is the virtue of civilization and war is its crime. War is only justified when the oppressors of humanity will heed no other appeal, and when the enemies of liberty will respond to no other demand. However high and pure may be the purposes of an appeal to arms in the beginning, war becomes immoral when continued for the purpose of subjugation, or for national aggrandizement.

COMMERCIAL EXPANSION.

We are in favor of expanding our commerce in the interests of American labor and for the benefit of all our people, by every honest and peaceful means, but when war is waged to extend trade, force commerce, or to acquire wealth, it is national piracy. Our creed and our history justify the nations of the earth in expecting that wherever the American flag is unfurled in authority, human liberty and political freedom will be found. We protest against the adoption of any policy that will change, in the thought of the world, the meaning of our flag. We insist that it shall never float over any vessel or wave at the head of any column directed against the political independence of any people or of any race, or in any clime.

OPPOSITION TO ASIATIC LABORERS.

We are opposed to the importation of Asiatic laborers in competition with American labor, and advocate a more rigid enforcement of the laws relating thereto.

TO PERPETUATE THE SPIRIT AND TEACHINGS OF LINCOLN.

The Silver Republican party of the United States, in the foregoing principles, seeks to perpetuate the spirit and to adhere to the teachings of Abraham Lincoln.

Prohibition National Committee:

Chairman, OLIVER W. STEWART, of Illinois.
Secretary, WILLIAM T. WARDWELL, of New York.

PROHIBITION CONVENTION.

Chicago, Ill., June 27-28, 1900.

Chairman pro tem. and permanent Chairman,
SAMUEL DICKIE,
of Michigan.

NOMINATED—

For President, JOHN G. WOOLLEY,
of Illinois.

For Vice-President, HENRY B. METCALF,
of Rhode Island.

The number of delegates present at this convention was 735, representing forty states. John G. Woolley was nominated for President on the first ballot, receiving 380 votes, as against 320 cast for Rev. Dr. Silas C. Swallow, of Pennsylvania. For Vice-President the names of Rev. E. L. Eaton, of Iowa; Thomas R. Carskadon, of West Virginia; Henry B. Metcalf, of Rhode Island; and James A. Tate, of Tennessee, were presented. Mr. Tate withdrew. Henry B. Metcalf was nominated on the first ballot, as follows:

CANDIDATES.	Votes.
HENRY B. METCALF, of Rhode Island	349
THOMAS R. CARSKADON, of West Virginia	130
REV. E. L. EATON, of Iowa	113
Whole number of votes, 592	
Necessary to a choice, 297	

The convention adopted the following platform:—

PROHIBITION PLATFORM.

PREAMBLE.

The National Prohibition party, in convention represented, at Chicago, June 27 and 28, 1900, acknowledge Almighty God as the Supreme Source of all just government. Realizing that this republic was founded upon Christian principles and can endure only as it embodies justice and righteousness, and asserting that all authority should seek the best good of all the governed, to this end wisely prohibiting what is wrong and permitting only what is right, hereby records and proclaims:

DEFINITION OF PARTY. PROHIBITION THE MOST IMPORTANT PARTY PRINCIPLE.

We accept and assert the definition given by Edmund Burke, that "a party is a body of men joined together for the purpose of promoting, by their joint endeavor, the national interest upon some particular principle upon which they are all agreed." We declare that there is no principle now advocated, by any other party, which could be made a fact in government with such beneficent moral and material results as the principle of prohibition, applied to the beverage liquor traffic; that the national interest could be promoted in no other way so surely and widely as by its adoption and assertion through a national policy, and the co-operation therein of every state, forbidding the manufacture, sale, exportation, importation, and transportation of intoxicating liquors for beverage purposes; that we stand for this as the only principle, proposed by any party anywhere, for the settlement of a question greater and graver than any other before the American people, and involving more profoundly, than any other their moral future, and financial welfare; and that all the patriotic citizenship of this country, agreed upon this principle, however much disagreement there may be as to minor considerations and issues, should stand together at the ballot-box, from this time forward, until prohibition is the established policy of the United States, with a party in power to enforce it and to insure its moral and material benefits.

OTHER AND LESSER PROBLEMS OF GOVERNMENT.

We insist that such a party, agreed upon this principle and policy, having sober leadership, without any obligation for success to the saloon vote and to those demoralizing political combinations of men and money now allied therewith and suppliant thereto, could successfully cope with all other and lesser problems of government, in legislative halls and in the executive chair, and that it is useless for any party to make declarations in its platform as to any questions concerning which there may be serious differences of opinion in its own membership, and as to which, because of such differences, the party could legislate only on a basis of mutual concessions when coming into power.

TRUSTS AND MONOPOLIES.

We submit that the Democratic and Republican parties are alike insincere in their assumed hostility to trusts and monopolies. They dare not and do not attack the most dangerous of them all, the liquor power. So long as the saloon debauches the citizen and breeds the purchasable voter, money will continue to buy its way to power. Break down this traffic, elevate manhood, and a sober citizenship will find a way to control dangerous combinations of capital.

THE FINANCIAL PROBLEM.

We propose as a first step in the financial problems of the nation to save more than a billion of dollars every year, now annually expended to support the liquor traffic and to demoralize our people. When that is accomplished, conditions will have so improved that, with a clearer atmosphere, the country can address itself to the questions as to the kind and quantity of currency needed.

THE OVERWHELMING ISSUE OF AMERICAN POLITICS.

We reaffirm as true indisputably the declaration of William Windom when Secretary of the Treasury in the cabinet of President Arthur, that "Considered socially, financially, politically, or morally, the licensed liquor traffic is or ought to be the overwhelming issue in American politics," and that "the destruction of this iniquity stands next on the calendar of the world's progress." We hold that the existence of our party presents this issue squarely to the American people, and lays upon them the responsibility of choice between liquor parties, dominated by distillers and brewers, with their policy of saloon-perpetuation, breeding waste, wickedness, woe, pauperism, taxation, corruption and crime, and our one party of patriotic and moral principle, with a policy which defends it from domination by corrupt bosses and which insures it forever against the blighting control of saloon politics.

We face with sorrow, shame, and fear the awful fact that this liquor traffic has a grip on our government, municipal, state, and national, through the revenue system and saloon sovereignty, which no other party dares to dispute; a grip which dominates the party now in power, from caucus to Congress, from policeman to President, from the rumshop to the White House; a grip which compels the chief executive to consent that law shall be nullified in behalf of the brewer, that the canteen shall curse our army and spread intemperance across the seas, and that our flag shall wave as the symbol of partnership, at home and abroad, between this government and the men who defy and defile it for their unholy gain.

PRESIDENT MCKINLEY ARRAIGNED.

We charge upon President McKinley, who was elected to his high office by appeals to Christian sentiment and patriotism almost unprecedented and by a combination of moral influences never before seen in this country, that, by his conspicuous example as a wine-drinker at public banquets and as a wine-serving host in the White House, he has done more to encourage the liquor business, to demoralize the temperance habits of young men, and to bring Christian practices and requirements into disrepute, than any other President this republic has ever had. We further charge upon President McKinley responsibility for the army canteen, with all its dire brood of disease, immorality, sin, and death, in this country, in Cuba, in Porto Rico, and the Philippines; and we insist that by his attitude concerning the canteen, and his apparent contempt for the vast number of petitions and petitioners protesting against it, he has outraged and insulted the moral sentiment of this country in such a manner and to such a degree as calls for its righteous uprising and his indignant and effective rebuke.

We challenge denial of the fact that our Chief Executive, as commander in chief of the military forces of the United States, at any time prior to or since March 2, 1899, could have closed every army saloon, called a canteen, by executive order, as President Hayes in effect did before him, and should have closed them, for the same reasons which actuated President Hayes; we assert that the act of Congress passed March 2, 1899, forbidding the sale of liquor "in any post-exchange or canteen," by any "officer or private soldier" or by "any other person on any premises used for military purposes in the United States," was and is as explicit an act of prohibition as the English language can frame; we declare our solemn belief that the Attorney-General of the United States in his interpretation of that law, and the Secretary of War in his acceptance of that interpretation and his refusal to enforce the law, were and are guilty of treasonable nullification thereof, and that President McKinley, through his assent to and indorsement of such interpretation and refusal, on the part of officials appointed by and responsible to him, shares responsibly in their guilt; and we record our conviction that a new and serious peril confronts our country, in the fact that its President, at the behest of the beer power, dare and does abrogate a law of Congress, through subordinates removable at will by him and whose acts become his, and thus virtually confesses that laws are to be administered or to be nullified in the interest of a law-defying business, by an administration under mortgage to such business for support.

LIQUOR POLICY IN NEW POSSESSIONS.

We deplore the fact that an administration of this republic claiming the right and power to carry our flag across seas, and to conquer and annex new territory, should admit its lack of power to prohibit the American saloon on subjugated soil, or should openly confess itself subject to liquor sovereignty under that flag. We are humiliated, exasperated and grieved, by the evidence painfully abundant, that this administration's policy of expansion is bearing so rapidly its first fruits of drunkenness, insanity, and crime under the hot-house sun of the tropics; and when the president of the first Philippine commission says: "It was unfortunate that we introduced and established the saloon there, to corrupt the natives and to exhibit the vices of our race," we charge the inhumanity and unchristianity of this act upon the administration of William McKinley and upon the party which elected and would perpetuate the same.

We declare that the only policy which the government of the United States can of right uphold as to the liquor traffic, under the national Constitution, upon any territory under the military or civil control of that government, is the policy of prohibition; that "to establish justice, insure domestic tranquillity, provide for the common defense, promote the general welfare, and secure the blessings of liberty to ourselves and our posterity," as the Constitution provides, the liquor traffic must neither be sanctioned nor tolerated, and that the revenue policy, which makes our government a partner with distillers and brewers and barkeepers, is a disgrace to our civilization, an outrage upon humanity, and a crime against God.

IN ALASKA AND HAWAII.

We condemn the present administration at Washington because it has repealed the prohibitory laws in Alaska, and has given over the partly civilized tribes there to be the prey of the American grog-shop; and because it has entered upon a license policy in our new possessions by incorporating the same in the recent act of Congress in the code of laws for the government of the Hawaiian Islands.

INCREASE OF LIQUOR EXPORTS TO CUBA AND THE PHILIPPINES.

We call general attention to the fearful fact that exportation of liquors from the United States to the Philippine Islands increased from $337 in 1898 to $467,198 in the first ten months of the fiscal year ending June 30, 1900; and that while our exportation of liquors to Cuba never reached $30,000 a year previous to American occupation of that island, our exports of such liquors to Cuba during the fiscal year of 1899 reached the sum of $629,855.

CALL TO MORAL AND CHRISTIAN CITIZENSHIP.

One great religious body (the Baptist) having truly declared of the liquor traffic "that it has no defensible right to exist, that it can never be reformed, and that it stands condemned by its unrighteous fruits as a thing un-Christian, un-American, and perilous utterly to every interest in life"; another great religious body (the Methodist) having as truly asserted and reiterated that "no political party has a right to expect, nor should receive, the votes of Christian men so long as it stands committed to the license system, or refuses to put itself on record in an attitude of open hostility to the saloon"; other great religious bodies having made similar deliverances, in language plain and unequivocal, as to the liquor traffic and the duty of Christian citizenship in opposition thereto; and the fact being plain and undeniable that the Democratic party stands for license, the saloon, and the canteen, while the Republican party, in policy and administration, stands for the canteen, the saloon and revenue therefrom, we declare ourselves justified in expecting that Christian voters everywhere shall cease their complicity with the liquor curse by refusing to uphold a liquor party, and shall unite themselves with the only party which upholds the prohibition policy, and which for nearly thirty years has been the faithful defender of the church, the state, the home, and the school, against the saloon, its expanders and perpetuators, their actual and persistent foes.

THE PARAMOUNT ISSUE.

We insist that no differences of belief as to any other question or concern of government should stand in the way of such a union of moral and Christian citizenship as we hereby invite, for the speedy settlement of this paramount moral, industrial, financial and political issue, which our party presents; and we refrain from declaring ourselves upon all minor matters, as to which differences of opinion may exist, that hereby we may offer to the American people a platform so broad that all can stand upon it who desire to see sober citizenship actually sovereign over the allied hosts of evil, sin, and crime, in a government of the people, by the people, and for the people.

ONLY TWO REAL PARTIES.

We declare that there are but two real parties to-day concerning the liquor traffic—perpetuationists and prohibitionists—and that patriotism, Christianity, and every interest of genuine and of pure democracy, besides the loyal demands of our common humanity, require the speedy union, in one solid phalanx at the ballot-box, of all who oppose the liquor traffic perpetuation, and who covet endurance for this republic.

The committee also reported three resolutions which were adopted, though not as a part of the platform:—

ADDITIONAL RESOLUTIONS.

Resolved, That it is the sense of this convention that the ballot should not be denied to any citizen of the United States on account of sex.

Resolved, That in the organization of the Young People's Prohibition Leagues, as presented by the representatives of the League from the current platform, we recognize an efficient agency for bringing about the suppression of the liquor traffic, legalized or otherwise, and aiding in the upbuilding of the Prohibition party.

Resolved, That we recommend to the National Executive Committeee and its chairman, the advisability of giving such substantial aid to the organization of Young People's Prohibition Leagues as may be reasonably practicable.

Socialist-Labor National Executive Committee:

Secretary, HENRY KUHN, of New York.

SOCIALIST-LABOR CONVENTION.

New York, June 2-8, 1900.

Chairman pro tem., THOMAS CURRAN, of Rhode Island.

Chairman, DANIEL DE LEON, of New York.

NOMINATED—

For President, **Joseph Francis Malloney,** of Massachusetts.

For Vice-President, **Valentine Remmel,** of Pennsylvania.

The convention of this party consisted of 83 delegates, representing nineteen states, and they nominated Joseph Francis Malloney, of Massachusetts, for President, and Valentine Remmel, of Pennsylvania, for Vice-President. The convention remained in session for seven days.

The platform adopted in 1896, with the exception of the "General Demands," was reaffirmed (see pp. 323, 324).

SOCIAL DEMOCRATIC (PARTY OF THE UNITED STATES) CONVENTION.

Rochester, N. Y., January 27, 1900.

NOMINATED—

For President, **Job Harriman**,
of California.

For Vice-President, **Max S. Hayes**,
of Ohio.

The following platform was adopted:—

SOCIAL DEMOCRATIC PLATFORM.

The Social Democratic party, of the United States, in convention assembled, reaffirms its allegiance to the revolutionary principles of international socialism and declares the supreme political issue in America to-day to be the contest between the working class and the capitalist class for the possession of the powers of government. The party affirms its steadfast purpose to use those powers, once achieved, to destroy wage slavery, to abolish the institution of private property in the means of production, and establish the co-operative commonwealth.

In the United States, as in all other civilized countries, the natural order of economic development has separated society into two antagonistic classes—the capitalists, a comparatively small class, the possessors of all the modern means of production and distribution (land, mines, machinery, and means of transportation and communication), and the large and ever-increasing class of wage-workers, possessing no means of production.

This economic supremacy has secured to the dominant class the full control of the government, the pulpit, the schools, and the public press; it has thus made the capitalist class the arbiter of the fate of the workers, whom it is reducing to a condition of dependence, economically exploited and oppressed, intellectually and physically crippled and degraded, and their political equality rendered a bitter mockery.

The contest between these two classes grows ever sharper. Hand in hand with the growth of monopolies goes the annihilation of small industries and of the middle class depending upon them; ever larger grows the multitude of destitute wage-workers and of the unemployed, and ever fiercer the struggle between the class of the exploiter and the exploited, the capitalists and the wage-workers.

The evil effects of capitalist production are intensified by the recurring industrial crises which render the existence of the greater part of the population still more precarious and uncertain.

These facts amply prove that the modern means of production have outgrown the existing social order based on production for profit.

Human energy and natural resources are wasted for individual gain.

Ignorance is fostered that wage slavery may be perpetuated.

Science and invention are perverted to the exploitation of men, women and children.

The lives and liberties of the working class are recklessly sacrificed for profit.

Wars are fomented between nations; indiscriminate slaughter is encouraged; the destruction of whole races is sanctioned, in order that the capitalist class may extend its commercial dominion abroad and enhance its supremacy at home.

The introduction of a new and higher order of society is the historic mission of the working class. All other classes, despite their apparent or actual conflicts, are interested in upholding the system of private ownership in the means of production. The Democratic, Republican, and all other parties which do not stand for the complete overthrow of the capitalist system of production, are alike the tools of the capitalist class. Their policies are injurious to the interest of the working class, which can be served only by the abolition of the profit system.

The workers can most effectively act as a class in their struggle against the collective power of the capitalist class only by constituting themselves into a political party, distinct and opposed to all parties formed by the propertied classes.

We, therefore, call upon the wage-workers of the United States, without distinction of color, sex, race, or creed, and upon all citizens in sympathy with the historic mission of the working class, to organize under the banner of the Social Democratic party, as a party truly representing the interests of the toiling masses and uncompromisingly waging war upon the exploiting class, until the system of wage slavery shall be abolished and the co-operative commonwealth shall be set up. Pending the accomplishment of this, our ultimate purpose, we pledge every effort of the Social Democratic party for the immediate improvement of the condition of labor and for the securing of its progressive demands.

SOCIAL DEMOCRATIC (PARTY OF AMERICA) CONVENTION.

Indianapolis, Ind., March 6, 1900.

NOMINATED—

For President, **Eugene V. Debs,**
of Indiana.

For Vice-President, **Job Harriman,**
of California.

The following platform was adopted:—

SOCIAL DEMOCRATIC PLATFORM.

The Social Democratic party of America declares that life, liberty, and happiness depend upon equal political and economic rights.

In our economic development an industrial revolution has taken place. In former years the tools of production were usually owned by the man who worked with them and who thereby became the owner of the product of his labor. Now, the machine—which is but the improved tool—is not owned by the laborer; it is owned by the capitalist, who thus becomes the master of the product, and the worker is dependent upon him for employment. The capitalist thus becomes the master of the worker and is able to appropriate to himself a large share of the product of his labor.

Capitalism, the private ownership of the means of production, is responsible for the insecurity of subsistence, the poverty, misery, and degradation of the ever-growing majority of our people; but the same economic forces which have produced and now intensify the capitalist system will necessitate the adoption of socialism, the collective ownership of the means of production for the common good and welfare.

The present system of social production and private ownership is rapidly converting society into two antagonistic classes —i. e., the capitalist class and the propertyless class. The middle class, once the most powerful of this great nation, is disappearing in the mill of competition. The issue is now between the two classes first named. Our political liberty is now of little value to the masses unless used to acquire economic liberty.

Independent political action is the chief emancipating factor of the working class. The trade-union movement and the voluntary co-operative movement are auxiliary measures.

Therefore the Social Democratic party of America declares its object to be:

1. The organization of the working class into a political party to conquer the public powers now controlled by the capitalist class.

2. The aiding of the trade-union movement as the main defensive measure calculated to improve the standard of living of the working class.

3. The encouragement of voluntary co-operation wherever such will do away with the profits of the middle men and thereby serve to educate the people and further improve their condition.

The working class and all those in sympathy with their historic mission to realize a higher civilization should sever connection with all capitalist and reform parties and unite with the Social Democratic party of America.

The control of political power by the Social Democratic party will be tantamount to the abolition of all class rule.

The solidarity of labor connecting the millions of class-conscious fellow-workers throughout the civilized world will lead to international socialism, the brotherhood of man.

While we believe that the overthrow of the capitalist system, as a whole, is certain, because this system is rapidly outgrowing its usefulness, we see that the development of economic conditions is gradual. We, therefore, consider it to be of primary importance for Socialist parties to elect Socialists to legislative and municipal bodies, in order that they may bring about all the Socialist reforms possible for the immediate amelioration and improvement of the condition of the people.

As steps in this direction, we demand the following:

1. Revision of our federal constitution, in order to remove the obstacles to complete control of government by the people irrespective of sex.

2. The public ownership of all industries controlled by monopolies, trusts, and combines.

3. The public ownership of all railroads, telegraphs, and telephones; all means of transportation and communication; all water-works, gas and electric plants, and other public utilities.

4. The public ownership of all gold, silver, copper, lead, iron, coal, and other mines, and all oil and gas wells.

5. The reduction of the hours of labor in proportion to the increasing facilities of production.

6. The inauguration of a system of public works and improvements for the employment of the unemployed, the public credit to be utilized for that purpose.

7. Labor legislation to be national and local.

8. State or national insurance of working people against accidents, lack of employment, and want in old age.

9. Equal civil and political rights, for men and women, and the abolition of all laws discriminating against women.

10. The adoption of the initiative and referendum, proportional representation, and the right of recall of representatives by the voters.

11. Abolition of war and the introduction of international arbitration.

Union Reform National Committee:

Chairman, R. S. THOMPSON, of Ohio,
Secretary, A. G. EICHELBERGER, of Maryland.

UNION REFORM NOMINATIONS.

Baltimore, Md., September 3, 1900.

For President, **Seth W. Ellis,**
of Ohio.

For Vice-President, **Samuel T. Nicholson,**
of Pennsylvania.

The nominations were made by direct vote of the people, which was counted and announced by the National Canvassing Board at Baltimore, Sept. 3, 1900. The number of votes cast was 1865 and thirty states and territories participated. The following is the vote in detail:

Candidates.	Votes.	Candidates.	Votes.
Seth W. Ellis, of Ohio	1561	Wharton Barker, of Pennsylvania	1
Samuel T. Nicholson, of Pennsylvania	254	John G. Woolley, of Illinois	1
William J. Bryan, of Nebraska	15	Ignatius Donnelly, of Minnesota	1
Eugene V. Debs, of Indiana	4	Scattering	27
William McKinley, of Ohio	1	Total	1865

The one receiving the highest number of votes is the nominee for President and the one receiving the next highest number is the nominee for Vice-President. Any citizen of the United States, 21 years of age or more, approving the principles of the party and declaring his intention of supporting the ticket was entitled to vote.

This party had its origin in Ohio, being a union of the minority parties which were unable to secure places on the official ballot under legislation enacted in that state. In the fall of 1898 the new party polled enough votes to secure official recognition, which led to a national conference, held at Cincinnati, March 1, 1899. Some 300 delegates were present from twelve states. A. G. Eichelberger, of Maryland, was temporary chairman, and R. S. Thompson, of Ohio, permanent chairman.

The following preamble and platform were adopted:—

UNION REFORM PARTY PLATFORM.

PREAMBLE.

Our present system of government vests the entire lawmaking power in representatives. The people elect these representatives, but have no control over their actions.

An experience of over a hundred years in the practical operation of this system has proved that it does not provide a government of, by, and for the people.

Representatives cannot always know certainly the will of their constituents, and even where that will has been clearly manifested it has been continually disregarded.

Legislative bodies, from municipal councils to the national congress, have been controlled by corrupt influences. Legislation has consequently been in the interest of the corrupt few and against the interest of the voiceless masses.

Under this system the people are disfranchised on all matters of legislation. They are allowed to vote for men, but are denied the right to vote for measures. The people are governed by laws which they did not enact and cannot repeal.

As the result of this system great abuses have arisen and politics has become a synonym for corruption.

The people have seen these abuses, but being disfranchised on all legislative questions have been unable to provide a remedy. They have become divided into parties and factions contending with each other in regard to the legislation needed. They have overlooked the fact that under our system of government they have power neither to enact legislation which they desire nor to prevent legislation to which they are opposed.

In search for relief the people have turned from one party to another, and have organized new parties without number.

But all such efforts have been fruitless, and must continue so to be as long as the people are disfranchised. They must be invested with the power to make their own laws before they can have laws made in their own interest.

So long as the people have no voice in legislation it is useless for them to contend among themselves regarding the legislation which they need, but cannot enact.

That we may have a government conducted in the interests of the people, and which will provide for the peace, prosperity, morality, and happiness of the entire nation, we must have a government which is in fact of the people, by the people, and for the people, and in which the people shall rule.

We, therefore, reserving to ourselves the right to our individual opinions on all questions of legislation, unite for the accomplishment of this end—the enfranchisement of the American people and the establishment of a government in which the will of the people shall be supreme. And to this do pledge our united labors.

And we invite all persons who believe in the principles of

liberty and the Declaration of Independence to unite in support of the following

PLATFORM:

Direct legislation under the system known as the initiative and referendum.

Under the "initiative" the people can compel the submission to themselves of any desired law, when, if it receives a majority of the votes cast, it is thereby enacted.

Under the "referendum" the people can compel the submission to themselves of any law which has been adopted by any legislative body, when, if such law fails to receive a majority of the votes cast, it will be thereby rejected.

The election occurred on November 6, 1900.

FORTY-FIVE STATES VOTED.

POP[...]

STATES.	William McKinley, Republican.	William J. Bryan, Democrat.	John Wool[...] Prohib[...]ist
Alabama	53,669	96,368	1[...]
Arkansas	44,800	81,142	
California	164,755	124,985	5[...]
Colorado	93,072	122,733	3[...]
Connecticut	102,572	74,014	1[...]
Delaware	22,537	18,863	
Florida	7,314	28,007	2[...]
Georgia	35,053	81,700	1[...]
Idaho	27,198	29,414	
Illinois	597,985	503,061	17[...]
Indiana	336,063	309,584	1[...]
Iowa	307,778	209,266	[...]
Kansas	185,955	162,601	[...]
Kentucky	226,799	234,902	[...]
Louisiana	14,233	53,671	
Maine	65,435	36,822	[...]
Maryland	136,212	122,271	[...]
Massachusetts	238,866	156,997	[...]
Michigan	316,269	211,685	1[...]
Minnesota	190,461	112,901	[...]
Mississippi	5,753	51,706	
Missouri	314,092	351,913	[...]
Montana	25,373	37,146	
Nebraska	121,835	114,013	[...]
Nevada	3,849	6,347	
New Hampshire	54,803	35,489	
New Jersey	221,707	164,808	
New York	821,992	678,386	2[...]
North Carolina	133,080	157,733	
North Dakota	35,891	20,519	
Ohio	543,918	474,882	1[...]
Oregon	46,526	33,385	
Pennsylvania	712,665	424,232	2[...]
Rhode Island	33,784	19,812	
South Carolina	3,579	47,236	
South Dakota	54,530	39,544	
Tennessee	123,394	145,744	
Texas	120,483	267,243	
Utah	47,089	44,949	
Vermont	42,568	12,849	
Virginia	115,865	146,080	
Washington	57,456	44,833	
West Virginia	119,780	98,791	
Wisconsin	265,866	159,285	1[...]
Wyoming	14,482	10,164	
Total	7,207,386	6,358,076	20[...]

OTE.

ene V. ebs, ocial ocrat.	Wharton Barker, Populist.	Joseph F. Malloney, Socialist-Labor.	Seth H. Ellis, Union Reform.	J. F. R. Leonard, United Christian.	Total vote.
....	3,796	....	....	....	155,240
....	972	....	341	....	127,839
7,572	....	....	....	....	302,336
714	389	684	....	....	221,382
1,029	....	908	....	....	180,140
57	....	....	....	....	42,003
601	1,070	....	....	....	39,226
....	4,584	....	....	....	122,733
....	213	....	....	....	57,682
,687	1,141	1,373	672	352	1,131,897
,374	1,438	663	254	....	664,094
,742	613	259	....	707	530,867
,605	....	....	....	....	353,766
456	1,662	408	....	....	466,489
....	....	....	....	....	67,904
878	....	....	....	....	105,720
908	....	391	147	....	264,511
,607	....	2,599	....	....	414,271
,826	833	903	....	....	544,375
,065	....	1,329	....	....	316,311
....	1,644	....	....	....	59,103
,128	4,244	1,294	....	....	683,636
708	110	111	....	....	63,746
823	1,104	....	....	....	241,430
....	....	....	....	....	10,196
790	....	....	....	....	92,353
,609	669	2,074	....	....	401,050
,869	....	12,622	....	....	1,547,912
....	737	....	....	....	292,556
518	110	....	....	....	57,769
,847	251	1,688	4,284	....	1,040,073
,494	275	....	....	....	84,216
,831	638	2,936	....	....	1,173,210
....	....	1,423	....	....	56,548
....	....	....	....	....	50,815
169	339	....	....	....	96,124
415	1,360	....	....	....	274,827
,846	20,961	162	....	....	413,339
717	....	102	....	....	93,062
....	367	....	....	....	56,152
....	....	....	....	....	264,095
006	....	866	....	....	107,524
187	267	....	....	....	220,610
095	....	524	....	....	442,894
....	....	....	....	....	24,646
173	49,787	33,319	5,698	1,059	13,956,672

ELECTORAL VOTE.

Counted on February 13, 1901.

STATES.	PRESIDENT.		VICE-PRESIDENT.		Number entitled to vote.
	William McKinley, of Ohio.	William Jennings Bryan, of Nebraska.	Theodore Roosevelt, of New York.	Adlai E. Stevenson, of Illinois.	
Alabama	..	11	..	11	11
Arkansas	..	8	..	8	8
California	9	..	9	..	9
Colorado	..	4	..	4	4
Connecticut	6	..	6	..	6
Delaware	3	..	3	..	3
Florida	..	4	..	4	4
Georgia	..	13	..	13	13
Idaho	..	3	..	3	3
Illinois	24	..	24	..	24
Indiana	15	..	15	..	15
Iowa	13	..	13	..	13
Kansas	10	..	10	..	10
Kentucky	..	13	..	13	13
Louisiana	..	8	..	8	8
Maine	6	..	6	..	6
Maryland	8	..	8	..	8
Massachusetts	15	..	15	..	15
Michigan	14	..	14	..	14
Minnesota	9	..	9	..	9
Mississippi	..	9	..	9	9
Missouri	..	17	..	17	17
Montana	..	3	..	3	3
Nebraska	8	..	8	..	8
Nevada	..	3	..	3	3
New Hampshire	4	..	4	..	4
New Jersey	10	..	10	..	10
New York	36	..	36	..	36
North Carolina	..	11	..	11	11
North Dakota	3	..	3	..	3
Ohio	23	..	23	..	23
Oregon	4	..	4	..	4
Pennsylvania	32	..	32	..	32
Rhode Island	4	..	4	..	4
South Carolina	..	9	..	9	9
South Dakota	4	..	4	..	4
Tennessee	..	12	..	12	12
Texas	..	15	..	15	15
Utah	3	..	3	..	3
Vermont	4	..	4	..	4
Virginia	..	12	..	12	12
Washington	4	..	4	..	4
West Virginia	6	..	6	..	6
Wisconsin	12	..	12	..	12
Wyoming	3	..	3	..	3
Total	292	155	292	155	447

William McKinley was elected President and Theodore Roosevelt as Vice-President.

During this period Congress was divided politically as follows:

Fifty-seventh Congress.

Senate—27 Democrats, 54 Republicans, 4 Populists, 3 Silverites, 2 vacancies.............................Total 90
House—149 Democrats, 195 Republicans, 6 Populists, 2 Silverites, 5 vacancies.............................. " 357

Fifty-eighth Congress.

Senate—33 Democrats, 57 Republicans ....Total 90
House—178 Democrats, 208 Republicans .... " 386

Election of 1904

Democratic National Committee:

Chairman, THOMAS TAGGART, of Indiana.
Secretary, UREY WOODSON, of Kentucky.

DEMOCRATIC CONVENTION.

St. Louis, Mo., July 6–9, 1904.

Chairman pro tem., JOHN SHARP WILLIAMS, of Mississippi.

Chairman, CHAMP CLARK, of Missouri.

NOMINATED—

For President, **Alton B. Parker,** of New York.

For Vice-President, **Henry G. Davis,** of West Virginia.

This convention consisted of 1006 delegates. The permanent organization was delayed by contesting cases. The Committee on Resolutions was unable to report a platform until Saturday morning, after an all-night session. On the first ballot Alton B. Parker, of New York, was nominated. The following is the vote:—

CANDIDATES.	Votes.
ALTON B. PARKER, of New York	658
WM. R. HEARST, of New York	178
FRANCIS M. COCKRELL, of Missouri	42
RICHARD OLNEY, of Massachusetts	38
EDWARD C. WALL, of Wisconsin	27
JOHN S. WILLIAMS, of Mississippi	8
GEORGE GRAY, of Delaware	8
GEORGE B. MCCLELLAN, of New York	3
NELSON A. MILES, of Massachusetts	2
CHARLES A. TOWNE, of New York	2
ARTHUR P. GORMAN, of Maryland	2
ROBERT E. PATTISON, of Pennsylvania	1
BIRD S. COLER, of New York	1
Whole number of votes, 1006	
Necessary to a choice, 671	

Idaho, Washington and West Virginia changed to Parker, giving him more than the necessary two-thirds.

After the call the nomination was made unanimous.

For Vice-President, Henry G. Davis, of West Virginia, was nominated on the first ballot, which was, after the call, made unanimous.

A contest in the Committee on Resolutions resulted in eliminating from the platform all reference to money or monetary standards, and so it was adopted without debate by the convention. The nomination of Alton B. Parker followed immediately, after which the convention took a short recess. Upon reassembling to nominate for Vice-President, it was profoundly agitated by the announcement of the following telegram from Alton B. Parker:

"I regard the gold standard as firmly and irrevocably established and I shall act accordingly if the action of the convention to-day is ratified by the people. Inasmuch as the platform is silent on the subject, I deem it necessary to make this communication to the convention for its consideration, as I should feel it my duty to decline the nomination except with that understanding."

The proceedings which ensued were dramatic; after many conferences and exciting discussion the following resolution was authorized by a vote of 798 to 184, to be sent in reply:—

"The platform adopted by this convention is silent on the question of the monetary standard because it is not regarded by us as a possible issue in this campaign, and only campaign issues were mentioned in the platform. Therefore there is nothing in the views expressed by you in the telegram just received which would preclude a man entertaining them from accepting a nomination on said platform."

After this action the convention adjourned. The platform adopted follows:—

DEMOCRATIC PLATFORM.

The Democratic party of the United States, in national convention assembled, declares its devotion to the essential principles of the Democratic faith which bring us together in party communion.

Under them local self-government and national unity and prosperity were alike established. They underlay our independence, the structure of our free Republic, and every Democratic extension from Louisiana to California, and Texas to Oregon, which preserved faithfully in all the States the tie between taxation and representation. They yet inspire the masses of our people, guarding jealously their rights and liberties and cherishing their fraternity, peace, and orderly development. They remind us of our duties and responsibilities as citizens, and impress upon us, particularly at this time, the necessity of reform and the rescue of the administration of government from the headstrong, arbitrary, and spasmodic methods which distract business by uncertainty and pervade the public mind with dread, distrust, and perturbation.

FUNDAMENTAL PRINCIPLES.

The application of these fundamental principles to the living issues of the day is the first step toward the assured peace, safety, and progress of our nation. Freedom of the press, of conscience, and of speech; equality before the law of all citizens; right of trial by jury; freedom of the person defended by the writ of habeas corpus; liberty of personal contract untrammeled by sumptuary laws; supremacy of the civil over military authority; a well-disciplined militia; the separation of church and state; economy in expenditures; low taxes, that labor may be lightly burdened; prompt and sacred fulfillment of public and private obligations; fidelity to treaties; peace and friendship with all nations, entangling alliances with none; absolute acquiescence in the will of the majority, the vital principle of republics—these are doctrines which Democracy has established, as proverbs of the nation, and they should be constantly invoked and enforced.

CAPITAL AND LABOR.

We favor enactment and administration of laws giving labor and capital impartially their just rights. Capital and labor ought not to be enemies. Each is necessary to the other. Each has its rights, but the rights of labor are certainly no less "vested," no less "sacred," and no less "unalienable" than the rights of capital.

CONSTITUTIONAL GUARANTEES.

Constitutional guarantees are violated whenever any citizen is denied the right to labor, acquire and enjoy property or reside where interest or inclination may determine. Any denial thereof by individuals, organizations, or governments should be summarily rebuked and punished.

We deny the right of any executive to disregard or suspend any constitutional privilege or limitation. Obedience to the laws and respect for their requirements are alike the supreme duty of the citizen and the official.

The military should be used only to support and maintain the law. We unqualifiedly condemn its employment for the summary banishment of citizens without trial, or for the control of elections.

We approve the measure which passed the United States Senate in 1896, but which a Republican Congress has ever since refused to enact, relating to contempts in Federal courts and providing for trial by jury in cases of indirect contempt.

WATERWAYS.

We favor liberal appropriations for the care and improvement of the waterways of the country. When any waterway like the Mississippi River is of sufficient importance to demand special aid of the Government, such aid should be extended, with a definite plan of continuous work until permanent improvement is secured.

We oppose the Republican policy of starving home development in order to feed the greed for conquest and the appetite for national "prestige" and display of strength.

ECONOMY OF ADMINISTRATION.

Large reductions can easily be made in the annual expenditures of the Government without impairing the efficiency of any branch of the public service, and we shall insist upon the strictest economy and frugality compatible with vigorous and efficient, civil, military, and naval administration as a right of the people too clear to be denied or withheld.

We favor the enforcement of honesty in the public service, and to that end a thorough legislative investigation of those executive departments of the Government already known to teem with corruption, as well as other departments suspected of harboring corruption, and the punishment of ascertained corruptionists without fear or favor or regard to persons. The persistent and deliberate refusal of both the Senate and House of Representatives to permit such investigation to be made demonstrates that only by a change in the executive and in the legislative departments can complete exposure, punishment, and correction be obtained.

CONTRACTS WITH TRUSTS.

We condemn the action of the Republican party in Congress in refusing to prohibit an executive department from entering into contracts with convicted trusts or unlawful combinations in restraint of interstate trade. We believe that one of the best methods of procuring economy and honesty in the public service is to have public officials, from the occupant of the White House down to the lowest of them, return, as nearly as may be, to Jeffersonian simplicity of living.

EXECUTIVE USURPATION.

We favor the nomination and election of a President imbued with the principles of the Constitution, who will set his face sternly against executive usurpation of legislative and judicial functions, whether that usurpation be veiled under the guise of executive construction of existing laws or whether it take refuge in the tyrant's pleas of necessity or superior wisdom.

IMPERIALISM.

We favor the preservation, so far as we can, of an open door for the world's commerce in the Orient, without an unnecessary entanglement in Oriental and European affairs, and without arbitrary, unlimited, irresponsible, and absolute government anywhere within our jurisdiction.

We oppose, as fervently as did George Washington himself, an indefinite, irresponsible, discretionary, and vague absolutism and a policy of colonial exploitation, no matter where or by whom invoked or exercised. We believe, with Thomas Jefferson and John Adams, that no government has a right to make one set of laws for those "at home" and another and a different set of laws, absolute in their character, for those "in the colonies." All men under the American flag are entitled to the protection of the institutions whose emblem the flag is. If they are inherently unfit for those institutions, then they are inherently unfit to be members of the American body politic. Wherever there may exist a people incapable of being governed under American laws, in consonance with the American Constitution, the territory of that people ought not to be part of the American domain.

FILIPINOS AND CUBANS.

We insist that we ought to do for the Filipinos what we have done already for the Cubans, and it is our duty to make that promise now and upon suitable guarantees of protection to citizens of our own and other countries resident there at the time of our withdrawal, set the Filipino people upon their feet, free and independent to work out their own destiny.

The endeavor of the Secretary of War, by pledging the Government's indorsement for "promoters" in the Philippine Islands, to make the United States a partner in speculative legislation of the archipelago, which was only temporarily held up by the opposition of the Democratic Senators in the last session, will, if successful, lead to entanglements from which it will be difficult to escape.

TARIFF LEGISLATION.

The Democratic party has been and will continue to be the consistent opponent of that class of tariff legislation by which certain interests have been permitted, through Congressional favor, to draw a heavy tribute from the American people. This monstrous prevention of those equal opportunities which our political institutions were established to secure has caused what may once have been infant industries to become the greatest combinations of capital that the world has ever known. These especial favorites of the Government have, through trust methods, been converted into monopolies, thus bringing to an end domestic competition, which was the only alleged check upon the extravagant profits made possible by the protective system. These industrial combinations, by the financial assistance they can give, now control the policy of the Republican party.

We denounce protection as a robbery of the many to enrich the few, and we favor a tariff limited to the needs of the Government economically administered, and so levied as not to discriminate against any industry, class, or section, to the end that the burdens of taxation shall be distributed as equally as possible.

We favor a revision and a gradual reduction of the tariff by the friends of the masses and for the common weal, and not by the friends of its abuses, its extortions and its discriminations, keeping in view the ultimate ends of "equality of burdens and equality of opportunities," and the constitutional purpose of raising a revenue by taxation—to wit, the support of the Federal Government in all its integrity and virility, but in simplicity.

TRUSTS AND UNLAWFUL COMBINES.

We recognize that the gigantic trusts and combinations designed to enable capital to secure more than its just share of the joint products of capital and labor, and which have been fostered and promoted under Republican rule, are a menace to beneficial competition and an obstacle to permanent business prosperity.

A private monopoly is indefensible and intolerable.

Individual equality of opportunity and free competition are essential to a healthy and permanent commercial prosperity, and any trust, combination, or monopoly tending to destroy these by controlling production, restricting competition, or fixing prices should be prohibited and punished by law. We especially denounce rebates and discrimination by transportation companies as the most potent agency in promoting and strengthening these unlawful conspiracies against trade.

INTERSTATE COMMERCE.

We demand an enlargement of the powers of the Interstate Commerce Commission, to the end that the traveling public and shippers of this country may have prompt and adequate relief for the abuses to which they are subjected in the matter of transportation. We demand a strict enforcement of existing civil and criminal statutes against all such trusts, combinations, and monopolies, and we demand the enactment of such further legislation as may be necessary to effectually suppress them.

Any trust or unlawful combination engaged in interstate commerce which is monopolizing any branch of business or production should not be permitted to transact business outside of the State of its origin. Whenever it shall be established in any court of competent jurisdiction that such monopolization exists, such prohibition should be enforced through comprehensive laws to be enacted on the subject.

RECLAMATION OF ARID LANDS.

We congratulate our western citizens upon the passage of the law known as the Newlands irrigation act for the irrigation and reclamation of the arid lands of the West, a measure framed by a Democrat, passed in the Senate by a non-partisan vote, and passed in the House against the opposition of almost all the Republican leaders by a vote the majority of which was Democratic. We call attention to this great Democratic measure, broad and comprehensive as it is, working automatically throughout all time, without further action of Congress, until the reclamation of all the lands in the arid West capable of reclamation is accomplished, reserving the lands reclaimed for home-seekers in small tracts and rigidly guarding against land monopoly, as an evidence of the policy of domestic development contemplated by the Democratic party should it be placed in power.

ISTHMIAN CANAL.

The Democracy, when entrusted with power, will construct the Panama Canal speedily, honestly, and economically, thereby giving to our people what Democrats have always contended for—a great interoceanic canal, furnishing shorter and cheaper lines of transportation and broader and less trammeled trade relations with the other peoples of the world.

AMERICAN CITIZENSHIP.

We pledge ourselves to insist upon the just and lawful protection of our citizens at home and abroad, and to use all proper measures to secure for them, whether native-born or naturalized, and without distinction of race or creed, the equal protection of laws and the enjoyment of all rights and privileges open to them under the covenants of our treaties of friendship and commerce; and if under existing treaties the right of travel and sojourn is denied to American citizens, or recognition is withheld from American passports by any countries on the ground of race or creed, we favor the beginning of negotiations with the governments of such countries to secure by treaties the removal of these unjust discriminations.

We demand that all over the world a duly authenticated passport issued by the Government of the United States to an American citizen shall be proof of the fact that he is an American citizen and shall entitle him to the treatment due him as such.

ELECTION OF SENATORS BY THE PEOPLE.

We favor the election of United States Senators by the direct vote of the people.

STATEHOOD FOR TERRITORIES.

We favor the admission of the Territory of Oklahoma and the Indian Territory. We also favor the immediate admission of Arizona and New Mexico as separate States and a territorial government for Alaska and Porto Rico.

We hold that the officials appointed to administer the government of any Territory, as well as with the District of Alaska, should be bona fide residents at the time of their appointment of the Territory or District in which their duties are to be performed.

CONDEMNATION OF POLYGAMY.

We demand the extermination of polygamy within the jurisdiction of the United States and the complete separation of church and state in political affairs.

MERCHANT MARINE.

We denounce the ship-subsidy bill recently passed by the United States Senate as an iniquitous appropriation of public funds for private purposes and a wasteful, illogical and useless attempt to overcome by subsidy the obstructions raised by Republican legislation to the growth and development of American commerce on the sea.

We favor the upbuilding of a merchant marine without new or additional burdens upon the people and without bounties from the public treasury.

RECIPROCITY.

We favor liberal trade arrangements with Canada and with peoples of other countries where they can be entered into with benefit to American agriculture, manufactures, mining, or commerce.

MONROE DOCTRINE.

We favor the maintenance of the Monroe Doctrine is its full integrity.

ARMY.

We favor the reduction of the army and of army expenditures to the point historically demonstrated to be safe and sufficient.

PENSIONS.

The Democracy would secure to the surviving soldiers and sailors and their dependents generous pensions, not by an arbitrary executive order, but by legislation which a grateful people stand ready to enact.

Our soldiers and sailors who defend with their lives the Constitution and the laws have a sacred interest in their just administration. They must, therefore, share with us the humiliation with which we have witnessed the exaltation of court favorites without distinguished service, over the scarred heroes of many battles; or aggrandized by executive appropriations out of the treasuries of a prostrate people, in violation of the act of Congress which fixed the compensation or allowances of the military officers.

CIVIL SERVICE.

The Democratic party stands committed to the principles of civil-service reform, and we demand their honest, just, and impartial enforcement.

We denounce the Republican party for its continuous and sinister encroachments upon the spirit and operation of civil-service rules, whereby it has arbitrarily dispensed with examination for office in the interests of favorites and employed all manner of devices to overreach and set aside the principle upon which the civil service was established.

THE RACE QUESTION.

The race question has brought countless woes to this country. The calm wisdom of the American people should see to it that it brings no more.

To revive the dead and hateful race and sectional animosities in any part of our common country means confusion, distraction of business, and the reopening of wounds now happily healed. North, South, East, and West have but recently stood together in line of battle from the walls of Pekin to the hills of Santiago, and as sharers of a common glory and a common destiny we should share fraternally the common burdens.

We, therefore, deprecate and condemn the Bourbonlike, selfish, and narrow spirit of the recent Republican convention at Chicago, which sought to kindle anew the embers of racial and sectional strife, and we appeal from it to the sober common sense and patriotic spirit of the American people.

THE REPUBLICAN ADMINISTRATION.

The existing Republican administration has been spasmodic, erratic, sensational, spectacular, and arbitrary. It has made itself a satire upon the Congress, the courts, and upon the settled practices and usages of national and international law.

It summoned the Congress into hasty and futile extra session and virtually adjourned it, leaving behind its flight from Washington uncalled calendars and unaccomplished tasks.

It made war, which is the sole power of Congress, without its authority, thereby usurping one of its fundamental prerogatives. It violated a plain statute of the United States, as well as plain treaty obligations, international usages and constitutional law; and has done so under pretense of executing a great public policy, which could have been more easily effected lawfully, constitutionally, and with honor.

It forced strained and unnatural constructions upon statutes, usurping judicial interpretation and substituting congressional enactment decree.

It withdrew from Congress their customary duties of investigation which have heretofore made the representatives of the people and the states the terrors of evil-doers.

It conducted a secretive investigation of its own and boasted of a few sample convicts, while it threw a broad coverlet over the bureaus which had been their chosen field of operative abuses, and kept in power the superior officers under whose administration the crimes had been committed.

It ordered assault upon some monopolies, but, paralyzed by its first victory, it flung out the flag of truce and cried out that it would not "run amuck," leaving its future purposes beclouded by its vacillations.

APPEAL TO THE PEOPLE.

Conducting the campaign upon this declaration of our principles and purposes, we invoke for our candidates the support, not only of our great and time-honored organization, but also the active assistance of all of our fellow-citizens who, disregarding past differences upon questions no longer an issue, desire the perpetuation of our constitutional Government as framed and established by the fathers of the Republic.

Republican National Committee:

Chairman, GEORGE B. CORTELYOU, of New York.
Secretary, ELMER DOVER, of Ohio.

REPUBLICAN CONVENTION.

Chicago, Ill., June 21–23, 1904.

Chairman pro tem., ELIHU ROOT, of New York.

Chairman, JOSEPH G. CANNON, of Illinois.

NOMINATED—

For President, **Theodore Roosevelt**, of New York.

For Vice-President, **Charles W. Fairbanks**, of Indiana.

This convention was composed of 994 delegates. Theodore Roosevelt, of New York, was unanimously nominated for President on a roll call of states.

For Vice-President, Charles W. Fairbanks, of Indiana, was unanimously nominated by acclamation. Only one name was presented for each office.

The platform adopted by the convention follows:—

REPUBLICAN PLATFORM.

Fifty years ago the Republican party came into existence dedicated, among other purposes, to the great task of arresting the extension of human slavery. In 1860 it elected its first President. During twenty-four of the forty-four years which have elapsed since the election of Lincoln the Republican party has held complete control of the Government. For eighteen more of the forty-four years it has held partial control through the possession of one or two branches of the Government, while the Democratic party during the same period has had complete control for only two years.

This long tenure of power by the Republican party is not due to chance. It is a demonstration that the Republican party has commanded the confidence of the American people for nearly two generations to a degree never equalled in history, and has displayed a high capacity for rule and government which has been made even more conspicuous by the incapacity and infirmity of purpose shown by its opponents.

REPUBLICAN ACHIEVEMENTS SINCE 1897.

The Republican party entered upon its present period of complete supremacy in 1897. We have every right to congratulate ourselves upon the work since then accomplished, for it has added lustre even to the traditions of the party which carried the government through the storms of civil war.

We then found the country, after four years of Democratic rule, in evil plight, oppressed with misfortune and doubtful of the future. Public credit had been lowered, the revenues were declining, the debt was growing, the administration's attitude toward Spain was feeble and mortifying, the standard of values was threatened and uncertain, labor was unemployed, business was sunk in the depression which had succeeded the panic of 1893, hope was faint, and confidence was gone.

We met these unhappy conditions vigorously, effectively, and at once.

We replaced a Democratic tariff law based on free trade

principles and garnished with sectional protection by a consistent protective tariff, and industry, freed from oppression and stimulated by the encouragement of wise laws, has expanded to a degree never before known, has conquered new markets, and has created a volume of exports which has surpassed imagination. Under the Dingley tariff labor has been fully employed, wages have risen, and all industries have revived and prospered.

We firmly established the gold standard, which was then menaced with destruction. Confidence returned to business and with confidence an unexampled prosperity.

For deficient revenues supplemented by improvident issues of bonds we gave the country an income which produced a large surplus and which enabled us only four years after the Spanish war had closed to remove over one hundred millions of annual war taxes, reduce the public debt, and lower the interest charges of the Government.

The public credit, which had been so lowered that in time of peace a Democratic administration made large loans at extravagant rates of interest in order to pay current expenditures, rose under Republican administration to its highest point and enabled us to borrow at 2 per cent even in time of war.

We refused to palter longer with the miseries of Cuba. We fought a quick and victorious war with Spain. We set Cuba free, governed the island for three years, and then gave it to the Cuban people with order restored, with ample revenues, with education and public health established, free from debt and connected with the United States by wise provisions for our mutual interests.

We have organized the government of Porto Rico, and its people now enjoy peace, freedom, order, and prosperity.

In the Philippines we have suppressed insurrection, established order, and given to life and property a security never known there before. We have organized civil government, made it effective and strong in administration, and have conferred upon the people of those islands the largest civil liberty they have ever enjoyed.

By our possession of the Philippines we were enabled to take prompt and effective action in the relief of the legations at Pekin and a decisive part in preventing the partition and preserving the integrity of China.

The possession of a route for an isthmian canal, so long the dream of American statesmanship, is now an accomplished fact. The great work of connecting the Pacific and Atlantic by a canal is at last begun, and it is due to the Republican party.

We have passed laws which will bring the arid lands of the United States within the area of cultivation.

We have reorganized the army and put it in the highest state of efficiency.

We have passed laws for the improvement and support of the militia.

We have pushed forward the building of the navy, the defense and protection of our honor and our interests.

Our administration of the great departments of the Government has been honest and efficient, and wherever wrongdoing has been discovered the Republican administration has not hesitated to probe the evil and bring offenders to justice without regard to party or political ties.

Laws enacted by the Republican party which the Democratic party failed to enforce and which were intended for the protection of the public against the unjust discrimination or the illegal encroachment of vast aggregations of capital, have been fearlessly enforced by a Republican President, and new laws, insuring reasonable publicity as to the operations of great corporations, and providing additional remedies for the prevention of discrimination in freight rates, have been passed by a Republican Congress.

In this record of achievement during the past eight years may be read the pledges which the Republican party has fulfilled. We promise to continue these policies, and we declare our constant adherence to the following principles:—

THE PROTECTIVE TARIFF.

Protection which guards and develops our industries is a cardinal policy of the Republican party. The measure of protection should always at least equal the difference in the cost of production at home and abroad.

We insist upon the maintenance of the principles of protection, and therefore rates of duty should be readjusted only when conditions have so changed that the public interest demands their alteration, but this work cannot safely be committed to any other hands than those of the Republican party. To intrust it to the Democratic party is to invite disaster. Whether, as in 1892, the Democratic party declares the protective tariff unconstitutional, or whether it demands tariff reform or tariff revision, its real object is always the destruction of the protective system.

However specious the name, the purpose is ever the same. A Democratic tariff has always been followed by business adversity; a Republican tariff by business prosperity.

To a Republican Congress and a Republican President this great question can be safely intrusted. When the only free trade country among the great nations agitates a return to protection, the chief protective country should not falter in maintaining it.

We have extended widely our foreign markets, and we believe in the adoption of all practicable methods for their further extension, including commercial reciprocity wherever reciprocal arrangements can be effected consistent with the principles of protection and without injury to American agriculture, American labor, or any American industry.

THE GOLD STANDARD MUST BE UPHELD.

We believe it to be the duty of the Republican party to uphold the gold standard and the integrity and value of our national currency. The maintenance of the gold standard, established by the Republican party, cannot safety be committed to the Democratic party, which resisted its adoption, and has never given any proof since that time of belief in it or fidelity to it.

ENCOURAGE THE MERCHANT MARINE.

While every other industry has prospered under the fostering aid of Republican legislation, American shipping engaged in foreign trade in competition with the low cost of construction, low wages, and heavy subsidies of foreign governments has not for many years received from the Government of the United States adequate encouragement of any kind. We therefore favor legislation which will encourage and build up the American merchant marine, and we cordially approve the legislation of the last Congress which created the Merchant Marine Commission to investigate and report upon this subject.

MAINTAIN THE NAVY.

A navy powerful enough to defend the United States against any attack, to uphold the Monroe Doctrine, and watch over our commerce is essential to the safety and the welfare of the American people. To maintain such a navy is the fixed policy of the Republican party.

EXCLUDE CHINESE LABOR.

We cordially approve the attitude of President Roosevelt and Congress in regard to the exclusion of Chinese labor, and promise a continuance of the Republican policy in that direction.

ENFORCE THE CIVIL SERVICE LAW.

The civil service law was placed on the statute books by the Republican party, which has always sustained it, and we renew our former declarations that it shall be thoroughly and honestly enforced.

ADMINISTER PENSION LAWS LIBERALLY.

We are always mindful of the country's debt to the soldiers and sailors of the United States, and we believe in making ample provision for them and in the liberal administration of the pension laws.

ARBITRATION.

We favor such Congressional action as shall determine by arbitration.

PROTECT AMERICAN CITIZENS ABROAD.

We commend the vigorous efforts made by the administration to protect American citizens in foreign lands, and pledge ourselves to insist upon the just and equal protection of all our citizens abroad. It is the unquestioned duty of the Government to procure for all our citizens, without distinction, the rights of travel and sojourn in friendly countries, and we declare ourselves in favor of all proper efforts tending to that end.

OUR POLICY REGARDING CHINA.

Our great interests and our growing commerce in the Orient render the condition of China of high importance to the United States. We cordially commend the policy pursued in that direction by the administrations of President McKinley and President Roosevelt.

ENFORCE THE CONSTITUTIONAL PROVISIONS REGARDING ELECTIVE FRANCHISE.

We favor such Congressional action as shall determine whether by special discriminations the elective franchise in any state has been unconstitutionally limited, and, if such is the case, we demand that representation in Congress and in the electoral colleges shall be proportionately reduced as directed by the Constitution of the United States.

COMBINATIONS OF LABOR AND CAPITAL.

Combinations of capital and of labor are the results of the economic movement of the age, but neither must be permitted to infringe upon the rights and interests of the people. Such combinations when lawfully formed for lawful purposes are alike entitled to the protection of the laws, but both are subject to the laws, and neither can be permitted to break them.

M'KINLEY AND ROOSEVELT.

The great statesman and patriotic American, William McKinley, who was re-elected by the Republican party to the Presidency four years ago, was assassinated just at the threshold of his second term. The entire nation mourned his untimely death, and did that justice to his great qualities of mind and character which history will confirm and repeat.

The American people were fortunate in his successor, to whom they turned with a trust and confidence which have been fully justified. President Roosevelt brought to the great responsibilities thus sadly forced upon him a clear head, a brave heart, and earnest patriotism, and high ideals of public duty and public service. True to the principles of the Republican party and to the policies which that party had declared, he has also shown himself ready for every emergency, and has met new and vital questions with ability and with success.

SETTLEMENT OF THE COAL STRIKE.

The confidence of the people in his justice, inspired by his public career, enabled him to render personally an inestimable service to the country by bringing about a settlement of the coal strike which threatened such disastrous results at the opening of the winter in 1902.

ROOSEVELT'S FOREIGN POLICY.

Our foreign policy under his administration has not only been able, vigorous, and dignified, but to the highest degree successful. The complicated questions which arose in Venezuela were settled in such a way by President Roosevelt that the Monroe Doctrine was signally vindicated and the cause of peace and arbitration greatly advanced.

PANAMA.

His prompt and vigorous action in Panama, which we commend in the highest terms, not only secured to us the canal route, but avoided all foreign complications which might have been of a very serious character.

IN THE ORIENT.

He has continued the policy of President McKinley in the Orient, and our position in China, signalized by our recent commercial treaty with that empire, has never been so high.

THE ALASKAN BOUNDARY.

He secured the tribunal by which the vexed and perilous question of the Alaskan boundary was finally settled.

Whenever crimes against humanity have been perpetrated which have shocked our people, his protest has been made and our good offices have been tendered, but always with due regard to international obligations.

Under his guidance we find ourselves at peace with all the world, and never were we more respected or our wishes more regarded by foreign nations.

DOMESTIC QUESTIONS.

Pre-eminently successful in regard to our foreign relations, he has been equally fortunate in dealing with domestic questions. The country has known that the public credit and the national currency were absolutely safe in the hands of his administration. In the enforcement of the laws he has shown not only courage but the wisdom which understands that to permit laws to be violated or disregarded opens the door to anarchy, while the just enforcement of the law is the soundest conservatism. He has held firmly to the fundamental American doctrine that all men must obey the law, that there must be no distinction between rich and poor, between strong and weak, but that justice and equal protection under the law must be secured to every citizen without regard to race, creed, or condition.

His administration has been throughout vigorous and honorable, high-minded and patriotic. We commend it without reservation to the considerate judgment of the American people.

People's Party National Committee:

Chairman, J. H. FERRIS, of Illinois.
Secretary, C. Q. DE FRANCE, of Nebraska.

PEOPLE'S PARTY CONVENTION.

Springfield, Ill., July 4–6, 1904.

Chairman pro tem., L. H. WELLER, of Iowa.

Chairman, J. H. MALLETTE, of Texas.

NOMINATED—

For President, **Thomas E. Watson**, of Georgia.

For Vice-President, **Thomas H. Tibbles**, of Nebraska.

The roll of the convention was made up of 927 delegates; 698 votes were recorded on the vote for President—334 for Thos. E. Watson, 319 for Wm. V. Allen, and 45 for Samuel W. Williams. The name of Wm. V. Allen was then withdrawn and Thomas E. Watson was unanimously chosen by acclamation. Both nominations were made on the first ballot.

The following platform was adopted:—

PEOPLE'S PARTY PLATFORM.

The People's party reaffirms its adherence to the basic truths of the Omaha platform of 1892, and of the subsequent platforms of 1896 and 1900. In session in its fourth national convention, on July 4, 1904, in the city of Springfield, Ill., it draws inspiration from the day that saw the birth of the nation as well as its own birth as a party, and also from the soul of him who lived at its present place of meeting. We renew our allegiance to the old-fashioned American spirit that gave this nation existence, and made it distinctive among the peoples of the earth. We again sound the key-note of the Declaration of Independence that all men are created equal in a political sense, which was the sense in which that instrument, being a political document, intended that the utterance should be understood. We assert that the departure from this fundamental truth is responsible for the ills from which we suffer as a nation, that the giving of special privileges to the few has enabled them to dominate the many, thereby tending to destroy the political equality which is the corner-stone of democratic government.

DEPLORE MILITARY RULE.

We call for a return to the truths of the fathers, and we vigorously protest against the spirit of Mammonism and of thinly veiled monarchy that is invading certain sections of our national life, and of the very administration itself. This is a nation of peace, and we deplore the appeal to the spirit of force and militarism which is shown in ill-advised and vainglorious boasting and in more harmful ways in the denial of the rights of man under martial law.

TRANSPORTATION MONOPOLY.

A political democracy and an industrial despotism cannot exist side by side; and nowhere is this truth more plainly shown than in the gigantic transportation monopolies which have bred all sorts of kindred trusts, subverted the governments of many of the states, and established their official agents in the Naticnal Government. We submit that it is better for the Government to own the railroads than for the railroads to own the Government, and that one or the other alternative seems inevitable.

We call the attention of our fellow-citizens to the fact that the surrender of both of the old parties to corporative influences leaves the People's party the only party of reform in the nation.

MONEY AND BANKS.

Therefore we submit the following platform of principles to the American people:—

The issuing of money is a function of government, and should never be delegated to corporations or individuals.

The Constitution gives to Congress alone power to issue money and regulate its value.

We therefore demand that all money shall be issued by the Government in such quantity as shall maintain a stability in prices, every dollar to be full legal tender, none of which shall be a debt redeemable in other money.

We demand that postal savings banks be established by the Government for the safe deposit of the savings of the people.

LABOR ORGANIZATION.

We believe in the right of labor to organize for the benefit and protection of those who toil; and pledge the efforts of the People's party to preserve this right inviolate. Capital is organized and has no right to deny to labor the privilege which it claims for itself. We feel that intelligent organization of labor is essential; that it raises the standard of workmanship; promotes the efficiency, intelligence, independence, and character of the wage-earner. We believe with Abraham Lincoln that labor is prior to capital, and is not its slave, but its companion, and we plead for that broad spirit of toleration and justice which will promote industrial peace through the observance of the principles of voluntary arbitration.

CHILD LABOR QUESTION.

We favor the enactment of legislation looking to the improvement of conditions for wage-earners, the abolition of child labor, the suppression of sweat-shops, and of convict labor in competition with free labor, and the exclusion from American shores of foreign pauper labor.

We favor the shorter work-day, and declare that if eight hours constitutes a day's labor in Government service, that eight hours should constitute a day's labor in factories, workshops, and mines.

INITIATIVE AND REFERENDUM.

As a means of placing all public questions directly under the control of the people, we demand that legal provision be made under which the people may exercise the initiative, referendum, and proportional representation and direct vote for all public officers with the right of recall.

Land, including all the natural sources of wealth, is a heritage of all the people, and should not be monopolized for speculative purposes, and alien ownership of land should be prohibited.

We demand a return to the original interpretation of the Constitution and a fair and impartial enforcement of laws under it, and denounce government by injunction and imprisonment without the right of trial by jury.

DEMAND GOVERNMENT OWNERSHIP.

To prevent unjust discrimination and monopoly the Government should own and control the railroads, and those public utilities which in their nature are monopolies. To perfect the postal service, the Government should own and operate the general telegraph and telephone systems, and provide a parcels post.

As to those trusts and monopolies which are not public utilities or natural monopolies, we demand that those special privileges which they now enjoy, and which alone enable them to exist, should be immediately withdrawn. Corporations being the creatures of government, should be subjected to such governmental regulations and control as will adequately protect the public. We demand the taxation of monopoly privileges, while they remain in private hands, to the extent of the value of the privileges granted.

REGULATE INTERSTATE COMMERCE.

We demand that Congress shall enact a general law uniformly regulating the power and duties of all incorporated companies doing interstate business.

Prohibition National Committee:

Chairman, OLIVER W. STEWART, of Illinois.
Secretary, JAMES A. TATE, of Tennessee.

PROHIBITION CONVENTION.

Indianapolis, Ind., June 29–July 1, 1904.

Chairman pro tem., HOMER L. CASTLE,
of Pennsylvania.

Chairman, A. G. WOLFENBARGER,
of Nebraska.

NOMINATED—

For President, **Silas C. Swallow,**
of Pennsylvania.

For Vice-President, **George W. Carroll,**
of Texas.

The number of delegates present at this convention was 758; 39 states and two territories were represented.

Silas C. Swallow for President and George W. Carroll for Vice-President were each nominated on the first ballot.

The Convention adopted the following platform:—

PROHIBITION PLATFORM.

The Prohibition party, in national convention assembled, at Indianapolis, June 30, 1904, recognizing that the chief end of all government is the establishment of those principles of righteousness and justice that have been revealed to men as the will of the Ever-Living God, desiring His blessing upon our national life, and believing in the perpetuation of the high ideals of government of the people, by the people, and for the people, established by our fathers, makes the following declaration of principles and purposes:—

1. The widely prevailing system of the licensed and legalized sale of alcoholic beverages is so ruinous to individual interests, so inimical to public welfare, so destructive to national wealth, and so subversive of the rights of great masses of our citizenship, that the destruction of the traffic is, and for years has been, the most important question in American politics.

2. We denounce the lack of statesmanship exhibited by the leaders of the Democratic and Republican parties in their refusal to recognize the paramount importance of this question and the cowardice with which the leaders of these parties have courted the favor of those whose selfish interests are advanced by the continuation and augmentation of the traffic, until to-day the influence of the liquor traffic practically dominates national, state, and local government throughout the nation.

3. We declare the truth, demonstrated by the experience of half a century, that all methods of dealing with the liquor

traffic which recognize its right to exist, in any form, under any system of license or tax or regulation, have proved powerless to remove its evils, and useless as checks upon its growth, while the insignificant public revenues which have accrued therefrom have seared the public conscience against a recognition of its iniquity.

4. We call public attention to the fact, proved by the experience of more than fifty years, that to secure the enactment and enforcement of prohibitory legislation, in which alone lies the hope of the protection of the people from the liquor traffic, it is necessary that the legislative, executive, and judicial branches of government should be in the hands of a political party in harmony with the prohibition principle, and pledged to its embodiment in law and to the execution of those laws.

5. We pledge the Prohibition party wherever given power by the suffrages of the people, to the enactment and enforcement of laws prohibiting and abolishing the manufacture, importation, transportation, and sale of alcoholic beverages.

6. We declare that there is not only no other issue of equal importance before the American people to-day, but that the so-called issues upon which the Democratic and Republican parties seek to divide the electorate of the country are, in large part, subterfuges under the cover of which they wrangle for the spoils of office.

7. Recognizing that the intelligent voters of the country may properly ask our attitude upon other questions of public concern, we declare ourselves in favor of:—

The impartial enforcement of all law.

The safeguarding of the people's rights by a rigid application of the principles of justice to all combinations of capital and labor.

The recognition of the fact that the right of suffrage should depend upon the mental and moral qualifications of the citizen.

A more intimate relation between the people and government by a wise application of the principles of the initiative and referendum.

Such changes in our laws as will place tariff schedules in the hands of an omni-partisan commission.

The application of uniform laws for all our country and dependencies.

The election of United States Senators by vote of the people.

The extension and honest administration of the civil service laws.

The safeguarding of the peoples' every place under the government of the people of the United States, in all the rights guaranteed by the laws and the Constitution.

International arbitration, and we declare that our nation should contribute in every manner consistent with national dignity to the permanent establishment of peace between all nations.

The reform of our divorce laws, the final extirpation of polygamy, and the total overthrow of the present shameful system of the illegal sanction of the social evil, with its unspeakable traffic in girls by the municipal authorities of almost all our cities.

Socialist-Labor National Executive Committee:

Secretary, HENRY KUHN, of New York.

SOCIALIST-LABOR CONVENTION.

New York, July 3–9, 1904.

Chairman pro tem., WM. W. COX, of Illinois.

At each session presiding officers were chosen for the day.

NOMINATED—

For President, **Charles H. Corregan,** of New York.

For Vice-President, **William W. Cox,** of Illinois.

The eleventh national convention of the Socialist-Labor party, composed of 38 delegates, representing 18 states, assembled in Grand Central Palace, New York City. On the fourth day the convention, without division, nominated Charles H. Corregan for President and William W. Cox for Vice-President. After six days spent in deliberation the convention adjourned, having adopted the following platform:—

SOCIALIST-LABOR PARTY PLATFORM.

The Socialist-Labor party of America, in convention assembled, reasserts the inalienable right of man to life, liberty, and the pursuit of happiness.

We hold that the purpose of government is to secure to every citizen the enjoyment of this right; but taught by experience we hold furthermore that such right is illusory to the majority of the people, to wit, the working class, under the present system of economic inequality, that is essentially destructive of their life, their liberty, and their happiness.

We hold that the true theory of politics is that the machinery of government must be controlled by the whole people, but again taught by experience we hold furthermore that the true theory of economics is that the means of production must likewise be owned, operated, and controlled by the people in common. Man cannot exercise his right of life, liberty, and the pursuit of happiness without the ownership of the land on and the tool with which to work. Deprived of these, his life, his liberty, and his fate fall into the hands of the class that owns those essentials for work and production.

We hold that the existing contradiction between the theory of democratic government and the fact of a despotic economic system—the private ownership of the natural and social opportunities—divides the people into two classes: the Capitalist class and the Working class; throws society into the convulsions of the class struggle; and perverts government to the exclusive benefit of the Capitalist class.

Thus labor is robbed of the wealth which it alone produces, is denied the means of self-employment, and, by compulsory idleness in wage slavery, is even deprived of the necessaries of life.

Against such a system the Socialist-Labor party raises the banner of revolt, and demands the unconditional surrender of the Capitalist class.

The time is fast coming when in the natural course of social evolution, this system, through the destructive action of its failures and crises, on the one hand, and the constructive tendencies of its trusts and other capitalist combinations, on the other hand, will have worked out its own downfall.

We, therefore, call upon the wage-workers of America to organize under the banner of the Socialist-Labor party into a class-conscious body, aware of its rights and determined to conquer them.

And we also call upon all other intelligent citizens to place themselves squarely upon the ground of working class interests, and join us in this mighty and noble work of human emancipation, so that we may put summary end to the existing barbarous class conflict by placing the land and all the means of production, transportation, and distribution into the hands of the people as a collective body, and substituting the Co-operative Commonwealth for the present state of planless production, industrial war, and social disorder—a commonwealth in which every worker shall have the free exercise and full benefit of his faculties, multiplied by all the modern factors of civilization.

SOCIALIST DEMOCRATIC (PARTY OF AMERICA) CONVENTION.

Chicago, Ill., May 1–6, 1904.

The chairmen of the convention were elected daily.

NOMINATED—

For President, **Eugene V. Debs,**
of Indiana.

For Vice-President, **Benjamin Hanford,**
of New York.

The following platform was adopted:—

SOCIAL DEMOCRATIC PLATFORM.

THE DEFENDER OF INDIVIDUAL LIBERTY.

We, the Socialist party, in convention assembled, make our appeal to the American people as the defender and preserver of the idea of liberty and self-government, in which the nation was born; as the only political movement standing for the program and principles by which the liberty of the individual may become a fact; as the only political organization that is democratic, and that has for its purpose the democratizing of the whole society.

To this idea of liberty the Republican and Democratic parties are utterly false. They alike struggle for power to maintain and profit by an industrial system which can be preserved only by the complete overthrow of such liberties as we already have, and by the still further enslavement and degradation of labor.

Our American institutions came into the world in the name of freedom. They have been seized upon by the capitalist class as the means of rooting out the idea of freedom from among the people. Our state and national legislatures have become the mere agencies of great propertied interests. These interests control the appointments and decisions of the judges of our courts. They have come into what is practically a private ownership of all the functions and forces of government. They are using these to betray and conquer foreign and weaker peoples, in order to establish new markets for the surplus goods which the people make, but are too poor to buy. They are gradually so invading and restricting the right of suffrage as to take unawares the right of the worker to a vote or voice in public affairs. By enacting new and misinterpreting old laws, they are preparing to attack the liberty of the individual even to speak or think for himself or for the common good.

By controlling all sources of social revenue, the possessing class is able to silence what might be the voice of the protest against the passing of liberty and the coming of tyranny. It completely controls the university and public school, the pulpit and the press, arts and literatures. By making these economically dependent upon itself, it has brought all the forms of public teaching into servile submission to its own interests.

Our political institutions are also being used as the destroyers of that individual property upon which all liberty and opportunity depend. The promise of economic independence to each man was one of the faiths in which our institutions were founded. But under the guise of defending private property, capitalism is using our political institutions to make it impossible for the vast majority of human beings to ever become possessors of private property in the means of life.

Capitalism is the enemy and destroyer of essential private

property. Its development is through the legalized confiscation of all that the labor of the working class produces, above its subsistence wage. The private ownership of the means of employment grounds society in an economic slavery which renders intellectual and political tyranny inevitable.

Socialism comes so to organize industry and society that every individual shall be secure in that private property in the means of life upon which his liberty of being, thought, and action depend. It comes to rescue the people from the fast increasing and successful assault of capitalism upon the liberty of the individual.

INTERNATIONAL SOCIALISM VS. INTERNATIONAL CAPITALISM.

II. As an American Socialist party, we pledge our fidelity to the principles of International Socialism, as embodied in the united thought and action of the Socialists of all nations. In the industrial development already accomplished, the interests of the world's workers are separated by no national boundaries. The condition of the most exploited and oppressed workers, in the most remote places of the earth, inevitably tends to drag down all the workers of the world to the same level. The tendency of the competitive wage system is to make labor's lowest condition the measure or rule of its universal condition. Industry and finance are no longer national but international in both organizations and results. The chief significance of national boundaries, and of the so-called patriotisms which the ruling class of each nation is seeking to revive, is the power which these give to capitalism to keep the workers of the world from uniting, and to throw them against each other in the struggles of contending capitalist interests for the control of the yet unexploited markets of the world, or the remaining sources of profit.

The Socialist movement therefore is a world-movement. It knows of no conflicts between the workers of one nation and the workers of another. It stands for the freedom of the workers of all nations; and, in so standing, it makes for the full freedom of all humanity.

THE WORKERS VS. THE SHIRKERS.

III. The Socialist movement owes its birth and growth to that economic development or world process which is rapidly separating a working or producing class from a possessing or capitalist class. The class that produces nothing possesses labor's fruits, and the opportunities and enjoyments these fruits afford, while the class that does the world's real work has increasing economic uncertainty, and physical and intellectual misery as its portion.

The fact that these two classes have not yet become fully conscious of their distinction from each other, the fact that the lines of division and interest may not yet be clearly drawn, does not change the fact of the class conflict.

This class struggle is due to the private ownership of the means of employment, or the tools of production. Wherever and whenever man owned his own land and tools, and by them produced only the things which he used, economic independence was possible. But production, or the making of goods, has long ceased to be individual. The labor of scores, or even thousands, enters into almost every article produced. Production is now social, or collective. Practically everything is made or done by many men—sometimes separated by seas or continents—working together for the same end. But this co-operation in production is not for the direct use of the things made by the workers who make them, but for the profit of the owners of the tools and means of production; and to this is due the present division of society into two distinct classes, and from it has sprung all the miseries, inharmonies, and contradictions of our civilization.

Between these two classes there can be no possible compromise or identity of interests, any more than there can be peace in the midst of war, or light in the midst of darkness. A society based upon this class division carries in itself the seeds of its own destruction. Such a society is founded in fundamental injustice. There can be no possible basis for social peace, for individual freedom, for mental and moral harmony, except in the conscious and complete triumph of the working class as the only class that has the right or power to be.

SOCIALISM THE ONLY SAVING FORCE.

IV. The Socialist program is not a theory imposed upon society for its acceptance or rejection. It is but the interpretation of what is, sooner or later, inevitable. Capitalism is already struggling to its destruction. It is no longer competent to organize or administer the work of the world, or even to preserve itself. The captains of industry are appalled at their own inability to control or direct the rapidly socializing forces of industry. The so-called trust is but a sign and form of this developing socialization of the world's work. The universal increase of the uncertainty of employment, the universal capitalist determination to break down the unity of labor in the trades unions, the widespread apprehension of impending change, reveal that the institutions of capitalist society are passing under the power of inhering forces that will soon destroy them.

Into the midst of the strain and crisis of civilization, the Socialist movement comes as the only saving or conservative force. If the world is to be saved from chaos, from universal disorder and misery, it must be by the union of the workers of all nations in the Socialist movement. The Socialist party comes with the only proposition or program for intelligently and deliberately organizing the nation for the common good of all its citizens. It is the first time that the mind of man has ever been directed toward the conscious organization of society.

Socialism means that all those things upon which the people in common depend shall by the people in common be owned and administered. It means that the tools of employment shall belong to the creators and users; that all production shall be for the direct use of the producers; that the making of goods for profit shall come to an end; that we shall all be workers together, and that opportunities shall be open and equal to all men.

TO SECURE IMMEDIATE INTERESTS OF THE WORKERS.

V. To the end that the workers may seize every possible advantage that may strengthen them to gain complete control of the powers of government, and thereby the sooner establish the co-operative commonwealth, the Socialist party pledges itself to watch and work in both the economic and the political struggle for each successive immediate interest of the working class; for shortened days of labor and increase of wages; for the insurance of the workers against accident, sickness, and lack of employment; for pensions for aged and exhausted workers; for the public ownership of the means of transportation, communication, and exchange; for the graduated taxation of incomes, inheritances, and of franchise and land values, the proceeds to be applied to public employment and bettering the condition of the workers; for the equal suffrage of men and women; for the prevention of the use of the military against labor in the settlement of strikes; for the free administration of justice; for popular government, including initiative, referendum, proportional representation, and the recall of officers by their constituents; and for every gain or advantage for the workers that may be wrested from the capitalist system, and that may relieve the suffering and strengthen the hands ot labor. We lay upon every man elected to any executive or legislative office the first duty of striving to procure whatever is for the workers' most immediate interest, and whatever will lessen the economic and political powers of the capitalist and increase the like powers of the worker.

But, in so doing, we are using these remedial measures as means to one great end—the Co-operative Commonwealth. Such measures of relief as we may be able to force from capitalism are but a preparation of the workers to seize the whole powers of government, in order that they may thereby lay hold of the whole system of industry, and thus come into their rightful inheritance.

To this end we pledge ourselves, as the party of the working class, to use all political power, as fast as it shall be intrusted to us by our fellow-workers, both for their immediate interests and for their ultimate and complete emancipation. To this end we appeal to all the workers of America, and to all who will lend their lives to the service of the workers in their struggle to gain their own, and to all who will nobly and disinterestedly give their days and energies unto the workers' cause, to cast their lot and faith with the Socialist party. Our appeal for the trust and suffrages of our fellow-workers is at once an appeal for their common good and freedom, and for the freedom and blossoming of our common humanity. In pledging ourselves, and those we represent, to be faithful to the appeal which we make, we believe that we are but preparing the soil of the economic freedom from which will spring the freedom of the whole man.

APPENDIX

APPENDIX.

Formation of National Conventions.

The meeting of a National Convention is provided for by the assembling of the National Committee of the party at some period usually about six months prior to the meeting of the convention, at which time the National Committee formulates a call for the National Convention and publishes the ratio and number of delegates to which each state is entitled in the same, together with the manner of choosing them. It is usual for the committee at this time also to select the place where the National Convention shall be held and to appoint an executive committee to take charge of the arrangements incident to the meeting of the convention. A few days before the meeting of the convention the National Committee, or its Executive Committee, meets for the purpose of arranging the program of the proceedings. The selection of the persons to be presented as officers of the convention is made at this time —namely, the temporary and permanent chairmen, and the secretary. The convention usually ratifies the selections of the National Committee, although instances are known where others have been selected by the convention.

The temporary organization of the National Convention is intended to prepare the way for the permanent organization, which preliminary work consists of the appointment of the standing committees of the convention, the Committee on Credentials being the most important, as it reports a roll of delegates entitled to seats in the convention. After this has been accomplished the permanent organization takes place, and the business of the convention is proceeded with. The contesting delegations in nearly all National Conventions consume one or two days, and sometimes more, in pressing their claims before the Committee on Credentials. All notices of contest are filed with the National Committee, in writing, which papers are passed to the Committee on Credentials with the official roll as reported by the National Committee.

Appendix.

It is usual at the close of the convention, or at some time during its meeting, for each state delegation to select some person as the state member of the National Committee. These, when reported to the convention, are usually summoned to meet before the convention closes its business. At this meeting the committee organizes and the National Chairman and Secretary are chosen, unless for some reason the matter is deferred to some future day. The members of the National Committee are chosen for four years, or until the meeting of the next National Convention, when the same process brings about a new organization.

Democratic Conventions.

In Democratic National Conventions the state has always been the normal voting unit. The casting of the vote of the state as a unit, by the will of a majority of the delegation, has always been recognized as legitimate and regular; and when the vote of a state has been divided and the minority of the delegation allowed a voice, it has been by the will of the delegation, not of the convention. In this there is the probability that an unavailable candidate might be nominated by the concurrent vote of a number of states none of which could possibly be carried by any Democratic candidate. In order to prevent this, the celebrated "two-thirds rule" has always been the law of Democratic National Conventions: it requires two thirds of the vote to secure the nomination of a candidate. It has never been formally settled whether the two thirds is of all the delegates present or of all the delegates admitted; but in the nominations of Douglas and Breckinridge in 1860 the former method was employed. Each state is entitled to two delegates for each electoral vote. Delegates are also admitted from each one of the territories and from the District of Columbia, but with no right to vote, unless granted by the convention; since their constituents cannot vote at the elections. The parliamentary rules of the National House of Representatives usually govern the action of the convention, when not in conflict with its own orders.

Republican Conventions.

A Republican National Convention consists of two delegates for each electoral vote in the states; and delegates are also admitted from each one of the territories and from the District of Columbia, but with no right to vote, unless granted by the convention; since their constituents cannot vote at the elections. The voting unit has always been the congressional districts or the individual delegate. Among party managers there has always been a lurking desire to introduce the Democratic unit system of a state voting and the " two-thirds rule," but only one serious attempt has been made to enforce it. In 1876 the state conventions of Pennsylvania, New York, and Illinois instructed their delegations to vote as a unit, though a strong minority had been elected under instructions from their local conventions to vote for other candidates. The National Convention sustained the minority in their claim of a right to cast their votes without regard to the instructions of the state conventions. Since the call for the convention of 1888 was issued by the National Convention, it may be laid down as the Republican theory that the local conventions in the congressional districts are to select delegates, instructing them, but not irrevocably; and that the state conventions are only to select the four delegates corresponding to the state's senatorial share of the electoral votes, with two additional delegates if the state elects a congressman-at-large. Any usurpation of powers by the state convention is usually summarily set aside by the National Convention. The rules of the National House of Representatives are usually adopted for the government of the convention, when not in conflict with its own orders.

Other Conventions.

The conventions of other parties which appeared from time to time have usually followed the Republican rather than the Democratic model. Many reasons may be assigned for this, the principal one being that most new party organizations fail to appoint or choose delegates in regularly organized conventions. As a rule they are appointed or chosen at mass-meetings or public gatherings, and it would be hard to define or enforce a two-thirds rule in such bodies, majority rule and individual freedom being more popular.

Appendix.

Presidential Succession in Office.

The act of Congress entitled "An act to provide for the performance of the duties of the office of President in case of the removal, death, resignation, or inability both of the President and Vice-President," approved January 19, 1886 (first session, Forty-ninth Congress), Statutes, vol. 24, p. 1, provides:

"That in case of removal, death, resignation, or inability of both the President and Vice-President of the United States, the Secretary of State, or if there be none, or in case of his removal, death, resignation, or inability, then the Secretary of the Treasury, or if there be none, or in case of his removal, death, resignation, or inability, then the Secretary of War, or if there be none, or in case of his removal, death, resignation, or inability, then the Attorney-General, or if there be none, or in case of his removal, death, resignation, or inability, then the Postmaster-General, or if there be none, or in case of his removal, death, resignation, or inability, then the Secretary of the Navy, or if there be none, or in case of his removal, death, resignation, or inability, then the Secretary of the Interior shall act as President until the disability of the President or Vice-President is removed or a President shall be elected: *Provided*, That whenever the powers and duties of the office of President of the United States shall devolve upon any of the persons named herein, if Congress be not then in session, or if it would not meet in accordance with law within twenty days thereafter, it shall be the duty of the person upon whom said powers and duties shall devolve to issue a proclamation convening Congress in extraordinary session, giving twenty days' notice of the time of meeting.

Sec. 2. That the preceding section shall only be held to describe and apply to such officers as shall have been appointed by the advice and consent of the Senate to the offices therein named, and such as are eligible to the office of President under the Constitution, and not under impeachment by the House of Representatives of the United States at the time the powers and duties of the office shall devolve upon them respectively."

SUMMARY.

1. Secretary of State.
2. Secretary of the Treasury.
3. Secretary of War.
4. Attorney-General.
5. Postmaster-General.
6. Secretary of the Navy.
7. Secretary of the Interior.

Appendix.

Mode of Counting the Electoral Vote.

The two Houses of Congress are jointly required to be together on the second Wednesday in February succeeding every meeting of the electors chosen to elect a President and Vice-President.

Respecting the powers conferred and the purposes implied by such joint meeting, there has been a great deal of controversy. The prevailing opinion seems to be that such meeting is not a joint meeting in any sense, but the two bodies are assembled together each maintaining its own organization for the purpose of witnessing the opening and counting of the electoral vote.

The following relating to the law and history, with the precedents cited, leaves the reader free to exercise his own judgment as to the nature and responsibility of the two Houses of Congress in the performance of this duty.

The following changes in the Constitution relating to the counting of the electoral vote are cited:

The original clause of the Constitution, article II, section 1, paragraph 3, which was in force until February 25, 1804, and read as follows:

"The electors shall meet in their respective States, and vote by ballot for two persons, of whom one at least shall not be an Inhabitant of the same State with themselves. And they shall make a List of all the Persons voted for, and of the Number of Votes for each; which List they shall sign and certify, and transmit sealed to the Seat of the Government of the United States, directed to the President of the Senate. The President of the Senate shall, in the Presence of the Senate and House of Representatives, open all the Certificates, and the Votes shall then be counted. The Person having the greatest Number of Votes shall be the President, if such Number be a Majority of the whole Number of Electors appointed; and if there be more than one who have such Majority, and have an equal Number of Votes, then the House of Representatives shall immediately chuse by Ballot one of them for President; and if no Person have a Majority, then from the five highest on the List the said House shall in like Manner chuse the President. But in chusing the President, the Votes shall be taken by States, the Representation from each State having one Vote; A quorum for this Purpose shall consist of a Member or Members from two-thirds of the States, and a Majority of all the States shall be necessary to a Choice. In every Case, after the Choice of the President, the Person having the greatest Number of Votes of the Electors shall be the Vice President. But if there should remain two or more who have equal Votes, the Senate shall chuse from them by Ballot the Vice-President."

This clause has been superseded by the Twelfth Amendment. The following is the new paragraph now in force:

"ARTICLE XII.

The Electors shall meet in their respective states, and vote by ballot for President and Vice-President, one of whom, at least, shall not be an inhabitant of the same state with themselves; they shall name in their ballots the person voted for as President, and in distinct ballots the person voted for as Vice-President, and they shall make distinct lists of all persons voted for as President, and of all persons voted for as Vice-President, and of the number of votes for each, which lists they shall sign and certify, and transmit sealed to the seat of the government of the United States, directed to the President of the Senate;—The President of the Senate shall, in presence of the Senate and House of Representatives, open all the certificates and the votes shall then be counted;—The person having the greatest number of votes for President, shall be the President, if such number be a majority of the whole number of Electors appointed; and if no person have such majority, then from the persons having the highest numbers not exceeding three on the list of those voted for as President, the House of Representatives shall choose immediately, by ballot, the President. But in choosing the President, the votes shall be taken by states, the representation from each state having one vote; a quorum for this purpose shall consist of a member or members from two-thirds of the states, and a majority of all the states shall be necessary to a choice. And if the House of Representatives shall not choose a President whenever the right of choice shall devolve upon them, before the fourth day of March next following, then the Vice-President shall act as President, as in the case of the death or other constitutional disability of the President. The person having the greatest number of votes as Vice-President, shall be the Vice-President, if such number be a majority of the whole number of Electors appointed, and if no person have a majority, then from the two highest numbers on the list, the Senate shall choose the Vice-President; a quorum for the purpose shall consist of two-thirds of the whole number of Senators, and a majority of the whole number shall be necessary to a choice. But no person constitutionally ineligible to the office of President shall be eligible to that of Vice-President of the United States."

The acts of Congress executory of the electoral system are cited as follows: Act March 1, 1792, obsolete; Statutes at Large, volume 1, page 239; act of January 23, 1845, Statutes at Large, volume 13, page 567; act of January 29, 1877, Statutes at Large, volume 19, page 227. This last act created the "Electoral Commission."

Under the foregoing statutes many very important contests have occurred in counting the electoral vote. The history of each event from 1798 to 1877 is compiled in an octavo volume containing eight hundred pages, entitled "Counting the Electoral Votes, Proceedings and Debates of Congress relating to," compiled by order of the House of Representatives, 1876, by Hon. William M. Springer, of Illinois, and George Willard. This volume is designated "House Miscellaneous Document, No. 13," second session, Forty-fourth Congress, to which reference is made that the reader may find all matters relating to this complex question.

The crisis reached in the counting of the electoral vote in 1877 by the Electoral Commission caused so much dissatisfaction that Congress attempted to remedy the apparent defects of the old law, and after a long struggle, on February 3, 1887, a statute was completed under which the electoral votes have since been counted. This law is so comprehensive and minute in its details that it is given in full. The supplementary act of October 19, 1888, is also appended.

"STATUTE.

An act to fix the day for the meeting of the electors of President and Vice-President, and to provide for and regulate the counting of the votes for President and Vice-President, and the decision of questions arising thereon.

Be it enacted by the Senate and House of Representatives of the United States of America in Congress assembled, That the electors of each State shall meet and give their votes on the second Monday in January next following their appointment, at such place in each State as the legislature of such State shall direct.

SEC. 2. That if any State shall have provided, by laws enacted prior to the day fixed for the appointment of the electors, for its final determination of any controversy or contest concerning the appointment of all or any of the electors of such State, by judicial or other methods or procedures, and such determination shall have been made at least six days before the time fixed for the meeting of the electors, such determination made pursuant to such law so existing on said day, and made at least six days prior to the said time of meeting of the electors, shall be conclusive, and shall govern in the counting of the electoral votes as provided in the Constitution, and as hereinafter regulated, so far as the ascertainment of the electors appointed by such State is concerned.

Sec. 3. That it shall be the duty of the executive of each State, as soon as practicable after the conclusion of the appointment of electors in such State, by the final ascertainment under and in pursuance of the laws of such State providing for such ascertainment, to communicate, under the seal of the State, to the Secretary of State of the United States, a certificate of such ascertainment of the electors appointed, setting forth the names of such electors and the canvass or other ascertainment under the laws of such State of the number of votes given or cast for each person for whose appointment any and all votes have been given or cast; and it shall also thereupon be the duty of the executive of each State to deliver to the electors of such State, on or before the day on which they are required by the preceding section to meet, the same certificate, in triplicate, under the seal of the State; and such certificate shall be inclosed and transmitted by the electors at the same time and in the same manner as is provided by law for transmitting by such electors to the seat of Government the lists of all persons voted for as President and of all persons voted for as Vice-President; and section one hundred and thirty-six of the Revised Statutes is hereby repealed; and if there shall have been any final determination in a State of a controversy or contest as provided for in section two of this act, it shall be the duty of the executive of such State as soon as practicable after such determination to communicate, under the seal of the State, to the Secretary of State of the United States, a certificate of such determination, in form and manner as the same shall have been made; and the Secretary of State of the United States, as soon as practicable after the receipt at the State Department of each of the certificates hereinbefore directed to be transmitted to the Secretary of State shall publish, in such public newspaper as he shall designate, such certificates in full; and at the first meeting of Congress thereafter he shall transmit to the two Houses of

Congress copies in full of each and every such certificate so received theretofore at the State Department.

SEC. 4. That Congress shall be in session on the second Wednesday in February succeeding every meeting of the electors. The Senate and House of Representatives shall meet in the Hall of the House of Representatives at the hour of one o'clock in the afternoon on that day, and the President of the Senate shall be their presiding officer. Two tellers shall be previously appointed on the part of the Senate and two on the part of the House of Representatives, to whom shall be handed, as they are opened by the President of the Senate, all the certificates and papers purporting to be certificates of the electoral votes, which certificates and papers shall be opened, presented, and acted upon in the alphabetical order of the States, beginning with the letter A; and said tellers, having then read the same in the presence and hearing of the two Houses, shall make a list of the votes as they shall appear from the said certificates; and the votes having been ascertained and counted in the manner and according to the rules in this act provided, the result of the same shall be delivered to the President of the Senate, who shall thereupon announce the state of the vote, which announcement shall be deemed a sufficient declaration of the persons, if any, elected President and Vice-President of the United States, and, together with a list of the votes, be entered on the Journals of the two Houses. Upon such reading of any such certificate or paper, the President of the Senate shall call for objections, if any. Every objection shall be made in writing, and shall state clearly and concisely, and without argument, the ground thereof, and shall be signed by at least one Senator and one Member of the House of Representatives before the same shall be received. When all objections so made to any vote or paper from a State shall have been received and read, the Senate shall thereupon withdraw, and such objections shall be submitted to the Senate for its decision; and the Speaker of the House of Representatives shall, in like manner, submit such objections to the House of Representatives for its decision; and no electoral vote or votes from any State which shall have been regularly given by electors whose appointment has been lawfully certified to according to section three of this act from which but one return has been received shall be rejected, but the two Houses concurrently may reject the vote or votes when they agree that such vote or votes have not been so regularly given by electors whose appointment has been so certified.

If more than one return or paper purporting to be a return from a State shall have been received by the President of the Senate, those votes, and those only, shall be counted which shall have been regularly given by the electors who are shown by the determination mentioned in section two of this act to have been appointed, if the determination in said section provided for shall have been made, or by such successors or substitutes, in case of a vacancy in the board of electors so ascertained, as have been appointed to fill such vacancy in the mode provided by the laws of the State; but in case there shall arise the question which of two or more of such State authorities determining what electors have been appointed, as mentioned in section two of this act, is the lawful tribunal of such State, the votes regularly given of those electors, and those only, of such State shall be counted whose title as electors the two Houses, acting separately, shall concurrently decide is supported by the decision of such State so authorized by its laws; and in such case of more than one return or paper purporting to be a return from a State, if there shall have been no such determination of the question in the State aforesaid, then those votes, and those only, shall be counted which the two Houses shall concurrently decide were cast by lawful electors appointed in accordance with the laws of the State, unless the two Houses, acting separately, shall concurrently decide such votes not to be the lawful votes of the legally appointed electors of such State. But if the two Houses shall disagree in respect of the counting of such votes, then, and in that case, the votes of the electors whose appointment shall have been certified by the executive of the State, under the seal thereof, shall be counted. When the two Houses have voted, they shall immediately again meet, and the presiding officer shall then announce the decision of the questions submitted. No votes or papers from any other State shall be acted upon until the objections previously made to the votes or papers from any State shall have been finally disposed of.

Sec. 5. That while the two Houses shall be in meeting as provided in this act, the President of the Senate shall have power to preserve order; and no debate shall be allowed, and no question shall be put by the presiding officer except to either House on a motion to withdraw.

Sec. 6. That when the two Houses separate to decide upon an objection that may have been made to the counting of any electoral vote or votes from any State, or other question arising in the matter, each Senator and Representative may speak to such objection or question five minutes, and not more than once; but after such debate shall have lasted two hours it shall be the duty of the presiding officer of each House to put the main question without further debate.

SEC. 7. That at such joint meeting of the two Houses seats shall be provided as follows: For the President of the Senate, the Speaker's chair; for the Speaker, immediately upon his left; the Senators, in the body of the Hall, upon the right of the presiding officer; for the Representatives, in the body of the Hall not provided for the Senators; for the tellers, Secretary of the Senate, and Clerk of the House of Representatives, at the Clerk's desk; for the other officers of the two Houses, in front of the Clerk's desk and upon each side of the Speaker's platform. Such joint meeting shall not be dissolved until the count of electoral votes shall be completed and the result declared; and no recess shall be taken unless a question shall have arisen in regard to counting any such votes, or otherwise under this act, in which case it shall be competent for either House, acting separately, in the manner hereinbefore provided, to direct a recess of such House not beyond the next calendar day, Sunday excepted, at the hour of ten o'clock in the forenoon. But if the counting of the electoral votes and the declaration of the result shall not have been completed before the fifth calendar day next after such first meeting of the two Houses, no further or other recess shall be taken by either House.

Approved, February 3, 1887. (Statutes, vol. 15, p. 373.)"

"SUPPLEMENTARY STATUTE.

An act supplementary to the act approved February third, eighteen hundred and eighty-seven, entitled "An act to fix the day for the meeting of the electors of President and Vice-President, and to provide for and regulate the counting of the votes for President and Vice-President, and the decision of questions arising thereon."

Be it enacted by the Senate and House of Representatives of the United States of America in Congress assembled, That the certificates and lists of votes for President and Vice-President of the United States, mentioned in chapter one of title three of the Revised Statutes of the United States, and in the act to which this is a supplement, shall be forwarded, in the manner therein provided, to the President of the Senate forthwith after the second Monday in January, on which the electors shall give their votes."

First Events.

First presidential election occurred January 7, 1789.

First presidential succession act was passed by Congress March 1, 1792.

First president elected by the House of Representatives, no choice having been made by the people at the election of 1800, was Thomas Jefferson, February 17, 1801.

First regular caucus of members of Congress for the nomination of a presidential candidate was held February 25, 1804, in Washington.

First election in which the electors were required by the Constitution to ballot separately for President and Vice-President, was that of 1804.

First declination of a nomination for Vice-President was by John Langdon in 1812.

First recorded popular vote was that of the election of 1824, the total vote cast was 352,062.

For the first time all presidential candidates were nominated by conventions in 1832.

The "two-thirds" rule adopted by the Democratic convention May 21, 1832.

First platform ever adopted was issued in May, 1832, by the National Republicans.

First election of Vice-President by the Senate, no candidate having received a majority of the electoral votes cast, took place in 1837, Richard M. Johnson being elected.

First time the unit rule was adopted was in the election of 1840 by the Whig convention.

First national committee was organized in the election of 1848 by the Democratic convention.

Presidential electors chosen in the election of 1848 for the first time under the law requiring their appointment on the Tuesday next after the first Monday in November of the election year.

First National Republican convention held at Philadelphia, Pennsylvania, June 17, 1856.

First army vote occurred in the election of 1864.

List of Presidents and Vice-Presidents of the United States.

	Presidents.	Vice-Presidents.
1.	George Washington..1789–93.	John Adams..........1789–93.
	George Washington..1793–97.	John Adams..........1793–97.
2.	John Adams ......1797–1801.	Thomas Jefferson...1797–1801.
3.	Thomas Jefferson....1801–05.	Aaron Burr ....1801–05.
	Thomas Jefferson....1805–09.	George Clinton.......1805–09.
4.	James Madison......1809–13.	George Clinton.......1809–12.
	James Madison......1813–17.	Elbridge Gerry.......1813–17.
5.	James Monroe ......1817–21.	Daniel D. Tompkins ..1817–21.
	James Monroe ......1821–25.	Daniel D. Tompkins ..1821–25.
6.	J. Q. Adams ....1825–29.	John C. Calhoun......1825–29.
7.	Andrew Jackson ....1829–33.	John C. Calhoun......1829–33.
	Andrew Jackson ....1833–37.	Martin Van Buren ....1833–37.
8.	Martin Van Buren...1837–41.	Richard M. Johnson...1837–41.
9.	William H. Harrison.1841–41.	John Tyler...........1841—
10.	John Tyler* ....1841–45.	
11.	James K. Polk ......1845–49.	George M. Dallas.....1845–49.
12.	Zachary Taylor......1849–50.	Millard Fillmore .....1849—
13.	Millard Fillmore*....1850–53.	
14.	Franklin Pierce......1853–57.	William R. King......1853–57.
15.	James Buchanan.....1857–61.	John C. Breckinridge.1857–61.
16.	Abraham Lincoln....1861–65.	Hannibal Hamlin.....1861–65.
	Abraham Lincoln....1865–65.	Andrew Johnson......1865—
17.	Andrew Johnson* ...1865–69.	
18.	Ulysses S. Grant ....1869–73.	Schuyler Colfax......1869–73.
	Ulysses S. Grant ....1873–77.	Henry Wilson........1873–77.
19.	Rutherford B. Hayes.1877–81.	William A. Wheeler ..1877–81.
20.	James A. Garfield....1881–81.	Chester A. Arthur....1881—
21.	Chester A. Arthur*..1881–85.	
22.	Grover Cleveland....1885–89.	Thomas A. Hendricks.1885–89.
23.	Benjamin Harrison ..1889–93.	Levi P. Morton ......1889–93.
	Grover Cleveland....1893–97.	Adlai E. Stevenson....1893–97.
24.	William McKinley.1897–1901.	Garret A. Hobart.....1897–99.
	William McKinley...1901–01.	Theodore Roosevelt...1901—
25.	Theodore Roosevelt*.1901–05.	

* Succeeded at death of President.

Number of Delegates in National Conventions

where the representation is made on a basis of Apportionment of Members of Congress.

STATES.

State	Delegates.
Alabama	22
Arkansas	18
California	20
Colorado	10
Connecticut	14
Delaware	6
Florida	10
Georgia	26
Idaho	6
Illinois	54
Indiana	30
Iowa	26
Kansas	20
Kentucky	26
Louisiana	18
Maine	12
Maryland	16
Massachusetts	32
Michigan	28
Minnesota	22
Mississippi	20
Missouri	36
Montana	6
Nebraska	16
Nevada	6
New Hampshire	8
New Jersey	24
New York	78
North Carolina	24
North Dakota	8
Ohio	46
Oregon	8
Pennsylvania	68
Rhode Island	8
South Carolina	18
South Dakota	8
Tennessee	24
Texas	36
Utah	6
Vermont	8
Virginia	24
Washington	10
West Virginia	14
Wisconsin	26
Wyoming	6
Total	952

TERRITORIES.

Territory	Delegates
Alaska	4
Arizona	6
District of Columbia	2
Hawaii	6
Indian Territory	6
New Mexico	6
Oklahoma	6
Grand Total	988

Necessary to a choice in the Republican convention, a majority; necessary to a choice in the Democratic convention, two-thirds of the vote. In the Democratic convention the District of Columbia and Alaska are allowed 6 delegates each.

General Index.

GENERAL INDEX.

General Index.

Index of Names.

Index of Names.

Index of Names.

Index of Names.

Index of Names.

Index of Names.

Subject Index.

Democratic Platforms.

(See also Subject Index to Liberal-Republican Platform.)

Subject Index.

Republican Platforms.

Subject Index.

Subject Index.

SUBJECT INDEX.

Abolition Party, Liberty-Abolitionist, Free-Soil, and Free-Soil Democratic Platforms.

Liberal Republican Platform.

Subject Index.

National Republican and Whig Platforms.

Prohibition Platforms.

Independent National (Greenback), Greenback, Greenback National, Anti-Monopoly, National People's, People's Party, Silver Party, National Party, and People's Party (Middle-of-the-Road).

Subject Index.

Labor Platforms.

Subject Index.

Platforms not indexed by subjects.

ELECTORAL VOTE.

State	Votes	State	Votes
Alabama	11	Nebraska	8
Arkansas	9	Nevada	3
California	10	New Hampshire	4
Colorado	5	New Jersey	12
Connecticut	7	New York	39
Delaware	3	North Carolina	12
Florida	5	North Dakota	4
Georgia	13	Ohio	23
Idaho	3	Oregon	4
Illinois	27	Pennsylvania	34
Indiana	15	Rhode Island	4
Iowa	13	South Carolina	9
Kansas	10	South Dakota	4
Kentucky	13	Tennessee	12
Louisiana	9	Texas	18
Maine	6	Utah	3
Maryland	8	Vermont	4
Massachusetts	16	Virginia	12
Michigan	14	Washington	5
Minnesota	11	West Virginia	7
Mississippi	10	Wisconsin	13
Missouri	18	Wyoming	3
Montana	3		

Total, 476. Necessary to a choice, 239.